God's Galloping Girl

Recollections of the Pioneers of British Columbia

God's Galloping Girl is the third volume in a series of editions of important documents of the colonial and early provincial history of British Columbia.

The first volume is *The Reminiscences of Doctor John Sebastian Helmcken*, edited by Dorothy Blakey Smith. J. S. Helmcken was British Columbia's pioneer doctor, first Speaker in the legislature, and one of the negotiators of the colony's entry into Confederation.

The second volume is *A Pioneer Gentlewoman in British Columbia*, edited by Margaret A. Ormsby. The author of these recollections, Susan Allison, settled in the Similkameen Valley in the 1860's.

GOD'S GALLOPING GIRL

The Peace River Diaries
of Monica Storrs, 1929-1931

Edited with an introduction by W. L. Morton
with the assistance of Vera K. Fast

Based on materials provided
by the late R. D. Symons.

Preface by R. D. Symons.

UNIVERSITY OF BRITISH COLUMBIA PRESS

VANCOUVER

GOD'S GALLOPING GIRL

The Peace River Diaries of Monica Storrs, 1929-1931

Canadian Cataloguing in Publication Data

Storrs, Monica, 1888-1967.
    God's galloping girl
    Includes index.
    ISBN 0-7748-0110-7 (Bound).—
    ISBN 0-7748-0207-3 (Pbk.)

    1. Storrs, Monica, 1888-1967. 2. Frontier and pioneer
life—Peace River district. 3. Anglican Church of Cana-
da—Biography. 4. Peace River district—History.
I. Morton, William L., 1908-   II. Fast, Vera K., 1929-
III. Title.
FC3845.P42S86   971.1'1   C79-091108-6
F1089.P3S86

International Standard Book Number 0-7748-0207-3
Printed in Canada

In memory of Alfred T. Adams a special grant to scholarly publishing has been donated to this book.

This book has also been published with the assistance of grants from:

The Canadian Federation for the Humanities, using funds provided by the Social Sciences and Humanities Research Council of Canada

The Anglican Foundation of Canada

The Hamber Foundation

The Leon and Thea Koerner Foundation.

CONTENTS

Illustrations   ix

Preface   xi

Introduction   xv

Robert D. Symons (1898-1973)   xxx

Monica Storrs: Companion of the Peace
                R. D. Symons   xxxi

Text of the Diaries   1

Notes   287

Index   303

ILLUSTRATIONS

Map

Plate 1. Monica Storrs before she left England
      2. Early photograph of Monica in the North Peace
      3. Fort St. John, c.1928
      4. May Birley during World War I
      5. Kenneth Birley at Fort Vermilion, 1912
      6. Douglas and Frank Birley
      7. Interior of May Birley's house
      8. Pouce Coupe, c.1935
      9. Rally held at May Birley's, 3 May 1930
     10. Four children off to Taylor School
     11. Brother Wolf on Charlie Lake
     12. Letitia Petter with students at Baldonnel, 1932
     13. Scout troop raising flag at camp
     14. Donella Chiulli and Lucy Lohman, 1930
     15. Group portrait with Father Luc Beuglet, O.M.I.
     16. Brownie Enrolment at Fish Creek, 1932
     17. Lawrence and Dave Chiulli with furs
     18. Anton Framst getting in the hay, 1930
     19. Eden Robinson with the first tractor on Bear Flat
     20. Providence Hospital, Fort St. John
     21. Hudson's Hope, 1929
     22. Logs being hauled at Baldonnel
     23. Ferry crossing the Peace at Taylor Flat
     24. George, Lila, and Dorothy Maginnis camping, 1930
     25. St. Martin's Church, Fort St. John
     26. Monica making her district visits
     27. Church Hall at Baldonnel
     28. Roy Cuthbert and Tony Flatt
     29. Adeline Harmer
     30. Monica Storrs outside "The Abbey"

PHOTO CREDITS

We wish to acknowledge the many individuals who contributed prized personal photographs to make up the picture section, in particular Mrs. Hope Symons of Silton, Saskatchewan, who was one of Monica's Companions, and Mrs. Cora Ventress of Fort St. John, who contacted many people mentioned in the book for photographs from the period. Mrs. Symons contributed Plates 2, 10, 11, 26, 28, and 30, and Monica's late sister, Mrs. Petronella Moor, sent Plates 1 and 29. Plates 4, 5, 6, 7, and 13 come from Douglas Birley, Plates 9, 12, 22, 25, and 27 from John Simpson, Plates 14 and 15 from Lucy Lohman Scheck and Plates 17 and 20 from Ross H. MacLean. We are also grateful to Alene Darnall Peck for Plate 16, Helen Robinson, for Plate 19, Mrs. R. Oakley, for Plate 18, Mrs. Lila Goodings, for Plate 24, and numerous other residents of Fort St. John for suggesting other possibilities. Plate 3 is from the collection of the Provincial Archives of British Columbia and Plates 8 and 23 are from the Glenbow-Alberta Institute. The Hudson's Hope Historical Society provided Plate 21.

PREFACE

The editor welcomed the chance to edit the diaries of Monica Storrs and much enjoyed doing so. In the process, three things become clear. One is that the diaries are a remarkable story of devoted service in circumstances of considerable hardship and difficulty. Another is that they are a social document of frontier history, detailed, vivid, and realistic. The third is a comment on the geography, political and physical, of British Columbia. The Peace River Block, the scene of the diaries, shows that the great Pacific province is not only mountainous, but also transmontane, and is not only coastal, but also continental.

The gist and substance of the documents here edited are to be found in Monica Storrs' own extraordinary devotion to the cause of charity and of the Christian faith. They also make up a fresh chapter in the missionary history which is so great a part of general Canadian history. As such, that part of the story clashes with the other aspect of the document, that it is a stark, realistic account of late frontier life in North America, its hardships augmented by the Great Depression. Christian spirituality is in stern conflict with North American frontier materialism at its most barren and its worst. The wonder is how Monica went on serenely between the faith by which she lived and the reality in which she moved.

Because the diaries are so extensive, it has not been possible to print them in their entirety. Yet it is the intensity of detail that makes the diaries an authentic, personal, and revealing document of the frontier. The sheer burden of homestead life on men, women, and children, the struggle to survive and to win improvements, and the dangers have seldom been so patiently and directly recorded.

It seemed better, therefore, to provide the complete text of a portion rather than extracts from the whole. The first two years were chosen because as they wheeled to their close, Monica Storrs was settled in Peace River. She had made friends and won acceptance for herself and her work, her Sunday Schools, her girl guides, her boy scouts. English institutions brought to a raw frontier, they were perhaps not the best way to touch the hearts and minds of the young. Yet what alternatives were there? That behind them was goodwill, self-sacrifice, and deep affection did much to transcend the oddities of guiding and of scouting to country children of many denominations. As a result Monica had found her work to do in the wide miles of the North Peace, and in the Abbey. She had a base and a "Sanctuary for that work."

She continued to send her reports home for nearly eight more years. The Second World War brought Monica's regular diaries to an end; indeed, the last printed leaflet is dated May, 1939, although there are later, isolated handwritten entries still extant. She wrote "after 1940 the War destroyed all my desire to write any more of our trivial doings." However, she did keep a notebook diary, entitled "Alaska Highway Log, August 13th to September 1st, 1949" and a tiny, pocket-sized diary of her trip to Grafton, Australia, in 1950, but these are short, succinct records in no way resembling her earlier writings.

The work of preparing for print the first two years of the diaries has been much helped by the work of the previous editor, the late R.D. Symons, and the editor who worked on the manuscript after his death, Norah McNiven of Atlanta, Georgia. His foreword is included. Needless to say, he bears no responsibility for the text and notes as printed here.

The actual text used, and which is reproduced here, was a typewritten and multigraphed copy of a similar document in the possession of the Archives of British Columbia. No original letters written by Monica Storrs in her bold, fluent hand exist for the early years of the diaries. That makes it important how the present copy came into being. Monica Storrs wrote directly to Miss Muriel Causton, a friend and aide in England. Miss Causton typed, multigraphed, and distributed the diaries to a growing circle of friends and helpers. Thus, in the old way of missionaries, accounts of the mission fed the work of the missionary. In later years, the diaries were printed.

The resultant text was good and required little editing. What took most effort was to convert the capital letters which concealed the identities of persons named into names wherever possible, by means of later use of the name, or by identification from other sources.

Otherwise, the printed text is almost wholly that of the typewritten text. A few errors, typing or other, have been corrected; a uniformity of usage has been, with slight change, imposed; and the abundance of capital letters has been pruned, without, I think, detracting from the vigour and emphases of Monica Storrs' style. Ellipses which appeared in the original, but which are not a genuine break in the text have been deleted.

I have to thank first Mrs. Vera Fast, my research assistant, who, as part of her graduate work, helped me greatly with the work of identification. The notes were prepared by her, and much was learned by her in interviews in England with some of those who knew and remember Monica.

Then too, I must thank, very warmly, for much help given by letter, or through Vera Fast, the late Mrs. Petronella Moor (nee Storrs) and Miss Eleanor Higginbotham. To their names I must add that of the late Bishop Christopher Storrs, who knew of and helped the beginning of this edition, but did not live to see it finished. I can only say that without this loving help, no warmth or verisimilitude would have been possible.

Finally, I acknowledge my many debts to the staff of the University of British Columbia Press, and especially to the Senior Editor, Dr. Jane Fredeman. The idea of publication was theirs in the first place, and only their enterprise and help made possible this publication, in part, of the Peace River diaries of Monica Storrs, church woman, church worker, a handmaiden at once of the church and the district she served for all of twenty-one years.

INTRODUCTION

I

The diaries, offered here in part, are the stories of an encounter, of the meeting of a woman and a river, of Monica Storrs, English gentlewoman and church woman, and of the Peace River, its valley and its plateau.

Monica Storrs came as a daughter of the Church of England to Peace River in 1929 to help carry on the work of the Sunday School and related activities, such as organizing girl guides, in the new and scattered settlements, almost roadless, almost schoolless, greatly mixed in origin and in religion. A daughter of the dean of Rochester Cathedral, she had been delicately and tenderly reared in that exquisite yet sturdy refinement of the Victorian afterglow. If refined, she had yet the quiet resolution and resilient heart to meet and accept conditions of frontier life such as she had never met. She was nevertheless to surmount all trials and to come to love the Peace. Her home in England on retirement was to be named "Peacewood."

She had learned, it seems evident, that Peace River was not merely a region, but also a state of the mind and an adventure of the spirit. She had met and imbibed the mystery and the mystique of the mighty Peace. From the time it enters white men's history with its strange, intriguing name, the river of the Peace, the river and its country have been both provocative to the imagination and haunting to the memory, and not without reason.

The Peace is ancient, older than the Rockies it cleaves through. It arises from the confluence of two rivers of the Rocky Mountain Trench, the Finlay and the Parsnip, west of the mountains. They meet head on, join and turn at right angles to the east and the range of the Rockies. That the Peace cuts through, having worn down the channel of Peace River Canyon as the Rockies imperceptibly rose. Bursting free, the river enters a great plateau through which it carves with curve and terrace its valley six to eight hundred feet below the level of the plateau. Its riverine thrust never fails in power and majesty; rightly is it called, with affection, the mighty Peace.

If its force impresses, so does the land it traverses. An intimate union of mountain and plain, of forest and of parkland prairie, the Peace River country brackets mountain and prairie. It also reaches out at once to the prairies, to the Pacific, and to the Arctic, a nodal region. Nor is Peace River central only geographically; it is also meteorologically central. Over the lands of the Peace, Pacific and Arctic weather combine and alternate. Normally there is the sunshine and wind of the southern prairies through the summer of long days and short nights. But in winter, Arctic air currents or blizzards bring stern frosts or level-driving snow. Or, when the Chinook blows, with its "blink" making the air as clear as leaded glass, warm Pacific air comes surging through the passes of the Pine and the Peace to raise the temperature and melt the snow. These changes govern much of the life recorded in the diaries below.

This region was the last unoccupied frontier of agricultural land in North America. But because it was the last frontier, it terminated a continental region. It is the penultimate region of the vast central basin of North America, which American, Canadian, and European farmers and artisans, traders, and soldiers had been settling since the process began in Ohio in the last quarter of the eighteenth century. The fact is made explicit by the square land survey which began on the Ohio and ended on the Peace. It was the last West, and in opening its own chapter of history, it closed that of the occupation and settlement of agricultural North America.

These archaic origins and that historical stop largely explain why Peace River was a condition of the mind and an adventure of the spirit. It combined first and last things, and perhaps what is last is even more compelling to the mind of the believer than what is first. There is the same excitement, but there is added a sense of finality, making the last opportunity more poignant than the first.

Thus for many Canadians and Americans, and for many newcomers from over the sea, to go to Peace River had an urgency and a promise which transcended all careful calculation of means and the impact of the brute realities of the first frontier years. It was this which made Peace River a state of mind. How it might vault over all earthly reason is touchingly told in Ralph Allen's novel *Peace River*. A Saskatchewan family, dried out in the drought years, set out for Peace River. That they never reached it was no great matter. The exaltation of trying resolved all their difficulties on the way.

It was, it may be supposed, something of this spirit which kept Monica Storrs at her trips by horse and car in British Columbia's Peace River District from 1929 to 1950, which brought her back in after years, and which left her, when her work in Canada ended, with an abiding love of Peace River.

II

The reality Monica Storrs encountered was indeed the river itself, but in the detail of her work it was much more the land of the Peace River District. The river gave its name to its adjacent land because it was the river that made travel through the country easy in the summer seasons. Rising west of the Rockies, it conjoins the mountain country and the prairie, except for the few but impossible miles of the canyon. The river, that is, entered our history as a highway from the plains to the mountains. It is a noble highway, ranging in breadth from hundreds of yards to a half and even a full mile, broad, steady, ongoing. Only winter checks its flow; only the spring mountain water makes it dangerous. It is, in spite of its power, a peaceful and benevolent river.

Its haunting name came from a treaty of peace between Indian tribes in conflict. Those who inhabited the lands of the Peace east of the mountains were first named by the fur traders, like the river itself, for the abundant beaver. The Beaver Indians and the Beaver River and its tributaries yielded quantities of pelts to the trapper and the fur trader, first to those trading from Hudson Bay, the great company of that name, then to the bold Nor'Westers from Montreal. Even before the North West Company came to "the Athabasca," as the whole new country was named, Cree Indians acting as middlemen for the Hudson's Bay Company had trade with the Beaver Indians, and to the latter's disadvantage. Sometime after the Crees were weakened by the great smallpox epidemic of 1781, the Beavers negotiated a treaty to ease their position with the Crees at Peace Point on the river which thereafter became the river of the peace. Such was the simple origin of the name Peace. The land and its position in North America were to supply the evocative overtones of the name.

The lands of the Peace are not, of course, as simple as the contrast of mountain and prairie suggests. It has different and integrating parts, and those parts themselves their significant divisions. The first, the eye-catching element, is the valley of the Peace, deep, winding and curving in slow amplitude, and at any point coming from or going into far, blue distance. Along the bottom of its course are bench lands, low points on the river curves; above in some places are terraces; at the top, six to eight hundred feet above, is the plateau. It was in the river bottom that the beavers worked, the Indians hunted and camped, the fur traders built their forts and the missionaries their chapels and churches. The plateau was little known and little used, except for travel up the tributaries and for hunting the deer and the buffalo. It was along the valley bottom that the lands of Peace River were entered and used by man.

Yet it was the plateau lands that were to be the challenge and the prize of agricultural settlement when the frontier of North America at long last reached the Peace. Would this unexplored country, a country which combined forest and prairie much as the whole district conformed mountains and plains, would it, with its late and early frosts, receive and reward the farmer? In the valleys of the Peace and its tributaries, the Smoky, the Pine, and countless others, were great forests, in the main of white spruce, as befitted the northern forest, but also of forest poplars. On the hills also the spruce stood in dark ranks, elevating the slopes. The prairie so called was not the short grass rolling plain of southern Saskatchewan and Alberta, but rather the long grass meadows and shifting groves, "bluffs," of poplar and willow of the parkland running from Manitoba across northern Saskatchewan and Alberta. The bluffs of white poplar were the "ghostly trees" of the diaries. It was in its way exciting country, full of game, well stocked with fruit, raspberry, strawberry, and that staple of the Northwest, the saskatoon, or revealingly, the "pemmican" berry, used to sweeten pemmican. Much of it lay open to the plough as it lay open to the traveller. But on the plateau the summer frosts smote silently on quiet nights; could wheat be ripened on the plateau? No one knew until this century, for the bottom lands were ample for the gardens and farms of fur trader and missionary.

The fur traders came first to the Peace. When in the late 1770's some of the traders from Montreal crossed the divide between the Saskatchewan and the Mackenzie, they entered "the Athabasca," the country of the great head tributaries which farther north joined to make up the Mackenzie. One of the tributaries was the Peace. That great advance made necessary a pooling of resources, the North West Company. For the next forty years the Nor'Westers were to draw from the Athabasca country the abundant beaver pelts which made them formidable rivals of the Hudson's Bay Company. Control of the Athabasca might mean control of the fur trade of Canada. The contest which led the Hudson's Bay Company to invade the Athabasca and which was to force the coalition of the companies in 1821 had begun.

The Nor'Westers, nevertheless, could not rest, but had always to seek new fur country. They began their advance up the Peace and over the mountains from Fort Chipewyan with the beginning of Fort Vermilion on the Peace in 1788, McLeod's Fort in 1792, Fort Dunvegan in 1805, and Rocky Mountain House the same year. Fort St. John, the name of the town in Monica's district, began to trade on the Peace in 1806. These were the post names to govern in Peace River, with Hudson's Hope added by the united company at the foot of the Peace River Canyon after 1821. The fur traders had followed in the course Alexander Mackenzie had set to and across the Rockies on his way to the Pacific in the second quest for the western sea, access to which would relieve the Athabasca of the burden of the long canoe route back to Montreal. He reached the sea in 1793 but opened no path to it. What the fur traders had done had been to reveal the Peace as part of the transcontinental route which was to grow into the Dominion of Canada from sea to sea. They had also revealed that the Peace River country was not merely a passage, but a nodal area, reaching out not only to east and west but also to north and south. The history of Peace River was to be a long, painful effort to realize that character.

In ascending the Peace the traders entered the lands of the Beaver Indians. They were Déné, of Athapascan stock, different from the Crees but allied to the other Athapascan tribes, the Chipewyan and the Dogribs, allied also to the Sekanees who lived across the Rockies on the upper Peace. With both tribes in the rich beaver country of the Peace relations were good, except for the sudden outburst of violence in the killing of the traders at Fort St. John in 1824. Among the Indians some "freemen," men who took their discharge in the northwest, French-Canadian canoemen mostly, served as a link between the independent, sometimes resentful, Beavers and the fur trade. Their descendants and successors account for the French names which occur in the diaries and which are common in Peace River.

After the death of Father Aulneau in 1738, the northwest was without missionaries. Not until the 1840's did they appear on the Peace. In 1859 Father Henri Faraun of the Oblates of Mary Immaculate founded missions at Dunvegan and Vermilion. The missionary church in the north, the Church of England, did not enter the Peace until 1868. For both churches these missions were the final outreachings of great efforts sustained against the constant pull of the long distances of the far northwest. In this effort Peace River tended to lose out to the pull of the Mackenzie River to the north and the pull of the populous tribes to the west along the coast. The result was that the Anglicans had established the bishopric of Athabaska in 1874, subdivided in 1884, to cover first the whole Mackenzie drainage area, then the Peace River country. In 1876 Bishop W.C. Bompas opened an agricultural mission at Fort Vermilion, and in 1878 a similar one at Fort Dunvegan, both on the lower Peace, both a curious foretelling of the future economy of the region. The Romans, better supported and better manned, by the 1870's had missions at Fort Chipewyan, Fort Vermilion, Lesser Slave Lake, and at Lac la Biche, also in eastern Peace River. The groundwork was laid for that intermixture of creeds Monica Storrs was to encounter.

Little was done in that portion of Peace River that from 1858 was part of the colony, and after 1871 the province of British Columbia. How did any part of Peace River east of the Rockies, that northwestward thrust of prairie and parkland, come to be part of the province? The answer is to be found in the history of the gold rushes.

The gold rush of 1857 made the colony of British Columbia. Its extension up the Fraser to the Cariboo country and over the divide between the Fraser and the Peace at Fort (Prince) George brought part of the Peace River country into the colony of British Columbia and into the Anglican diocese of Caledonia. The gold seekers, "panning" the beds of the mountain rivers, traced the Parsnip and the Finlay and passed the canyon of the Peace eastward. In the black sands of the shores of the river they found fine gold, enough at least for wages. Thus the gold seekers crossed the Rockies; thus characters such as Nigger Dan and Twelve-Foot Davis became part of Peace River lore. To keep some measure of control of the miners, the British government extended the boundary of the colony eastward to the 120th meridian of longitude and north to the 60th parallel of latitude in 1863. So it was that the Peace River country came in its upper half to be part of British Columbia. And thus the mountain colony and province became also in part a prairie province.

In time the new boundary was to become a real dividing line between the Province of British Columbia and the Province of Alberta and between the Diocese of Athabaska and that of Caledonia, the latter with some consequences for Monica Storrs. In more recent times, the British Columbia part has yielded to the essentially nodal character of Peace River, and it has become an area of provincial integration rather than division. In Monica Storrs' day, although it was part of British Columbia and of Caledonia, it was served by and dependent commercially on Edmonton and, for aid and fellowship, on the Dioceses of Athabaska and Edmonton.

Peace River yielded little gold, and the concern which divided it soon passed. Once more its continental significance, its place in the integration of Canada, slowly emerged. What first caused the renewal of its old place in the continental fur trade was the project of building a transcontinental railway to unite Canada and British Columbia after Confederation.

A single railway line from the Ottawa River to the Pacific Ocean meant that much care must be given to the route chosen for it. As far as Red River there would be little debate; the line must follow the north shore of Lake Superior to Thunder Bay and from there proceed as straight as rock and water allowed to the Red. Beyond, the route was indicated by the history of the fur trade. It should keep to the north, to avoid the deep valleys and independent tribes of the Plains. At the Rockies it should pass by one of the lower passes. These were all to the north; one was the Pine Pass of the Peace River country. The surveys, therefore, under Sandford Fleming set out to trace a line by the park belt country of the northern prairies and to examine the northern passes of the Rockies. Thus the detailed, scientific exploration of Peace River began. The Peace might be the passage to the Pacific and the long heralded riches of the region might be realized. All this was not to be. The choice of a southern route by the Kicking Horse Pass violated the indications of history and retired Peace River once more to its original remoteness. A slow half century was to pass as the region, step by slow step, regained the destiny for which it had prepared by time and history.

Thus the railway, and history, passed Peace River by in the 1880's. There life continued on much the old lines. The Indians pursued their ancient ways, moving from camp to camp, living on yet abundant game, trapping in winter, trading in spring. The Hudson's Bay Company went on, but changing its ways. Its flour mill, first at Vermilion, then at Peace River Crossing, pointed to the future. Its steamboats brought something of the future. But it had new rivals in small free traders, then a sterner opponent in the French firm of Revillon Frères.

Travellers came and went, from Captain William F. Butler of *The Great Lone Land* to Warburton Pike of *The Barren Ground of Northern Canada*. Their vivid accounts of the river and the land filled out the growing image of a land of immense and brooding promise, waiting to be waked.

Canada, busy pushing its newly created destiny, was not wholly unmindful of the Peace. It took note of its frontier behind the active frontier of the southern plains. The Geological Survey of Canada, with its enormous task of verifying, correcting, and extending the work of the fur trade explorers, came in the 1880's and 1890's under the tireless geologist G.M. Dawson and the ever optimistic botanist John Macoun. Canada was assessing its far out heritage.

The Peace River remained, however, far out until in 1898 the Yukon gold rush once more raised the possibility that Peace River might be the route to new gold fields. Most of the gold rush went by sea from Seattle and Vancouver to Skagway. But hopeful Edmonton was not to be excluded. Some sought the trail of '98 by the Mackenzie, others by the Peace. Either way they then had to traverse a tumult of little known mountains. Practically no one made the goal; some perished; a few joined relics of past gold rushes, panning the sands of the Peace River or gardening and trapping along its banks. Peace River resumed its somnolent but expectant waiting.

What was really awaited was the filling of the southern prairies by settlers. When that neared completion, Peace River's time would come. The government of Canada began its preparation for settlement in 1899. Indian Treaty No. 8 was made with the Beaver, Cree, and Chipewyans, thus carrying the Dominion's system of treaties into British Columbia as far as the Rockies. In 1906 the Canadian government took up the "Peace River Block" in British Columbia. The Block was made up of the lands given to it by the province as a grant for the building of the Canadian Pacific Railway. The surveying of its 500,000 acres began, bringing the square-mile survey to the foot of the Rockies in that province of surveys made according to local circumstances. If, however, the style of the survey was alien and the lands held by Canada until 1930, it opened the way to settlement, gave British Columbian Peace River its own identity, and constituted the region in which Monica Storrs was to do her work.

By 1914 that country, then, had everything needed for settlement on the prairie model except railways. Once more the railway had passed Peace River by. Responding to the rush of prairie settlement, the Canadian government in 1903 had launched an enormous project, the building of a second transcontinental to the north of the Canadian Pacific from Quebec to Prince Rupert. It was to be built by the Grand Trunk Pacific Railway of Canada from a point east of Winnipeg to the Pacific. Had it really renewed the historic project of a railway on the old fur trade route to the Rockies and the ocean, it might well have passed through Peace River by the Pine River Pass. That route was explored, but once more the railway chose a more southern route, that by the Yellowhead Pass.

This cutting down of the hopes of Peace River might have been made right by a third railway with transcontinental ambitions, the Canadian Northern. Private, opportunistic, cheaply built with provincial guarantees, the Canadian Northern was a railway man's railway, well fitted to cross the muskegs of the Athabaska River and thread the Pine River Pass. It too, however, turned to the Yellowhead, paralleling the Grand Trunk Pacific, but striking southwest for Vancouver. Neither railway fully served the new ambition to thrust the Canadian frontier as far north as possible and develop Professor Morris Zaslow's Middle North.

In so failing, the opportunity to open the Peace was left to the equally aspiring ambitions of the Province of Alberta and the city of Edmonton. The city and the province had their own Peace River country to add to the provincial frontier and the hinterland of the city. They too had northern dreams to realize. Out of feverish hope and speculation came two provincially supported lines, the Alberta and Great Waterways to Fort McMurray of the tar sands, and the Edmonton, Dunvegan and British Columbia to, as the name signified, Peace River. Slowly, delayed by war and difficulties of construction, the line, which became the Northern Alberta Railway, crept forward. By 1924, after a detour to the rising settlement of Grande Prairie, it had reached Pouce Coupé in British Columbia and could bring Monica Storrs almost to her destination.

The advance of the railway caused other stirrings than the coming of settlers. In far Vancouver, rivalry was stirred by the sight of Edmonton annexing to its hinterland the Peace River District of British Columbia. In 1912, with the backing of the provincial government, the construction of the Pacific Great Eastern Railway to Prince George was begun, with a view to eventual extension over the Pine Pass to Peace River. Again the nodal character of Peace River was stirred, if it was not to be finally achieved until 1958, when the railway reached Fort St. John. In that year it was to complete the ties with the coast and join those which the Alberta Northern Railway had begun and those which the Alaska Highway of the Second World War and the Pine Point Railway of the early 1960's opened with the Yukon and the Mackenzie Valley. Peace River was at long last to be knit to all its orientations.

Monica Storrs had to do, of course, not with the land of Peace River, but with its people, its new people. Her concern, her mission, was with the settlers and the frontier. Hence her diaries came to be the great social document of Peace River Settlement, and of the frontier, that they are. And settlers now were moving to Peace River. Before 1914 the scattered squatters by the posts and the casual farmers selling their surplus grain and cattle for local use were being joined by deliberate farmers who meant when the railways came to sell their grain for export.

These people were relatively few, men who had read of Peace River and sought the region for its promise; they were mostly men of some sense of adventure, of some capital, come to exercise an almost complete freedom of selection, and able and willing to wait a few years for the coming of the railway. And fresh literature of travel, observation, and experience came from settlers and travellers in Peace River writing to tell prospective settlers of the resources and promise of the District. Of these it is easy to name A.M. Besanzon, himself a successful early settler, and his booklet, *The Peace River Trail*, and Captain J.T.O. Galloway and his sprightly account of observations as an engineer. The settlement of Peace River was opening with the usual harbingers of rush and boom, the journalist and the historian.

Two things checked and delayed the response to the touch of the railway. One was the Great War; another was the ancient doubt as to whether wheat, a sure crop on the valley bottom, could ripen on the plateau.

The war passed, and then were added to the incomers first the soldier settlers who chose to go to Peace River, then a new influx of settlers, immigrants from the United Kingdom and the United States and incomers from the Prairie. In their push and enthusiasm the old fear of the plateau frosts, the issue on which Macouns, father John and son James, had strongly divided, was settled. They went onto the high land and grew their crops successfully. What they had really done was to

bring in the new strains of short season wheats, notably Marquis, king of
wheats. They had been bred for the prairies where frost had been a hazard
too. Naturally they ripened on the plateau. The future of the Peace was
assured. The victory was strikingly confirmed when a Peace River
farmer, Herman Trelle from Wembley, three times was hard spring
wheat champion at Chicago in the 1920's.

The new, far frontier, the last west, the best west, it was easy to affirm,
was now in full travail. The railway had still to be extended—Monica
Storrs in 1929 was beyond railhead—roads had to be built, school
districts formed, towns brought into being. Above all, a wildly mixed
population had to learn to live together and make life something more
than mere subsistence on a frontier. It was to this exciting, confused, and
socially barren frontier that Monica Storrs came in the autumn of 1929.
It was a year that was to add to the poverty of the frontier, the hardships
of depression, and, because the Peace was not drought stricken, to the
numbers and variety of its settlers, as farmers left the wind-scourged
prairies. In such conditions a church worker, a Sunday School teacher,
would find much to do and observe both in her own work and in work
beyond, which demanded to be done. The result was both an account of
personal work and devotion and a commentary of acute and vivid
observation of a frontier struggling to cease to be a frontier.

III

The coming of Monica Storrs to Peace River requires some explanation. Why should an Englishwoman, gently born and gently reared,
come to the hardships and disordered beginnings of mass settlement
in Peace River? There are in fact adequate explanations.

One was, if not the most important, significant. There was already
in her family a tie with Canada. Her grandfather, Rev. John Storrs, had
been curate of St. George's, Halifax, and then rector of St. John's, Cornwallis, and her father, also Rev. John Storrs, was born in Nova Scotia.
That long and intimate connection was honoured and was a lively
memory in the family. Moreover, it was part of a tradition felt strongly
by many English people, and not least by Church of England people,
with the world missions of their church to support and their many relatives overseas to remember and help. That tradition was one that quietly
held that the wealth and civilization of England, at their height in the
golden years before 1914, should be available and be given to those in
need of support on the far frontiers of the empire. It was in fact one of the

"burdens of Empire"; but of empire in one of its most innocent forms, the obligation and the desire to help those who in founding outreaches of empire needed a helping hand to establish themselves. The history of the Anglican Church in Western Canada from the days of John West is in large part a history of missionaries sent and supported. In the days of settlement it was largely money, helpers, and clothing that were sent to turn the sharp edges of frontier poverty and to mitigate the destitution of all things, churches, schools, hospitals, of friends and neighbours to talk with, or to turn to in time of need. It was not the less sincere and helpful if done in part in the name of empire.

Monica Storrs, moreover, was prepared to serve when the opportunity came to go to Peace River. Born on 12 February 1888 at St. Peter's Vicarage, Grosvenor Gardens, London, she was the fourth child of Rev. John Storrs, later to be dean of Rochester. Her eldest brother, Ronald Storrs (1881–1955), was to serve in the Foreign Office and become, as Sir Ronald Storrs, Governor of Jerusalem and Judea in the 1920's. There were two other older brothers, Francis (1882–1918) and Bernard (1884–1967). Younger were her brother, Christopher Storrs (1889–1977), who was to enter the Church and become bishop of Grafton, New South Wales, and her sister, Petronella, later Mrs. Moor (1896–1978). When she was two years old, Monica developed tuberculosis of the spine, which left her completely bedridden, and it was not until she was nearly twelve that she learned to walk again. During these early invalid years, she was educated by her parents and by tutors. After she was again able to move about freely, Monica attended a Francis Holland Church of England School for Girls on Graham Street, just off Eaton Square in London.

Her upbringing was clerical and gentle. She became a church woman through and through, firm, charitable, and profoundly convinced of the importance of the Christian way of life and of the strength of Christian truth. Somewhat Anglo-Catholic in spirit as she was, she was in no way evangelical, much less aggressive, her quiet insistence on the Christian way was to explain why in time some were to speak of her as the "Angel of the Peace." (She would, privately, have laughed gently at the term). But Bishop R.F. Brown, who knew and aided her, was to say: "There was in this small, smiling woman, with an innate wit and incisive intellect, a rare faculty—an uncommon gift of spiritual perception. To know her was to know God better. In other words, there was a sort of 'magnificat' quality about her."

In more immediate ways also Monica Storrs was prepared. From the time of her father's appointment as dean of Rochester Cathedral in 1913 and in fellowship with her close and lifelong friend, Miss Adeline Harmer, daughter of Bishop Harmer of Rochester, she had been active in the service of the cathedral church and of the diocese. In this these young women were taking part in a movement in the Church of England to rely on the laity, both men and women, more and more to help in the pastoral work of the church, particularly that of the Sunday Schools and of the new organizations, the boy scouts and girl guides. These last were not necessarily dependent on, or centred on the church, and were certainly not denominational. They did, however, with their discipline and observances, join readily with church work in Sunday School and informed services and became, in effect, auxiliary to Sunday Schools and genuine church work. Monica became a divisional commander with the guides, and thus it was natural that much of her work in Peace River was to be with guides and scouts. These efforts gave her useful ties with the many and varied families which had no connection with, or inclination to, the services of the Church of England. In all things she was concerned about spiritual matters. Even during World War I, when she and her sister worked as volunteers in a munitions plant on Sundays, she arranged with the local vicar for a service for the workers during the lunch hour.

To these activities Monica added her work as general secretary for the United Kingdom of the Girls' Diocesan Association, and later with the Village Evangelists and the Bishop's Messengers in the dioceses and parishes of the Church of England. In many ways her own creation, the latter organization of church workers and children to supplement the work of the clergy was a forerunner of and an education for her work in Peace River. (It was not, it is to be noted, a preparation for some of the brutal harshness of frontier life. The ultimate Monica was to face was the sight of children shrinking at the use of the name of Jesus. To them it meant not love, but anger and profanity; it was a warning of violence. Monica Storrs had, she said, to become "unshockable" to deal helpfully with those so lost to Christian and civilized life.) As well she was instrumental in starting a local chapter of the League of Nations.

Finally, and sadly, Monica was freed, by the deaths of her mother in 1923 after many years of ill health and of her father in 1928, of the ties of her deep attachment to her home. She was free to go where called. First she entered St. Christopher's College, Blackheath. Here she met Eva Hasell, who told her of the spiritual and physical needs of the settlers in the Peace River country. Monica felt called to minister to these needs and left for Canada on 27 September 1929. She was now forty-one years old and described herself as "middle-sized and middle-aged, and fatally English." This "gently born and gently reared" woman of cultivated taste went out to an unknown, materialistic, and sometimes hostile pioneer environment, where mud, mosquitoes, bitter cold, and lack of privacy awaited her. She stayed for twenty-one years.

From Canada there were in the 1920's many calls from the church in

Canada to the church in England. In the great rush of immigrants to the Canadian West after 1896 about one-third, some hundreds of thousands of people, came from Great Britain and Ireland. Many were escaping from unemployment and poverty and needed help until settled. The Church of England was active both in helping people to migrate and in following them to their new homes with its service. It was in fact an enormous and almost unmanageable task. This was the more so, perhaps, as the clergy, notably Bishop Lloyd of the English settlement at Clark's Crossing, now Saskatoon, Saskatchewan, tended to see it as a carrying of England overseas. (It was this aspect of "empire" which sometimes stood in the way of non-Anglicans accepting Anglican help.)

To aid the work of the church some organizations were created to raise and direct funds and to bring help to the clergy. The first of these was the Fellowship of the Maple Leaf. Its roots lay in an association named the Maple Leaf Workers, founded in 1903 by a Mrs. Stamford, sister of Bishop George E. Lloyd. Dr. Lloyd himself became the prime mover in a reorganization of this society which resulted in the founding of the Fellowship of the Maple Leaf (F.M.L.) in 1917. The main function of the F.M.L. was to supply dedicated Anglican young people to serve as teachers in Western Canada. The emphasis was on young women trained at St. Christopher's College, Blackheath, although other qualified applicants were also accepted. The F.M.L. also followed a policy of limited financial assistance to dioceses where this was necessary. Monica Storrs was regarded by the F.M.L. as one of their own, and in her work in Fort St. John she received a monthly stipend of about seventy-five dollars from the organization. In later years she was elected to its governing body in which her sister-in-law, Mrs. Francis Storrs, was also active. When Monica retired to England in 1950, she and Marguerite Fowler of St. Faith's Mission in Manitoba, who is mentioned in the early pages of the diaries, were asked to undertake recruitment for the F.M.L., which they did.

The second organization germane to Anglican work in Peace River was the Sunday School by Post, which used the mails to forward Sunday School lessons, pictures, and books to homes beyond the regular reach of clergy and teachers. The idea was conceived by a Mrs. Gwynne in Grenfell, Saskatchewan, in 1905, but was adapted and greatly developed by Bishop Lloyd and Miss Bolton in 1906. Monica Storrs was very solicitous for this work and spent much time and energy ensuring that children become enrolled in it.

The third pertinent organization was the Fellowship of the West. Three Montreal priests, Geoffrey Guiton, Elton Scott, and R.K. Naylor had been deeply moved by reports, given by Miss Hasell among others, of the desperate need for clergy in the Peace River. With the encouragement of Bishop John Cragg Farthing and Dean (later Bishop) Arthur Carlisle, they organized the Fellowship of the West in 1929. Their plan was for a priest and a layman to go in pairs into the dioceses of Athabaska and Caledonia—later also Edmonton—during the summer vacation and then, during any free time in the winter months, to lecture and report on their work to raise funds for the fellowship. The work of the mission expanded, and Rev. George Wolfendale, first resident Anglican priest in Fort St. John during Monica's time, was one of the missioners, as were his successors until the parish became independent.

The operative agent in bringing Monica Storrs to Peace River was the work done under the heading of the Western Canada Sunday School Caravan Fund—later the Western Canada Sunday School Caravan Mission Fund—by two women of unusual force and devotion, Miss F.H. Eva Hasell and Miss Iris Sayle. Of the two, Miss Hasell was the leader, not to say the driver. A person of indomitable will, she had been trained in nursing and car driving and maintenance during the First World War. Her policy was to purchase large durable vans and outfit them to be at once the conveyance, office, and sleeping quarters of two women, one trained in driving and maintenance, the other in Sunday School work. Her ideas and her aid, for she put her private means as well as her will behind the work, were accepted by hard-pressed bishop on bishop in the Prairie Provinces and British Columbia.

Miss Hasell began her work in 1920 and was joined by Miss Sayle in 1926. Summer after summer these invincible ladies pioneered in dioceses from Fredericton to the Yukon and Caledonia. Each van they drove was left for a new team and fresh work, while the tireless pioneers went in search of a new van and a new diocese or area.

In the winters Miss Hasell lectured extensively throughout Britain. She was usually accompanied by Iris Sayle, who, as an artist, had painted the photographs taken of their work and these lantern-slide lectures attracted large audiences and raised sizeable sums of money for their work.

Miss Hasell also wrote three books and some plays and smaller booklets in her forceful, lively fashion, describing her labours and adventures. and the sale of these also fed the work. There really had never been anything like it, and Miss Hasell became as well known in the Canadian West as Monica was, if more quietly, in Peace River.

Miss Hasell, as it happened, served the diocese of Caledonia in 1928, and visited the Peace River section of the diocese—on foot—and advised Bishop Rix of the diocese that a woman worker was needed at Fort St. John in what was to become known as the North Peace, as it was north of the river and somewhat less accessible. In England she told Monica of the need and that she should go to meet it. Monica, prepared, accepted the commission and, paying her own expenses, made her way to the North Peace in October 1929.

Such was the manner of her coming. As to what kind of person she was, what she encountered in Peace River, how she built the "Abbey," her home and headquarters, and how she came to do and did the work that made her known and loved on the Peace, it is good furtune to have it told in his own words by R.D. Symons, friend, sympathizer, and supporter, who knew her for many years in the North Peace River, a region he knew and intimately loved.

Robert D. Symons
1898–1973

In 1914, when he was sixteen, R.D. Symons came to Canada from England. He got off the train at Maple Creek, Saskatchewan, and became a ranch hand in the Cypress Hills. From then on he spent his life on the Prairies and in the Peace River District of British Columbia, except for his First World War service with the 217th Batt., C.E.F., and the 7th City of London Fusiliers (7th Foot).

As cowboy, game warden, and rancher, he travelled widely by horseback, canoe, snowshoes, dog team, and later by car, often fighting mud or snow. Always carrying a pencil and sketch pad, he came to know and love the West. In a number of works of fiction and autobiography he celebrated its spirit and inspired many others to seek and see the beauty of the Prairies. His books, among them *Many Trails, Hours and The Birds, The Broken Snare, Still the Wind Blows, Where the Wagon Led, North by West,* and *Silton Seasons,* are illustrated with his own line drawings and paintings.

Besides other honours, in 1970 the University of Saskatchewan gave him an honorary L.L.D.

He met Monica Storrs about 1940 and later married Hope Onslow, one of Monica's assistants as a Companion of the Peace. As long as Monica remained in the Peace, they were closely associated with her, and they continued to keep in touch after she retired to England in 1951.

During the last years of his life Bob Symons undertook to edit Monica's diaries. This manuscript was in the hands of the publisher at the time of his death and provided much valuable material for the present volume.

Monica Storrs: Companion of the Peace

R.D. Symons

It was not altogether by accident that Monica Storrs accepted a call to the Canadian mission field, for she had a very strong sense of tradition and loyalty; so that when the call came from Canada she did not hesitate, remembering her grandfather's service to the Church of England there. The east window of St. John's Church, Wolfville, depicting the Ascension on the upper half and the women at the tomb on the lower, has the following inscription: "To the glory of God and in loving memory of John Storrs, Rural Dean for 35 years, Rector of Cornwallis and Upper Horton, who died 1881." The lectern Bible, also in memory of the Rev. John Storrs, was presented by his grandson and grand-daughter, Sir Ronald Storrs and Monica Storrs. As Monica once said to me, "I feel deep roots in Canada."

Her brother Christopher followed in the ministerial tradition to become a bishop in Australia. He died late in 1977. Among his delightful childhood memories of Monica he wrote: "She was my elder by a year, a delightful companion, with a wide interest in music, art, astronomy and books of every kind. She had a genius for friendship and later on for making friends of an audience. She would hold them enthralled by the vivid, humorous accounts she gave of her work and experiences.

"My earliest memory of her goes back to the time when somewhere between four and six years old we shared a double bed at night. On the blankets and sheets Monica would see 'little people,' some grand, some humble, whom I could never see but who became, night after night, real to me because of their intense reality to her. I can remember nothing of their significance and behaviour, but they meant a great deal to her in the days when she lay a helpless invalid for many years. Psychologists will perhaps interpret this experience. Then there was the long wheel chair in which I was eventually allowed to push her at Westgate-on-Sea—on that wonderful Kent coast which, with Dr. Frederick Trevis, helped her towards eventual recovery.

"One of our day-dreams together—I almost hesitate to put this on paper—was a plan to assassinate Queen Victoria! I can't remember whether we were ambitious to succeed Her Majesty or simply to win notoriety by this dastardly deed. But I recall that out of a number of schemes which we devised, the most reputable was the presentation to the Queen of a box of poisoned chocolates, which we felt sure would tempt her to her death.

"Later again on one of her teenage birthdays a letter has survived the waste paper basket which tells of Monica's reaction to a minor domestic tragedy. Here it is, dated February 18, 1905, written to me by our youngest sister: 'O dear, dear, dear. Have you heard the fatal tidings of Monica's gold watch? Given last Sunday (her birthday) by Father at 10:30, worn in church, lost and was seen no more on the road home. Father in fits, Mother mad, everyone very unhappy but Monica, who is quite calm.' How prophetic!

"Monica's power as a speaker came from the breadth of her humanity and the depth of her humility. The most moving moment that I remember out of all the addresses which she gave us in Australia was when she spoke to a large Cathedral group about the very earliest days of her twenty-one years in Canada. She said that for the first weeks at Fort St. John she was very unhappy. She had come out with such hopes and expectations of happy service and friendship, and everything seemed to be going wrong. She felt estranged from the people, who seemed to suspect, criticize or even dislike her. At last one evening in the home of May Birley (who became later her dearest friend and supporter) she broke down and cried. Her weakness accomplished what her strength could not. I cannot remember what May said to her in detail, but apparently she had given the impression to the little community that she had come to bring culture and civilization as well as religion to this outlying township. I am sure there was no real superiority-complex in Monica; but (as Australians also know!) the English migrant sometimes gives that impression. Anyhow May's wise words and Monica's blend of common sense and humility made this conversation a completely new beginning of her twenty-one years work in Canada. It was, I repeat, an astonishingly moving moment, when she made this frank confession to her Australian audience at Grafton.

"I have only one thing more to add. My father became dean of Rochester fifty-two years ago at a time when it was not uncommon for the bishop of a diocese and the dean of its cathedral to live in a state of 'cold war,' with rivalry, suspicion and even plain dislike poisoning the relations between palace and deanery. At Rochester we were blessedly free from this disgrace. Bishop Harmer and my father, Mrs. Harmer and my mother, their daughter Adeline and my sister were constant and devoted friends, and after the death of their parents Adeline and Monica lived many years together, and it would be hard to exaggerate how much Monica owed to this partnership with so wise, practical, congenial and devoted a companion.

"To conclude, my debt to Monica is unpayable. The width of her interest and her knowledge, her fun and generous sympathy and her faith in God through Christ, which was completely natural and found room in it for every kind of human experience—these together made her the greatest inspiration that has been given to me in my life."

I can speak for her humour, for both my wife Hope and myself knew her so well when we were at Fort St. John. Hope had been with Monica (as one of her "girls," or "Companions of the Peace") for several years before I met her.

Hope Onslow (now Hope Symons) has many treasured memories of Monica, but some she remembers so well follow, and they are very typical of both women!

"With her overpoweringly strong personality, Monica was one of the most maddening people I've ever lived with and also one of the ones who have helped me and taught me most; never too tired, bored or impatient to tell of the stars, the classics in music and literature and many other things as we'd be driving home from Fort St. John in the cutter on a glorious, below-zero night or riding the twenty-two miles across the Pine River for hours in the spring thaw Peace River gumbo. So often when I'd be miserable and dejected and wanted to be morose, Monica would somehow lift me up by her indefatigable *joie de vivre* and the perhaps agonizingly cold ride would be forgotten in the interest of listening; and really she'd be so dead tired herself. So often I've been to sleep in church on a Sunday evening after a long cold winter ride and after coming into the cosy warmth of the big wood stove, but Monica even beat me once by going to sleep standing up saying the Creed!

"She always expected the rest of us to be as terrific as herself, but if we didn't come up to scratch, she was amazingly patient and very often would just laugh at an incompetence.

"Once when I'd only been out from England a very few weeks, on a pitch dark fall Sunday evening, before there was any snow to help one see the way, Monica and I came out of Evensong at St. Martin's. For some reason we only had one horse between us, so Monica said, 'Ride ahead, Hope, and make the cocoa and I'll walk with the lantern. Jenny will take you straight home, you won't need to see where you are going.' I did so want Monica to ride so that I could walk and see a little by the light of that lantern, but I had my orders so nervously rode off. There wasn't a *glimmer* of light, and this supposedly trustful mare, instead of stepping up briskly in the direction of her oat bundle and our cocoa, meandered onto the side of the road and tried to settle down to eating the dried grass. I kept kicking and we gradually proceeded south. After a while I had an uncomfortable feeling that we had got to the crossroads where I knew I was supposed to turn on to the east trail home, but the wretched Jenny certainly wasn't turning, in fact she seemed to be scrambling up a bank. I was terrified by this time and had visions of her going on south which led straight down to the Peace River and wilderness, but I was also fearful of looking an idiot in Monica's eyes, but my fear of being lost was the stronger so I just got off Jenny and held her there halfway up the bank and waited till that welcome lantern came along, to find that we *had* gone past the crossroads. Once more Monica put us on the right trail east and cheerfully said, 'Now she's really heading for home, you won't have any further trouble.' Reluctantly I rode on, but soon I was aware that we were not on the trail, were going through bushes and suddenly we were right up alongside a building. Then I was embarrassed as well as nervous as I thought this must be the log shack of a Norwegian bachelor, old Moik, and I was afraid he'd wake up and wonder why I was calling on him at that hour! Jenny seemed content to stay there. I really didn't know what to do and was sitting in misery when that glorious light, Monica's lantern, suddenly appeared away to my left. I yelled and she heard me, but there was no relenting, and again I was sent on on the last lap across some flat scrubby prairie. 'Jenny will turn in at the gate'; but Jenny didn't! I was uneasy again, so very soon, when I felt that gate must be close, I rode looking behind me every step and sure enough that blessed light appeared behind me but suddenly turned sharp off to the side. Wicked Jenny had taken me a hundred yards or more beyond the gate! I yelled again before the light could disappear into the house and I would be lost forever. And so, I never got home that night in time to make poor Monica her cocoa!"

On our visits back and forth, Monica often regaled us with accounts of her lecture tours in England. One of her best was about the time she had been invited to a large country house in Shropshire to speak of her work in Canada.

This she was ever ready to do, and after dinner the guests assembled in the drawing room to hear her. These guests belonged mostly to county families and included a number of retired army officers of high rank, now returned from service in India and other parts of the Empire.

Prominent among them was a tall, long-legged, ex-cavalry man who occupied one of the front row chairs, and who obviously felt a little ill at ease from being so close, and under the gun so to speak. (Your army man

MISS STORRS ON THE HALFWAY

is easily embarrassed at being eyeball to eyeball with the missionary breed.)

At the end of a long and inspired address on the hardships suffered by settlers and their families in Western Canada, during which she made several references to her long rides on horseback, she finally ended by asking if any of the guests would like to ask a question which, she added, she would do her best to answer.

No one spoke. Slightly flustered, Monica put the question again.

Finally, to the everlasting honour of the British cavalry, the officer mentioned rose slowly on his long legs, looked around to see if anyone else would speak, satisfied himself that no one would, and adjusting his monocle said, 'Ha–rumph–Er, yes Miss Storrs, I should like to ha–ask if I may—do you ride with a short or a *long* stirrup.'

"Oh," said Monica, "I'm afraid I ride with a *long* stirrup."

"Just so. Har–rumph—very right and proper—thank you Miss Storrs—Ha!" replied her questioner and sat down.

No more questions were asked, but typically the collection for the starving children of the Peace exceeded Monica's fondest expectations.

Monica's sister Petronella, (later Mrs. Moor, younger by nine years), wrote to her brother: "Monica had a large share in my upbringing. Very Spartan it was—but great fun. I'm afraid she found me a hard nut to crack and I remember hearing her say to our mother, 'I don't know *what* to do to make Pet good.' Nor did anyone, but Monica battled bravely on, and I certainly owe an enormous debt of gratitude for her wise help and unfailing love and friendship.

"She had a passionate loyalty to the family and was never so happy as when she could gather us, nephews, nieces, great nephews, great nieces and cousins of every degree to stay with her and Adeline at their home in Liss. When Hitler started persecuting the Jews she adopted two boys from Berlin, Hugh and David, aged twelve and ten. I asked her how she had chosen them. 'Oh, I asked the woman there to send the two who seemed most in need of a home.' So simple! She took them to Canada with her, brought them up as sons and saw them launched into life.

"A few months before she died, one of them, David, and his charming wife came to England on leave and stayed at Peacewood, a great joy to her.

"She had a Franciscan outlook, and when 'tramps' came to the door begging, asked them in and gave them a meal. One very tough looking customer confided to her afterwards that he had really come to prospect for a break-in; but wouldn't trouble as 'the lady had been so kind.'

"She always made mild fun of us when we complained of trivialities—the weather, the heat, the cold or our own minor ailments.

"But in any real trouble or difficulty one's first reaction was to talk it over with Monica."

This too was typical. No man or woman ever entered the gate of the "Abbey" without being offered food, a bed, and a chance to tell their troubles. They might be atheists, they might be thieves or vagrants, they might be bishops or businessmen or young people in trouble—yet they were to her all God's children.

But to return to her young days, here are a few memories from Miss Evelyn Gedge, daughter of the famous (blind) Canon Gedge: "Eaton Square and Graham Street school remembered Monica as having been a long time immobile (and then wearing some neck support) from two to twelve years old.

"But when she came home from her first time in Fort St. John, having had a bit of pneumonia, I found her in a nursing home, momentarily, in South Kensington, sharing the great joke: the doctor had come to examine her, but seemed more excited by her back than her chest, so she called him to order, to which he replied with amazement at what he had found—two or three bits of spine missing, but the remnant joined together so perfectly . . . .

"My father was greatly valued by Monica and she by him, and when we set out to walk seven miles from his Rectory to the Cathedral or vice versa, I have vivid memories of the gain of her mind and memories as we walked and talked.

"The big work which we owed to her was the bringing to birth of a Volunteer Movement, called Bishop's Messengers.

"She enlisted one of the Canons, later Bishop King, as its pivot, and she drove him ruthlessly to guide some six or eight of us. Twice a year we had two days under her leadership, retreating in the crypt of the Cathedral under Canon King, and conferring on the work of helping in mission visits up in the Deanery.

"The first Rochester Diocesan Mission we were summoned to help was with Bishop Walpole (father of the writer Hugh Walpole), but Monica's mother was badly ill, and so another of the Bishop's Messengers went on this work.

"But all of us helped in various spots, owing to her creative spirit, from time to time, and it was thanks to this that a big work, begun in October, 1948, secured one of Monica's Messengers as Hon. Slave, to receive demands for Village Evangelists' help in parishes all over England, and also to receive offers of help from priests and lay. Village Evangelists had done big work for some fifteen years, and now left the work to be done by Bible Missions, but had visited some four thousand parishes, and that was, as it were, her work.

"And later when she came home from Canada, she herself gave invaluable help in Village Evangelist mission after mission.

"Village Evangelists had a final conference at Swanwick in 1967 with the Archbishop of York, Bishop of Coventry, Dean of St. Paul's, etc., to help us, and though Monica was already far from well, she was determined to come, and it was wonderful to have her there. A week later she had that final stroke."

For Monica's Spartan qualities—referred to by her sister—I can speak; for this quality permeated not only her view of things practical such as eating and other bodily requirements and comforts, but also her tastes in the arts.

I remember how she gently rebuked me on one occasion when I had remarked how dear to me was the music of Chopin. "Yes," she said, "very pretty, but not deep. Chopin has none of the glorious solemnity of Bach, after all."

She had a large number of books, whole shelves of them running the length of the roomy sitting-room at the Abbey. But you would look in vain for anything of a purely frivolous nature. It was all good solid reading. Needless to say, to the many local visitors who called on her, these shelves were barely glanced at; and it was a rare thing for anyone to borrow a book.

It was largely by coming in contact for the first time with good taste in things pertaining to art, literature, or furnishings (home-made chairs, very delightfully constructed by local carpenters, fabrics from India, plain stained floors, and so forth, that readers of the "Women's Magazines," American paperbacks, and so forth, judged (most incorrectly) that Monica felt herself "superior." Poor Monica! who thought her guests would enjoy the Brandenburg concerto!

She quite often shocked her hearers by sayings, the impact of which was perfectly obvious to her, but pure Greek to her listeners. Once a visiting lady remarked what a pity it was that her nephew, who had done so well in college and had such a bright financial future, had decided to *throw it all up* to go into the ministry.

Monica's reaction was to say, "How glorious!"

She sometimes referred to "a splendid failure!" Perhaps it was the case of a man who failed in business by being "too honest," or it might be someone who lost his money but turned to God. It took people some time to understand that she was speaking "not as the world speaks."

She believed fervently that trials, errors, difficulties—even tragedy—had a very real purpose, that each was an opportunity for testing faith, and that "bad" things only occurred that we might build something better upon them.

Of her teen years Monica herself told us: "When I was about fifteen, I went all modern and cynical. I read a tremendous variety of books dealing with the incompatability of science and religion, as well as a lot of other rubbish. This made me feel very grown up and sophisticated, and I remember that I told Father and Mother that religion was outdated and I would have none of it and so on in the same foolish strain. I suppose I wanted their attention and expected a jawing. But my wise parents barely raised an eyebrow and would not be "drawn." Things in the family went on as if no bombshell had burst; family prayers, grace at table and so forth went on as usual, and I was given not even the satisfaction of being considered naughty and rebellious. Of course my atheism broke down over this and I returned to grace, but that made as small a ripple as my rebellion.

"It was as though they knew, and left all with the Holy Spirit. I only realize now what it must have meant to those wonderful parents of mine. From then on thanks be I have never again been bothered with doubts."

Monica's cousin, Iris Tower, wrote of early (1913–23) work with the Girls' Diocesan Association, a movement which was to spread into most dioceses during the years of World War I. It attracted girls of the upper classes of eighteen upward, girls under great temptation to frivolity during and as a result of the war. Gatherings known as "weeks" were held; happy and harmonious times with a chaplain and a lecturer. To many girls these proved a turning point in their religious life.

She ended her time with it as general secretary for the United Kingdom which meant exploring new avenues and starting a branch of the League of Nations at Rochester.

Then came the great sorrow of the death of her mother in 1923. Her care now was for her father and keeping up the happy hospitality of the deanery. She continued her connection with the girl guides and became divisional commissioner. She had already started guides in Palestine when on a visit to her brother Ronald in Jerusalem. The guide company there consisted of Jews, Moslems, and Christians. Later, in Canada she formed the first company north of the Peace River.

While still needed at the Rochester deanery to replace her mother, she knew that she must prepare and wait for her life's work. In the meantime she acted as "Bishop's Messenger" and was active in the Girls' Diocesan Association, the guides, and in mission work with the "Village Evangelists." After her father's death in 1928, she studied hard at St. Christopher's College, Blackheath, in further preparation.

Always she felt that her life was too easy, too secure, too complacent. "How easy it seemed to be good," she once told me, "under those circumstances. I needed a much greater challenge. In dear, safe old England one was welcomed and recognized—even respected far above one's worth. Was this, I used to think, going forth with only faith to sustain? The Son of Man had not where to lay his head; he had to rub out corn between his hands! And there was I with good meals, a soft bed, and a motor car to drive!"

The call came at last. A call that would test her faith in many things, in people, in her own ability, and almost (but never quite) in greater things.

She would be tested by many circumstances. By loneliness, by sense of failure, by perils of storms and subarctic climate, but above all by the blackness of real and imagined *rejection* by the people she strove (perhaps too hard!) to understand in the same measure that she loved.

It was upon all these things that she built that "something better." She became unshockable; she learnt to love the sinner even as she hated the sin. She had to hear of things she had not known existed. She found out what the world, the flesh, and the devil *really* meant; as she would never have known them in the Rochester deanery, among people who had taken St. Paul's advice to "think on these things which are of good report," and in so doing never saw the unspeakable under the carpet.

That call came from the far-flung Peace River country of northwestern Canada; to be more precise, the land north of the Peace River with Fort St. John, the only settlement of any account. The call came from Eva Hasell, undaunted, clever woman. It was to the land north of the Peace that Miss Hasell and Miss Sayle penetrated in 1928 to assess the need for, and possibilities of, some sort of mission to carry the gospel to isolated settlers, and give Sunday School classes to their children, who were growing up (in many cases) with no religious background.

Christianity had indeed made its debut many years before, in the establishing of a mission to the Indians and Métis by the Oblate Fathers; but even when the settlers began to come, there were not many of that faith—a few Irish, a few French-Canadians.

Also there had been a small log Anglican chapel built in 1898 near the Old River Post. It was built by a priest called Rev. Henry Robinson from White Fish Lake, who subsequently married the sister of Bishop Young of Athabaska. With so very few parishioners the work was not successful, and the next incumbent was withdrawn. Therefore, there had been no Anglican service north of the Peace for some years.

However, by the time of Miss Hasell's visit the new settlers were multiplying; the bulk of them were Protestants, many of them half-hearted members of the numerous sects from south of the border. Their education was limited, their experience of church life confined to casual attendance at "camp meetings."

Miss Hasell knew the West. She knew its people, and she knew the conditions, having worked in the northern settlements of Saskatchewan and Alberta. Miss Hasell is now best remembered for her work in assisting the Sunday School by Post and the founding and inspiriting of the Sunday School van service which travels far and wide on the prairies and in the Peace River country whenever roads permit; it is staffed by dedicated young women, obtained by voluntary recruitment from Canada and the United States, but mostly from Britain.

Few people have properly appreciated the fact that these girls, many from well-to-do homes, were willing to forego big money and careers to spend a few years in unselfish devotion to the work of helping young minds to see beyond the crass materialism of the age.

Miss Hasell saw the desperate need for this work and for a worker so dedicated as to be, as far as possible, unshockable. Wrote Monica, "With this information they returned to Montreal, and so interested many

Anglicans there, that a group was formed called the 'Fellowship of the West.' And the North Peace Parish owes more to that Fellowship than can be realized, far less repaid.

"In 1929 they sent up a priest and a young layman from Montreal, to make a further survey. In August 1931 the little Church of St. Martin was built, and consecrated by Bishop Rix of Caledonia. The Bishop came all the way from Prince Rupert (a *real* journey in those days) and on the same morning, August 23, he ordained our first Minister, the Rev. George Wolfendale, [as priest] in the Church—his salary being guaranteed by the Fellowship of the West.

"Meanwhile, early in 1929, Miss Hasell saw me in England, where I was preparing for God's call. Miss Hasell said: 'Can you ride? Go to the Peace River in British Columbia—fine country; lots of fine people going in; NO CHURCH; lots of children; lots of mosquitoes—just the place for you, Storrs.'

"And so, in fact, it proved.

"I couldn't really ride (as some of you remember) and the horse soon found that out, of course!"

Typically, Monica omitted to mention that it was she who largely made it possible for the first priest (Mr. Wolfendale) to be appointed; she paid half his stipend from her own small resources.

The May Birley she writes of was a sister to the Miss Nina Birley who also occurs so often in her diary. These two maiden sisters lived near their brother Kenneth, who was a real old-timer.

They came from the Isle of Man. Kenneth had been with the R.N.W. Mounted Police until 1913, when he became post manager at Fort St. John for Revillon Frères, rivals in the fur trade to the Hudson's Bay Company. He married Mary Beaton, daughter of Frank Beaton, Hudson's Bay Company factor at Fort St. John whose wife, Mary's mother, was one of nature's real ladies though she spoke only Cree.

After the withdrawal of the "French company," Kenneth and Mary settled down to farming.

The two maiden sisters came out to be near their brother. Nina, the elder, took a homestead nearby and built a cozy little house in which the two lived in delightful Edwardian style, with trophies from India on the walls, plenty of books, and nice china for "tea-time." Miss Birley loved her old fashioned garden with its herbs and hollyhocks.

Monica soon found others to make friends with, men mostly (for they outnumbered women), and these were to prove a strength to her in many ways. There was Duncan Cran, a surveyor, who became the first churchwarden, in which post he remained many years. A lean bachelor of many gifts, Duncan was until his death a dedicated and hard-working church-man. We shall meet many more as we read her own account;

some warm, some lukewarm, and some cold, but all people of the hardy and adventurous breed which has made Canada.

In Peace River Monica remained, except for visits to England in 1930 and 1933. In December, 1938, she went for some time, coming back to Peace River in July 1939. The highlights of her years in Canada were probably the building of her home, "The Abbey," in 1931, and the erection of the churches: St. Martin's, Fort St. John, in 1931, the Church Hall of St. John, Baldonnel, 1931; the Church of the Good Shepherd, Taylor, 1933, St. Matthias, Cecil Lake, and St. Peter's, Hudson Hope, both consecrated in 1938. There was also the beautiful little Chapel of the Holy Cross at the Abbey, built after the temporary one in the house. The windows are all on the south side, looking straight down the Coulee to the Peace.

In 1939, while in England, Monica "set about adopting" two non-Aryan boys from Germany. She wrote: "You may possibly have heard of the little scheme I had for taking two small non-Aryan refugees back with me to the Peace River. These are Hubert (né Horst) Schramm, aged twelve, and David (né Arwed) Lewinski, aged ten. They were rescued under a Church of England guarantee from impossible conditions in Germany, and proved to be delightfully vigorous, friendly little boys, who would make fine Canadian citizens.

"But, alas, after two months of negotation Ottawa has refused to admit them under this guarantee, or to let me adopt them in Canada, unless I previously adopt them in England, which by British law is impossible. So I have been obliged most regretfully to leave them behind in charge of a friend in London, while going myself straight to Ottawa for another attempt at close quarters to obtain their admittance.

"If this fails, I shall be very anxious for the soul of Canada, which can close its doors to such harmless immigrants, and dreadfully disappointed by my own loss in not being allowed to give them a home. But I shall still be more than thankful that they are brought safely away from an atmosphere of increasing contempt and hostility, and whether in England or Canada, will now have a fair chance in life."

In 1940 Monica finally managed to adopt the boys and they were allowed to come to Canada with other children being evacuated from Britain.

On June 25, 1947, Monica was received at Buckingham Palace. As Monica had never spent money or thought on clothes, her relatives and friends gathered around to make sure she was suitably dressed. They offered everything and anything. However, after looking at a splendid array of dresses, she finally rejected them all for one reason or another, in favour of the green velvet she had worn on "state" occasions in the North Peace. She did, however, accept shoes from one, a hat from yet another,

ST. MATTHIAS' CHURCH
CECIL LAKE

handbag and accessories from yet others, and was voted quite "proper."
How very typical of Monica!

In January, 1950, Monica left Fort St. John for Australia to visit her
brother, Bishop Christopher Storrs and his family. She returned to the

Peace River country only briefly, and in November of that same year, she left Canada to retire in England. She was now sixty-two.

In England, together with Adeline Harmer, Monica acquired a lovely little wooden house near Liss, in Hampshire, which she named Peacewood. It stood among natural chestnuts, birches and Scotch pines on a slope grown with grass and bracken, overlooking a misty-blue vista of rolling downland, in a seclusion rarely found so close to tarmac roads and innumerable other dwellings.

Although she had presumably "retired" to England, it was an energetic, enthusiastic retirement, for Monica immediately became involved with Village Evangelists, the Victoria League, and the English-Speaking Union, with the Fellowship of the Maple Leaf, with giving talks to various groups around the country and corresponding with various individuals across the world. It was a whirlwind retirement. Peacewood, like Monica, was always open to friends and strangers alike, and her sister, Petronella Moor, comments that she became "fair game for the unbalanced as well as for others." In 1958 she took time off for a visit to Canada. She spent a week or two in the North Peace, visiting old friends. The Abbey property had been vacant for some time, during which it had been sadly vandalized by boys. Unknown to her a group of devoted parishioners quietly got together and tidied and thoroughly cleaned the little chapel, and then asked Monica to conduct a little service to which they all gathered. She was her witty and amusing self and in splendid health.

In 1963, shortly after we left the ranch and came to live in Saskatchewan, Monica visited Canada for the last time. After a spell at Fort St. John she came to us for a few wonderful days. The weather was fine (it was midsummer), but like many people visiting the prairies for the first time, she found the countryside rather bare and featureless. She did enjoy the long stretch of sky-blue water which is Last Mountain Lake, and the soft groves of Manitoba maples and ash and poplar which grew in the hollows and filled the coulees; and she thought our great prairie skyscapes and sunsets almost the equal to anything she had seen in the North Peace.

In early December of 1967 Monica, although far from well, attended a long and final Village Evangelist conference at Swanwick. Very shortly after she suffered a fatal stroke (really a coma) and died on 14 December, just two months before her eightieth birthday.

Her funeral service was held at Liss, where she was also buried, on 1 January 1968; a memorial service was held at St. Martin's Church, Fort St. John. It was a fitting tribute to one who for twenty-one years had walked on snowshoes, ridden on horseback, slogged through mud, and in all ways disciplined "her patrician, middle-aged body as she went about her Master's work."

R.D. Symons sketched his portrait of Monica Storrs largely in the words of those who knew her intimately. He delineated Peace River, the region he knew and loved, in his own words.

You will look in vain on the map of Canada for a province called "Peace River." Yet in daily conversation throughout the West, one hears the Peace River country spoken of as though it were capitalized; as though it were a legal and surveyed division of Canada. It is, however—though of empire size—no more than a region, so that one crosses no boundary to enter it, for it was left out in the arbitrary provincial dividing of the West, and it actually occupies adjoining parts of two provinces. Yet the name stubbornly persists, so that a person from Grande Prairie, Alberta, will preferably refer to himself as a Peace Riverite rather than an Albertan; while another from Fort St. John is apt to use the same title rather than that of a British Columbian.

So do we retain that fierce price in regional citizenship; which perhaps need no more weaken our allegiance to the Great Dominion of which we are a part, than allegiance to England is vitiated whether a man calls himself a Yorkshireman or a man of Kent.

There is a boundary to the Peace River country, to be sure, but it is not marked, and it follows a jigsaw line, at the behest of a vague height of land, a barely perceptible ridge which divides a maze of streams, sending some southward and eastward to the Athabaska and more northward to the Peace to swell that great river already fed from the north by a similar number of creeks and rivers. It is this whole vast basin of the Peace which is properly named for that river, and occupies parts of the two provinces mentioned.

This northwesterly extension of Canada's great interior plain, extending from Manitoba to the Rockies, pushes far to the north of Edmonton and westerly until it laps against the mountains at a point almost due north of the southern Pacific shores of British Columbia. It comprises a far-flung stretch of plains, valleys, and hills; of mixed prairies and shrouded forests, timbered foothills, and grassy river-flats and, towards the north, of heaving muskegs misted in spring with the soft tender green of tamaracks.

Once beyond the scrubby height of land and truly in the basin, the most surprising thing is to find again those flowery and park-like prairies which we thought we had left far to the south, and it was these prairies—broken indeed by islands of woodland and patches of dark spruce—which first enticed agricultural settlers to this new frontier.

The only important surveyed line does not enclose this Eldorado, but rather divides it. This line is the 120th meridian, and it forms the boundary between Alberta on the east and British Columbia on the west. And one wonders why, for there is no natural boundary. Yet the mountain province was fortunate to have a share of the plains when the boundary was extended northward, the surveys left the Rockies at Intersection Mountain and carried the line straight north along the 6th meridian (so-called in terms of western land survey; but actually the 120th meridian in terms of world geography). This line cut the drainage basin of the Peace into two parts, leaving a pie-shaped triangle of interior plains joined, in an unnatural way, to British Columbia, like a bread basket held on the arm of a shopper.

And a bread basket it was to prove, for the British Columbia Peace River area is the only important grain-growing region of that mineral-rich but otherwise agriculturally poor province. Only here, west of Alberta, does one see the familiar row of lofty grain elevators at each small town or hear the autumnal hum of wheat combines. Fortunately for the beauty of the region, there are plenty of areas which cannot be put under the plough. Steep river hills, narrow valleys, numerous creeks and coulees, big clumps of spruce, wide marshes, and lakes; these will not allow the passage of farm machinery, and remain in their pristine state, adding to the general charm of the landscape, allowing for the continuance of game and other animals, providing a safe haven for song birds, and permitting gay patches of wild flowers to thrive in peace, and delight the eye and nose. The scent of wild roses is everywhere in June; while as summer wanes, there are wild strawberries to pick and bitter little cherries to make into a syrup which rivals the famed product of the Canadian maple.

Through this many-hued land, from the junction of two rivers west of the mountains, the great Peace River—high-banked and majestic—flows to its appointed meeting place with the Mackenzie River system. It threads the mountains by way of the Peace River Pass, passing through a canyon, beyond which is now the great dam which has flooded not only a large part of the Peace but also its parent waters, the Parsnip and the Finlay. The Peace River, like the 6th meridian, divides rather than encloses the region, and the names of the divisions are North and South Peace.

It is that part known in British Columbia as "The Land beyond the Peace" within which most of the activities recorded here are concerned. The deeds had to do with people, and there were few people until the arrival of the Northern Alberta Railway (successor to the original Edmonton, Dunvegan and British Columbia Railroad) at Grand Prairie, the region was ripe for settlement. By the time the Kaiser's war started, Alberta's share was filling with settlers and a fair number of land-seekers had penetrated a hundred and more miles with their ox wagons across the 6th meridian, and the little "towns" of Pouce Coupé (named for an Indian Chief), Dawson Creek, and Rolla began to serve their needs. Pouce Coupé soon became the "capital" and provincial administrative centre, with a government agency, a police post, and a land office.

Until 1920, indeed, except for a mere scattering of white trappers, gold seekers, fur traders, and pioneer ranchers (such as Vern MacLean), the North Peace remained largely wilderness, the hunting ground of the wild, mounted Beaver Indians, who looked sullenly at the white man's intrusion with the ploughs which would bury their horse pasture and their moose range.

With the cessation of hostilities in Europe, the trickle of settlers suddenly swelled, as numbers of soldier settlers took up homes near the trading post of Fort St. John, on the high prairies of North Pine and the valley of the Montney Creek—or more correctly "Montagnais"—named for another nomad chief. Prominent among these new settlers of the North Peace were names which will occur frequently in Monica Storrs' diary.

The little crossroads village of Fort St. John now came into being, and the Hudson's Bay Company moved their post from the deep valley to the higher plateau upon which was now built a fur trader's store, a log "hotel" or stopping house, an Indian sub-agency, a police post, and a small Chinese eating-house, all of which accommodated the freighters, the teamsters, and the landseekers. There was also a telegraph station of the Yukon telegraph line. The village was connected with Grande Prairie in Alberta by a rough wagon road, while a wooden cable-ferry took travellers and their beasts across the Peace.

But except for the chop of the settler's axe and the tramping of his plough team, the land north of the Peace still slumbered. Church there was none; nor library; nor any of the conveniences of modern life. Books and music were known only to those few—mostly from Britain—who had brought these along as essentials. The restless Americans seeking new frontiers; the dried out and impoverished farmers from the prairies; these had had little use for things cultural or religious. They were faced with bush and ragged scrub to be cleared, log homes to build before winter overtook them, a garden to plant, cows and horses to be provided for. Their only recreation even had to do with the body—baseball games in the summer, dancing in winter. Even hunting was only for the pot.

To the north was a wilderness (of which much still remains) sweeping to the Arctic with only a lonely police post or Hudson Bay Fort making a tiny spot on the map, at Fort Nelson, at Lower Post on the Liard, at a few locations up the Mackenzie. To the west the great Continental backbone thrust up its peaks and dared any but the boldest to penetrate its mineral secrets. To the south lay the jungles of the Brazeau Forest and the timbered whale's back of the Swan Hills. And to the east, still only a partly settled northern Alberta.

Isolation was the theme. In the choosing of good land, individual settlers were often miles apart, while in the overall picture the islands of settlement barely altered the general wilderness characteristics, and suffered a common isolation from the only city—Edmonton—five hundred miles away.

To one unfamiliar with frontier patterns, the many faces of its growing society are indeed hard to reconcile into a whole, and the first reaction of a visitor to a region in the process of settlement may well be one of puzzlement, if not of shock and even repulsion, because the ordinary norms of community life do not appear to exist. Only years of living together would finally make ancient history of the petty feuds, the mistrust between neighbours, the bitter gossip, the mischief-making which divided people of different backgrounds, different cultures, and different motivation who were thrown together higgledy-piggledy and by chance.

All these causes of friction, together with the envy of the less successful for the more fortunate, can be traced to the fact that the majority of such settlers came, not from a wish to live in undisturbed and Arcadian peace, but rather because they found the older settlements too constricting, too much under the rule of law, too competitive, and they were seeking a freedom based on elbow room, freedom (according to their lights), and the opportunity to tell others to go to hell. And the "to hell with so and so" does not make for a tightly knit and happy social life.

The pioneer life was hardest on people of real loyalty, real faith, real appreciation of good values. For a settler's wife reared in an atmosphere of church-going, of the reading of good books, of a certain privacy, of interesting conversation, the experience of living in such a society must at times have been very hard to bear. The constant visits from neighbours, often actuated by mere curiosity, the constant borrowing and not returning, the impudent stares, the impertinent personal questions, the rough language and the lack of any religious appreciation—the name of Jesus used only as an exclamation of annoyance—all these must have brought many hours of tears and depression to the young wives of soldier-settlers who could remember family life in a different environment. And these same young wives, and often their husbands, because they minded their business, would be thought of as snobs and interlopers.

But there—if you have read Mrs. Moodie's book, *Roughing It In the Bush*—I can only add that what she wrote of the Ontario backwoods of

1837 was repeated in the Peace River country almost a hundred years later. However, because people are good and generous as well as dishonest and mean, there is another and brighter side to this picture. In time of real need—and on the frontier that is often—animosities were laid aside and misunderstandings forgotten. The spirit of God still operates and calls deep into people's souls, so that a sick child, a burned barn, a man's broken leg, at once brought offers of help, offers of transportation, offers of a day's work to repair the damage.

It was in this mutual aid in times of necessity that Monica Storrs could see hope; it was on the same that she slowly built a greater appreciation of neighbour for neighbour, welded together by mutual understanding of the healing power of religion. I know better than many, how utterly she felt failure, because so many people persisted in rejecting her ministry; but I also know, better than she ever did, what changes she did finally bring about. "If people want to be missionaries, why don't they go to the *heathen* in Africa," I have heard said of her. And I have also heard her blessed as few of us will ever be, especially by the young wives for whom her coming meant the end of loneliness and of isolation and removal from things spiritual.

The frontier in time moved north, and one will look in vain for much that once was old Fort St. John. Only in the western foothills will one find some ranch folks in log houses, people who still find a horse the best transport when unbridged creeks must be crossed in flood, where the branding fire glows ruby red until the work is done and a big supper is eaten by a kerosene lamp.

It is on these lonely trails that one may yet understand the work of Monica Melanie Storrs, whose ministry commenced while the land still slumbered between two wars.

"Quite as wonderful as inheriting the walls and traditions of centuries is to acquire a bit of nameless, untouched bush and start everything from the very bottom."

Monica Storrs, 1931

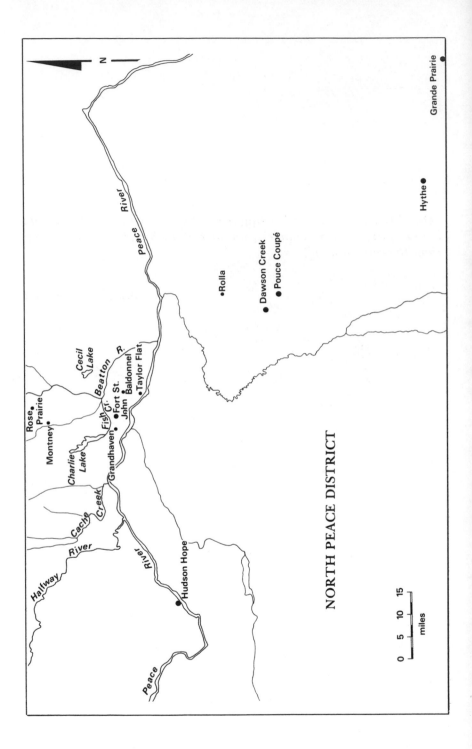

NORTH PEACE DISTRICT

Grande Prairie

Hythe

Rolla

Dawson Creek

Pouce Coupé

Peace River

Cecil Lake

Beatton R.

Fish Cr.

Taylor Flat

Fort St. John

Baldonnel

Rose Prairie

Montney

Charlie Lake

Grandhaven

Cache Creek

River

Halfway River

Hudson Hope

Peace River

N

0 5 10 15
miles

Extracts from Monica Storrs' Diaries 1929[1]

The train went almost into the boat,[2] and the moment I crossed the gangway I found Muriel Hooper[3] saying good-bye to her Father with most admirable firmness and calm, and sending him right away so as not to watch the ship's departure. Directly after that I fell into the arms of Sylvia and Iris Tower[4] who had most angelically motored up all the way from Ellesmere for a quarter of an hour together. We found our cabin and had a tiny talk, but in no time the all-ashore bugle went, and they had to bundle off. After that there was the usual rather awful pause waiting for the gangways to go down, and at last the slow gliding off and the endless waving to and from the shore. After a bit we went down and found heaps of sweet letters and telegrams, and above all Gundulf's[5] adorable bag of tricks which has been my daily delight ever since.

Saturday, September 28

The fair promise of our start was not fulfilled, but within two or three hours of going to bed I woke up to find the whole world swinging and poor Hooper in a very bad way. After that there is nothing more to tell for at least thirty-six hours during which I lay in profound meditation while poor Hooper suffered *far* more. Towards the afternoon I got really anxious lest she should hurt herself, and ventured to send for the doctor. But when he found it was only seasickness he said coldly: "I'm afraid you must console yourself with the thought of 750 sufferers," and promptly withdrew.

Our beautiful plans for a Sunday School soon faded away while I lay all day and all night vaguely thinking of the past, and poor Hooper's attention was strictly confined to the present.

Sunday, September 29, Michaelmas.

Not much of a Sunday or Saint's Day either as the ship was still rolling like an acrobat. There was a Morning Service but I wasn't there, alas, though about mid-day I did crawl up on deck and had a cautious luncheon. Monday was much the same; and Tuesday found Hooper after a short renaissance back in bed again and very depressed. She hated the cabin and yet couldn't leave it; and all my devices whether physical (brandy) or mental (reading aloud) or aesthetic (gramophone) were equally useless.

On *Wednesday* morning (October 2) an inspiration was sent me. I opened the folding harmonium (mercifully labelled "wanted on the voyage") and played Handel's "Largo" as far as I knew it by heart, making good use of the swell. In less than half an hour Hooper was on deck—and she has been perfectly well ever since! It's true that the sun had come out and the sea steadied down at about the same time, but I don't believe that had much to do with it.

This is a beautiful ship and all the stewards are delightfully kind and friendly. The passengers are a little disappointing from our point of view, being nearly all rich Canadians or New York merchants and their families. They look and sound like profiteers, but I expect we should get fond of lots of them if the Atlantic had only allowed us to start earlier. As it is I don't think we shall have made any friends for the future.

Margaret Robertson,[6] the other girl who is going with Hooper to work under Miss Fowler on the Swan River, is unfortunately travelling third, and was incapacitated almost as long as Hooper so we have only seen her for odd moments the last day or two. But I like her very much and wish I could carry her on to Fort St. John with me.

Besides Hooper's cure there were two other great events yesterday. First we passed quite close to a huge ice-berg, so close that I thought it must be a bit of C.P.R. scene-painting; but they all said it was real, so I photographed it from the top deck. I was surprised at the colour, having expected it to be like greenish glass whereas it was really pure white and glistening in the sun like a small escaped snow mountain. I supposed it reminded everybody of the *Titanic*, but we didn't say so till today.

Then at 3 P.M. (Wednesday, October 2) we sighted the first land, Belle Isle on the Starboard bow, and a little later the coast of Newfoundland further off on the Port bow. This meant that we were beginning to enter the St. Lawrence River and should have calm-going for the rest of the voyage.

It was an extraordinary feeling—that first sight of the huge New World—and of the land where Father was born. I'm afraid it was not altogether a friendly feeling I had for it, but something very near resentment for not being the coast of England. But all the same it made me feel rather like a little Columbus.

My word—what a man was Columbus!

But whether a benefactor to the world is quite another question.

Thursday, October 3.

This morning the land had quite disappeared; but the sea was smooth and the wind gone down so I suppose we are sheltered by Labrador though we can't see it. It has been wet and misty all day and more like coming up the English Channel to Plymouth than anything else I can remember.

We hear that there will be a mail taken off after dinner tonight by the pilot boat and sent home by the *Duchess of Atholl;* so Hooper and I (and almost everyone else) having several dozen letters to answer have been doing nothing else all day. Before luncheon however I had one break-away and went upstairs for the first time to the little gymnasium. It's the most ridiculous place full of elaborate devices for working off your meals and keeping down your weight. There is a dummy outrigger sculling boat, two dummy bicycles where you can sit and pedal and race each other while an indicator opposite shows who is winning. But the absurdest part is two dummy horses on which you sit, and when you turn an electric switch they trot, canter or gallop to taste! The only feeble part is that they haven't yet trained them to shy or bolt, so it is no real practice!

Every night since we started the clocks have been put back an hour, so now we are six hours behind Home. Hooper and I find this most disturbing. Because by the time we are awake in the morning (that is providing we have had at all a decent night) all our people are already having luncheon, which seems to make them *so* superior; and after that they get out of hand and we don't know what they are doing. What it will be like when I get nearly across Canada I don't like to think. I shall have lost control of them altogether—unless by good luck I can be putting them all to bed.

Our greatest daily excitement has been the opening of a marvelous series of little parcels which we *both* found waiting for us on board, Hooper's from some cousin in Beckenham, and mine from Gundulf. The only day we were actually too ill to open them was Saturday, so on Sunday afternoon we both opened two which was really against the rules. Of course, my series has been *far* the nicest, but I have naturally tried to conceal the fact from Hooper.

On Friday I found Vinolia Soap,
On Sunday, Eau de Cologne (for Saturday) and Ginger,
On Monday, a travelling Laundry outfit,
On Tuesday, a Rothenburg Top,[7]
On Wednesday, a round box of Creme de Menthe sweets,
On Thursday, a tiny portrait of the Angel Donor,
and the last one *I don't know yet.*

Havergal,[8] *Toronto*
October 7, 1929

We had a quite pleasant journey here from Montreal on Saturday. The railway coach was just like a long cinema. We all sat in twos in very deep chair-shaped seats facing forwards, while very solemn Archdeacons dressed as super-railway Guards in gloves walked up and down announcing (quite unintelligibly) the name of the next station and discouraging all attempts to open a window. We arrived here at nine and had supper, talked to Pop[9] and went to bed. It certainly is a delightful place and a fine bit of work. Yesterday morning she took us to the nearest Church for Holy Communion. Yesterday Robertson also turned up from Quebec and the marvellous Pop found her a third bed, so we are all together here in great luxury. In the morning I had a walk with Pop. After luncheon she drove us into the City, where after a walk round she and Hooper went to tea with Canon Plumptre[10] while Robertson and I went to Mrs. Warren,[11] the Dominion Guide Commissioner. The latter is a very opulent and most kind lady, who is lending us her car this morning and treats us with almost super-motherly interest and care. Last night we went to Evensong at Canon Plumptre's church, St. James, a nice large church with a good congregation and enormous choir.

The country so far has been pretty but monotonous—flat, with large flat lakes rather like Norfolk Broads only surrounded by little thin trees—birches, and white poplars and maples chiefly—all made rather lovely just now by the colouring, but normally an anaemic effect, I should think. I suppose it is due partly to the rocky soil and partly to the cold. Mrs. Warren's car is just coming so this must stop.

Train Crossing Saskatchewan
3.45. October 9, 1929

I have just parted with Hooper and Robertson or rather they departed from me at Brandon three hours ago; and so Swan[12] now gleams ahead as the last link with the familiar world. Pop brought us to the station and after a lot of confused battling over our sleepers, we were at length torn from her and started off in the 9 P.M. Vancouver Express. Our berths were awfully funny. Hooper got a lower one because she is a bad train-sailor too and seemed to think she would feel the motion less. Robertson and I had uppers both with strangers below; so it wasn't at all easy to be independent of the ladder in getting up, though of course easy enough to swing out on the bar and jump down. It is awfully funny dressing and undressing in the top bunk because there is nowhere to put anything nor is there quite room to kneel up. So you have to learn to get up lying down! We slept perfectly well, at least Robertson and I did and I think Hooper did too; and in the morning we all went bust and had breakfast in the Restaurant Car—the very *smallest* breakfast you could discover cost a dollar each. However, as nearly all the rest of the day we lived on victuals supplied by Mrs. Warren, we can't really complain. I can't tell you how good Mrs. Warren was. She not only supplied us like that, but also gave us a free grant of books at the Guide Headquarters, lent us her car most of the day, and sent word of our approach to Winnipeg where we were greeted by two distinguished Guiders this morning at 9 o'clock.

Really we enjoyed yesterday very much. There is enough room in the Tourist carriages and the people are awfully friendly and although you can *never* open a window, it's not so appallingly stuffy as I had been led to fear. All yesterday was Ontario forest and lakes, pretty deadly country until we got to the shores of Lake Superior which are rather lovely, surrounded by low hills covered with little trees all gold and red. But most of the forest is flat and yet rocky, so that nothing can grow except mile after mile after mile of these tiny little spindly trees whose only beauty is the temporary one of colour. It looks an awful country to live in, and perfectly *fearful* to get lost in as there is no difference for mile upon mile. Personally I even prefer the prairie which began this morning after Winnipeg. It is of course flat and monotonous but it has at least the difference between plough and grass-land, and there are clumps of bush and you do see farms and cattle, and the distant horizon. Already there is a good deal of snow about, which is rather a shock to see so soon. The really dreary part is the buildings of course, such hopeless looking houses and shacks and shanties and nothing else. Still I was prepared for all that of course, and as it's *not* England, it doesn't really matter.

We have just left a place called Broadview, where the clocks went back another hour so we arrived at 4 and left at 3.15!

From this point also the snow has become more general and all the roofs are white. I got very fond of Hooper and Robertson and think they got fond of each other which is capital as they will be thrown very much together now. Miss Fowler met them at Brandon and carried them off. I felt a little desolate at first, but was not allowed to feel it long because a large family of stout Presbyterians—father, mother, son and Scotch lady friend—all "took pity" on me, and came and talked Church doctrine and lent a pamphlet about the enormities of the United Church[13] under the cover of which the mother quietly borrowed the Mary Webb novel[14] I was trying to read! This I suppose is one of the penalties of travelling alone!

The soil is quite black here and the snow has vanished, so it is evidently still purely local.

In train for Edmonton
Thursday, October 10, 6 p.m.

Last night, having learned that the train would arrive at Edmonton today at 3.30 instead of midnight, I spent a good two shillings at Moose Jaw imparting to Swan the happy tidings. But this foresight had a fatal effect upon the train, which broke down for two hours in the middle of the night, so that we reached Calgary at 9.30 this morning, exactly an hour after the departure of the Edmonton train; so I spent another fortune, first in informing poor Swan of the new change of time (9.30) and then in cloaking my four little light cruisers at the baggage office for the nauseating sum of sixpence apiece! After that it was not yet 10 and the next train wasn't till 2.50 and I didn't know anyone and it was raining.

I asked the Enquiry Office whether there was a Cathedral or a Museum. They said no Museum but a Cathedral—at least a United Church! I repudiated this as civilly as possible, and started off to look.

Calgary is rather an awful town, so glaringly hideous and blatant in every part. And the people, instead of the sort of simple open-spacey country-folk one imagines, seemed more ultra-towney and over-dressed, and the women more touched up than anywhere I can think of at Home. I found myself getting miserable for the first time and in danger of hating the whole business when suddenly I found a policeman with quite an English voice who directed me straight to the little Anglican Cathedral.[15] It's an unpretentious little building something like Luton Church, but it was Homely and not the least blatant anyway; and the organist was practising very loud old favourites—as it might have been John[16]—so I stopped there till after 12 and got quite straight again.

After that I explored the rest of the town, had luncheon at one of those funny places where you pick up a tray and run around loading it yourself, and finally at 2.50 started off again Northward in this train.

The country is still prairie, but it hasn't been quite so dead flat this afternoon. There are a few swellings and a river or two and far on the Western horizon I saw the foothills of the Rockies very rugged and blue, giving a new feeling of hope and variety to the whole landscape.

Taken altogether the people seem very friendly and not at all aggressive. The girls in food-shops are the worst—very curt and bored; but the railway officials, though incredibly middle-aged and dignified, are perfectly kind and friendly, and as for our fellow-travellers during the last three days, they almost drove me back into my stoney British reserve.

Pouce Coupé
(only till tomorrow I hope)
October 16, 1929.

Swan and the Archdeacon[17] saw me off on Monday at 4 (from Edmonton). The journey took exactly twenty-five hours, and is 450 miles to the North West. The chief feature about it was the badness of the permanent way, so that the train rocked all the time like a very energetic cradle (why *do* we rock cradles?) and you had to take care not to be thrown out of your bunk. The country seemed to be all waste woods and bush, varied by flat prairie. When you went to sleep and when you woke up, and all next day—hardly any change. The colour just now is all a faded brown and the trees are all either white poplars or more rarely spruces. Really I think I begin to like the spruce best as at least they look alive and give a little colour, whereas the poplars look like millions and millions of thin spikey ghosts. It's funny looking out of the train to see no real trees, no hedges, or lanes, no real hills, no villages or stone churches, no gardens or large houses or fine barns or yellow ricks. It seems as if the Creator had started making a landscape, and then abandoned it as too large to finish.

We got to Hythe[18] about 5 on Tuesday and a Pouce Coupé man brought me as far as here (sixty miles) for five dollars (a guinea). I found Hasell and Sayle[19] waiting for me in the hotel[20] and they showered information over me till after midnight. They really are a wonderful pair. Everybody round here calls them "the Gurrls" and the common remark to me is "My! Ain't them Gurrls just It!"

I went down with them yesterday morning to see the Caledonia Van, and off they went in it for their last week's work up here, while I returned to the hotel in hopes of finding a seat in a truck (lorry) going back to Fort St. John. It's another sixty-four miles of more difficult road and in a returning truck would cost about five dollars, but if I have to get a car to go on purpose it will be at least £7—which is rather too tough. Nothing came through yesterday, and this morning I thought of starting to walk, but have got too much small luggage and no rucksack available. Also it would take about three days and lodging is doubtful; and *finally* it would lose me this precious chance of catching an extra mail. So I've got to be patient and if nothing comes to-day the District Road Inspector[21] has promised to take me when he goes on business to-morrow (Friday).

This is a very nice large clean hotel with *twenty* little bedrooms and far the best view I have yet seen in Canada. It is a wide sweep of long low hills like English downs only hairy instead of smooth, that is, they are clothed all over by the faded ghostly little poplars. In the foreground is a little stream, the Pouce Coupé River, crossed by the road to Hythe. By day it's all no colour but grey and faded brown but yesterday at sunset the hills turned blue and pink and it was really rather lovely. I am afraid though that these hills, low as they are, are higher than anything at St. John, except the actual banks of the Peace River which I am told are 800 feet high. Pouce Coupé is the "County Town" of the Peace River Block. I had plenty of time yesterday to admire it. It looks like a cross between a soldiers' permanent camp during the War, and a home for lost bathing machines. The bathing machines are apparently thrown down more or less haphazard on the waste ground, but there are two or three broad mud roads among them with raised pavements made of logs or planks. When you reach the bathing machines you find that one is a bank, another a Government Office, and another a general store, and of course there are two or three garages, each far larger than any other building except the hotel. I called on the doctor's wife yesterday afternoon, a very refined English woman from near Porchester. Her husband [Dr. Watson] is the only doctor west of Hythe, that is, he has a little practice of about 10,000 square miles. They do *say* however, that Fort St. John is to have a doctor and a hospital quite soon, but nobody knows whether it is to be this winter or not. It's rather sad that everyone first thinks that I have come to be a nurse there, and when they learn the truth their jaws drop with a crash. Nevertheless they are all most kind and friendly, and the complete absence of any sort of class distinction really is delightful. Everybody—farmers, mechanics, lorry-drivers, store-keepers, hotel servants—all drift in and out, give me a nod and start off with a conversation as if we'd all been born and brought up together.

I also went to call on the Matron[22] in the little tiny hospital. She was in bed with lumbago but sent for me to go up, and in her room I found a woman whose mother lives in Kent, and who immediately asked me to go and stay with her whenever I wanted a change. The Land-inspector came and had a very nice talk this morning and the village schoolmaster, who is a very dandy young gentleman of forty-two joined me for dinner last night. He is a tremendous talker and evidently glad of any microphone, as he turned up again in the school-break this morning.

Some of the men and boys are delightfully picturesque, that is the rougher ones who still wear slightly cowboy clothes especially the most enchanting big hats almost too good to be true.

Extracts from letters written to two people, which accounts for a certain repetition in places.

Fort St. John
Feast of St. Luke, 1929 (November 22).

At last I've got here, exactly three weeks to the day. I found your two letters here—which arrived together yesterday, so the time taken was seventeen days, and means I think that a letter posted on Monday is pretty safe to get here on the following Thursday fortnight—provided of course that the last bit of road is not too bad.

After a very chic evening drinking tea with the hotel-keeper's wife in her private apartment till mid-night yesterday, I was finally rescued this morning by the District Road Engineer, a nice little Canadian called Mr. Clark. The first thirty-five miles or so were tame enough through alternating ploughed fields and unclaimed bush. Then came eighteen miles of solid forest and then the long steep muddy hill down to the Peace River. Half-way down we came upon another car completely embedded in the mud and stayed for about an hour, trying to dig it out, lever it out, push it out, pull it out, putting chains on the wheels and hauling with a rope both backwards and forwards—but all in vain. So at last we had to skin round the edge of the road past it, and sent up a horse team kept for such emergencies at the ferry below.

The river is about half a mile wide and its banks at that point about 800 feet high so it is rather fine. We crossed in a wooden ferry pushed by a tiny petrol boat and drove up a corresponding steep and tortuous road on this, the North side. After that about seven miles of more or less flat bush brought us at last to this abode at 2.30.

Miss Birley[23] greeted me with a genial indifference to the fact that I was two days late, and proceeded at once to give me some cold meat, cheese and tea in the kitchen, which is also the dining room.

She is younger than I expected, perhaps about thirty-five, dark and slim and very kindly, humorous and happy-go-lucky. She announced at once that she was *no* housekeeper and never let house-keeping trouble her. And when I asked when meal-times were she said, "Whenever anyone comes in—but I prefer to give you breakfast in bed, because I have it about 7 or 7.30 and *don't sit down to it.*" I protested against this plan, but shall have to accept it at the start, at least as far as having it in my room (though that will be cold later) because I rather gather she wants me out of the way at that hour. It seems also that we have dinner somewhere between 12 and 1 o'clock and supper somewhere between 6 and 7. Afternoon tea is, of course, not the custom, but if anyone drops in at *any* time, tea is produced; so though you may miss it five days in the week, you may quite likely get it five times on the sixth day to make up.

My window looks West on to rough scrub beyond which I can just see the tops of distant hills. But the foreground is a little marred by a tall bran-new wooden garage and some other rather ramshackle farm sheds. Outside there are turkeys and chickens and two pigs and (somewhere about) three cows and three horses. Inside, there is a spotted white setter called Rowdy and two cats. Miss Petter,[24] last but not least of the party, is a school-teacher aged twenty-one who runs the nearest school[25] (East Fort St. John [Baldonnel]) which is three miles off, and has twenty children.

Miss Birley has long gone to bed, so I think I must too. To-morrow morning she is going to take me round to a few salient people in her brother's Ford car (there *is* a brother with the next-door farm, I'll tell you more about him next time) and after that as soon as my breeches come I am to be introduced to a nag called Buster.

The weather is quite warm at present and she says *may* continue so until Christmas or *may* drop to 40 or 50 below at any moment—so jolly! Once she remembers it 68 below [Fahrenheit] but that is quite exceptional, and I don't believe it's anything like as cold as that normally. I think they rake up all the records they can remember to frighten new-comers!

Fort St. John
October 19, 1929.

. . . [This house] is an oblong grey bungalow with an excellent hall-sitting-room, entered immediately by the front door, and off this are three very small bedrooms, a little kitchen where we also feed and wash up and wash our clothes etc., and a tiny larder, store and lamp-room. The bedrooms are distinctly cramped, but the sitting-room-hall is palatial and furnished with Oriental rugs, South African relics, and tiger skin, a sofa and table and some perfectly good books and magazines. There is also a *radio* set of *six* valves; but she owns that it seldom functions and when it does you only get Seattle, U.S.A. She professes to be very excited about my gramophone and when, if ever, my trunks come up from Pouce Coupé with the records, I shall give her a fine concert. The view to the front of the house (East) is, first a little attempt at a garden, then flat scrubby bush, very dull. But the back-view from my window is *nearly* charming, in fact if only the house had been built fifty yards farther back, it would have been lovely. For we are close to the top of a long wooded gully which runs down a mile and a half to the river, and from the clothes line can see over the tops of the trees right across to a lovely line of distant blue hills. I'll send you photographs of the house and of Miss Birley, as soon as I can get them taken and developed . . . .

Would you believe it, Fort St. John has just started a picture house and has a film every Saturday night! And Miss Birley and two of the little nephews have just gone off to it, fetched by a garage friend in his car.

This morning I was taken to have a preliminary look at Fort St. John which is five miles to the North West. It is a perfectly hideous scattered dump of about a dozen wooden shanties, vaguely springing up on each side of a straight mud road which crosses a high plateau with a fine view

of distant hills. The contrast between the view and the buildings is so
pitiful that it makes me rather despair of the future of Canada. Of course,
these shanties will go in time, but I doubt whether anything more
comely will supersede them. I was introduced to the post-master and the
two stores, and we had dinner in the "Hotel" which is a kind of barn
with four linoleum-topped tables at one end.[26] There we were joined by
a very highly dressed lady at in a black silk toque with long bead tassels
who I learnt afterwards was a homesteader's wife aged about sixteen and
living about eleven miles away.

I must say the work seems to be rather baffling. In the first place there
is a veneer of advanced civilization that is so difficult to cope with.
Everyone tries to have a car, even if they can't pay for it, and the roads are
few and often impassable. Everyone tries to dress in public as if they were
in a town—hence the lady at dinner in the barn. Everyone has to go to a
dance as often as possible. On the other hand the distances are
tremendous, everything is five, seven, ten or twenty miles from
everything else. There is only one real road, and the country is all alike—
just rough bush, broken by clearings and a little shack or shanty *about*
every half mile, but generally *miles* from the road and reached by more or
less definite trails.

Also Miss Birley says the settlement itself is as full of small gossip as
the worst English village, the people are fed up with the Church for
neglecting them for so long, and still more put off by the few odd
preachers who have drifted through. Also she says that horses can't go far
in the very cold weather as they get short of breath—and even if I could
borrow a car and the roads were open at such times—petrol is 2/6 a
gallon and starting up is a problem!

By the way: we have two stoves burning wood; two oil lamps; a water
butt outside; a rubber bath, but not enough water till it rains or snows.
Now *never* say I tell you nothing.

We eat very good bread, butter, eggs, apples, cheese, macaroni,
potatoes and jam. Salt beef and tinned milk—both quite good—turnips,
carrots, one cabbage a week. No fish of course, but you know that's no
loss to me. Now *never* say I haven't told you everything.

There are attached to this house: two cats and a dog; lots of Rhode
Island chickens; several cows and horses at present at large in the woods;
two pigs, who devour the washing-up water. Isn't that convenient? So
the bacon goes on coming backwards and forwards! Isn't that
convenient? Except that we don't have bacon. Now NEVER say . . . .

October 25.

Last Sunday was the first Sunday (not spent in a ship or train) that I can remember without any kind of Service within reach, unless you count the queer little Sunday School. We have by now a rough routine of life, more or less as follows: Miss Birley calls me when there is some water boiled, but won't let me help her in any way before breakfast which is about 8.30. Directly after that Miss Petter goes off to her little school at East Fort St. John which is three miles away. She rides the mare called Papoose and wears marvellous cowboy trousers made of thick leather which I envy very much. After breakfast Miss Birley and I wash up, and then I do my room and the sitting room which is all she will entrust to my care, because she says English people are far too thorough for Canada and make an unnecessary labour of everything. She's English herself, but I see what she means. I take out the floor mats and shake them outside and sweep every corner and long for a mop and a dust-pan to finish off, and ask for a duster, and move all the ornaments as I dust. *She* snatches the broom, charges around, moves nothing, has no dustpan, pushes the dust over the rugs and over (partly under) the door-mat out of the door, and doesn't dust at all—and the annoying thing is that the apparent result is just the same!

After that I clean shoes and then have my own Matins. After that she cleans out the animals and cooks the dinner and I feed and water the horse, and then either go out visiting—or don't.

We have dinner about 12.30 when Mr. Birley often joins us. He is great fun really. I have great fun quarrelling with him over Canadian misnomers such as "trucks" for lorries—"street cars" for trams—"canned meat" for tinned meat, and also over Canadian and English ways of ploughing and milking, etc., (me not knowing the first thing about either but never mind that!).

On Sunday he produced for me a temporary mount named Buster, a huge black farm horse looking rather like Haig's horse of the ill-fated memorial.[27] I pounded on him to the East Fort St. John School where Miss Hasell has already started a Sunday School for me to water. About fourteen children turned up which isn't bad seeing the whole school every day has only twenty and most of them are three or four miles away. Only one of the mothers who teach turned up, so I took the other class, and at the end tried to teach the children to sing "All Things Bright and Beautiful" which was jolly up-hill work! Afterwards I asked who would like to be Wolf-cubs and of course they *all* would; so I told them to get their parents' leave and we are to start in the dinner hour on Tuesday week.

There is a huge preponderance of boys here;[28] in this school for instance they are seventeen to three, mostly young; so I hope to start a pack of Cubs and the three little girls will have to be Cubs too, for all practical purposes anyway!

They are funny gauche sort of children, slow and very off-hand, though I don't think they mean to be rude. I suppose I shall get to understand them before long.

On Monday morning at *last* my luggage arrived, and I had a regular field-day, unpacking and squeezing everything into my funny little room which is about nine feet by twelve feet . . . .[29] The chief problem is books and papers. And the only solution I can find is to put the trunk trays on the top of the trunks and fill them with carefully arranged heaps of Mothers' Union, Society for the Propagation of Christian Knowledge,[30] Scout and Guide literature. There is no chair, but I don't mind, as there isn't really room for one; so I cover the long trunk with its papers etc. all over with Ronald's[31] flag of Cyprus, and when I go to bed, put my clothes on the top of that. So now you know. Also, under the washing-stand is a shelf which holds the gramophone records and quite a lot of books and the rest of the books remain in the book-box which mercifully is allowed to stay on the verandah.

The kitchen and sitting-room each have a wood stove and there are logs outside which we split and fetch in about once a day. For water, we are dependent upon last winter's ice which is cut out of the river or lake and stored in a little shed packed with sawdust. This is brought in and melted as occasion requires, but there is not enough for any baths until the snow comes. There is also a well about 100 yards away at the bottom of the coulee (a sort of dry ravine) at the back of the house, but it hasn't much water and is only used for the animals.

The food is very good, and amusing, because it really does depend upon circumstances. For instance, we finished the salt beef last week, and shall have no more meat until Mr. Birley kills. Also the cows happen to be dry at present, so we drink "Carnation milk" which isn't at all bad. Also the hens are going on strike, so we have three eggs a week and take them in turns. But don't imagine for a moment that food is short or bad. We have heaps of bread and butter and jam and cheese and soup and bacon and grocery things, and supplies of apples and carrots and turnips and celery and potatoes, and yesterday, greatly daring, Mr. Birley killed and we ate a chicken. Also, at every single meal, we have either tea or coffee which I think is rather a bore, but they insist that the water, though perfectly safe, is very nasty! And I don't like not to fall in with their little ways.

Miss Birley really is a delightful person; and I've hardly ever met anyone so kind. She is more than a hostess; she is a Guardian Angel, always genial and placid and very amusing and quite full of consideration and really thoughtful care. She works all day without a pause, in the house and among the animals without ever getting hurried or fussed, and always having time to stop and do something else for anybody. She wears a grey jumper, or a short brown leather jacket, with breeches and stockings, and when she takes me out in her brother's car (an occasional privilege) she dresses just the same and never wears a hat. I must say this country is the Eldorado in that respect that appearances really *do* seem to be nothing. The men can look like tramps or cowboys or mechanics or bank-managers, nobody notices. The women can go out in fur coats or silk dresses and fleshy stockings or breeches and heavy boots—nobody notices. When I started visiting, I asked Miss Birley whether I should wear a hat, and she said, "Just as you like, nobody will notice," so I didn't.

Another frequenter of the house besides Mr. Birley is Tommy Hargreaves (I don't call him Tommy),[32] a kind little man who runs the local garage. He is more or less at home here and it takes nice practical forms such as making me a three foot square map of the district, and taking me all round one part of the district in his car one afternoon, over the most impossible trails, "to show me the way about." I came back far more bewildered than I started but that was hardly his fault; and of course, he can't do it often, because it's losing him his own day's work.

On Wednesday therefore I embarked on my first real round of *District Visiting*. Miss Birley is letting me have her horse, as much as I like. She insists on cleaning him out. I feed him (and pay for his feed) and water him and of course saddle and bridle him, etc. He is a sturdy little bay called Rama, and supposed to have *endless* endurance. The Canadian saddle is a funny ponderous building with a horn in front and a high back, more safe than comfortable. It has no buckles, but you fasten it on by passing a long strap round and round through two rings and pulling for *all* your worth. Rama hates the tightening process and tries to bite in self-defence, otherwise he is as mild as milk. I don't know why Miss Birley said he was as obstinate as the devil, unless she meant that he is inclined to shy especially at cars, and at fallen trees, etc., in the twilight. He only jumps sideways or revolves a little, and soon recovers his equilibrium. We were out on Wednesday from 11 till 6.30, but stopped a good while for dinner in one house. Then I followed up to about six other houses on a round of about sixteen miles, nearly all along these funny little trails through bush and over rolling prairie. The women were awfully nice and welcoming. I'll tell you more about them and their homes next time; this letter is much too long already.

Rama was rather lazy, and I had some trouble in teaching him that District Visitors *always* either trot or canter—but he got his vengeance later. Yesterday I decided to go shorter, so only went ten miles and visited six people between 1.30 and 6.30. I started a bit worn inside the knees, having resolved the day before to ride with a straight leg and full length stirrup like the Canadians and to practise sitting tight for a trot. But half-way through yesterday my left leg punctured completely;[33] for three miles I had to implore Rama to walk as smoothly as possible, and for the last two I had to dismount and lead him. So he got his revenge!!!! It's only a very mild sore really, and it gave Mr. Birley a fine laugh at me for riding so long and gripping so tight before my knees were used to a Canadian saddle. But how was I to know they weren't used? Anyway I'm on the ground to-day, and to-morrow and hope to be all right for Sunday. If not I can easily walk to that school as it's only three miles away, and the others are not started yet.

My great hope is to get another Sunday School started at Fort St. John proper on Sunday week. That's five miles away. The children are ready, and there are many more of them, but the teachers are the difficulty. Together with the Sunday School I hope to start Scouts and Guides on Saturdays, the former in the mornings, the latter in the afternoons, and I hope to get a bed somewhere in Fort St. John for the Saturday nights and to hold that Sunday School on Sunday at 11, so as to get across to East Fort St. John for that one at 2.30. There are still two more schools to be considered at the two ends of the line; but I think they'll have to wait a bit. Meanwhile will you pray for these first two schools:

(1) *Fort St. John.* Sunday School, Scouts and Guides.

About to be started, i.e., as soon as I can get teachers and if possible an Assistant Scout Master.

(2) *East Fort St. John.* Sunday School already started. Teachers a difficulty. Wolf-cubs starting next Tuesday. N.B. You will realize that four-fifths of even this plan is still in the future. I am only telling you to get your prayers as soon as possible. The teachers say the boys are rough and need a man, but so far nobody can produce a man, though I think we shall find one eventually who is both suitable, and willing to help at least.

Fort St. John
November 3, 1929.

This will get duller and duller every week until it peters out in pure bathos and pious platitudes, so here goes.

This week has been windy and colder, but no snow yet and no frost to-day, though of course all shallow water is frozen.

The sunsets are most beautiful, and the Northern Lights after dark are quite amazing. I never saw them before, and first thought it was a strange form of search-light, and then of moon-rise.

Almost every cold clear night there come great feathers and streamers of pearly light all emanating from the Northern horizon and sweeping right across the sky. Usually the colour is pearly-white, but sometimes it is red or orange or rose. The streamers move slowly about the sky, and I'm told that on *very* still cold nights they can be heard *swishing* which seems too uncanny for words! The whole business seems precious uncanny to me and even rather fearful, but of course, everyone is quite used to it here, and practically indifferent.

I am going to try and keep *Monday* as a Sabbath, i.e., wear a skirt all day, do no visiting, but do washing and mending and other home chores instead. I started this last Monday, but in the afternoon got an attack of conscience and went off for three visits. However, my left leg being still skinned, I compromised and went on foot, taking about the smallest possible circuit, i.e., only five miles altogether.

These three women were rather typical specimens. The first was a dear little Welsh woman very small and neat and refined, living in a log shack entirely surrounded by herds and herds of pigs. The shack consisted as they almost all do of rooms divided by a very slight wooden partition with no floor. Sometimes they are wonderfully neat and clean and sometimes more or less pigsties, but always about the same size and design, i.e., a living-room-kitchen, and a common family bedroom with one, two or three double beds as the size of the family requires. The shacks look very small and humble from outside, and are really indistinguishable from cattle sheds, though the men build them wonderfully well, and there is something rather dignified in the strong simplicity of the big logs.

Unluckily everybody's ambition is to have a "frame house"—that is, one built not of logs but of planks on a wooden frame. This is a frame house but not so bad as most. They look exactly like cheap summer-houses in England, only the bare planks look more gimcrack being quite naked and neither painted nor stained. However, practically nobody up here has reached the nouveau riche stage of building a frame house.

On Tuesday I had to ride again because there was thirteen miles to go and simply wasn't time to walk. I went first to East St. John School for the dinner-hour and started the oddest little troup of Scouts, i.e., one Guide (aged fifteen), ten Scouts, two Brownies and four Cubs—rather a difficult team to organise efficiently!

After that I went off on a voyage of discovery to find one of the mothers who was taken on as secretary for the Sunday School by Post for this Diocese, and having received the papers for the first time was in rather a panic and had sent imploring me to go and help her. It was about four miles farther along fairly vague trails, and I had to go at foot's pace because of my stupid old legs. However, it was fine practice in disassociation and I got there in the end. Mrs. McDonald is a nice woman from Winnipeg.[34] She lives about twelve miles from Fort St. John and practically never goes there or anywhere else. We had a field day over the Sunday School lists and papers and a long talk about her family during tea. Then I came away and home in triumph about 6.30.

On Wednesday I visited in and around Fort St. John. I went into the school which has two rooms and over forty children and discussed with the two teachers [Miss House and Miss Richards] and the children, times for Sunday School and Scouts and Guides. The latter make rather a problem as all the little children have to go home directly after school because of the distance and dark but could come on Saturdays, whereas all the big ones have to work at home on Saturdays, but could stay on after school. In the end we arranged for Sunday School at 11 A.M. on Sunday, Guides at 4 on Thursdays and Scouts at 4 on Fridays. This suits the big ones and I am going to try to fit in a dinner-hour for Wolf-cubs and Brownies. The trial is that it necessitates riding three days a week into Fort St. John five miles each way, and is therefore very uneconomical of time.

However, I chose four leading girls and started with them on Thursday and five leading boys and started with them on Friday. The boys are simply enormous, they range from fourteen to sixteen but look about nineteen and terrific cowboys. The difficulty is that they already know all there is to know about outdoor life, and don't seem to have the wits or imagination to care about any other side of Scouting. At present they are keen because they seem to think I am going to lead them out to track and shoot bears and wolves in a new way!

When I got back that evening Miss Birley investigated my stupid remaining sore and found it a bit septic. So she "drew" it, and put on marvellous dressings and made me stay about the house all yesterday till the evening. To-day it is so much better that riding is no longer an ordeal but a pleasure.

On Friday night we all went to a mysterious money-raising function at the East St. John School called "Shadow-Box Social." The ladies each took supper for two in a box and before supper their shadows appeared one by one on a sheet and the men bought them by auction. When all the shadows were sold they shared their supper with their purchasers! Being quite new to the place and rather shy I was allowed not to sell my shadow, but to share my supper with some little boys, and the rest of the evening till about 2.30 A.M. I tried to fraternise with the mothers and skilfully avoided dancing. These dances are very funny. The light was one or two dim oil lamps, the music a fiddle, a concertina and a guitar.

The women were in all sorts of rigs from full working-dress to full evening-dress, the men in any old shirts and trousers as rough as you please. Everybody brought their children, because they couldn't leave them at home. But there was nothing for the children to do and the little boys were hopelessly naughty! There was a little girl of about eighteen months awake all the time and very miserable, and two real babies who slept most of the time through all the noise and heat.

Mr. Birley and I escaped at about 2.30, but no one else left for at least another hour. I believe they are going to have another dance like this at Fort St. John on Armistice Night—but I shall not be there.

To-day being the first Sunday with two schools, I rode into Fort St. John last night in order to knock five miles off the sixteen to-day and spent the night with a funny old woman [Mrs. Millar].[35] She has a very clean bran-new little house only a mile from the school and the Postmaster kindly let me put up Rama in his stable. This plan is rather a bore and costs an extra six shillings a week, but I think it is worthwhile, if only as not interfering with Miss Birley's one late morning in bed, and at the same time giving me a chance of a private Service before seeing to Rama and getting in good time to school.

The beginning was rather typical of these conditions:

1) The boy who had promised to light the stove didn't come as his father sent him off to collect some cattle.

2) The [policeman's] wife [Mrs. Devlin][36] who is going to be a teacher suddenly went away for the week-end.

3) One's daughter who is going to be another teacher, arrived forty-five minutes late.

4) Another——'s niece—didn't arrive at all.

5) About twenty children came but spread over their arrivals from 10.45 to 11.45, the late ones all having been plucking chickens, or hunting horses or killing pigs—all such virtuous occupations that I couldn't be carping—but it made school rather difficult.

They seemed nice children, though nearly all boys as usual, and *fearfully* shy and ignorant. I spent about twenty minutes trying to teach them "All Things Bright and Beautiful" word by word and note by note and line by line, and at the end produced a sound like two mice squeaking in another world!

After that I rode six miles to East St. John, carrying all the hymn-books and my night-clothes, etc., in two saddle bags which jumped about terribly and threatened to break loose at every moment. This house is half-way between the two, so I got a quick luncheon on the way and arrived in time for 2.30. This school was very badly attended to-day, and the children awfully late again. They are a dreadfully shy, slow little lot too, and for singing they are almost heart-breaking. Do you know

they can't sing a NOTE, not a song or a comic song or anything? In vain I
slaved away at "Sun of My Soul" and "While Shepherds Watched" and
gave the most *moving* renderings on the portable harmonium. In vain I
tried deep breathing and later on scales, *simply nothing can be heard.*
Did you know there were children in the world who never sing anything
at all? I didn't.[37]

Oh dear, this must stop.

November 10, 1929.

Miss Birley is, among other things, amazingly hospitable. Having
already a full house and a *very* full life, she is always ready to invite
anyone who is or has been ill to stay here and promptly gives them her
room and sleeps herself in the kitchen.

Last week we had a tired nurse up from Pouce Coupé Hospital, and
this week we are going to have a woman recovering from a buggy
accident [Mrs. Anderson], and her husband. The room is very small and
quite full of things already, so where their clothes and Miss Birley's
possessions are going to live I can't imagine; or what we shall do if Miss
Birley gets another of her knock-out sick headaches and they are all left
to my tender mercies!

Monday is my holiday but last Monday I had to ride eight miles to the
post first, and shall have to to-morrow also because I am so late with the
letters. This is a great annoyance to poor Rama whose Sabbath it also
breaks, and he has written no letters either!

The rest of Monday is sacred to washing and mending clothes and
cleaning the room and house generally. I enjoy it very much, especially
washing and ironing although the water is now so short that it has to be
a good stiff purse [*sic*] before we can part with it. After supper we also
mark the day by having a full-sized gramophone concert and not a
furtive record or two as on other nights. Everybody here loves the
gramophone, and Miss Birley says it's the best tone she has ever heard.
Also she likes most of the best music—especially the "Toccata and
Fugue" and the "Ride of the Valkyrie." Mr. Birley is not so high-brow,
he prefers a well-known song and a hymn with a familiar tune. Miss
Birley and Miss Petter both beg me to play them to sleep when they go to
bed and two or three times a week as a great concession I do it.

On Tuesday I had the dinner-hour Scouts and Cubs at East St. John
and a very primitive show so far, but great fun, as they get so gorgeously
excited over team-games. Afterwards I took the only big girl of that part

on her pony, to see the only other girl who lives three miles further on
and is temporarily crippled by a bicycle accident. They are both going to
be Guides, so we had an amusing afternoon over knots and things, while
I pursued a disjointed conversation in French with her mother (they are
French Canadians) [the LeClercs].[38]

On Wednesday I had a bit of luck in the shape of a motor-drive with a
nice Mr. Travis,[39] the agricultural expert of this district, who took me up
to Charlie Lake and the Mountainy [Montney] Prairie,[40] two parts I
haven't seen yet. The Montney Prairie is a large scattered region with
no school yet and too remote for me to tackle this winter, but Charlie
Lake (grisly name!) is different. The school is only ten miles from here
and the teacher [Miss Bell][41] is nice and quite keen for me to do something. So I hope to try and go there once a month *as soon as* I can get
someone to take East Fort St. John Guides and Scouts. These are still in
the stage of leaders only—five delightful girls on Thursday and six
immense, funny boys on Friday. The brightest is an Italian called Dave
Chiulli,[42] aged sixteen, who talks the most marvellous Italian-Canadian
tongue and is awfully keen for me to go and see his mother who still only
talks Italian. Another huge boy called Johnny Donis[43] looks quite
grown-up and most picturesque as he dresses like a perfect cowboy with
the *huge* hat, and a beaded and fringed leather coat and riding trousers
covered with long hair.

All Friday poor Miss Birley lay quite helpless in bed with one of her
absolutely knock-out sick-headaches. They really are awfully bad when
they come and make her almost deaf and quite bed-ridden. I long to do
something for her, but apparently nothing can be done until they wear
themselves out in a day or two. So all I could do was to turn entirely
domestic, and try to become a general farm-hand. It's rather pathetic
how slow and stupid I am at it all. Kind Miss Birley puts it all down to
"English thoroughness" but that's just her tact, and doesn't take in
either of us for a moment.

All the same I had rather fun fetching the water and cleaning the
house and washing the kitchen floor and splitting the logs and feeding
the animals and cleaning out the stables and chicken-house. But the sad
part was that it took me nearly all day (except three hours away for the
Scouts) without any cooking except poached eggs for supper—whereas
Miss Birley does it all, and cooks all our meals and often goes out and
nurses somebody as well! Yesterday she recovered and went out for the
day to get a child, who is losing its sight, taken to hospital. So I had
another day's practice till 5.30 when I rode over to Fort St. John for the
night. I sleep at the house of a funny old girl called Mrs. Millar who gives
me supper and breakfast and talks *without ceasing* except when we are
actually asleep. She gives me a nice clean bedroom which is

unencumbered by a washing-stand because as she truly says there is only one lamp in the house and it's warmer to wash in the kitchen!

This morning when I appeared for breakfast she said: "Did you hear a moaning and a groaning in the night, Miss Storrs? No? Well I did, and first I thought it was you in a nightmare and decided I couldn't help any and then I thought it was Thorson's bull and was glad I'd got my bar'l of water inside but now go and look out of the window my Golly yes I'll say so." I looked out of the window and saw a poor white horse lying up against the house, stone-dead. We couldn't make out what it had died of or whose it was, so I went off and reported it to the one policeman, but it was a very pathetic sight.

It was a hard white frost this morning, but it hasn't once touched zero yet so nobody calls it cold. Still everything looked very lacey and lovely all sparkling in the sun. I had twenty-six children at Fort St. John, ranging in age from five to seventeen, and as usual they trickled in all through the hour and all said that according to their clocks they were in perfect time! The policeman's wife came and played the harmonium and next Sunday we are going to bud off a kindergarten class for her. The children are three-quarters boys as usual, but very friendly and well-behaved in a funny gauche way, and I am getting rather fond of them. But you should see the school. It is left in complete chaos and perfectly filthy, so much so that it took the children and me nearly twenty minutes getting it swept and dusted and cleared up before we could begin the School. It's rather a trial; but as I'm only there by courtesy and pay nothing except for fuel, I can't complain. After that I rode back here, had luncheon and went on to East St. John where only eleven of the total possible seventeen turned up, and only one girl, but they were all very sweet and seem to be sharpening up a bit, even sang a little.

The water in the well is getting awfully low and is as hard a liquid as emery paper. But on Tuesday there was just enough rain to wash Miss Petter's head so I bagged her lather and did mine too. But we both had to rinse in the hard, and both look like Strewelpeter [*sic*] in consequence. However, when the snow comes we shall have *Baths*. They will be comic ones out of a kettle in a tin tub in the kitchen—won't it be FUN?

Also Mr. Birley really is going to kill a cow. It's not definitely stated when but *soon*. And then we shall have meat. Miss Birley says "we shall have roast beef every day for 6 months." So if I come home with a fine pair of horns glancing through my scarlet halo you won't say anything, will you?

To-morrow is Armistice Day, but nobody takes any notice of it in connection with the War. It's simply a general holiday with a turkey shoot in the afternoon and a dance at night. Rather sad, but apparently for one reason or another these people hardly felt the War at all though, of course, some of them must have served. I think the chief reason may be that no one here is old enough to have lost a son.

Monday was Armistice Day, but a pathetic travesty of the real thing here. It has been joined to the traditional Autumn Festival called Thanksgiving (imported from the States) and is really neither a Memorial nor a Thanksgiving Day nor even a Harvest Festival, but a Social Beano vaguely based on the ideas of all three. In the afternoon the whole neighbourhood collects at what is called a "Turkey Shoot," where the men, and women too, shoot at targets or play poker or dice, and the prizes are turkeys of which everybody has a great many to dispose of. In the evening it all turns into a dance which goes on till 4 or 5 next morning. The Birleys went and took Miss Petter, the little school-teacher, who adores these entertainments. Miss Birley being English and having lost a brother in the War feels the incongruity, but says it can't be changed. I didn't go to the Turkey Shoot or the dance, but heard afterwards that the latter was pretty typical of the bad sort of Fort St. John revels. Most of the men got drunk and before the end were brawling and fighting, and the one police officer of the District was far too drunk himself to interfere. It's especially sickening because all the little girls from twelve upwards go to these dances.

On Tuesday I rode to East St. John as usual for the dinner hour Scouts and Cubs, who are *still* in a very preliminary stage of team games. It's great fun because they know almost *nothing* about games and get awfully excited, and it's a lively job making them keep the rules. Afterwards, I went on another four miles for two visits, and at the second one found a nice family hard at work finishing off their very superior log house. The father and big son were putting on the roof of wooden shingles, and the mother and small son were "chinking," that is, filling the chinks between the logs with mud and clay. Everybody builds their own houses like that and they are perfectly weather-proof and some very nice looking. It does make our laborious, expensive professional way of building at Home—at least in the country—seem absurd. The woman was very glad to stop for a bit and take me into their small temporary shack, where she produced a row of piping hot loaves out of the oven, and gave me a huge slice with home made wild raspberry jam. They are about twelve miles from Fort St. John, and she seldom sees anyone; but like most of the women here, she is very refined and good-looking, and the tiny over-crowded shack marvellously clean and fresh.

I got back to East St. John school by a new trail over high and gently undulating bushland, rather like a faded English park, beautified by the distant hills and the usual glorious sunset. I found Petter just ready to ride home (she generally starts about 5.45), so as the two horses love being together we galloped hard for a good part of the three miles which was great fun, in the moonlight. Petter is a very pretty, refined little girl from Vancouver, but too young and inexperienced, I think, for sole charge of a school and completely independent existence up here. The school, though there are only nineteen children, is a big responsibility for her quite alone (all boys but two) and the life is difficult really with these rather wild dances and some pretty rough young men. She thirsts for a good time, but she needs a lot of wisdom and I am only so thankful that she has got such a splendid friend as Miss Birley.

On Wednesday I rode for the first time to *Taylor's Flats*.[44] This is another tiny settlement quite close to the river, and nine miles down hill from here. When we got there I had dinner with a nice old couple right on the river bank near the ferry. The river is getting full of ice which will soon stop the ferry, and after that, there will be no crossing until the ice is thick enough to drive and ride across. To-day there is an awful rumour that we are to be reduced to one mail a fortnight, so if I suddenly miss a week you will know the reason why.

I visited two or three other people, especially the two women who promised Miss Hasell to hold a Sunday School but haven't started yet. They are both English and new arrivals having a hard time. They live in two tiny huts, in one of which the school-mistress (our Mrs. Anderson) normally occupies the only little bedroom, and the father, mother, and boy sleep in the little kitchen where they have also been feeding nine newcomers. Taylor's Flats is a good example of what is going on up here. Until about three weeks ago it had three or four families and only eleven school children. Then suddenly six new families arrived in one week, bringing twenty-eight new children. The school is much too small for this influx, and so they don't go. The first two women are quite game to start on Advent Sunday if I can find a big enough room, and I have promised to go down and help them once a month which will mean throwing one of the Fort St. John Schools on its own resources. I tried to find a room at the back of the one little store, but had no luck, and then it was time to start home, so I must go down again all next Wednesday and finish the visiting. The nine miles back was rather tedious, all along the road—the first six uphill and straight as an arrow except at the beginning where it climbs a rather interesting little narrow defile. I had to lead Rama in the most narrow and winding part for fear he should suddenly meet a car and not have room to shy in safety! His shying is really perfectly harmless, but he requires a little level space for his sudden manoeuvres. (N.B. He's a perfectly good horse really).

I shall try to go to the Flats on Wednesdays as often as may be necessary to get things going. Mrs. Anderson is a Church woman and very friendly, but won't be well enough to start work again for at least a fortnight. Meanwhile, I am trying to make friends with her for future use.

Thursday was only the little Guide leaders at Fort St. John, and Friday the Scouts, each preceded by a visit or two on the way. That particular little group of girls attracts me very much. They are awfully natural and friendly, and I long to give them something better than these beastly dances to think of, but doubt whether anything else will hold its own against them.

The boys are immense and loutish, great fun over knots and tracking, but heartbreakingly stupid over mental things like the Law and the Promise.[45] The trouble is that I can't let in the younger boys till the leaders are enrolled, and I can't enrol the leaders till they know the Law, and they can't or won't learn it.

On Saturday I started at 10.30 to ride to Charlie Lake (eleven miles north) to have dinner with the school-teacher and discuss possibilities for her school. However, about four miles short of the place I met her driving out in a buggy to Fort St. John for a music lesson, having quite forgotten our arrangement! This is very typical of everybody here, even school mistresses; and the worst of it is that the impossibility of letting people know if you are going to fail them, which to most of them acts as a deterrent, is here regarded as a good excuse. People say, "It was difficult to come, and I couldn't let you know, so I didn't come!" Miss Bell couldn't say when she would get back to Charlie Lake, so I turned round and followed her back to Fort St. John and discussed preliminaries with her at the back of the store while she waited for her music lesson. She thinks seriously of starting Guides herself after Christmas, and also contemplates a possible young man for Scouts, whom I must go over and see. She says the people are very Bolshie and mostly don't want a Sunday School, but I can't take that on trust, and must aim at something if it's only once a month. The difficulty is visiting up there, because it's so far to go at the start, and the only place where I could sleep the night before has only one bedroom, which is hers! However, we can't let trifles like that stand in the way.

I spent the rest of the day visiting round Fort St. John especially a nice Italian family called Chiulli, whose eldest son, Dave, is to be my senior Patrol leader if he ever knows the Law. Mrs. Chiulli has been out here three years, but can't talk *a word* of English. She was so thrilled by my pigeon [*sic*] Italian that she begged me to stay for dinner and supper, and failing that, produced a huge flagon of awfully sour raisin wine, supposed to recall to us both the vintage of the Campagnia. We sipped this (and she kept filling me up again to the top!) and made laborious small talk about her life there and here, her married daughter still in Italy, and the few towns we both knew. She was very touching and said it was the first conversation *outside* her family she had had for ages, and I promised to go again, though what we shall talk of next I can*not* imagine.

I had supper with the chief store-keeper and his family [the Finchs],[46] and then went to bed as usual on Saturdays with old Mrs. Millar. She has only one lamp, so I have to undress and wash in the kitchen—but she has lots of good water so I usually do it thoroughly. This time just as I had finished and was polishing off my feet (neatly dressed in a blue viyella nightgown) the door opened and in walked a married daughter and her large strange husband! Afterwards I murmured to Mrs. Millar the possibility of washing in my room next week, and she said, "Oh Pete, he don't mind—he's a married man!"

Apparently this was an unanswerable argument.

When I got to Sunday School I nearly wept as usual at the dirt and confusion of the room. It always looks as if there had been a free fight the night before, books and papers littered about, piles of rubbish, and a broken chair, and thick dust on everything. While I was tackling it, a strange man turned up dressed like a trapper and said he'd heard I was going to have a meeting. I said "Yes, but it's only a Sunday School."

"That's all right, I'll stay."

"But I don't think you'd be interested—it's only children."

"That's all right. I like kids."

So he stayed, and I must say was very harmless, and the [children] paid no attention to him at all.

We budded off a little class of non-readers, taken by the policeman's wife in the next room. What she taught them I don't know, but it was supposed to be the Lost Sheep. We started to learn "While Shepherds Watched," in preparation for Christmas. The children were quite reverent and good, but I think they must most of them be tone deaf. Afterwards I visited a sick mother and then the usual ride to East St. John and the tiny afternoon School there.

I got home at five to find the house full of visitors. Tommy Hargreaves is really a garage-owner, but he is used to clipping horses which is supposed to qualify him for cutting our hair. He did mine last night very conscientiously—but it is just as well for the moment that I'm over 5,000 miles from Home.

Today has been my Sabbath as usual. I'm ashamed to own how much I enjoy it. The thermometer reached zero in the night and the first thing this morning was pretty parky [cold], but warmed up to only 3 or 4 degrees of frost at mid-day. It's funny taking a big hammer out to the water butt and filling the kettle with ice.

Must stop and go to bed.

Fort St. John
Monday, December 9, 1929.

Petter was driven to school in a sleigh by Mr. Birley and got her cheeks frozen. All the meat and bread and milk and apples and eggs and jam froze solid, and all the windows became perfectly opaque, and our hot water bottles froze into awfully distorted shapes the moment they fell out of bed—if not before.

On Tuesday the wind abated a little, but it was much too cold and the snow too drifty to ride, so I walked to East St. John for the dinner hour and found Petter and seven little boys shuddering round the stove. After that I went up the ride trail to Mr. Simpson's[47] to discuss our plans in the light of the new state of the roads. It was only two and a quarter miles further, but it was heavy going, and at times rather difficult to find the trail. We discussed plans and agreed that as the roads were impassable for cars and he had no sleigh as yet, we must abandon next Sunday at Taylor's Flats or rather postpone it to the first in the New Year, and we agreed instead to try for a Service at East St. John on the Sunday before Christmas, and at Fort St. John the Sunday after, and to leave Charlie Lake alone a big longer. I started back at 4.30, and didn't get in till 7 o'clock, which for five and a half miles was very ridiculous, but the trail was deep for one half mile, and the road *much* deeper.

Wednesday was quite a still day and very bright and lovely, and started at only 22 below, so I decided to ride down to the Flats, partly to see what the road was really like, and partly to pave the way for a future Service. It turned out to be heavier going than I had expected, and so cold that I had to lead Rama for quite two and a half miles out of the seven each way. There wasn't a sign of movement or traffic anywhere, and the whole world was pure white and glistening with almost intolerable brightness. Miss Birley had given me the usual sandwiches for luncheon so I crept with Rama into the log stable for mutual shelter and refreshment. It was a fearfully draughty barn open at both ends and full of huge cracks, but it had some cows and pigs steaming away in it; so Rama and I huddled up together and were glad Bethlehem was not in this country. However, the sandwiches were frozen so hard that after I had cracked one with

difficulty I gave the rest to the pigs to make what they could of, and
started up the hill, home.

That evening Ritchie,[48] the future Scoutmaster, came to supper. He is
really very nice and intelligent, and came in useful as we were busy
making sixty little muslin bags for sweets for Petter's Christmas tree.

From Thursday till this morning the glass dropped into the [minus]
30's, reaching 40 [below] at night, but not with any certainty lower.
Apparently, although it has been known to drop to *68* [below]—that
only happened once in living memory and 40 [below] is really the
normal low level.

It isn't at *all* bad really, in fact, indoors, except for the actual fact that
everything freezes and you can't see out of the windows, and the house
goes off like rifle fire all night, and the front door warps and won't quite
shut, *indoors,* so long as you keep the stoves going, it's deliciously warm.
I suppose it's because the houses are entirely of wood and so small, and
there are no halls or passages or lobbies or stairs to get cold. And yet,
when I put my water jug *close* beside the banked up stove at night, it's
always frozen quite solid in the morning.

Of course we dress up absurdly to go out, and I'm afraid you would
laugh dreadfully at my appearance! I wear two pairs of woollen
stockings (one turned down at the knees), plus one pair of bed socks, plus
moose-hide moccasins which all the men wear here, and which are much
better in the snow than boots. I wear a perfectly close fitting sort of fur
cap (made by self!!!) with ear flaps coming over the ears and a perfectly
hideous short coat of brown duck lined with sheep-skin, and with a big
furry collar turned right up like an Elizabethan ruff, and held close
round by your splendid red woolly scarf. This picture is rounded off by
two pairs of men's mitts, the inner ones of wool and the outer of horse-
hide, which look just like clumsy animals' paws, and feel pretty well like
that too.

I've only been a tiny sleigh journey so far. I was walking to Fort St.
John for Guide meeting (school dinner hour) on Thursday and was
within a mile of the school when a woman caught me up, driving on
home, and gave me a lift. Her hands were almost frozen so I drove and
was just saying to her with great satisfaction, "This is the first sleigh
drive of my life," when she replied, "Yes, and both your cheeks are
freezing!" I got a handful of snow at once and rubbed them hard, and
they quickly came right again, but if that can happen after only five
minutes driving, just think what it must be for the men who drive all day
as traders and freighters.

Later in the day my nose got caught a tiny bit too, so I was reduced to
buying a tiny pocket mirror to look into from time to time when walking
alone and see whether anything is going white.

Don't be deceived into imagining *any* hardship. It's wonderfully healthy here; there is no "flu", no chilblains, very little rheumatism, no comsumption, hardly even any bad colds—and the only heroes are the people who drive sleighs all day, and the people *who get up first and light the stove!*

I walked over again on Friday for the Scouts. There are going to be eighteen at Fort St. John so next term we are going to form a third Patrol. I can hardly bear to hand them over to Mr. Ritchie, they are such fun.

The actual road within three miles from Fort St. John was pretty well beaten by the end of the week, that is to say the sleigh ruts were sufficiently packed to make tiny little footpaths—rather like walking on a *concave* tightrope and good for the balance. But beyond the three miles it was still very rough and drifty, though quite passable everywhere, and by Saturday even one or two cars struggled down to Taylor's Flats. But the trails are killing—that is the untrodden ones—you either plough through what is like very deep sand, or else strike a patch which seems quite hard; you start briskly on the top of the snow, and just before the finish of each step it lets you through to well above the knees—rather like walking across a very extensive crisp and brittle cold apple tart.

Yesterday, it being still 37 or 8 below, I decided to abandon all idea of riding for the week-end and to walk between the two Sunday Schools to-day. So I packed my rucksack with night gown and Sunday School books and walked into Fort St. John for the third time this week. We went to bed at 40 below, and woke up to find it zero! Evidently this was too much for the children, for there were only two girls and seven boys at School. Of course, this weather does rather demoralise the homes and the children, and added to that they can think of nothing else just now but the School Concert next Friday, which is the great event of the year.

They also trickled in late as usual, so we couldn't get done till 12.30, which gave me exactly two hours to walk the eight miles to East St. John. Mrs. Millar had given me a large cheese sandwich to eat as I went so by a little extra pressure I got there just in time, and found *two* little boys, only one of whom could read—all the rest of the School being also overcome by the Concert and weather (though whether by last week's rigour or to-day's ease-up I can't make out!)

We had a little lesson about the expectation of the Prophets and finally the Annunciation to Mary; and then Mr. Simpson turned up to plan next Sunday's Service. We prepared every detail, I hope wisely, and agreed not to be hurt if *nobody* came, and all the rest of it. Then I started back at 4.30 and had a fine last hour's walk singing over all the favourite carols by the after-glow, first of a glorious sunset and later by the moon and Jupiter rising almost hand in hand.

Fort St. John
December 23, 1929.

Last Monday (16th) I jumped my day off as I wanted to visit for next Sunday's Service. It wasn't too cold, only 10 below, so I rode round the trail North of East St. John and visited three new families. The first was quite unusually English, a nice man and his wife from Banbury and Chester respectively, and four tiny children. They were most welcoming and made me stay to dinner and I had a very happy time with them. They are the first couple I have met who have been out for nine or ten years (but in Saskatchewan, not here), and haven't picked up a trace of either accent or slang. I could hardly believe I wasn't in the Midlands as I sat there with them. Afterwards I wandered on to a young Canadian woman married to a very Canadianised Englishman and spent a long time with them also and their first baby. They also were awfully welcoming and insisted on producing tea and cake so I got a lot of food that day. The people round the East St. John School certainly are the most friendly, partly, I think, because they are the most English and partly because rather scattered, that is, each little shack about a mile from its nearest neighbour. I visited one more family that seemed a good deal poorer, and then came home pleasantly fast, as Rama was excited and the snow was mostly firm enough to gallop. In the evening we filled sixty green and red muslin bags with candies for the school party on Wednesday.

All Tuesday Miss Birley was over at the school rehearsing with Miss Petter for the concert which she privately told me was going to be very bad. I did chores in the morning and rode to Fort St. John school for the dinner hour bearing a rucksack full of clothes and toys for two very poor families thirty miles up the river. We also found that the Sunday School collection had a dollar over after paying five dollars for their firewood, so they voted to send a cake to one of the poor families and I went on to Mrs. Millar to ask her to make it. After that, one or two little visits delivering notices of the Fort St. John Service on the 29th, and then the usual five and a half miles home, by road this time and lighted by a brilliant moon.

All Wednesday Birley and Petter and Mr. Birley were at school preparing the tree and stage for the Great Event of the Year. I offered to help but was not a bit sorry that they preferred me to stay at home to mind the house and animals, make sandwiches, clean up generally and have some supper ready whenever they dashed in. So I had a nice domestic day alone, swept up the house, cleaned out the stables, fed the beasts and felt a perfect (unskilled) settler. I also managed to find in the book box twenty quite suitable books to give the children myself, and wrote all their names in just as the others returned. Then a hurried supper, and we dressed in our best *Summer Sunday* dresses with huge coats on the top and at 7.30 Mr. Birley arrived with the waggon box sleigh already containing Mrs. Birley and the three little boys. We all huddled together under rugs in the straw, and had a pretty cold but rather jolly drive to the school singing carols and chanties—at least Petter and I did, nobody else seemed to know any.

The school was pretty well packed. It is just one room with an entrance lobby, and it's rather marvellous how they had decorated it with paper and spruce branches and a Christmas tree in the corner. Light is always a difficulty as none of these schools have any, and generally each concert or dance smashes a lamp for Miss Birley. However she lent two and Mr. Birley lent one and for once they all came home alive. The desks were cleared away and we sat on backless benches, at least the lucky ones did, but I and all the men and a few women stood behind in a tight squash round the stove. We *had* to be too hot or everybody else in the hall would have been cold. The concert began with the singing of the "First Nowell" unaccompanied. Afterwards we had a series of recitations and tiny plays, redeemed by one boy of about twelve who really *could* act. That lasted till about 10.30, then came Father Christmas (who they *will* spoil by calling Santa Claus) and a present and a bag of sweets for every child in the district, about fifty, plus another for each one in the school, plus my little lot, so they did pretty well and were very much excited. After that came what is called Rough House, which means that the children run riot while the grown-ups make coffee over the stove and collect and redistribute the sandwiches and cakes which they have all brought. It's a chancy sort of supper very much catch as catch can. After that Petter asked me to organise one game for the children (this was a dangerous innovation!), so a mother and I introduced a short bout of Oranges and Lemons[49] (only they had to choose between horses and cars) which we had to teach the victims, but they madly enjoyed the Tug of War at the end. After that it turned into a dance for the grown-ups which continued till about 3. It is apparently the universal plan in these parts to end everything with a dance while the poor little kids hang about till well into the morning getting awfully in the way, and either dog-tired or hopelessly out of hand. There are always three or four babies, luckier than the others because they can sleep on a chair or in a basket through all the racket, and several infants of two or three who can't and usually get fractious instead.

Luckily for me, Tommy suddenly arrived with his car, almost the only one (still unfrozen) and offered early lifts home, so Miss Birley and I thankfully escaped at about 1 o'clock, and carried off the two smallest Birley boys, who were too exhausted to make effective protest. Petter who *adores* dancing came home with Mr. Birley and the eldest boy aged twelve in the sleigh at the bitter end. I forgot to say that the band was composed of a violin, two guitars and a *comb* and made a very effective noise for the purpose.

On Saturday the 21st, before going over to Fort St. John, I went to the East St. John School to tidy it up for the next day's Service. It required a lot of dusting and sweeping and I brought in and set up again the Christmas tree that had been thrown away, and decorated a bit with the odd spruce branches that were lying about in the snow. Then I lit the stove and practised hymns and chants on the tiny harmonium but did it so badly that I decided to bring over Mrs. Devlin in Tommy's car at whatever cost if they could both come. So I walked to Fort St. John instead of riding, found Tommy and Mrs. Devlin, and luckily both were agreeable.

Sunday morning was cold still, the temperature was not low, only just zero, but there was a fierce North wind which made it feel much colder. And for the first time *nobody* came to Sunday School! At least, nobody but Mrs. Devlin and one little red-headed boy of six called Roddy H. who always turns up. I told him the Christmas story with the aid of pictures and we had a little prayer and he went off with a Sunday School magazine feeling, I hope, that the morning had been a success.

Then Mrs. Devlin and I gathered up all the hymn books and joined Tommy and came home in great splendour and luxury to dinner.

Tommy then drove Mrs. Devlin and me, in good time, to the school where we were joined by Mr. Simpson. He brought in a nice little plain white wooden cross which he had got a friend to make for him, and I contributed a special new blue tablecloth and picture of the Nativity. For about half an hour after the Service was due to start we only had a funny farouche little boy called George C.[50] At about 3.00 the first sleigh arrived bringing a bunch of mothers and children; about 3.30 the second, and a little later, a third. We began the Service after the first sleigh, and finally rolled up twenty-three people, chiefly mothers and boys except for two men.

Mr. Simpson took shortened Evensong. We read the Christmas psalm and sang three Christmas hymns. He managed to give a tiny address on the value of coming together, and altogether I admired his spirit immensely. I really think that the women at least enjoyed it. They warmed up a lot at the end, forced a collection of $2.60 (about 11/-) upon us, and asked us to arrange another Service as soon as possible. So I was very much encouraged, though Mr. Simpson had the blues about his incompetence and the absence of men. I bucked him up all I could, and agreed to aim at much the same Service next Sunday at Fort St. John.

On the way home the car skidded in loose snow and ran into a drift where it stuck deep and all our efforts with shovels and chains and sacks failed to move it. Finally Tommy made Mrs. Devlin and me walk on toward home while he went to the nearest farm to get a team to pull him out. We had about two and a half miles to go, and had got in a good time before he turned up and carried her back to her husband. That little trip cost me a guinea but it was worth it because she plays *so* much better than I ever could. Luckily also this was an exception, as Taylor's Flats can produce *two* musicians of its own.

On Monday I rode over to X., a little place seven and a half miles off where there are two stores and a house. The stores supply the new settlers who are filling up the district North of us called the Montney.

My first object was to place two notices of next Sunday's Service, then to visit the family of one storekeeper. He has got seven tiny children who look like real slum kids and live in a miserable bare house like a really poor family in England. But the monstrous thing is that their father is fairly raking it in at his store, but simply won't supply his own family. They are not starving or the policeman could interfere, but they are just utterly dirty and squalid, *quite* unlike any other family here. For all the other children I have seen are well dressed and beautifully clean and even the roughest two room shacks are never bare and squalid. But these little children are always wonderfully sweet and welcoming and not at all shy. They are three miles from school and very tiny, so I don't see them except when I can get over for a visit. I took them each a tiny Bible picture book and they were fearfully excited, and insisted on my writing the full name in each one. The trouble is that practically none of them can read a word; and although the mother promised to read all the stories to them—well, I hope she will.

After that I visited the latest arrival in the *Roman Priest*.[51] He has just come, and I was determined to make friends with him at once. He was busily occupied in arranging the lower room of his little house as a Church. Above it is the sort of loft he sleeps in. He is a youngish Mission Priest born in Ontario but used to the West; and he told me that he intends to hold Midnight Mass on Christmas Eve. I had a sneaking longing to ride over for this but was very suspicious of my own motives especially as I knew it would make me too fast asleep in the early morning to join spiritually in our own Service. Afterwards I heard that quite forty people came which is rather wonderful as there are not much more than a dozen Roman Catholic families within twenty miles.

But more than that I learned a tremendous thing—that he has been given ten acres of land in the settlement where the Roman Catholics propose to build a *Hospital,* a *Church* and a *School.* This really means that they will get a flying start up here after all, and our poor old Church will come trundling behind—when it does come. But it's a wonderful work they are undertaking anyway, though of course it is only projected at present. Apparently there is an Order of "Black Sisters"[52] who do all the nursing in pioneer parts and it is they who will run the hospital. I am awfully glad that they are coming in such force, and must try not to be too sorry that we are late again.

Most of Tuesday I visited in Fort St. John to tell people about next Sunday's little Service. It started by being a much warmer day but about 4.30 the North wind sprang up and the sky turned a sort of heavy leaden grey which looked very strange above the almost pure white world, and everybody said there was going to be a blizzard. So not wanting to be caught in one, Rama and I turned our noses East and came home as hard as we could. It was rather exciting trotting back in the gathering dusk over the silent snowy road and between the feathery white trees and knowing that it really *was* Christmas Eve; and what some people call an "Old-fashioned Christmas" too! Although in the end there was no blizzard, but the night turned crisp and fine. After supper we had all the Messiah records on the gramophone, "There were Shepherds," "He was Despised," "Behold the Lamb of God," and my three carols: "O Come All Ye Faithful," "Hark the Herald Angels Sing," and "Good King Wenceslas." At 11 o'clock we went to bed when all of you were beginning your Christmas Service.

On Christmas morning I got up at 7, and having extracted permission and a few logs from Miss Birley overnight, lighted the stove and the lamp and held my own Service as well as I could.

Some time later Miss Birley assembled a very special Christmas breakfast—Grapenuts, coffee, and an egg. Then we exchanged our own little presents and found to our amusement, that *neither* of us had given the other anything, but the horses, dogs and cats had been very generous to us both! After that we dashed at the housework and after that I dashed at my little sacred dump of parcels and had a marvellous time unpacking chocolates and pudding and handkerchiefs and books and toys, until the three little Birley lads arrived to spend the day with us, and we had to switch on to them.

Their names are Douglas, aged twelve, called Bolshey, Frank, aged nine, called Snookey, Harold, aged six, called Deric. These are funny little boys, but Miss Birley manages them admirably and they are perfectly good and nice whenever they come here. We helped them to open their presents and admired them all very specially. I gave them each a brilliantly self-colored *iron* elephant specially trained to act as a money-box. They professed great admiration, but Snookey left his scarlet one behind for two days!

After that I read them half a dozen chapters out of a classic volume called *Billy Whiskers' Adventures* (i.e., "Memoirs of a Super-Goat") while Miss Birley produced the dinner. I longed to read them something very different, but they were so excited that I don't think they would have listened to anything that didn't *butt!* Then we had one of Miss Birley's own turkeys and puddings and just when we were finishing, Tommy Hargreaves arrived, so everything started again, and ended at about 3 with crackers and caps and musical instruments all going strong. Lastly we had a field day of all my toys and all their toys and managed to break one or two before Mr. Birley at length arrived and took away his sons, but said they were expecting us *both* to supper!

This was rather a blow to me as I longed for an evening of recollection; but of course it was impossible to refuse. So I went out for a short walk just before sundown when everything was looking *most* lovely.

I went along the top of the coulee, ploughing through very deep soft snow, and getting a fine view down the long ravine with its curving white banks and bluffs to the much steeper slopes of the Peace River valley beyond. Even the stupid little poplars really did look their best, because last night's wind had dusted them all with fresh snow, and everything was covered with white lace very delicate and sparkling, (not just heavy wads of cotton wool like you see on evergreens). And the setting sun gleamed upon them and made very long blue shadows in the snow.

Just before 7 o'clock we went over to Mr. Birley's house for supper. There was no other guest but one bachelor farmer, and the entertainment after supper was provided by Mr. Birley's new gramophone, a "Victor" portable, supposed to be by the same firm as my His Master's Voice (only made in Canada) and costing £6—but by Mr. Birley's own confession *immeasurably* inferior to mine. After about one and a half hours of only shouting against the music, the three little boys thought it would be more fun to compete more seriously. So they provided themselves with an accordion, a mouth-organ, and a collection of whistles out of crackers, and starting off the gramophone with the loudest possible records, they began to *bray* against it till the house nearly fell down. None of the grown-ups seemed to think this was at all an undesirable performance, but I was not sorry that we came home before 11 o'clock.

Next morning Miss Birley was sent for to attend to a Christmas Day accident. A runaway sleigh had thrown a woman [Mrs. Michaud] out and badly injured her leg. Miss Birley said it had certainly been dislocated and possibly broken, but the swelling was so great that she couldn't tell for certain. She therefore did her best to persuade the patient to go out to Pouce Coupé. It would mean sixty miles in a sleigh, but the road isn't too bad now, and she would get a doctor and proper treatment (though not X-rays nearer than 100 miles at least). But the woman refused to go, largely I'm afraid on account of her small children; so she has to stay at home and be nursed as well as possible by an elder son. Of course for this and many other emergencies which happen continually the Roman Catholic hospital would be a Godsend . . . .

For most of Boxing Day my humble function was to replenish the water supply by keeping a fire going outside in the garden and melting snow over it in a large tub. It is *not* skilled work, but about as much as I am good for at present in the colonist line! The temperature was very comfortable at zero but next day it bumped up to freezing (a jump of 32) and seemed absurdly warm. I was involved that night in a supper party with Mr. Birley and family at the McDonalds. Mr. Birley drove us in the waggon-box sleigh. The journey each way took an hour and a half and was rather like pigs going to market, except that you have rugs over you instead of a net, and can *just* see over the side. The driver stands or kneels in front and the horses loom up very high, and go a fine pace, even a canter whenever the snow is not too deep or rough to allow it. There is no jarring or rumbling or vibration, but only an occasional heave and sway from side to side, so it's rather like sailing over a gently swelling sea. There is no noise except the dull soft pad of hoofs and the faint clink of harness and at intervals Mr. Birley's rather high sing-song voice calling "Get up now—Jessie—Bay."

The McDonalds' house is a great deal too small for their possessions. It has one room downstairs and one up, with a staircase going up through the ceiling of one to the other. The downstairs one is kitchen, dining-room, drawing-room, school-room, pantry, larder, scullery, etc., and has pretty well full furniture for all the functions. Anyhow, it has two stoves and a dining-room table, and a sofa and two easy chairs and eight upright chairs and piano and a roll-top desk and one or two occasional tables, and a big gramophone on legs, besides all the pots and pans and food stores *and* the staircase! Upstairs is the bedroom which they intend to cut into two one day. Luckily there are only three children—two boys and a girl. Mr. McDonald, wearing his blue farm overalls, was very bulky, placid and silent, rather the cut of a Canadian John Bull. Mrs. McDonald, who has been a school-teacher and is therefore a lady of culture, was very eager and hospitable and talked incessantly. Supper consisted of the almost universal beef, potatoes, and carrots, followed by bottled wild strawberries or raspberries, (a *very* strong point up here), tea and home-made candies.

Helen, the little girl of ten, is very sweet, and I had the great happiness of giving her a delightful little dancing doll, one of an enchanting collection of toys sent from Ellesmere.[53] I took it really to show her, and we made it dance on a little table while Helen knelt in front and gazed with popping eyes. As we were leaving I said "Would you like to have the dancing doll for your own?" Helen who is usually fluent and collected enough, became crimson and stammered violently: "Oh I don't know—*I don't know*"; and then took it into her arms and gazed at it as if it were a new-born child. So I think she really knew all right.

The drive home was delicious—very dark; in fact I can't think how Mr. Birley kept to the trail which was as vague as possible. Whenever we went through deep snow the horses kicked it all over us, causing a sort of short sharp snowstorm but between these diversions the eldest boy Douglas and I studied the few stars that were showing. It's wonderful what a good observatory is a waggon sleigh. You are lying down and looking up, and except for the passing trees there is nothing else to see except the whole sky. I told him the story of Perseus and Andromeda, and showed him Jupiter and Orion, Sirius and Aldebaran. And when I explained the last as the Eye of the Bull he exclaimed "Oh that's easy. I shall always remember the bullseye." Somehow I hadn't thought of it that way before! We got home soon after midnight, the other little boys having slept soundly all the way.

On Saturday morning early there blew a "Chinook." This is the *Warm West Wind* which comes from time to time from the sea through the passes in the mountains, and very often causes a thaw. It brought us up to *just* above freezing and though of course it didn't melt the snow it brought a hazy look and soft moist feeling in the air which made me rather homesick.

I spent the day riding to Taylor's Flats to visit a few people and place the notices of our first little Service on Sunday week, and among other things took a note from Miss Birley to an elderly Cockney bachelor who has been a trapper out in these parts for over forty years. But though he has picked up all the Canadian slang, he still treats the letter "H" in a way that was pure music to my ears. "Well Miss Storrs. Hi don't 'old with the sheep-skin coat. It's hall very well if you don't sweat. But hif you sweats hon a cold day, the sheep olds *hin* the sweat hand it freezes hon you. Hand there's nothink more honpleasant that frozen sweat."

The ride back was so lovely and warm that it seemed like the beginning of spring and was hard to realise that there are three good months of winter still ahead.

December 29 to January 5, 1930.

For once I did not go to sleep at Fort St. John on Saturday, because there was to be no morning Sunday School. But after my own Service on Sunday morning, and a general tidy-up, I packed sandwiches and tea for two, and started to meet Mr. Simpson at Fort St. John School. He had to walk or ride there ten miles, so I had promised to meet him with nourishment. The trail to the school was fearfully drifted since I last rode over it a fortnight ago. The snow was deep and cakey and poor Rama floundered in and out at foot's pace nearly all the way. I found the school rather tidier than usual and the fire lighted but no fuel and no water and no Mr. Simpson. I went out and collected logs and put snow in the kettle and immediately a mother arrived with two kids *an hour too early*. She warmed herself at the stove while the children helped with desks and books. Then Mr. Simpson arrived so we had a little rehearsal of plans in the freezing lobby while a few more people trickled in. Eventually there were about twenty-five, chiefly women and children again; plus three or four men of whom one was Ritchie, the Roman Catholic Scoutmaster. We had Evensong again and sang the chants quite respectably—also "Hark the Herald Angels Sing," "Once in Royal David's City," and "Abide with Me." Mr. Simpson had asked me to give the address so I started with the children about the real meaning of Christmas, and tried to go on to the grown-up people about trying to keep in closer touch with God in the coming year. It was all very nervous and muddled. At the end I gave each child a Christmas card—all out of a lovely framed batch sent by the Greenhithe Girls' Friendly Society,[54] and shook hands with everybody as they melted away. The congregation was technically speaking disappointing, that is to say not one of the three or four leading men and women were there. I think they feel it definitely beneath them to come to a Service without a parson. But those who did come were nice and liked it I think; and I was especially glad of the presence of Miss House, the head school-teacher, a girl of twenty-two or three, who had not previously professed much interest.

Mr. Simpson was riding a pretty lumbering farm horse, so we joined forces for the return and called ourselves the Church cavalry. Only as the paces of his mount practically forbade trotting, we were very slow and ponderous cavalry, and I was quite stiff with cold by the time I got home. Mr. Simpson wanted to discuss plans at greater length, so I asked him to supper on Tuesday.

On Tuesday I conceived the idea of a small tea-party for the Senior Guides and went into Fort St. John to invite them and fix up with Mrs. Millar for next Saturday.

Mr. Simpson duly arrived for supper, soon after which Miss Birley and the Andersons went off to the New Year Dance.

Mr. Simpson stayed on and we talked tremendously, chiefly about religion. While we were talking we suddenly realised that midnight was passed, and the New Year had come. So we knelt down and prayed by turns, for pardon and strength and guidance, and then he started on his five and a half mile walk home. It was pretty dark and he couldn't find the way to the road. So I had to escort him to the gate, and a funny walk we had floundering and tumbling in and out of the deep snow.

You've no idea (well perhaps you have but I hadn't) when you see a wide white field or trail between woods what a variety of experience either can provide especially, but not only, at night. Part of it may be quite hard and smooth, and generally as slippery as ice; but a minute later it turns into a sea of deep soft powder like sand, up to the knees or higher. A little farther there may be a sleigh trail making deep ruts which you walk in if you can see them and fall into if you don't. And then suddenly the whole drift is frozen on the top and you climb up and walk along three feet higher up on a crisp shell of frost which makes a hollow noise like walking over a thin metal bridge. That is fine while it lasts, much the best of all until suddenly you reach the part that *just* won't hold; and then each step you climb up two or three feet and just as your full weight is on *that* foot you go through with a plop the whole length of your leg again and are held in a sort of Plaster of Paris splint. This sort of snow provides the finest exercise of all.

New Year's Day, 1930, was a perfectly lovely day, only about zero and beautifully sunny. I kept it as a whole holiday and in the afternoon went for a walk down the top of the coulee. I started in Miss Birley's snow-shoes, but alas, haven't got the trick of them yet. They seemed to sink almost as far as the unaided foot, and got terribly entangled in each other besides. So after a trial trip I abandoned them and reverted to nature's way. It was heavy going and rather laborious, but rather lovely, especially the receding white banks of the coulee and the distant blue ridges of the hills beyond. After supper I played Beethoven's "Fifth Symphony" and read some of Ronald's present, *The Universe Around Us*, by Sir James Jeans,[55] a marvellous book.

Thursday was a foul cold morning, down to 20 below again, and dark and snowy. It was my last chance of a dash to Taylor's Flats to fix up about the school and fire etc., for Sunday's Service. But it looked so cold that I couldn't be bothered to catch Rama (who was out in the pasture) and decided to walk instead. Miss Birley promised if Tommy *should* come along, and the road proved passable, to come along and meet me in the evening. The road wasn't bad really, and the wind being behind me didn't matter, so I did the seven miles in two and a half hours. The little school was in a horrible messy condition and of course *icy* cold, and fearfully short of seats—only in fact about twelve desks, several of them very small and one or two broken—and there were books and papers and piles of litter all over the table and in every corner. I cleared up as well as I could and then called on the nearest trustee (a Swedish agnostic)[56] and got him to promise that the fire should be lighted an hour beforehand on Sunday, and a couple of planks put in for seats. Then I visited the Englishwoman who is going to play my tiny harmonium and told her the hymns, called at another house for Mrs. Anderson's mail, ate my sandwiches and was given a cup of tea and started for home again. However, for two miles I got a lift and in a sleigh with four very agreeable men, and for the last three miles the angelic Tommy and Miss Birley actually loomed up with a car, so I got home very lazily and found an immense Christmas mail.

That was the last car on the road, for the night brought a blizzard and next morning the snow was about twice as deep and all drifted and a stiff North wind was still blowing.

It was Friday, and the day of Miss Birley's long-planned bridge party. She had asked twenty-one people, making with ourselves and Mr. Birley a grand total of twenty-five for supper at 7 o'clock and bridge afterwards. She had killed, plucked and cooked three of her own turkeys, and a fat chicken and made no end of trifles and pies, all marvellously good. And now it looked as if nobody could *possibly* come!

However we carried on with the preparations. Mr. Birley came in and made a huge table exactly filling the sitting-room. Miss Birley finished the cooking and Miss Petter made very ornamental scoring-cards for everyone while I laid the table for eighteen as a sort of compromise with probability. Of course there wasn't enough in the way of implements and we had to extemporise a good many of most things like cups and forks, and especially seats, because this house only has four upright chairs and they are very wobbly. Eventually we found a plank out in the snow and spread it across five stools (whose height was equalised with books) and that did all one side of the table. At 3.30 just when both the gale and the preparations were at their height, a man arrived from Charlie Lake asking Miss Birley's help for a woman taken suddenly very ill up there. He could give no useful information, but made it sound pretty serious; so after a moment's hesitation on account of the party, Miss Birley decided to go off to Charlie Lake at once and Mr. Birley said he'd drive her in the small sleigh. So Petter and I piled clothes and rugs upon her and gave her hot water bottles and rugs while she collected all the remedies she could think of and set off at once for this freezing twelve-mile drive in the teeth of the icy wind. She told us to carry on with whoever came, and not to bother if she didn't come back that night.

So we carried on, feeling rather headless horsemen, and eventually Ritchie, the Scoutmaster, arrived, having walked from his little shack three miles away through heavy drifts, then three bachelors and a man and wife from Taylor's Flats arrived in two sleighs, but *nobody* from Fort St. John. We gave them nearly an hour's grace owing to the weather which was still pretty fierce and then started supper, four women and seven men (I forgot to say that Mrs. Anderson was also there with her husband and brother-in-law). We were just lamenting the absence of Miss Birley when the door burst open and in she came, covered with snow and dreadfully cold, but having seen the patient and sponged her down and given remedies and left instructions, had come back like the wind (and with it) to her own party.

We feasted her and Mr. Birley (who had to rub down his horses and put them to bed first), and considering we were only fifteen instead of twenty-five, made a marvellous mess of the turkeys, tarts and trifles. Directly we'd finished supper the *men* swept it away into the kitchen and washed up every blessed thing and put them all away in no time (chiefly in the wrong places but what matter?).

Don't you see our men-guests at a home dinner-party doing that?

Afterwards we played progressive bridge from about 10 P.M. till *3.30* A.M. I had only played once before and am notoriously M.D.[57] over cards, but I enjoyed this immensely. Nobody played really well except Petter, and everybody was friendly and funny and completely *un*serious about it. At 3.30 we finished up with prizes and two of the bachelors started on their long icy drive home. But the other guests had still farther to go, so Miss Birley said they couldn't possibly go, but must *camp here*. So we shared out blankets and rearranged bedrooms, and ended by sleeping most happily and decently two married couples, three spinsters, and three bachelors in this little house of three small single bedrooms! Of course this was accomplished by piling up ladies in the kitchen and bachelors on the sitting-room floor.

Between 9 and 10 on Saturday we got up and shared out basins and cleared up the worst traces of last night's orgy and had a delightful amusing breakfast, all ten of us, while the wind still howled and the men announced they were staying for the week-end! However, after washing up and doing wood and water and other odd jobs for us, they started to melt away and our bridge party actually began to draw to an end.

But before the Taylor's Flats people departed, I had to consult them about the next day's Service. The trouble was that the temperature was still 25 below, wind blowing and snow drifting, and I couldn't think *how* I could get across the twelve miles from Fort St. John after Sunday School *in time*—the state of the road being unknown but certainly bad. And what made it worse was that the only hymn book with tunes was at

Fort St. John; and while they could have a perfectly good Service without me they certainly could not without a *Tune Book*. The Taylor's Flats people were quite sure:

a) that I couldn't possibly make it;
b) that probably Mr. Simpson wouldn't make it;
c) that anyway at this temperature no congregation would come;
d) that this weather would certainly last a third day.

Among them they broke my spirit, and I consented to let them take a notice of postponement. But how were we to tell poor Mr. Simpson who lived five and a half miles away, half of which distance was up his own trail off the road?

Mr. Birley solved that by suggesting a big notice at the foot of his trail. So I wrote out very big on a large square notice-board:

"MR. SIMPSON
I HAVE POSTPONED SERVICE
MONICA STORRS, JANUARY 4.
Will come and see you early in the week."

And one of the men promised to tie it to a large stake and plant it bang in the middle of the trail just before it joined the road.

So that settled it and the last sleigh departed leaving me relieved but also rather sadly disappointed and ashamed.

The next thing was to go to Fort St. John for my little Guide tea-party at Mrs. Millar's. So as Ritchie had to go that way too, he waited while I packed a rucksack with Sunday School books, and chocs, and crackers, and we started off together on foot. It was still pretty cold, and our faces felt as if they were being flayed by the wind, but didn't actually get frozen for a wonder. The wind had made a fine mess of the trail, though, and we spent about one and a half hours floundering into drifts and pulling one another out before we reached the little shack which is on the way. We were so cold that we agreed to go in and light a fire and eat anything we could find. The shack was pretty bleak and cheerless at first, but we lit the stove and gradually thawed ourselves in his funny little composite room. A quarter of it was occupied by the stove where we crowded on two stools, a quarter of his wooden home-made bed of planks and boards, a third quarter was used as a granary half full of oats for the pigs, and the last quarter contained Ritchie's photographic chemicals, all of course frozen like rocks.

"Now," said Ritchie, "let's have dinner." So he rummaged round and produced a baking sheet with some bannocks, a sort of water scones, all frozen like iron of course. We put them on the stove to thaw and then he rummaged in his pockets and found two bits of cake he had saved from last night's feast! Then I robbed the Guides in advance of some of their chocolates and we had quite a good meal. We thought of having tea, but the water in the barrel was so unbreakable that we couldn't detach any for the kettle.

After this meal we felt much stronger, and went on to the town, where we parted and I found a little group of girls already assembled but, alas, diminished by the weather from nine to five. We had a lively tea, composed chiefly of cocoa and crystallised fruits, and then spent a hilarious evening playing writing games, guessing games, and Dumb Crambo,[58] none of which they had ever played before. It was great fun, and old Mrs. Millar, who of course took a leading part, enjoyed it most of all.

After that, Supper, Letters, BED.

(Hoping for a blizzard to-morrow to ease my conscience).

Week ending January 11, 1930.

After all, Sunday the 5th turned out a most lovely day, very cold but beautifully still and sunny. It was just what I didn't want, because it made it so perfectly sickening to have postponed the Taylor's Flats Service. And it was more sickening still when not a single soul turned up at Fort St. John Sunday School. Even Mrs. Devlin failed and little red-headed Roddy H. Of course it was between 20 and 30 below and no child is nearer than a mile and they have to come on week-days. And I am beginning also to realise that out here people simply *don't get up* on Sunday morning till hunger drives them. So these children who do come to Sunday School practically always have to get up, light the stoves and find their own breakfast. So although dreadfully disappointing, it is quite comprehensible when they fail in the real cold weather. Of course some of them are probably bored as well, now that the novelty has worn off, but I don't think that applies to all, anyway I certainly hope not! I said my own Matins, waited till 12 in case of a possible straggler and then walked home the long way round because though the trail is four miles against six, I felt pretty sure the road would be quicker, quite apart from the possibility of a lift. On the way I decided to discontinue both Sunday Schools till the end of January, and to try and do something by way of personal visiting instead. It was a horrid decision to make, but I have to accept the fact that ever since the real cold and snow began in December, the falling off has been continuous and worse every week. And I feel that anything is better than letting Sunday School deteriorate into either an intolerable burden or a weekly farce.

About 100 yards from Miss Birley's gate I was overhauled by an old French-Canadian who invited me into his little sleigh. It was his wife who was thrown out and so badly hurt twice lately, once about three months ago and again on Christmas Day. As we drove the short distance left to me I asked whether this was the offending team (i.e., pair) of horses. He was rather indignant and said "They are not at all an offending pair—they are perfectly good horses. They were frightened. It was just bad luck." He left me at the gate, and the *next* moment the blameless lambs bolted again; and though he did finally get them under control, it was not before they had smashed up most of their harness!

On Tuesday Rama who had not been used for four days was distinctly above himself. He was very cross and restless while being saddled and as I was leading him out of the stable he made a bold bid for freedom. Luckily I had the rope tight (being suspicious) and didn't let go. But the lamb dragged me off my feet and towed me on my back over the manure heap (mercifully now converted into a snow bank) and each time I tried to get up, pulled me over again and danced round in great excitement. By chance Miss Birley was quite near feeding the turkeys, so she came to the rescue and together we held him while I mounted. Then he started his pranks again (nothing but high spirits, of course) but luckily there was a good snowdrift close at hand so I charged him into that and held him in it bucking and bolting in *snow up to his belly* and that soon brought him to reason! Mind you I'm making a fine story of this. It was a *tiny* affair really.

It was the first dinner hour in the new term with the East St. John Scouts and we attempted knot-races. But it really is rather awful how slowly they get on even with the easiest and most elementary part of Scouting. Probably one reason is because it *is* school dinner hour and they are really a bit fagged; so we shall have to be content to go at snail's pace and stick chiefly to games. As a matter of fact I also started Company drill with them. That's not easy either because there is no room in the schoolroom with its fixed desks, and it's much too cold outside for anything that's not running. But there is just room to line up and form fours in the lobby. So we started in there and I think they rather enjoyed it.

After that I went on to the Simpsons to apologise to him about last Sunday and make a new plan. It had started snowing again in heavy thick flakes but was quite warm and very pleasant riding up the trail which was just indicated still by the tracks of somebody's sleigh. The Simpsons were most welcoming as always, and as they hadn't yet had dinner (about 3 o'clock) I had it with them. Mr. Simpson had seen the notice and bore no malice; and we agreed to hold the Service at Taylor's Flats next Sunday alive or dead. They have two absolutely speechless and fearfully solemn big sons and a funny little boy called Johnnie aged seven who means to be friendly. He produced his chief Christmas present and said, "*Here*—look at this." It was a Noah's Ark just like the ones we used to have a thousand years ago, except that being rather a cheap line the animals were even thinner and *more* inclined to fall over than in our day, and except for a liberal use of the primary colours were very much alike and difficult to distinguish as to species. We started making a procession up a cardboard lid into the ark and naming each pair as they came along but I was very bad at that. They nearly all seemed to be blue dogs or red pigs. So I said, "Here are the dogs, Johnnie."

"Them's not *dogs*. Them's timber wolves."

"Oh, I see. Well, here are the pigs."

"Them's not pigs. Them's heifer-ca'vs."

"Of course, heifer ca'vs—but look, here are the elephants anyway."

"Elephants! Them's billygoats!"

Later on he thrust a draughts board under my nose and commanded, "Here. Play chequers." I played; and was beaten. After that, Mr. Simpson pleaded for whist, and as I didn't want to be only pious with him I agreed.

Coming home was lovely for the first three miles, still snowing and deepening dusk. The actual trail was obliterated; but Rama and I both knew the way and pounded along quite fast in and out among the trees, surrounded by the curious muffled silence of the snowflakes. The last two miles was much heavier going and very cold, so I got home pretty well frozen; but soon thawed at supper.

On Wednesday I went to Taylor's Flats to re-announce the Service for next Sunday, and start making friends with the school children, in view of a monthly Sunday School. I arrived for the dinner hour as arranged with Mrs. Anderson. It is a tiny school with only twelve children at present, but twelve more waiting to come as soon as there are desks for them. The twelve range as usual from six to fifteen in age, boys and girls, so how can we start Scouts or Guides? Well, anyway I want to start with games and see what comes of it. They were awfully shy at first, and only two or three volunteered for the first game. But after a little while they all joined and we had a delightful time with ball games and team races in the snow. You see they really don't know any real games and the teacher hasn't time to teach any, so their dinner hours are perfectly deadly, anyhow in the winter. I mean to go down there every Wednesday when possible, and hope to lead on to some sort of Scouting. It was a glorious bright zero day. I visited a bit about the Service and got home again for supper, pretty cold but not to matter.

Thursday was only the Fort St. John Senior Guides' first little meeting of the term. They (six of them) came to Mrs. Millar's directly after school, and we worked with great excitement at making the Union Jack in all its stages out of coloured paper commonly used for Christmas decorations. The idea caught on very well and we made a complete set to teach the young ones in each Patrol. I slept at Mrs. Millar's and took the Scouts next day both at dinner hour, and Seniors at 4 o'clock.

Mr. Ritchie didn't turn up at all, I don't know why, but the trail was too bad to go and look for him; so I carried on without him and thoroughly enjoyed it. Of course he is charming and it is wonderful to have found a man to take the Scouts. But I do hate the prospect of giving them up, which I suppose I shall have to do as soon as he's enrolled. We shall have eighteen boys in this Troop, and it has great possibilities if we can handle it properly. At present they are not much beyond the knots and team-game stage. So I told them a short yarn about two boys saving each other from a raging torrent by throwing a rope across and making a bowline, and then we went out and did it in teams, and had great fun. Only three of the eighteen made a bad bowline and were drowned, so they are getting on a bit. We ended as usual with a big relay race round the school, and their excitement was enchanting. Later I had the six Seniors and made some paper Union Jacks to teach *their* little Juniors next Friday. I love these boys, but am not the least adequate to help them really and they don't know the *first thing* of what Scouting really means.

It was snowing again all day, and was rather a stiff ride back against the wind. But the next day, Saturday, was quite glorious—crisp and shining and beautiful in brilliant sunshine—so lovely that instead of being home-sick, I simply longed to have you all out here. The mail arrived, and my total of letters to answer reached sixty-three, so I stayed at home and did a bit of writing, varied by snow and log chores and a photographic expedition into the coulee with Petter. Miss Birley says that most winters have fifty per cent days quite as beautiful as this, but so far I have only experienced about three. Apparently this winter is exceptionally snowy and windy, instead of still and bright. But for all that it isn't a bit bad really.

Week ending January 19, 1930.

As far as I can see nothing new can happen till the Spring comes and the snow gives place to mud. I have seen practically everybody within the present reach, and started a tiny routine, which while interesting enough for me is not likely to produce any surprises worth writing about. Of course work at this moment has reached its lowest ebb—at least I'm sure I hope so—in fact I am really only killing time, or perhaps rather *Nursing the Constituency,* so don't be disappointed at the dullness and just skip the repetitions.

Last Monday I was blissfully doing nothing in and around the house. But [I] had one great treat. It was a dark day as well as cold; and in the afternoon Miss Birley was working double quick time at a pair of mitts for her brother when she suddenly observed that she could knit double the pace if she was being read to. You bet I dropped the iron and dashed for the *Oxford Book of Verse,* and we had quite a delightful English hour of poetry. You will wonder why it doesn't happen every evening. Well, you see, she and Petter have supper about 6 o'clock and I have it when I get in generally between 6.30 and 7 o'clock and then we wash up. After supper Petter has to prepare for school, and naturally requires comparative silence, or at least not more than a desultory conversation. That's the best chance of either writing a letter or reading a book. But it doesn't last long because at about 8 o'clock Mr. Birley arrives for the rest of the evening. Mr. Birley is a very nice man. He works like a navvy all day at his farm, and every evening he comes and sits with us for a smoke and a chat. He is a great raconteur, and loves to tell at length either anecdotes of his own career or the latest short story he has read. He tells these stories very well, and has an inexhaustible supply of them, but of course they require an audience. So the rest of the evening, though very pleasant, is pretty well dished for any other purpose. That's why we don't read poetry, or anything else much, at night. After all that talk about Monday, I forgot all about Sunday and Taylor's Flats!

Sunday was dark and cold and snowing a little, though not much. The Sunday Schools having been abandoned for the rest of the month anyway, I had nothing to do but to go to Taylor's Flats for the little afternoon Service. So after breakfast and chores I went to look for Rama who was out in the pasture with Papoose, the other horse. They come up to the fence every morning and evening for their sheaf of oats and that is when we catch them for use. But Sunday they didn't come, preferring to go hungry somewhere far down in the comparatively sheltered coulee, to facing the freezing North wind and getting their breakfast (I wonder which you and I would prefer?). The pasture is pretty extensive and very rough and steep, and the snow very deep and drifted, so after a short search I abandoned Rama and decided to walk. I went and told Miss Birley and asked for sandwiches early, and to my surprise she said, "All right. I'm coming with you," so for the first time since I've been here I had the excitement of a companion on the road. The snow was very heavy, but we made good speed and got there in exactly two hours—and found Mr. Simpson already arrived and the school almost full of children.

Of course Mr. Neilson, whom I had twice visited about it, had not lighted the fire as promised, so Mr. Simpson lighted it when he came and the little school was still freezing. Also he had not produced any extra bench to supplement the twelve small desks. So there were about twelve kids with nothing to sit on—and out of sympathy, I suppose, or general confusion, nobody else sat down either. I mobilised two or three big boys and we went out and found a couple of planks buried in snow, and collected four logs to put them on, and finally got everyone sitting on something. Meanwhile the little woman who was to play the harmonium suddenly struck at chants, and afterwards I wasn't sorry she had as she seemed to forget to pedal during most of the hymns! Meanwhile also Mr. Simpson implored me to give the address, so as there were over twenty children and not more than seven or eight grownups beside ourselves, I tried to talk to the children about the meaning of Christmas *and* the New Year, and fell very heavily between two stools. Altogether it was rather a melancholy little Service. The congregation [were] completely ignorant of the form of Service—or [their] way about the Prayer Book and apparently even ignorant of the four carefully chosen hymns: "Hark the Herald," "Lead Kindly Light," "Jesu Lover of My Soul," "Abide with Me." They couldn't even find the hymns because they all confused the number with the *page*, owing to Mr. Simpson having given out the *page* of each part of the Prayer Book Service. Even this latter plan was not fool-proof, because a few Prayer Books were in a different size and the pages differently numbered to his own. So each time he announced for instance: "We will now say the Creed on page 23," I had to add in a stage whisper: "Little books, page 34," and rush round inspecting. Lastly, nobody knew when to stand up and sit down and Mr. Simpson was too nervous to tell them.

The culmination was probably my officiousness, and the miserable poverty of the address. Anyway these were the only elements in the general feebleness of the Service that were definitely culpable. The only part that was a tearing success (humanly speaking, of course!) was the distribution of calendars and texts at the end. Everybody wanted them and they gave quite a warm feeling at the finish such as ought to have been associated with the address or hymns.

Well, anyway I am going down on the first Sunday of the month for a Sunday School, and what we have got to decide is whether Mr. Simpson shall come too, and try to precede the Sunday School with a short grown-up Service—like this but better.

When everyone had gone we ate our sandwiches (no time before) and Mr. Simpson started to drive us home in his borrowed sleigh. He took us three miles to where his trail leaves our road; and we were just starting to walk the second three when up drove Mr. Birley with his sleigh.

Goodness, what a lot of talk about all that! And there was nothing in it, as you see. And yet it is just possible that such utter nothingness may leave more room for God.

Tuesday was still pretty nippy, barely 20 below but a nasty cutting little wind. I rode as usual to Petter's school and found only nine children out of the possible eighteen. We stayed indoors and had knot races. It's a dreary little show that I give those little kids and yet Petter says they look forward to it. Afterwards I only went a mile farther and paid a long visit to Mrs. Michaud, the nice French-Canadian who was so badly hurt on Christmas Day. She was still in bed and having bad nights but the swelling is going down and they don't think the bone is injured. I sat with her a good while and played with two of her little boys and promised to send her via Miss Petter and one of the little boys who comes to school, a French book and some aspirin out of my First Aid box. Of course she is Roman Catholic and therefore not strictly my affair, but I do like the little sick-visiting, and she is having a deadly time, poor thing.

Wednesday was clear and crisp and beautifully sunny and I went down to the Flats School for the dinner hour, told the children something about Scouts and Wolf Cubs, asked them to think if they'd like to join and then played some team games with them in the snow. Then I went on another mile to visit a little boy who had been hurt tobogganing. Poor little fellow, he had a big lump under his chin and another on his leg, and looked very miserable, but of course I couldn't tell how bad it might really be.

Coming home at sundown it got colder and colder and colder. For the last two miles I had to lead Rama; and even then, almost running, it felt as if we were racing some deadly steely foe who was steadily overtaking us and must eventually cut us both to pieces. Poor little Rama who had started out a brown horse came home a white horse, being completely frosted all over. It was all I could do to undress and put him to bed, and took about twenty minutes, my hands were so numb. The sort of time when you long for a nice English groom to throw the reins to, and walk straight into the Baronial Hall. When I did walk in I found it was 36 below, which rather comforted me, because sometimes I have got cold like that for nothing or only zero, which is dreadfully stupid.

Thursday and Friday were Guides and Scouts at Fort St. John as usual, and the numbers were again reduced by the weather and the heavy snow which has made some trails almost impassable.

Would you believe it—no badges have come yet for either Scouts or Guides, though all were ordered at the beginning of November. It does make it hard to keep the zest going when both Headquarters (Canadian) are so dilatory that I cannot get a single Guide or Scout or even the Scout Master enrolled.

On Saturday I started to visit the McDonalds who live up a trail four and a half miles beyond Baldonnel School and whose children haven't turned up for over a week. A mile beyond the school the trail disappeared completely, and I could find no trace of the way; so having gone a long distance out of the way, I abandoned the attempt for that day and visited Alice LeClerc,[59] the French girl who is going to be a Guide, and Mrs. Michaud again, and gave a story book (*The Three Little Pigs!*) to her little boy, who was fearfully excited about the book though he took no manner of interest in the story.

That night Tommy arrived for the week-end, also Miss Bell, the Charlie Lake teacher, and they and Miss Birley and Petter all went to a dance at the Flats which I blissfully shirked.

Week ending January 28, 1930.

The weeks have started to fly past now at the most astonishing rate, I think chiefly because they are so much alike and there is so little to mark them one from another.

Last Sunday was rather sad because it had no Service or Sunday School of any kind; so I determined to go to the McDonalds without fail this time, as they are rather remote and hadn't even been to day school lately. It was a cold morning, 20 below, but lovely and bright, and snow apparently quite full of diamonds. Four miles of the way was quite familiar and not bad going, but for the last three and a half there was no visible trail and it was pretty tedious progress. The actual route was easy enough (once I'd found the right turn off the road which I failed to find on Saturday) because there are fences here and there and a shack or two, and some cuttings between trees, but the untrodden snow was very laborious. It made me realise the true value of that which we all so properly despise at home and do our best to avoid—THE BEATEN TRACK. Here it's just the other way round. The beaten track, or rather the broken trail is what we all look for, and complain bitterly when the wind or a fresh fall of snow wipes it out again.

The beaten track may just be human or horses' footprints, or it may (much better) be the two grooves made by sleigh-runners. But whatever it is, you always cling to it, as the firmest footing and the best way of avoiding drifts.

However, the McDonalds' trail was properly obliterated, so Rama and I floundered along with lots of jerks and plunges, and every now and then Rama stopped dead and looked round at me saying: "I've had enough of this." After a mile or so, I got off and led him, chiefly for the sake of warmth. The only drawback to that is when you occasionally slip back a foot or so and Rama doesn't. Then he occasionally and quite innocently kicks your heel or treads on your foot, when his spiked steel shoes through your soft skin moccasins give a nasty jar. This happened once or twice, and after that the terror of it gave wings to my feet.

We reached the McDonalds at last and found they hadn't been to school for at least a fortnight, because their sleigh had broken and Mr. McDonald was away logging in the bush. I had taken a book each for the boys and a cut-out model of a Palestine market for the little girl, Helen; and Mrs. McDonald wanted to divide the Sunday School by Post list with me, so there was lots to do, and I spent the afternoon with them. Mrs. McDonald said they simply couldn't get to Sunday School just now, while the trail was so bad, though she also told me of a much better trail than the one I had come by.

So after a lot of talk we agreed that she should invite the two neighbouring boys next Sunday afternoon, and I should come out again and hold a little group Sunday School in her house. Finally, she produced some tea and cake and I came home by the longer but quite decent trail round by the Simpsons. It had warmed up a lot in the afternoon and the return was lovely. The McDonalds' part is rather high and less systematically cleared than just round us, more like heath land as compared with farm land at Home. There are clumps of trees everywhere in the foreground, and off to the right the opposite bank of the North Pine River rises up very white and romantic looking. To the left and farther off (about eight miles at the nearest point), runs the long dark blue line of the opposite bank of the Peace; and in front of you along the whole Western horizon stretch the real mountains, I suppose about eighty or 100 miles away. As I rode home that evening they were dark silhouettes against the sunset sky. But in the morning, as I have pretty often seen them from Fort St. John, they are white and glistening like the delectable mountains in *Pilgrim's Progress,* only so far away as to be only *just* not out of sight. They give me a fool longing to ride on and on till I reach them, and never come back to this bald plateau again. And yet, do you know I believe this may prove to be rather beautiful country. Certainly, I haven't given it a fair chance, for when I came, the autumn was just over and it was all brown and dead, and since then it has been almost black and white, like a photograph. Perhaps it really will be all they say it is, perfectly lovely in the spring.

On Monday Miss Birley was not at all well. Apparently she used to be liable to slight attacks of pleurisy which was one of the causes of her leaving England. This was another of these attacks, the first since she has lived up here. She had the usual sharp pain in breathing, and was very hot and flushed; but I couldn't take her temperature because the only thermometer in the house has been broken by the frost. She wouldn't let me do anything for her, but said it must just run its course and would be all right in a day or two. Tommy Hargreaves, who arrived on some errand, stayed with us and immediately assumed charge of the kitchen. It was rather worrying because we couldn't tell how bad Miss Birley really was, and were obliged merely to do what she told us instead of vice versa. Incidentally, three people called (an almost unexampled number), and I had to be her go-between with them. One was the School Inspector who comes round once a year, and only called to say he was well pleased with Petter. The two others were the man with the frozen toe and the father of the Taylor's Flats' little boy who splintered his jaw while tobogganing last week. Both of these Miss Birley insisted on seeing, so I had to take them to the door of her room while she talked to them, and gave instructions. It was rather wonderful considering how feverish and ill she really was. By evening she was distinctly better.

On Tuesday I didn't want to go out, but she urged me to go the East St. John dinner hour, where I has the usual queer little mixed Scouting and games, and came straight back. Miss Birley got *much* better in the evening, and on Wednesday, after breakfast, she got up, but didn't do any work till Thursday.

Tommy stayed all the week. He is, as you know, the owner of the one garage at Fort St. John, but the state of the roads has made motoring impossible nearly all this winter and quite impossible now, so he shuts up his garage.

So I went down to the Taylor's Flats school to start something like Scouting there. This school has always been very tiny, only about fourteen children. But on Wednesday I found twenty-five and seven more coming next week. The absurd thing is that all these new ones have the same surname [Alexander], as their fathers are six brothers who have all moved in here together from Saskatchewan. They nearly all want to be Scouts but as nearly half of them are girls, and two-thirds of them are under twelve, and they quite fill the school, without moving, and the teacher has to stay all the time, and doesn't like the noise, [and] it is generally too cold outside to stop running for more than a moment, it's a little perplexing to know how to carry on. Of course, this is the problem of all the one-roomed schools, I suppose, but not many are so suddenly crowded up with new kids as Taylor's Flats.

This kind of school is a strain on the teacher too, because she has children from six or seven up to fourteen or fifteen years old, covering eight different grades, and has to keep them all going at different levels at once. How they do it at all is a marvel to me. But one rather sad result seems to be an atmosphere of strain in the teacher and of oppression in the school, quite different from the cheerfulness in our National Schools.

I took names and ages of recruits and tried to sort them out a bit, taught them two knots, distributed Sunday School magazines and ended up with the usual boisterous team games in the snow. Then I rode on another mile to visit the little boy with the injured jaw, Harry J. He had been very bad all the week, poor kid, with his whole face swollen right up to the eye. But on Thursday the abscess had broken inside his mouth, and I found him very much better and the swelling almost gone. I stayed a long time and read to him. He is rather a dear little kid of eight, and his people came out from Leeds last year, but have been short of work and rather miserable all this winter.

On Thursday—you know—Guides and Fort St. John and Friday Scouts, both of them mid-day and evening. We have great plans for a rally at Easter and a Summer Camp. I do *hope* they will come off.

On Saturday, we all seemed to have stayed at home until 4.30 when Miss Birley and Petter and Tommy went off in the sleigh to a bridge party down at the Flats. They said they *might* stay the night, or might not. I rather hoped they would, for although it was much warmer, I don't like these very late drives home for Miss Birley so soon after her attack.

Then I wrote letters, got my supper, fed the animals, and spent perfect ages preparing a little lesson for the tiny class at McDonalds tomorrow.

About midnight, it seemed pretty clear that they were staying the night; but I made up the stove in *case* of a return, and put out the tea things and went to bed. It was rather a queer feeling, not knowing whether I should wake up alone in the house or not, but as the door is never locked, it's quite simple!

However, I was not allowed to sleep in peace because Rowdy was so *dreadfully* worried. He wandered round and round the little house moaning and groaning and making such a fuss that at last I had to call him on to my bed. Once there, he spread out all over me and went sound asleep, but was so heavy that my sleep was not so sound! However, it was company anyway, and I had just got used to it and dropped off properly, when with the usual *crash* (as it always seems), the bridge party returned at 5 A.M., and Rowdy sprang up with a yell of rapture to welcome the adored Mamma.

Week ending February 1, 1930.

On Sunday I was due at the Simpsons for dinner and at the McDonalds for a little Sunday School afterwards. It was a lovely bright day—about 10 above zero and therefore delicious riding except for the heaviness of the trail. I got to the Simpsons in one and a half hours and had an immense dinner of pork and Xmas pudding washed down, as always, by strong tea. Then we all went on a mile or so farther to the McDonalds who as usual were *most* welcoming and nowhere near ready. At last the dinner dishes were washed and the house tidied a little and Mrs. McDonald got into a very smart afternoon dress. Then the three children were ferreted out of their respective funk holes and made to wash—and I only intervened just in time to prevent Jack from being forced to change his shirt—which would have put back Christianity in these parts for several years. Then Erving Foster, a very nice boy of twelve, arrived from the next homestead beyond, and the party was fully organised; i.e., one girl, four boys, two fathers and two mothers. I drove the fathers out at first, but they drifted back after a bit—because there was nowhere else to sit, poor fellows!

The lesson was the Boyhood of Christ, all of course, quite an unknown topic to these children. Then I taught them a prayer, taken from a Christmas card sent me by Hardcastle,[60] and we sang several hymns for the benefit of the grown-ups who thoroughly enjoyed that part. The kids were very nice too, even Jack was friendly and almost forthcoming, and afterwards showed me all his books. Finally, Mrs. Mac gave us all tea, after which I rode home, first straight towards a heavenly sunset, and then in the gloaming, feeling that fourteen miles was somehow well worth while, though it had been such a funny little Sunday School.

On Monday, Miss Birley and Tommy went off for a grand riding exhibition to visit Miss Birley's friends, the Palings.[61] They live twenty miles away down the river, far from the road and and from any other house. Mrs. Paling is English, from Cambridge, and it must be an awfully lonely life for her. They have no children either, and are pretty hard up, although they both have quite well-to-do relations at Home. Miss Birley is very fond of her, and not having heard from her at Christmas, wanted to see if all was well. So she and Tommy took Rama and Papoose and went off for the night, leaving me in charge of the house and Petter. I had a delightful day messing round with cleaning up and washing and melting snow, and was only just ready with supper for Petter when she came in at 6 o'clock. We also had a nice evening together, she preparing lessons as usual, and I writing letters. She is a charming kid, especially when you are alone with her. She told me that she was rather frightened of what she calls my "sarcasm," meaning the gentle irony which all English people employ to their friends' edification. It is gradually dawning upon me (and she made it clearer), that the sort of mild irony which is current coin in England is not liked here. If for instance, anyone treads on your toe and you exclaim: "D——

— you dirty beast," it's all right. But if you remark: "Bless your fairy weight," it is "sarcastic," and they are hurt!

On Tuesday morning I acted Miss Birley perfectly, lit the stoves, fed the pigs and Petter in bed (only Petter in bed, not the pigs), and made her sandwiches and filled her thermos and felt awfully important "getting her off to school."

After that, chores again, and a good clean-up of the house; and then being without a horse, walked over to Baldonnel School, and took over an hour as the snow was deeper than ever. After the usual hour with the kids I walked on to Mr. Simpson's to fix up next week's Service at the Flats. It is still snowing pretty hard though quite warm, and took me another hour to get there. They gave me some dinner which was unexpected and nice. Then Mr. Simpson and I worked hard at preparing the Service, always a slow process. Finally he actually hitched up his horses and took me back in his sleigh to the school where I was just in time to join Petter and the little boys, and come home with them in the cutter. We found Miss Birley and Tommy already home, having had a good visit.

On Wednesday at the Flats I chose two boys and a girl to be the leaders of the strange little Scout-Guide troop. They picked up their three Patrols and came out with four boys and two girls in each. I hope soon to get the girls into a Patrol by themselves at any rate for special Guide work; but as they have only forty-five minutes a week altogether, I can't really split them off from the boys at present, and as they do all their lessons together always it doesn't seem necessary, at least in this early stage.

After that I heard that Mrs. Herbie Taylor,[62] the ferryman's wife, was pretty ill across the river, so went over to see her. This was the first time I had been across on the ice, so I felt very bold and enterprising, though of course, teams and sleighs are going over every day. It isn't as exciting as it sounds, of course, because the river is so deeply covered with snow that you don't *see* any ice at all except in the occasional holes which people have cut to get water and then you can see the ice to be about two feet thick. So the river looks like a broad and winding white road dividing two hilly brown and white worlds. It is about half a mile wide, and Rama was by some strange instinct a little bit frightened, although of course at this time of year it's safer than Watling Street.

I found the old lady in the ferryman's shack at the other side. He is a halfbreed, but she is a squaw, quite pure Indian, and talks no English. She is evidently suffering from gastric ulcers, and has been pretty bad; so I urged him to feed her on milk only. But he said that however ill she was she insisted upon meat and he had to give it to her. But he agreed that beef was unsuitable, and added that he was making great efforts to

procure *moose* or *bear* meat as being more suited to a delicate stomach! I
couldn't feel quite satisfied with this plan, but nothing would shake
him, so I could only hope that moose and bear are as hard to find as
possible. Meanwhile, the old lady smiled very sweetly, and told me
(through his interpretation), that if she didn't die, she would make me a
pair of moose-hide gloves as a reward for visiting her. Then Mr. Taylor
showed me all the remedies he was giving her in a terrific row of very
large bottles, all nameless quacks bought at the Fort St. John store,
which has of course, no *real* medicines at all. It was all rather worrying,
as she is probably pretty seriously ill, and ought to go to a hospital. But
nothing would induce her to take the two days journey, and he is quite
confident of curing her with bear-meat and quack medicines—so
perhaps he will.

Coming back we galloped the half mile across the river which was
great fun, as the snow was more smooth and hard than on the road or
trails, and the banks looked fine standing up seven or eight hundred feet
on each side. Apparently it's quite safe to cross until well into *April*. Isn't
that funny?

Thursday was Guides and exactly as usual, so I'm not going to say
things about them except that we are *still* waiting for their badges to
come, and our patience is fast becoming the patience of despair. One of
the elder ones who has left school and has the use of a horse, rode with me
for three miles of the way home, and says she generally intends to do so,
which is very nice, especially for Rama, who gets dreadfully bored with
being alone.

Friday was Scouts, and chiefly devoted to a careful revision of the
Tenderfoot Test in preparation for Enrolment next week, as their badges
have at last come, and beaten the Guides' ditto's by one mail anyway. I
had a rather long evening meeting with the actual five boys and Mr.
Ritchie, discussing future plans and trying by a succession of games and
competitions to teach them the Scout Law. We broke up about 6 o'clock,
and I collected our mail at the Post Office, having for the first time
undertaken to bring it home. It was too much for my haversack, so Mr.
Pickell[63] lent me a big canvas mail bag, which I had an awful job to tie
on Rama's back, behind the saddle. He was very restless and irritable,
and wouldn't stand still; so after three false starts, I lashed it on once
more and tried to hold it in position with one hand. The next minute I
suppose it slipped and hit his leg or something. Anyhow, it was the last
straw, and his Christian spirit suddenly gave way. There was a violent
upheaval, and I flew over his head into a snowdrift as neatly as possible.
Rama cast one ironical backward glance and then cantered gaily off into
the darkness.

I wasn't the least bit hurt, thanks to the snowdrift, but immensely surprised and annoyed, being five miles from home and very hungry, because I had forgotten to bring my lunch sandwiches in the morning. There was no hope of catching the criminal of course, and my only hope was that he would carry the mail home safely and be found by somebody. It was quite dark except for the glimmer which snow always makes, so pretty hard to keep on the exact trail, but it wasn't really cold, so I floundered along quite happily only wondering whether Miss Birley might get into a fuss at my being so late.

However, after only about two miles I came round a corner straight upon Rama motionless in the snow. I crept up like an Indian and caught him, and then discovered that there was no need for any stealth because poor little Rama was tied and bound by the chain of his sins. The mail bag had heeled over and dragged the saddle right round under his belly and the halter rope had gone with it, and was round his legs and so were the reins, and he was properly shackled in the deep snow. I tried hard to release him, but it was almost impossible in the dark, and we were both getting crosser than ever, when by a sort of miracle a sleigh came along, and I had to shout hard to prevent it from running into us. The man driving was a stranger to me, but so kind, of course. He worked patiently at disentangling Rama, and took the mail bag for me and promised to drop it on Mrs. Birley sometime tomorrow. Rama seemed really sorry, and came home as good as possible, in fact he found the way when I had completely lost my bearings and was obliged to leave it to him. One thing I needn't have worried about anybody being fussed. In Canada we have no such custom. Tommy said, "Why on earth didn't you fasten the mail bag on properly?" Mr. Birley said, "What sort of cowboy are you if you can't stick on a poor little cayuse like Rama?" Bless their hearts! Cayuse = native pony (which Rama is not).

On Saturday Miss Birley and Petter went out for a little jaunt together, and I stayed at home intending to write letters. But the two little Birley boys came over, obviously hard up for occupation, so I started them to paint and cut out a model of a Palestine house, thinking in my innocence *that* would keep them quite happy and self-supporting. It did keep them happy, but it also kept me busy *all* the afternoon, advising over colours, helping over cutting out, preparing sticky paste, and assisting at the Grand Finale. So good-bye to letter writing; but it was rather fun and they were so *very* good, both of them. When Miss Birley came back she jeered at me and said, "You crazy mutt, you should have taken no notice of the brats, and they'd have gone home again." I never thought of that!

Alas, when the mail bag returned we discovered that Rama had put his foot through and *completely* smashed the two new choir boy records that we had been eagerly looking forward to for weeks!!

Week ending February 8, 1930.

Last Sunday was the last I hope without a Sunday School at Fort St. John, and it was also the first of the monthly ones at Taylor's Flats. So I had nothing to do in the morning, but prepare for the afternoon. I rode down to the Flats in good time, knowing how much warming and tidying up the school would require.

I took the picture of Christ and the Children (modern children) and the blue table cloth and the usual collection of hymn books, and had to rely on Mr. Simpson bringing the little harmonium, as he was to hold the short grown-up Evensong afterwards. The children were late of course, but they turned up well, i.e., twenty-four or five of them which is practically the whole day-school plus four mothers including who do you think? The runaway wife who thought better of it and got home again on Saturday! There she was bright and smiling just as if nothing at all had happened. But all the neighbours seem to think she has made a great mistake in coming home so soon. What they will live on now I don't know, as he has no work; and the teacher who boarded with them found a new billet while the wife was away. I'm rather worried about them really, for though he undoubtedly had a shock, I'm terribly afraid it can't have changed him very much.

The Sunday School went rather well, though it's awfully hard to design a suitable course of monthly lessons for children like that. I started with their Christian names, the Name of Jesus and His love for them. We sang "Do No Sinful Action," or rather began to learn it, and I gave them each a picture card of Christ and the Children, on the back of which they wrote (with great difficulty) the little prayer from Hardcastle's Christmas card, and promised to try and use it.

Almost at the beginning Mr. Simpson came in ready for the next Service, which followed on immediately as nobody new came for it, and nobody went away. Quite honestly I doubt whether the Flats are ready for an Anglican Service.[64] There are no Anglicans amongst them except the one woman who plays the harmonium, and they all seem to be utterly bewildered by the Prayer Book and its elaborate language and devious ways. Mr. Simpson gave a little address on the Good Samaritan, very nervously but quite clear and nice.

We sang four of the most familiar hymns— "Jesu Lover," "Lead Kindly Light," "How Sweet the Name of Jesus Sounds," and "Abide with Me," but nobody except the two Englishwomen and one father seemed to sing a note. Afterwards we had the usual friendly chat with the grown-ups, and then Mr. Simpson insisted on driving me the first three miles homeward in his little new-made cutter of which he was very proud. It was just a little box of planks on wooden runners. They are what almost everybody here makes and uses for light driving (answering to a two-seater), while for heavier work they use the big-waggon-box on sleighs. We tied Rama behind and progressed pretty slowly as his horses are ponderous beasts. At the third mile we parted and I was rather thankful to be on Rama again and come home at twice the pace. The only thing I remember about Monday is that in the afternoon May Birley was knitting and I read aloud to her one of Barrie's little plays "The Old Woman Shows Her Medals"[65]—do you know it? Most delightful and touching too, like everything that Barrie produced.

On Tuesday we had the first Enrolment, i.e., four Scouts at Baldonnel. We formed our little Horseshoe round the flagstaff outside the school, all standing in the snow. I tried to make it as impressive as possible without frightening them. But two of the boys' horses having a sham fight not five yards away made concentration a little difficult. Afterwards I visited three homes to tell them about the little Service to be at Baldonnel next Sunday. On Wednesday at the Flats I chose three leaders, two boys and a girl and they picked up their three Patrols and got on a little bit themselves. The difficulty in that school is the overcrowding of the one little room, and the complete absence of any atmosphere of welcome on the part of the teacher. She is the one who stayed here and was nursed by Miss Birley after her accident last term, and we are quite friends out of school; but on these occasions although invited by her to come, I always feel I'm there on sufferance which is a little disconcerting. Little Petter at the Baldonnel School is far more welcoming (of course, we live together so it would be sinister if she wasn't!). But she doesn't take any interest—I think because she doesn't really care about children. But far the most encouraging is the Fort St. John teacher who really is interested and comes out to cheer on the team games, and often gives me five or ten minutes overtime quite cheerfully because she thinks it's good for the children. After the Taylor's Flats dinner hour I visited the father of the two biggest children there. His wife is away in an asylum, and he has four nice children and a housekeeper (presumably a widow) who also has four children. I called on her ostensibly and found her very, very shy and uncommunicative. We had a lame, heavy conversation, in which we were presently joined by Neilson *from his bedroom* where he was sitting on his bed reading a book! For quite twenty minutes he continued to sit there and to talk to me through the hinges of the door. But eventually I managed to draw him from his cover, and he shuffled into full view in the sitting-room; but I think the real reason was his desire to know whether Miss Birley had a gobbler turkey to sell! After that I paid three more visits all nice but nothing to write about, and didn't go to the returned runaway wife lest she should think I was spying out the land by dropping in so soon.

Thursday was Guides as usual, but started with a short rehearsal of Horseshoe formation with the Scouts, so as to be as impressive as possible to-morrow. I started the Senior Guides at First Aid; and they had a crowded hour of great joy and gigglings restoring each other rather drastically from choking, fainting and nasal haemorrhage.

On reaching home I found that May Birley's friends Mr. and Mrs. Paling had arrived by sleigh for a visit. At least she was to stay over the week-end; but he had to go back to look after the cattle, etc., and return for her next week. They are both what you call Public School people, he from Sussex and she from Cambridge. They are quite a different type to all the other homesteaders, and it seems queer to see them in this sort of life, especially as their farm is far more isolated than any other I know of. They are sixteen miles from here, and seven miles from the Flats—not seven miles of nice country lanes, but seven miles of steep hilly bush with no sort of road whatever. Their little house is right on the river on the way to nowhere. They have had lots of bad luck and are very hard-up. For months they see nobody, and sometimes Mrs. Paling goes eight or nine months without seeing another woman; so no wonder one of the greatest events is her annual visit to Miss Birley. She is a wonderful housekeeper so what do you think was the entertainment provided for her? Two pigs to pickle and cure! The day before her arrival had been set apart for a great tragedy, the execution of May Birley's two beloved pigs—Romula and Rema. Tommy Hargreaves was the chief executioner assisted by Mr. S——p, the man whose frozen foot had been cured by May Birley, who offered his services as a Thank-offering. All the morning Tommy and he were preparing the sacrifice—erecting a wooden scaffolding to hang up the corpses and boiling a huge barrel of snow in preparation for the shaving. Poor May Birley hated it because she is devoted to all her animals and therefore not really suited for farming. Luckily I had just taught her how to work (I won't say play) the little portable harmonium. So directly she was warned that the sacrifice was about to take place she retired into the house and played "Abide with Me" till all was over! Tommy shot the pigs and killed each instantaneously with one bullet. Then he and S. shaved and cleaned and skinned and cut them up, and when I got home in the evening the whole house seemed to be full of pork. Miss Birley says it's a real test of friendship to butcher somebody else's pigs—and I'm inclined to believe it. After that it was her turn with Mrs. Paling and they worked at it for three whole days, making pies and brawn and lard and bacon and ham, till the house reeked with their efforts.

In the evening they all played bridge which was embarrassing because I wanted to practise next Sunday's hymns on Cordelia (the harmonium), and every time I gave warning of this intention it was received with hoots of rage and derision. However, I put a bold face on it, and as the game drew towards a conclusion prepared the ground by announcing at intervals, "Cheer up, the Organ Recital will commence in fifteen minutes—no charge for admission—silver collection only"—groans and jeers and hoots from the card-players. At last they had finished; and I began, frightfully bungling and inaccurately to practise "Lead Kindly Light." Immediately, to my astonishment, all the jeering stopped and one after another the card players drifted up and began to sing. Then they began to call for favourite hymns without any regard to the fact that I hardly got two notes right; and we ended by having a good hour of really delightful hymn-singing, Mr. Paling and Tommy joining as heartily as anyone.

Friday was the first Scout Enrolment at Fort St. John—luckily it was still warm enough to hold it outside, round the flagstaff—and thanks to yesterday's rehearsal the eighteen boys marched quite decently and formed their Horseshoe round the Flag without any outside interference. I enrolled Mr. Ritchie first and the five boys with as much dignity and solemnity as possible. Then we all said the Law and finished with a short prayer, and the National Anthem; and *immediately* after the Dismissal there were wild yells and the whole Troop broke up in somersaults and catherine wheels. This was quite unrehearsed and simply a reaction from the Awful Strain of the last ten minutes, but it made rather a good finale! After that we had a series of very exciting team games and finally I handed the Troop over formally to Mr. Ritchie, reserving the right to come in once a month as *District Scouter* (a post invented entirely by myself!), and to take all further enrolments until Mr. Ritchie should get his warrant. This sounds rather officious, *but if you knew* the anguish it cost me to hand them over at all, you wouldn't be so critical. They are, of course, the first Troop, the biggest Troop, and are bound to be the best Troop in the District; and Mr. Ritchie, though very nice, is of course quite a dark horse and a Roman Catholic dark horse too. Before I stop boring you with the Scouts I must give you a swift analysis of their nationalities or rather their original races; because of course their nationality is Canadian; but their *races* make rather a good sample of the population of North West Canada.[66]

Taking the three little troops together, and the leaders or enrolled boys only:

Two are Danish—one is Italian (Roman Catholic)—one is half Italian half German—two are American—one is French-Canadian—two are Scotch-Canadian—one is three-quarters Indian—one is *half* halfbreed, and half Canadian—one is English with a halfbreed mother.

Does that list give you rather a shock? Well, so it did me when I first realised it. You may say: what has all this got to do with our own people overseas?

It's quite true—only one of the boys so far enrolled is English, and he has a halfbreed mother. Only three of the Guides at present ready to be enrolled are English; and the father of two of these has run away, and the mother of the third (and I don't know what her nationality was).

Of the other Guides—one is French-Canadian—one is German-Italian—one is German-American—one is three-quarters Indian—two are American—and one is real Scotch.

But about this I must make three comments:

1. That among the newcomers and *younger* children there is a definitely larger proportion of British blood.

2. That all these queer varieties have cut the painter from their own Old Countries and only want to be Canadian.

3. *That* probably is not so very unlike the make-up of our own English population about 900 years ago.

The next great excitement is Uniform; but I will let you off any more of this for the present.

Afterwards I walked up to the City (as we call the cluster of shacks round the Post Office), bewildering poor little Rama with last charges; and outside the store we saw three strange females, two on skis and one walking. They looked perplexed so I hurried officiously to them and asked whether I could help. To my rapture (not exactly surprise), they answered in *Pure English* such as might have come from Rochester, Winchester, or even Crayford. It's so funny, you know, one almost ceases to notice the accent and language here, or even to realise the difference UNTIL you hear a Pukka English voice again, and then it's electrifying. They were almost as thrilled as I was and immediately made me go to tea with them in the absurd little Fort St. John Hotel. It turned out that they were three English spinsters from West Malvern who are touring North West Canada *on their legs*.[67] They had already wandered about 800 miles in the Peace River Country and were now planning to go to Fort Nelson about 300 miles due North of here. There is no road but a rough trail by which the trappers and traders go; and their plan is to walk and ski, as soon as they can hear of a team going up which can carry their luggage and help them to camp at night. There are no hotels or stopping places on the way. I was mad with envy and seized with wild longing to go with them and shake off these suburban surroundings for a little. They invited me warmly enough to join them; but couldn't promise *to come back here* afterwards, as they contemplated a far more ambitious dash to the East if it can be accomplished. This knocked me out, as I couldn't come home alone from Fort Nelson or wait about there indefinitely for a trader to come back with. So with deep disgust I tried to make a virtue of necessity and think how much better really to stick to my little guns here than yield to a pointless lust for adventure. But I haven't got over the disappointment yet; especially as they started off next day with all tackle in a sleigh going North, and left a note to say they might be back here in about three weeks after all!!! Wasn't that???

Meanwhile another stranger turned up the same afternoon, a nice little man sent up by the British Columbia Red Cross to look into the hospital problem here.[68] As usual it was assumed that Miss Birley would put him up, and she did. Luckily Petter was away for the week-end, so he slept in her room; and both the Palings being in Miss Birley's bed, she slept in the kitchen. You will notice that the only room that never gives hospitality is mine. That is, alas! true enough; and the only excuse is, that I am never away for more than one night, and it is the smallest room and the only *obstinately* single bed in the house.

"The little Gink," as May Birley would call this man (not to his face), was a well-trained guest, made his own bed and insisted on helping to wash-up supper. Mr. Birley drove him round in a sleigh all Saturday to interview the heads of the various warring cliques up here, and I gather he was rather disgusted by them. He and the Palings seemed to occupy us all Saturday except the time I took in preparing for Sunday School and Service and riding over to Mrs. Millar for the night.

Week ending February 15, 1930.

Last week was awfully dull. I really don't think there is anything to tell about it, but must have a try.

Sunday started fairly cold but turned out perfectly *lovely* in the afternoon. We started the Fort St. John School again after a whole month's lapse. Mrs. Devlin turned up and about sixteen children, who left certain bad gaps. We started to learn "Do No Sinful Action" and I took the lesson about Christian names and our belonging to Christ. Then I gave each a card with a text on one side (sent from Crayford), and dictated to them the little Prayer beginning:

"Jesus, loving Child in the Home,
Help me to be like You. . . ."

I hope to get all the children I can reach to use this prayer in time and have started using it altogether at the end of each Sunday School.

As the second Baldonnel (East Fort St. John) Service was to be that

afternoon and I had to play the Psalms and hymns on Cordelia, I didn't
go back to dinner but rode straight through and arrived before 2 o'clock
for a tidy-up and practice. Mercifully Georgie had for once remembered
to light the fire, so the school was quite warm and not *too* dirty. All one
can do to make a Church effect is to dust the desks (mostly much too
small for grown-ups!) hang a sacred picture on the back wall, and cover
the teacher's table with the blue Sunday School cloth and a white
wooden cross produced by Mr. Simpson. The only unexpected problem
at this school was the presence, *tightly* screwed into the end of this table,
of a large new pencil sharpener which no effort of ours could remove.
So we draped the table-cloth over it and produced a mysterious swelling
which intrigued the congregation very much.

Alas! there was [a] tiny congregation—no men, five mothers, and four
boys! But just at the last moment to my great surprise Miss Birley and
Mrs. Paling arrived, having walked the three miles through pretty heavy
snow. We had shortened Evensong with no Psalm, but Canticles and one
Lesson (the one ending "Seek Ye First the Kingdom of God") and for
hymns, "Holy, Holy, Holy," "Lead Kindly Light," "Fight the Good
Fight," and "Abide with Me." I played everything quite abominably;
but luckily the one real Anglican woman present has a capital voice, and
she and Mr. Simpson howled down my blunders pretty effectively. I gave
a rather confused address about realising the Presence of God without
external helps, doing the commonest work of life for Him and trusting
Him entirely. I quoted the little poem (given me by Evelyn,[69] I think),
which begins.

"Lord of all pots and pans and things. . . ."

At the end we had the usual friendly chatter, and agreed, however small
the number, to carry on this little Service once a month, on the last
Sunday.

In the evening Mr. Wood, the Red Cross Commissioner, returned
from a long round of visits in which Mr. Simpson was his charioteer.
The upshot of it all is that an English nurse recruited by Miss Hasell and
now waiting at Vancouver is to come up as soon as possible and occupy a
little empty house belonging to a Danish store keeper two and a half
miles the other side of Fort St. John [at Grandhaven].[70]

Monday was still nice, and Mr. Wood went off in the mail, which
should get him to Rolla in two days, where he should get something on
to Pouce Coupé, and from there to Hythe in time to catch the Friday
train to Edmonton. We were rather cruelly glad that he had to go off in a
series of cold open slow sleighs in order that he might get some idea of
what it's like for really suffering people with appendicitis or broken
limbs when they have to go out to hospital.

For the rest of the day I played about with Mrs. Paling who is rather a touching person. She is not really much older than me but seems (to me anyhow) *immensely* older, I think because she has a bun [of hair] and has lived for so many years *quite* alone with her much older husband. She is tremendously keen on books and music and simply adored the gramophone, especially all the sacred records, because they reminded her of Services in King's Chapel at Cambridge which was her home. She was so happy with May Birley and we were all frankly disgusted when Mr. Paling turned up again in the evening to take her back next day. We had one more evening chiefly of music. Everyone says my gramophone is the best they've ever heard (including Mr. Wood who comes from the great Metropolis of Vancouver) so I assent very modestly and resist the temptation to say "Of *course* it is."

It got tremendously warm that evening—about 30 above and almost a thaw. That started the question of how long the river will hold this year. It generally holds till about the middle of April and there is a dangerous period when it begins to weaken, and all the teams and trucks go on crossing until usually one is lost. May Birley says that last spring was the first in her memory in which no horses were drowned. A few years back the Palings were driving up the river from their house to Taylor's Flats (it is their only sort of highway). They were going on a visit somewhere and had all their luggage with them, and suddenly they struck a weak place in the ice and the horses went straight through. They had just time to jump out of the sleigh before that went, too. For a few seconds they could see the poor horses swimming hard in the hole, and then they disappeared, swept away under the ice by the strong river current. It was a heavy loss, the sleigh and all their clothes and things, but it was the horses they minded about so dreadfully.

We went to bed with windows open cheerfully expecting a Chinook; but a shrewd change took place about 6 A.M. and I woke up feeling as if the whole world was two large freezing ears. There had been a brisk wind blowing in at the window and the glass had dropped to 15 degrees [below] in an hour or so—not really what you'd call COLD, but a drop of 45 degrees in an hour, you can't help noticing even in bed. We rather fussed in the morning about Mrs. Paling having that sixteen mile drive in the open cutter; but she had to go because their cows and chickens couldn't be left. So we all lent her extra coverings and I was delighted at being able to give her two old fur coats, sent out for distribution by the Dean of Carlisle's daughter. Mrs. Paling was thrilled. She is an excellent needlewoman and is going to make the two into one beautiful new coat and a fur cap. And meanwhile I think they must have made all the difference to her on the drive home.

For the rest of the week we switchbacked up and down from spring sunshine, which even cleared the snow off the roofs, and melted the

icicles, to iron and steel 20 and 30 below; varied by driving snow storms.
Tuesday night went down to 40 [below], but Wednesday started at 30 and
improved up to 20 in the middle of the day to drop again with a bang
after sundown. That day, being one of those milestones which people of
my age usually ignore, I couldn't resist marking it in a quiet way by
wearing my green stockings enlivened with scarlet garters. May Birley
very wonderfully took the hint and provided an egg and coffee for
breakfast. (Later) we agreed that I should call her May, and that she
should produce coffee for breakfast whenever I wore green stockings—
provided that I honestly restricted these occasions to First Class
Birthdays, and Anglican Holy Days only.

The rest of the day I spent at Taylor's Flats; and had a pretty awful cold
return, Rama once more white all over from his own breath and the iron
entering into both our souls. As we stumbled along towards the sunset I
saw for the second time a queer little phenomenon called up here "Sun-
dogs." They are like two ends of a broken rainbow; but instead of being
in the part of the sky opposite to the sun they are on each side of him, and
only a few yards away. They are a recognised sign of cold, but on this
occasion were scarcely needed. We had a marvelous supper because May
had killed a CHICKEN and also cooked my second Christmas pudding;
and also I found most darling little presents from each of the animals:
Rama, Rowdy, Tom-Tom, Ambereyes (the black kitten), the purebred
hens—and the turkeys. Afterwards we had more gramophone, and I read
aloud "Mary Rose"[71] to May who loved it till quite near the end, and
then was furiously indignant at it for being so "unreasonable."

All Thursday it snowed again just as if it had never snowed before; and
all the trails were obliterated once more. I had Guides again, dinner hour
and evening at Fort St. John, and odd jobs in the settlement in between.
For some reason which I can't remember, I walked in and out that day,
and was for the first time rather tired coming home. Awful thought—
was it Anno Domini? "A heavy weight of years has chained and
bowed . . . ."

Friday was a very solemn day up here because apparently *St. Valentine*
is the one saint universally revered in Fort St. John. Naturally nobody
has the faintest notion when it is St. John's day, but we make up for it by
most thoroughly observing St. Valentine's, i.e., all the children make
wonderful productions representing golden or crimson or pink or
purple hearts suitably transfixed, and send them to each of the other
children and to a fair number of grown-ups, each one entreating about
thirty others to "BE MY VALENTINE."

Then in the evening everybody goes to a dance and they carry on
somehow till sunrise next day. This part, owing to a merciful lack of
transport, May and I safely missed; but Petter was fetched and returned
by an admirer. So all were satisfied.

On Saturday I had a little tea-party at Mrs. Millar's for all the Fort St. John girls whose birthdays had fallen in the same week as mine—plus the two school-teachers. There were twelve of us, and we spent a fiercely exciting afternoon from 3.30 to 6.30 playing Clumps,[72] Dumb Crambo, and Charades, all of which were quite new to the guests. It was another wonderful warm day with the sun shining, the glass *above* freezing, the snow soaking wet and spongy and a warm West wind, that all thought must be the long expected Chinook. But in the night it changed its mind once more; and the next morning was once more far below zero, and a stiff blast straight from the North Pole by way of encouragement to my little Sunday Schools.

Week ending February 22, 1930.

Sunday was biting cold again, with a drop of about 45° from Saturday night and a stiff North West wind. The chief result was once more to wither up the poor little Sunday School. Only seven children came, including, I am sorry to say, not *one* of the guests of last night's tea-party. They are a queer lot, aren't they? The brightest and best of the Guides, all older and mostly living no farther away than the kids who did come. Three of these arrived in a dog-sleigh looking very sweet. Luckily, they were all nearly the same age, i.e., little boys between nine and twelve (plus one of seven and a little girl of [?]), and so I was consoled for any disappointment by the very real joy of a tiny class all to myself— Mrs. Devlin being also apparently frozen up at home. The ride on to Baldonnel was cruel cold as it was eight miles into the teeth of the wind now shifted to due East. We had to go past our own (or rather Miss Birley's) gate and poor Rama made a frantic bid to go home. He even reasoned with me, pointing out that there would certainly be no one at Baldonnel and it was pure waste of time to go on. I had to be rather beastly to him, poor little man, although I knew he was probably right. There was no fire and the logs were so big and snow-sodden that I couldn't get one to go and was thankful to see Mr. Simpson arriving in a sleigh with Johnnie, and bundle of kindling and a thermos of tea!

No one else came, so I gave Johnnie a Sunday School magazine and we sang a few hymns, and Mr. Simpson read the Epistle for Septuagesima.

Then Rama and I came thankfully home.

(On Monday) Tommy arrived about something and incidentally cut our hair—May Birley's rather well and mine far too short so that it would simply horrify some of you. But alas, there's plenty of time to recover before you see it. Also in the afternoon I read Miss Birley "A Kiss for Cinderella,"[73] the first time for both of us. We thought the first two acts enchanting, but the last painfully feeble, almost impossible to have been written by Barrie.

Tuesday was pretty biting and windy still. Rama having jumped his fence and gone off with some friends, I was not sorry to walk to the Baldonnel Scouts, and afterwards on to the Simpsons to fix up finally about Taylor's Flats on Sunday week. They had a guest who made it impossible to talk shop, unluckily. He is an American bachelor between forty and fifty I should think; and says his father and mother are coming up to live with him. I was quite excited as it means the possibility of a real *Old* Couple.

Wednesday was lovely again and not nearly so cold. Tommy had recaptured Rama who will have to be kept in the stable quite sternly now until he promises not to go on jumping the fences. It was the day for Taylor's Flats—much the most difficult and unsatisfactory of my little enterprises so far. The school is a small single room with about twenty-eight children who quite fill it. About ten don't want to be Scouts and eighteen do. Those who do range from six to fourteen in age, and the boys and girls are about equally distributed. So there are not enough Guides for a Company or Scouts for a Troop, or Wolves for a Pack. The desks are clamped to the ground so we can't get into a circle or even sit on the ground in a corner because there isn't room. The children who are not joining in run about and make a noise all the time, and I can't stop them because they've a perfect right to do so. Finally, the oldest boy and girl who are two of the three leaders, and the only really keen ones so far, have to go home to dinner, and as often as not the girl has to stay behind and wash up afterwards. Last Wednesday, being a lovely day, I tried to carry on outside; but it was too cold for anything but running games, added to which the non-Scouts thought it good fun to snowball us, most of the time. I'll have to think out another plan for Taylor's Flats. It would be easy enough of course if there were any sort of other room to meet in. But there ain't, you see.

Afterwards I went on to look up the returned runaway wife. She was out, but her neighbour told me that up to the present the husband was a "Changed Man." He even does her washing for her. Why don't we all run away more often? I also looked in on Herbie Taylor, the father of the Flats, whose Indian wife I visited across the river a fortnight ago. He is a sturdy old halfbreed, very friendly and full of talk and when not acting as Charon he is Postmaster and has a shack this side of the river where his daughter does the washing, and he sells the stamps. He told me I needn't go on to see Mrs. Taylor to-day as she was much better and "only the gall stones instead of gastric ulcers." As it would have been two miles farther and it was getting late, I weakly yielded to this good news and was rewarded (or punished) by the production of an immense family photograph album, containing all the halfbreeds there can ever have been since Columbus, arranged in wedding-groups, and culminating in a terrific series of old Herbie himself at all ages, his wife ditto and his nine [*sic*] children ditto ditto DITTO. He explained each portrait so remorselessly that I couldn't even turn over two pages at once; and before I had finished admiring the Olive Branches he said "Wait a moment," and rushing up a sort of chicken ladder began rooting very noisily in the little loft above. At last he scrambled down again perspiring and very proud with his two most precious documents which it was obviously an enormous privilege to see—his confirmation card and his marriage lines, both over fifty years old. I had to read every word of both out loud, and he was so solemn that it was almost like a Service.

Thursday was Guides as usual and very much as usual, except that we are getting unusually desperate about the badges that haven't come yet. I took the Rules of Health with the six Seniors, and had the funniest discussion because they were so ingenious in explaining to me how in Canada it is impossible to keep any of them! The climax arose over teeth. I gave them a very impressive little account of germs in the mouth, and what they do, not only destroying the teeth but poisoning the system, etc. At the end, there was a little pause and then the Senior Patrol Leader remarked: "That's funny because my father has perfect teeth and excellent health, and he has never cleaned his teeth in his life, but always laughs at us for doing it"!!!

Friday is, I'm ashamed to say, still a holiday, that is, since Ritchie took over the Scouts a fortnight ago, and until I start at Charlie Lake as I hope to do next month. So all the morning I played round at house work and chores (having succeeded in snatching back my full share of these ever since the Palings' visit), and in the afternoon had a first short snowshoe potter with May Birley along the top of the coulee. She wore one [pair] of the nephew's snowshoes and lent me a little old pair of hers, meaning to be generous, of course. But these turned out to be much too small and narrow to stay on top of the snow, and also they kept on coming right off the feet; so I spent most of the time on my back with my legs tied in every sort of knot, and felt very much ashamed. However, coming back we exchanged shoes and the same thing happened to the scornful Miss Birley, which comforted me quite enormously. Anyhow it was tremendous fun, because at last you can despise all trails and strike right out into deep snow, and also it was first outing for pure *divertimento* since coming here, and therefore felt deliciously wicked. We now even contemplate doing something like it every week. I forgot to say that all last week Douglas Birley, the eldest nephew, was kept away from school. He slept at home and spent the days with May Birley. He is twelve, small and plain and very shy and sensitive, but a very dear little boy. He is *awfully* keen on Scouting (being one of the first four enrolled up here) and devours every book about it that I can lend him, besides giving me a stiff military salute every time we meet. He spent his odd moments learning Morse and I had a little flag practice with [him] nearly every day. He is slow but delightfully in earnest; and the other morning May was talking about April-fooling someone (rather long way ahead), when Douglas said quite seriously and rather sadly that he thought he might have to give that up now [he] was a Scout. I was hastily called in to adjudicate in this delicate case of interpretation of the First Law.

Saturday was mostly preparation for Sunday, and then the usual ride over to Fort St. John and night with Mrs. Millar. I found the dear old bird for the first time rather keen to start studying the Bible again, and promised to bring her some helps to this next week. This is a real chance, I do hope I shall hit on the plan that suits her best. Unluckily her main point of interest at present is the vexed old creation problem which seems just to have reached Western Canada. We talked about it a very little and this was Mrs. Millar's summary of the Problem of Evolution, given verbatim:

"Miss H. (a school teacher), told the children we were descended from monkeys.

"Mr. H. (an ex-ditto), told the children we were descended from fishes.

"Mrs. P. (a farmer's wife), says Mr. H. may well be descended from a fish, but SHE isn't.[74]

"I say—My Golly and how does she know that?"!!!! This is the slender thread on which I hope to hang a course of Devotional Bible Study.

Week ending March 1, 1930.

Last Sunday being a fine and not very cold day, Fort St. John Sunday School experienced a nice little Renaissance, that is, twenty-four children turned up. It doesn't sound many, does it? But it's quite good here and I was awfully pleased. Mrs. Devlin turned up too and carried off the tinies who can't read, i.e., six or seven adorable little boys and girls of six and seven, nearly all red-headed and very ruddy altogether. I also long to have them myself; and the awful thing is that I don't even know exactly how Mrs. Devlin deals with them. I've given her an Infant book and a bunch of pictures, and have to leave the rest to her. The remainder of the children I still take in a lump, because they are all almost equally untaught and there is no grown-up able or willing to help so far. We start with a short singing practice, two or three scales and one or two arpeggios and then learn a hymn. This School is actually beginning to produce a little sound, that is, some of the kids are starting to open their mouths anyway and a vague murmur emerges which includes quite a few right notes. The general effect of a hymn is rather like a very *ultra-modern* form of *faux-bourdon*, with a thin trickle of melody only just not quite submerged.

I tried to tell them something about the Forty Days in the Wilderness and led up to the question of whether we could each do something during Lent. At which one dear little boy of ten, the only one who has had a little home teaching, rather threw me out by saying:

"Mother *always* makes us fast in Lent. It's rather *fun!*"!!

Later on, another little boy said:

"Mother's teaching Leslie and me a hymn."[75]

This was most astonishing news, so I said: "Is she really? How lovely! What hymn?"

"I don't know."!!

At the end of this little School I appointed two Churchwardens, a boy and a girl, to count the collection each week for a month, and two Vergers, also a boy and a girl, to collect books, etc., and tidy up.

The eight mile ride on to Baldonnel was quite warm and lovely, though the road is still very drifted and heavy, and Rama stumbled a lot and fell on his nose once. At the end it was rather another sort of come down to find only three children! But luckily they were all the same age—two little boys and a little girl all aged about seven. I was glad, really, to have these three alone because they were bound to get neglected. So we had a nice little time round the harmonium learning the first two verses of "Do No Sinful Action"—and discussing their meaning, especially the second verse, "Christ is kind and gentle, Christ is pure and true, and His little children must be holy too." It was a great chance, really, and I was quite thankful for such a "poor" School, if only *only* I had the gift and grace to seize the chance it gives, and make it really profitable to them.

Monday was a perfectly glorious day, about 10° above and brilliant sunshine reflected from the snow like millions of diamonds. May and I did chores and washing all the morning, and in the afternoon had a delightful little snow-shoe expedition along the top of the coulee to the point where the ground drops abruptly 900 feet to the river. We wore the little nephew's snow-shoes and it was tremendous fun. I fell down about seven times (chiefly through interlocking my heels), and had the greatest difficulty in getting up again because of the impossibility of getting a purchase in the deep soft snow. It's really very funny trying to get up; wherever you put your hand or arm to get a leverage, it just sinks right down indefinitely, and all you can do, is to flounder and wallow till somehow your feet are under you again. Of course, it's nothing at all compared with ski-ing; only I imagine that ski-ing is not performed over quite such soft snow. The view at the end was very fine, but unluckily too wide and large to photograph. We saw several miles of the winding course of the river, which has cut itself a deep bed from 800 to 900 feet below the table-lands, North and South of it. On both sides, the banks stand up pretty steep, and are only broken by the openings of coulees like our own. Wherever you looked, of course, for miles and miles there was nothing but little ghostly trees and great slopes and fields of white. Winding along the valley between the slopes, was a broad ribbon of pure unbroken white, the frozen and snow-covered Peace River, never so peaceful as now, and far, far off, like little shining white clouds on the Western horizon, the line of the Rocky Mountains. Unluckily there was a stiff wind blowing and it was too cold to stay more than about five minutes. But this little outing filled me with a fierce longing for a big one—up the river to Hudson Hope, for instance. But there's no one free for that sort of thing, which would take a week altogether out and back; and anyway I mustn't play truant like that till after Easter.

After the Baldonnel Scoutlets on Tuesday I went on another three miles to visit a very nice Finnish mother who came to our last Service, and had asked me to go and see her and let her know when I was coming. Rama and I got the wrong trail, that is, one which has snowed up and was abandoned before Christmas, and had a very tedious time floundering in and out of the drifts for about an hour. At last we reached the Ohlands' shack, which is a wonderful example of the best kind of extreme simplicity. It is just one log room divided in two by a plain white curtain. On one side of this Mr. and Mrs. Ohland[76] and the three little boys sleep in two beds, and on the other side they cook, eat and live. It's all extremely bare, and as fresh and clean as a Dutch picture. Mrs. Ohland was tremendously welcoming, and made me sit up to the table while she bustled about talking. I was quite hopeful of a cup of tea, but rather staggered when she casually put her hand into the oven and as if it were accidentally, brought out a *Roast Chicken* and said I must eat it all!

It was quite embarrassing because she wouldn't eat any herself, but just talked and urged me on. And then, just as my strength utterly failed, she casually thrust another hand into a large pail, and brought out quarts and quarts of ICE-CREAM! Don't imagine that this is what happens whenever I visit a settler. It never happened before and I don't suppose it will ever happen again. But May Birley told me afterwards that Mrs. Ohland is famous for her amazing cooking and hospitality. When I left, she gave me a quart jar full of cream as a present for May; rather tiresome luggage on a horse, but it got home all right. The Ohlands are Lutheran, but she sends the boys to Sunday School when weather permits, and wants them to be baptised.

On Wednesday, I had one more dinner hour at Taylor's Flats, and then arranged with Mrs. Anderson, the teacher, to come in future, at the end of school (4.30) instead. It won't be ideal because she herself always has to stay behind with any children who are kept in for mistakes, etc., so that both she and I shall still be rather in each other's way. But at least I shall get rid of the children who don't want to join, and if the number who stay is reduced to ten or twelve keen ones, it will be more worth while than at present.

Afterwards I went to the Post Office, and there found old Mrs. Taylor who had been brought there from across the river. Her bed was partly veiled from the Post Office customers by a suspended sheet. Poor old Mrs. Taylor certainly seemed very ill, and I do wish she could go to the hospital; but neither she nor her husband will hear of that, so I suppose they must just muddle on with nursing her among the stamps and parcels. I asked whether she would like me to say a prayer and she said Yes. So I held my Messenger Cross[77] where she could see it, and prayed beside her, not in her language, of course, but she seemed to understand and smiled.

On Thursday, the first five Guides of the District were enrolled in the dinner hour outside the school as the boys had been before. I tried to make it an impressive and moving little ceremony, but this is very difficult with these children. It's not that they are irreverent, neither have they anything like the mischievous humour of Cockneys. But they seem to have a certain stolid matter-of-factness which it's very hard to fire with any sort of emotion or solemnity. All the same, I think that Guiding will come to mean something real to some of them anyway, beyond what it is at present, just "Lots of Fun." In the evening we practised bed-making; and Mrs. Millar's spare bed where I sleep every Saturday night was stripped and made up nearly a dozen times and I am sure more carefully than ever before. We had a few serious differences of opinion, the two principal ones being:

> 1. Whether the pillows should go outside or underneath the counterpane. They all held to the former as more pretty. But I got my way in the end—at least, in theory.
> 2. How often you should strip. The general opinion was, that to do it every day, (as sometimes in England), is morbid if not hysterical. Here we arrived at a compromise of *at least* twice a week!

On the way home I called for the butter as usual from a charming *very* Scotch family called Ogilvie.[78] The boy and eldest girl are preparing to be enrolled, and always rush at me with bowlines and sheep-shanks. To-

day they made me stop and listen to a new gramophone record called
"The Song of the Prune," of which the refrain was:

No matter how young a Prune may be

It has a wrinkled face.

We all enjoyed the song immensely, and now I call them the little
Prunes, which they think is *wonderfully* funny!

Friday was rather a trying day because Mr. Simpson was getting up a
dance that night in the new store just built at East Fort St. John, and
wanted me to help him prepare for it.[79] As we are partners in spiritual
matters, I hadn't the heart to refuse, so rode over on Friday morning and
spent most of the day helping him to make a barn into a ball-room. It is a
newly built plank shed with four walls and two doors, and of course,
nothing else at all, not even a stove or chimney yet. We exhumed extra
boards and planks out of the surrounding snow, and I helped in a small
way while Mr. Simpson rigged up a partition with shelves and hanging
nails for the women's cloakroom, and fixed a ladder near the ceiling for
the men's ditto, and nailed off another corner and made a rough table in
it, for the supper counter. Then I swept up and tried to make the rough
plank floor look like a dancing-floor, while he and another man
brought in a borrowed stove and chimney. I couldn't help admiring
their ingenuity. We finally curtained off the Ladies' Cloak Room (about
eight by five feet), with an old tarpaulin and decorated the whole with
my flag of Cyprus, fetched round half a dozen plank benches from the
school, and hung up two borrowed petrol lamps; and the ball-room was
complete.

Of course, I had to go to the dance too, which was a far greater trial.
The whole Birley family went as usual, including the tiny boy of six, Mr.
Birley driving us all in the waggon-sleigh. The room was quite full as is
always the case with these dances, and the band consisted of a trombone
and a comb. There should also have been a fiddler but he didn't turn up.

The tiny cloak-room was full of babies parked on and under the coats
and hats, and all apparently trained to survive the obvious perils of
being trodden on or suffocated. The supper is a funny part of these
entertainments. Every woman householder is supposed to bring
sandwiches or a cake, and the promoter is responsible for producing
coffee. Otherwise no one is responsible for anything. So between 12 and
1 o'clock, Mr. Simpson, who was busy trying to collect payments from
the men, suddenly called upon me to dispense the supper. I hurried to
the little bar we had made in the morning, and found it a confused mass
of coats, hats, cakes, milk and sleeping babies. Whichever you tried to
pick up, caused a frightful landslide of all the rest. It was like a
nightmare game of spillikins;[80] while hungry dancers clamoured round
and gobbled up each large sugary cake or ever it crossed the bar!

The coffee was to be made at the Post Office about a quarter of a mile away and should have come round much earlier, but somehow it got delayed, and finally arrived very late and half cold. Directly it started to go round, the cups ran out, apparently before any had had a DROP. We hastily melted some snow and started to wash up among the babies; and then mercifully Mr. Birley suddenly said he must go home—and so we came to the end of a Perfect Day.

Saturday, apart from household chores, was chiefly spent in preparing for Sunday, so you shall be spared any more details.

I sometimes fear you must be rather horrified at the awfully unspiritual character of these weeks. You can't be more shocked than I am, anyway. But this is what they *are* like, and it's no use deceiving you, is it?

(No ink at the store. Have to use liquid blueing!)

Week ending March 8, 1930.

Sunday was fine and deliciously warm, that is, only a few degrees of frost in the morning and almost a thaw at mid-day. The Fort St. John Sunday School really seems to be reviving and has at least reached the staggering total of thirty children. This doesn't at [all seem] many to shout about, but it includes everyone available within two and a half miles, so *if* they keep it up, I can't complain. I tried to tell them about the Forty Days in the desert, and showed them the beautiful pictures of the beautiful Hole New Testament[81] that Ethel gave me. It seems a shame to cut them out, as required; but they are so far better than any other pictures, that I have to do it as the whole book is much too heavy to carry about. Of course, everything seems odd to these children, Bible clothes included, so every picture requires most careful explanation, like every hymn. They are singing better though, and I think beginning faintly to like it. My ambition now is to get them each supplied with a New Testament, and I think I shall write to the kind Archdeacon at Edmonton who sent me the hymn books. Only about two children possess one at present, so we can never read the Gospels together, which is a great weakness.

Being the first Sunday in the month, it was Taylor's Flats day; so I rode straight through, and the twelve miles took exactly two hours, which sounds very leisurely but you must remember the snow. I got there just in time to cook up the fire and tidy and prepare the little school before the "Scholars" arrived. There was rather a bad falling off of children—only about twelve instead of about twenty-six as last time. On the other hand, there were more grown-ups—about fourteen—and they rather embarrassed me by coming at 2.30 with the children, instead of waiting till 3.15 for their own Service. The children seem even more ignorant that those at Fort St. John and far shyer too. So I told them about the Feeding of the Five Thousand from the point of view of the lad; and tried to get them to find out how a child's unselfishness can help Jesus.

At 3.15 Mr. Simpson arrived, and we had the grown-up Evensong, attended by about eight women and six men, besides those of the kids who wouldn't go away. I think it certainly went better than last month, chiefly because there were some better singers and it wasn't *all* a duet between Simpson and me. He read the Collect and Epistle for Quinquagesima and I tried to preach about it, and we finished with "The Day Thou Gavest Lord is Ended."

After the usual friendly chatter all round, Simpson and I were left to pack up the harmonium and books, etc. for him to fetch in his sleigh, and then he produced a thermos of tea for which I was most thankful, as there is no time for a mid-day meal on these Sundays, and finally we started for home, I riding and he on foot. Barely twenty minutes from home little Rama took it into his head to celebrate over 1200 miles of happy companionship by bucking me off again! He gave no warning; otherwise it was just like an eruption of Vesuvius; and I scrambled to my feet in the snow to see him galloping gaily away, with all the Sunday School books and pictures flapping wildly like wings.

Luckily there was a man on the road not very far ahead who caught Rama, and even offered me a lift in his sleigh for the last two miles. But that I declined with all the dignity which the situation allowed, and rode home blissfully unaware of a *small* cut on my cheek which gave the show away at once to the Birleys!

Monday was Sabbath as usual. I was very tired and glad of it. So we had the usual fuller share of household chores, and the usual washing of clothes and patching of breeches, and otherwise a real lazy day, too lazy to go out on snow-shoes with May and Douglas Birley.

Tuesday was rather a shameful day, about which the less said the better. I should have gone again to the Flats, to start a new regime with the Scouts and Guides there, who are rather a problem. And I was all ready to go when it began snowing pretty hard; and I let May persuade me that the children would not expect me and would want to go home early. She *swore* she really meant it, but I knew that I was slacking. The worst of it was that the snowing stopped and the sky cleared soon after, but—too late. So I tried to salve my conscience by an intensive Scouting practice with little Douglas, who is still kept away from school by some impetigo sores on his hands and feet. He is such a dear little boy, and a great delight to teach, because, though not clever or quick, he is so *tremendously* keen. We worked hard at knots and lashing and signalling and (except for my conscience) thoroughly enjoyed ourselves. He has dinner here every day while he is away from school, and May dresses his hands and he does odd jobs—logs, snow, etc.—for her. The other day she told me she wanted him to do a full half-day's work for her, cleaning out the stables, turkeys, chickens and pigsties. So she offered to hire and pay him like any other chore-boy. He immediately said he would do the work, but wouldn't take any money for it. May was quite surprised, for up to now he has always accepted any money without a murmur. But afterwards, Tommy told her that he has started refusing tips from him, too. All this has nothing to do with me. He simply found it out for himself from Scouts books and story books I have been able to lend him.

On Wednesday, besides the dinner-hour at Baldonnel, we started an after-school meeting for the enrolled Scouts—only three till Douglas returns. They are a funny trio—Maurice, an immense full-grown, very heavy and inexpressive French-Canadian; Jack [McDonald], the boy whose behaviour made me so wild when we all went to supper with his family after Christmas; and Erving [Foster], a *very* sharp and attractive little American. We started on the Morse Code, and I told them to cut themselves Scout staves and bring them next week. Then we discussed Troop plans in general; but not for long, because Helen and Harold have to wait for Jack and they all live from three to four miles away.

Of Thursday, I can remember hardly anything except that it was Guides as usual, and we started learning Morse by a game which they took to wonderfully quickly and played awfully well. They got so excited and shouted and laughed in a perfectly delightful way; and old Mrs. Millar kept poking her head through the door to see what was the joke.

Friday was my statutory once-a-month Scout Day at Fort St. John; so I met Mr. Ritchie at the school, and we solemnly enrolled one awfully keen little new boy; but though several more were ready, could not enroll them because there were no more badges. In the evening I also took the Seniors, who are tremendously keen to get their Second Class Badges and expect them to drop from the sky without any effort at all.

In the afternoon a big Guide called Eileen Brooks[82] who has left school, took me for a toboggan-ride behind a horse. The toboggan is a *very* simple affair. It's just a short piece of thin plank, curved up in front like a prow. You sit on this plank with your legs straight out in front and are hitched by a long rope to somebody's saddle-horse. Then off goes the horse at a spanking trot or gallop, and you fly over the snow just as if you were on a tea tray. Eileen is a good rider and her horse is very fast, so it felt just like the Edinburgh express, chiefly because you are so low—in fact on the ground. Where the trail is beaten hard it's pretty rough and makes a harsh grinding noise, but where the snow is soft you dip and rise over it with a soft swishing, just like a boat breasting the surf. Of course, the snow pours over and under you from all sides, and the horses' hoofs cover you with it from the front, so that you end by being almost smothered, but that's part of the fun. We went about five miles and only had one adventure. On the way back we met a sleigh; and Eileen pulled out into the deep snow to give the sleigh the trail as riders always do. But the toboggan was in a groove and refused to leave the trail, and the sleigh driver, who couldn't see over his horses' heads to anything so flat on the ground as us, came briskly on. So there we were, making for a head-on collision, and I rolled off the toboggan just before it flew under the horses' hoofs. Of course, it wasn't in the least dangerous because any fool can roll out of a toboggan, but it was great fun and the horses and sleigh driver were so taken aback!

On Friday night the Northern lights were turned full on. Of course, they very often are, but we don't always see them. First they looked like a full moon rising behind clouds and sending rays right out above the clouds. You could be sure it *was* the moon rising until you realised that it all radiated from the *North*. Later the rays turned into search light beams of milky light, and then these began to curve into strange shapes, like a very slowly moving snake curling round the Northern horizon, and fading into faint rose and green, like a rainbow seen in the dark. May says they are supposed to be reflections in the sky of the Polar ice and snow, and changing, of course with the atmospheric changes. Do tell me if you know of any other theory. The days are quite warm now and lovely, and the snow even shows signs of weakening on steep banks and round buildings. But at night it drops again to below zero and this morning it was still 5 below.

On Saturday I prepared for Sunday as usual and rode over in the evening to Fort St. John. Mrs. Millar's little grandson and daughter, Roddy and Thelma [Howes][83], came for the night by special arrangement. It was Thelma's sixth birthday and I wanted to give her a little treat, because birthdays are practically ignored up here. So I took her a lovely waddling crocodile sent me from Ellesmere, two little hankies, also from there, and a picture of Christ and His Mother surrounded by a crowd of sheep and little lambs.

The crocodile, whom they immediately christened "Pig," was rather a fearful success, as he had to waddle down an ironing board from 7.0 to 10 P.M. One of the hankies had to go to Roddy or he would have turned Bolshey on the spot. On the back of the card Thelma and I wrote out "Jesu, Tender Shepherd Hear Me," for her to learn with her mother and say at night. Then we had a wonderful supper lighted by tiny candles carried by those little wooden angels from Rothenburg. We carried them into the kitchen in a procession before supper, and the only drawback was that Roddy *would* call the Angels "the girls."

Afterwards, I said prayers with them both in bed. They were quite new to it, poor little darlings, and had great difficulty in understanding how they could talk to Jesus without seeing Him. But Thelma, at any rate, was quite keen to try.

Week ending March 15.

Last week really was a tame one with almost nothing worthy of record. Sunday morning was lovely with only a light frost. I have to stable Rama in a livery barn on Saturday nights now, because the Postmaster's horse and two cows all sleep indoors (rather tactlessly), and fill up his stable. The barn costs 2/- a night; but it means that once a week Rama is watered, saddled, and bridled for me, and I can start off for School as clean as a Rochester lady, so it's worth it. Last Sunday a new man brought out Rama, a complete stranger to me.

He said, "Are you always on the road? I thought you were a teacher."

"Well, yes, I am generally on the road, and I am a teacher too; a Sunday School teacher." "Oh Golly! And what do you get for that?"

I evaded this rather sudden enquiry; but isn't it funny, this simple and direct way of making friends!?

There were thirty children, which is top score so far. Mrs. Devlin takes all the children who can't read into the other class room and I have the rest. I feel pretty sure that we ought to sub-divide the latter, now that the number is large enough, and there are a couple of big Guides who would probably be fairly reliable teachers. But I haven't taken the plunge for two reasons:

1. The extreme difficulty of dividing up at all. You see, there are no chairs or benches, only small desks firmly clamped to the ground and all facing one way. So it is physically impossible to make little compact groups round a teacher; and I think that even two classes only, in such a room, would disturb each other pretty badly.

2. The two possible teachers don't *know* a word more than the younger children and would require heaps of coaching. This I would love to try and give them, but they are both rather grand young ladies and also are studying hard at High School exams, as well as very hard worked in their own homes. So I doubt whether they would give the time or take the trouble to prepare anything like enough (the tendency being

to think very easily that one knows all about everything). If they don't they'll do more harm than good, yet it would be very difficult to go back on the arrangement once it was made. So, at present, it looks like continuing to be a Catechism, and all learning together (though I tremble to think what St. Christopher's will say).

We took the story of the wonderful Sabbath in Capernaum. My hope is to give them just an outline of the life of our Lord up till Easter, or probably Ascension Day; and then something about the following Sundays till I go. We all embarked on a new hymn, introduced by an elder girl: "When He Cometh, When He Cometh, to Make up His Jewels." It's a pretty bad hymn, but has a swing, and they like and *do sing it*. So I think we must start with any hymns they *will* sing, and then gradually try to lure them on to better ones.

Baldonnel School rose in numbers from three to seven and ranged in age from seven to fourteen, with one child for each year—rather a difficult party to grade.

Monday was idle as usual, and I actually remember nothing about it. Tuesday was a glorious morning, and I actually took my coat off to ride down to the Flats; but before getting there a biting wind sprang up, and I had to put it on again quick.

I visited poor old Mrs. Taylor and found her still very ill. In fact, she looks to me unlikely to live, but may revive with warmer weather. I gave her two of the little lavender bags with texts attached, sent by Crayford. A daughter translated the texts for her, and I think she liked the scent. Of course, there is no lavender up here, so she was a little shy of it at first.

Then I visited the nice Englishwoman who was once a District Nurse near Hastings, and is now housekeeper to two bachelors. She is a homely, pleasant, middle-aged body, (like me), and there is furious betting in the community of the Flats as to which of the bachelors she will marry!

At 4.30 I returned to the school to find out who wanted to do Scouting and Guiding seriously. I found that all the boys except two had gone home, while eight girls had stayed. So we started again with this queer little party, and I learnt that someone had told the boys that if they became Scouts they would *have* to be soldiers and go to the next war and be shot. As a result of this rumour all the little heroes, except two, had faded away! So now the only surviving recruits are:

> One boy of fourteen who wants to be a Scout in spite of the above risk!
>
> One little boy, who ought to be a Wolf-Cub.
>
> Four girls old enough to be Guides.
>
> Four girls under eleven, who ought to be Brownies.

It's rather baffling, isn't it? I must go and see the mothers next week, and try to get to the bottom of the whole business.

Just before we left, there was a sudden short blizzard—pitch dark, and driving wind and snow—but it only lasted about fifteen minutes and afterwards was a lovely evening, though still pretty cold.

On Wednesday and Thursday the only excitement was that I rode May's other horse, Coronach. He is a thick ponderous colt of four, and had been driven in the sleigh but never ridden till Monday, when Mr. Birley saddled and rode him round the farm. He was as quiet as a mouse, so I said I'd take him on the road for two days as a final fool-proof test before Petter has him as a school horse. I felt very daring in theory, but actually it was about as adventurous as riding a towel-horse. Coronach seems to have been born broken-in, and all that remained to be done was to teach him to answer the helm. This he hated doing at first, especially going West. And we had an amusing tussle at the gate on Thursday, when I wanted him to go to Fort St. John. It took about twenty minutes to get him started; and then every 100 yards or so of the five miles, he stopped and tried to turn round as an official protest. So I reached the Guides half an hour late, and they had nearly given me up. Coming home, we had the same difficulty at first; but afterwards he came like a bird, and in fact, the only real drawback to him is his appearance, which is just like Lord Haig's proposed Memorial Charger.

Friday was perfectly glorious; in fact, all last week was steadily warming up—except at night, when it still dropped to below zero. I spent most of Friday preparing for Sunday, because a Guiding outing was to mop up the most of Saturday. But in the afternoon little Douglas lured me out to practise signalling, and we had great fun sending messages to each other from the tops of two straw piles in the field. Douglas *sends* almost professionally now, but his reading is awfully slow; and often enough when he has spelt out all the letters he can't make out the word! Afterwards I was still more demoralised and helped him to complete a big snowfortress, and then had a snow fight for the possession of it. The odd thing is that you can only play these games at the end of the winter, when the snow is nearly thawing, because in the real cold weather, it's far too dry and powdery like sand, and won't bind at all.

Mr. and Mrs. Simpson came to supper, ostensibly for him and me to prepare for his next Service on the 30th; but still more to make a "Jolly" for Mrs. Simpson. She is a nice, simple Welsh woman, who was once in service at Clapham, and always looks back to that time as her Golden Age. She has been rather lonely and unwell up here, and had a pretty hard time all last year. But she is better now, and I think thoroughly enjoyed an evening which began with chicken, continued with hymns on the harmonium, and finished in a blaze of glory with a rubber of whist.

Saturday was our absolutely first Guide Outing. We all met at

Baldonnel for a Camp-fire dinner and a Woodland Enrolment. Of
course "all" only means the ten Fort St. John Guides, the two teachers
who wanted to come too, and Alice Leclerc, the French-Canadian girl
who lives eleven miles from the rest, and for whose benefit we came to
Baldonnel. It was a Heavenly day, brilliant sunshine, and sparkling,
though soaking wet snow. The two teachers, three Guides, and I came
on horseback, the rest in sleighs. We found a clearing in the bush where
the snow was not too deep, and there made two patrol fires.

Everybody wanted to borrow my lovely little axe that the King's
School gave me, and I had the greatest difficulty in keeping it for a
moment. As it was the first day of using it properly, and as it was so busy
cutting down, we christened it "Brutus." The two Patrols each brought
a surprise feast, and had a race as to which would be ready first. The
Canaries brought eggs and bacon and canned beans, and the Buttercups
brought steak and onions and potatoes, so you can guess which Patrol
won.

Week ending March 15.

A very inglorious week on the whole, of which only my revolting
vow of candour compels me to give you the full details.

Sunday was a lovely day with a warm West wind blowing, and real
promise of the long expected Chinook which is to take the snow away. It
was so warm that I could tie my coat on to the back of the saddle and ride
in my orange jumper only, without cap or mitts. That's a great blessing
because you do get tired of being so clumsily dressed. Both Schools went
happily, and Fort St. John kept up its grand total of thirty, but
Baldonnel still had its little handful of seven only.

Monday was still warm and full of the softness of spring. The glass
actually went up to 50° and the top of the snow became wet and slushy
and round houses and barns it began to give place to pools of water and
mud. Everybody was in high spirits; because the farmers now need a
thaw pretty badly, both for the sake of the cattle and horses, and also that
they may prepare the ground for sowing. You see, after the snow goes,
there is first water and then mud; so it takes nearly a month before the
land can be worked, and if they don't get it sown before the middle of
May, there is danger of the crops being spoilt by autumn frosts before
they are ripe enough to cut. Apparently this has not been an unduly
hard, but an unduly *long* winter. The four months of deep snow and
practically no let up in the frost makes people fear a delayed spring; and

also makes it so much more expensive and difficult to feed the beasts. Nearly all the Birleys' reserve of oats is exhausted and they have to ration the horses as low as possible. But as soon as the real thaw comes we shall be within sight of grazing time again. All this seemed most hopeful last Monday, and we went to bed with the glass still at 50° and our windows wide open to the warm West wind, almost expecting to wake up and find the snow gone.

But in the middle of the night I woke up shivering instead, and found that the wind had suddenly jumped round to the North and had blown the house-door wide open and my bedroom door, too. The Chinook had turned into a blizzard, and the glass had fallen 60 degrees!

In the morning it was still 10 below and the snow driving furiously, and we were back again to New Year's Day. May said I couldn't possibly go down to the Flats, and I had a miserable day of indecision, waiting to see whether conditions would improve; then finally not going and despising myself for it. I had intended to go in the morning and visit as many as possible of the parents, because I hear that they believe Scouting is the first step to conscription and death at the front. It would certainly have meant a fifteen mile ride and been pretty beastly. But it was perfectly safe and possible to go, and there was no real reason for my shirking it. Petter, on the other hand, did walk three miles to school and was the hero of the day so we called her Captain Scott.

On Wednesday, it had risen to zero and was quite calm again but the snow deeper than ever and all the trails obliterated. Mr. Birley drove Petter and the boys to and from school in the sleigh. I rode over at dinner time, taught the little boys the Wolf-cub Law, and Promise, and undertook to enrol all who should know them perfectly next week. Then I rode on to visit a family of tiny children, and came back again to Baldonnel for the four Scouts at 4.30. We started flag-signalling which excited them very much, and Douglas Birley, who is much the smallest of the four, having been learning with me at home, appeared quite professional, and was awfully happy.

At Thursday's Guide we started acting little plays on the Guide Law. They did them pretty well and as usual they were terribly funny, which is not exactly the purpose, but seems inevitable. Afterwards I found Mrs. Millar in rather a poor way. Her chimney had caught fire the day before, and her little house had been within an ace of complete destruction. Luckily, being right in the settlement, it was seen by all the neighbours, and everybody had rushed and put it out for her. But the excitement had left her rather shaken and exhausted, so I was glad to be able to help her in a small way, by sawing up some logs for her stove. Then the Guides came again and we revised the six Rules of Health, and tried to sift all the reasons why none of them could *possibly* be kept out here.

Friday was the day for a new enterprise. I had promised Miss Bell, the teacher at Charlie Lake, to go up and see the elder boys at the end of school with a view to starting Scouts.

It was a warmer day, about 10 above, but dark and snowing just a little. Charlie Lake[84] is seven miles the other side of Fort St. John and as I had not yet ridden up there and didn't know what the trail was like, I promised May if I was late or tired coming back to stop off for the night with Mrs. Millar and come home on Saturday morning. On the way up I called at Fort St. John School to borrow Scout books to show the new boys, and then visited the Italian family called Chiulli. Mr. Chiulli had been ill in bed for some time; but nothing will induce him to go out to the hospital, so he will have to be cured by Nature like most people here. One of the boys, who was trapping about 120 miles North, shot himself in the cheek about a fortnight ago, and the bullet lodged just in front of his ear. He had to snow-shoe alone with this wound thirty miles to the nearest Indians. They brought him in a sleigh as far as here, and his brother took him in another the sixty miles out to Pouce Coupé. You or I would almost have made a fuss about this, wouldn't we? But I found him home again with a pad on his cheek, but otherwise carrying on with his father's work as if nothing at all had happened. Then I went on to Charlie Lake, by a very pleasant winding trail which runs chiefly along the banks of a creek. The land that way is very little cleared, and the trail runs through thin bush rather like very light English woodland, only the trees are all spruce and white poplar and of course there was no earth or flowers to be seen.

There is a little store where the teacher lodges, quite near to the school, kept by American Roman Catholics called Mr. and Mrs. Soman.[85] (The worst of Charlie Lake is that almost everyone there is American and Roman Catholic). I went there first to put up Rama and had a sort of tea-dinner meal in company with the Roman Catholic priest who is a great friend of the Somans. He and Mr. Soman had been out all the morning in the bush choosing logs with which to build their Church. Drat them, I wish it was ours. Their hospital is still hanging fire and so [is] the Red Cross alternative. We are beginning to think that neither will ever be built. Mrs. Soman is a quiet, kind woman. Mr. Soman is a terrible American rough-neck with a face and voice and bearing exactly like a caricature of a wild-west novelette! After a rather endless pause I went on to the school for closing time at 4.30. It's an unusually pretty little log building, very neat and well-kept. There are about twenty-two children, but only four boys over twelve, so I started with these, to avoid the mistake I made at the Flats of taking on all ages and both boys and girls at once. They were a dear little quartet and appeared very keen—so I left them three books to read up, and told them to bring cord to school next

Friday—and came away feeling rather pleased with this tiny new beginning. It was snowing hard, but not dark or cold, so I decided to come straight on home and not stop at Mrs. Millar's.

But Rama had decided otherwise; for before we had gone half a mile, he played his little devil's trick for the *third* time of asking, and planting me as firmly as ever, before bolting full steam for home! This time I didn't land in soft snow, but on a patch of bare brozen ground which came as rather a surprise to my right hip. I scrambled up and tried to hobble after Rama, but soon found there was no hope of walking as far as Mrs. Millar's, let alone twelve miles home. So there was no choice but to go back to the Somans and that turned out to be quite far enough. There was nothing the matter really but a bruised leg and hip; but I was rather thankful to lie down for a bit on the Somans' bed, where Richard and Dolores promptly came to entertain me. They are funny children, aged ten and seven, not at all Canadian but very American and therefore not at all shy or gauche, but very confident and full of a sort of social technique all their own. They were *tremendously* amused at my little tumble, and discussed it with as much interest and delight as if it had been the star turn at a circus. It was quite easy to laugh because the bump had given me the giggles!

Then they offered to read to me, and produced two little nursery story-books which turned out to be pretty fine instruments of torture. All the stories had to be read and Richard and Dolores took the reading in turns (with occasional sharp squabbles which I had to settle). Dolores spelt out the words very slowly with no expression at all, but rather new to the art. Richard, to show his superiority, read so fast in his high-pitched, nasal voice that I hardly distinguished a word. This went on until dark, and all the time I was wondering how on earth I should get home and what had become of Rama.

At last kind Mrs. Soman brought me some supper on a tray and then I thought I *must* get up, and not pretend to be an invalid any longer. So I limped into their little parlour behind the store, and to stave off any further reading rashly suggested cards. I was still hoping for some sort of rescue, but Mr. Soman had taken the Roman Catholic priest off to the settlement in the only sleigh, and so my hopes were very faint. The suggestion of cards proved a *ghastly* success and we played a game called rummy till far into the night. I longed to ask whether I might go to bed, but not knowing whether there *was* a bed, hesitated to open the subject.

Meanwhile, from 10 o'clock onwards, Mrs. Soman kept suggesting to Richard and Dolores that *they* should go to bed; but each time they replied, "Why should we? There's no school and nothing to get up for to-morrow," and that seemed final. At last I said to Richard, "Do you never get up except when you have to go to school?" "Of course not," said Richard, "nor does the teacher." As Miss Bell was sitting there, this was also final! At last I gave out and asked if I might go to bed somewhere and was quite thankful when Miss Bell said I might sleep with her. She had a funny little room with no door and nowhere to put anything down, but a good double bed; and except for being very stiff and achey it wasn't a bad night.

Before Miss Bell [joined] me, I heard two visitors come in, one a man called "Shorty" S. who stayed the night and slept somewhere in the kitchen and the other called "Slim" F. (quite a third of the young men up here seem to be called Shorty, Scotty, or Slim). I heard Slim say he was driving into Fort St. John in the morning, whereupon the Somans eagerly invited [him] to take me that far—and I inwardly decided to make him bring me all the way at whatever cost.

Next morning I was stiffer than ever and felt like a very old rheumatic old man. It was pretty obvious that even if Rama was at home, I shouldn't be able to make Sunday School to-morrow. So with deep reluctance I wrote a note each to the eldest Guide and Scout asking them to see whether Mrs. Devlin would take it, and if not, to let the others know as far as possible, that it was off. These notes we dropped at Fort St. John as Slim drove me through. All the way along we asked anyone we met whether they had seen Rama go by, but nobody had, so I got rather anxious, and more so when we got home and he wasn't there either.

Slim left me there and took Petter back to the Somans. It is her Mecca and she always loves to go there.

Rama was found and brought back next day; but I'll tell you that next week. The real tragedy took place on Saturday evening when May, after a talk with Mr. Birley, said she would rather I didn't ride Rama any more. She said he was developing a trick on me that he had hardly ever (or very seldom) played before. That as he has beaten me three times, he would almost certainly do it more and more if I continued to ride him, that she couldn't take responsibility for continuing to lend him, because apart from danger to me, it would make him a dangerous horse for anyone else.

All this is perfectly true and perfectly *sickening;* and of course he is her horse so I have no option but to agree to it. She says he always was tiresome about shying and obstinate and has bucked a few people but only very occasionally and at long intervals but this fortnightly attack is something quite new and mustn't be allowed to go on.

I shouldn't mind it, if it had happened in the first two or three weeks, when I was quite new to the game and indifferent to Rama. But after five months and over 1200 miles together it does seem sickening to have to break our partnership—just because he has an occasional devil and I am a feeble rider.

So I am to have Coronach instead, the despised younger brother. He is very thick-set and slow, and not good at answering the helm. He is also unshod and will have to be led if not carried over all slippery places and up and down hills until the frost goes finally. But what matter these trifles so long as he is fool-proof and *maintains an even keel?* It's partly a joke and partly a disgrace up here to be bucked. So I was not surprised when Mr. Birley walked in and said: "Well, you Timothy Eaton cowboy, and whoever told you that you could ride?" The only possible reply was to grin and say "Nobody."

N.B. Timothy Eaton is the Woolworth or general cheap store of Western Canada, and is the common expression for anything cheap or inferior.[86]

Week ending March 30.

This really will be short, because, alas! I did nothing whatever from start to finish, except a tiny little spasm to begin with.

On Sunday morning I very nearly had the blues. Quite apart from being in a sort of disgrace, and having lost Rama (to my horror he hadn't turned up here), I had to let down the Fort St. John Sunday School—for I could hardly conceive that Mrs. Devlin would take it alone—and didn't know what to do about the afternoon one at Baldonnel. Also, looking ahead, I couldn't think how to do without Rama, and yet couldn't help seeing the justice of May's position in refusing to continue to loan, if and when he should be found.

However, there was anyhow no question of riding that day, as I still felt like St. Catherine after her trouble with the wheel[87]—as if there was no whole part in my body—although, unluckily, there was no visible sign of any injury! at all!

Finally, I decided to start very early and walk to the Baldonnel School, so that at least one of them should not be let down. Douglas said he'd go with me, and so we started before 1 o'clock for the three and a half mile walk and we certainly needed the time. The thaw had begun and the snow was awful. In some placed quite hard and slippery, in others just wet slush. Sometimes it held you up quite well and the next step might let you through two feet or more with a most painful plump. I progressed with a sort of dot and go one walk, and felt I could at least give them a good lesson about Jacob when he halted on his thigh.[88] There were only five little boys at school, but those tiny little groups seem to me to be specially worth while, because they are almost like a baby study circle; and I was awfully glad I went.

When we got home, we were met by two of the big Fort St. John Scouts—Johnny [Donis] and Cecil [Pickell]—who had found and brought back Rama. Apparently retribution came upon him very quickly; for the effort of the buck must have loosened the saddle which slipped round under his tummy. He wandered off into the bush, and got hopelessly entangled in the halter-rope and reins. Finally he was found by a Charlie Lake man who tied him up until he should be claimed. Johnny and Cecil rode up to Charlie Lake and found him there, a little scratched and the saddle very much scratched but otherwise unhurt. Also they recovered the precious and invaluable officer's haversack given me by Mabel.[89] It had been found hanging under his tummy still, almost dragging on the ground and alas! kicked and torn to ribbons but still holding quite my New Testament, Scout Diary and note-case full of dollars.

The boys stayed to supper; and told me one *lovely* bit of news. Mrs. Devlin, as I expected, had said she couldn't take the whole Sunday School. But instead of jumping at the chance of dropping it, the Guide Leaders had approached Miss House, the day-school teacher, and she had taken it, and the children turned up well and there was no break after all.

You can't think how thankful I was. It sounds a small thing; but it means a lot that the children cared enough to ask someone else, and also that Miss House (contrary to *all* school teacher custom up here) rose to the occasion like that. She *is* a nice girl really, *much* the nicest of the four teachers I come across, and getting steadily more friendly and helpful about the Scouts and Guides. But she told me at the start that she couldn't help with Sunday School, so this was really ripping of her.

On Monday, being holiday, I hobbled about doing my washing and other chores, but it wasn't really a great success; and finally May clapped me into bed for Tuesday and Wednesday and persuaded me to throw up the sponge for the rest of the week. There was *nothing* the matter really except a bruised hip and general shake-up. But I couldn't walk or ride for a few days, and as you can't get anywhere at all without either walking or riding, it seemed more sensible to give in, and cook up for next Sunday.

I read Streeter's book *Adventure* which is interesting, though not nearly so good as *Reality*. Also that old book, Glover's *Jesus of History*,[90] and a little poetry, and played the gramophone. Also I was entertained pretty continuously by the smallest Birley boy—Deric, aged six—who spends a large part of every day in this house; and finding May too busy to attend to him, spent most of these days in my room. He is a very sweet, friendly little boy, and loves wandering politely in and out of my bedroom and digging out new story books and toys from under the bed. All the week the thaw went on, and the stillness of the snow began to give way to pools and streams, and these, finally, to torrents of water. Deric was very much excited by these, and after I had made him some little paper boats I was able to read for quite a while.

On Friday we had another horse pow-wow, and May was still adamant about Rama. But it was agreed that Petter should ride him to school again, as she did before I came. He never has minded going to school or given the least trouble about it. His only little outbursts seem to have been connected with what he regards as over-time trips like Charlie Lake and the Flats, or as unfair loads, like the mail sack.

I am to have Coronach and the new regime was to start on Sunday. But Coronach was out in the bush with some of Mr. Birley's horses; and when Mr. Birley came in on Saturday afternoon he hadn't found him. So I prepared to start pretty early next morning for a good long walk or rather wade to the two schools, with a forlorn hope of being able to get from one to the other in time, and the monthly Service to follow. However, just before bed-time, Mr. Birley came over again, and said he would lend me one of his horses, Buster, if I liked to go over and get him in the morning soon after 9 o'clock. That was an immense relief, and another proof of Mr. Birley's *real kindness* in spite of his elaborate pose of callous indifference, and you can bet I jumped at it.

Week ending April 8, 1930.

On Sunday morning all the pools were frozen as usual at this sort of turning point in the year, and as usual also they promised to melt into deep slushy lakes by noon. I went over to Mr. Birley's at 9 o'clock and found, rather to my annoyance, that Coronach had repented and come home, so I had to ride him instead of the more dignified and experienced Buster. Coronach had only once ridden Westward, and that had been rather a tussle. I had a fairly long day ahead with the two Schools and the Service, and was not yet in full fighting trim; so I didn't want to have to urge and argue with him all the way—and in fact, secretly rather longed for a bus! However, after the first sharp conflict of opinions the little horse was better than I expected; and apart from tacking like a barge for the first mile or so, and nervous moments getting round or across the ice, he gave less trouble than I expected. It's rather disappointing that for the moment anyway the warmer weather works against and not for Sunday School. You see, the roads are just becoming impossible for sleighing, and too deep in mud and water for anything but riding, and all the children haven't got horses. In fact, I found out afterwards that the trail from Fort St. John and the school (a mile exactly) was one continuous bog only broken by a series of lakes from one to two feet deep. The lakes froze at night, but by School time had thawed too much to walk across, so we had a poor Sunday School but the dozen or so little boys who came were all very hearty and sweet.

Then we plodded back the seven miles to the other school, and only had two slight squalls when poor Coronach had to be driven, hotly protesting, past first May's and then Mr. Birley's gate.

The Sunday School there was tinier still—only five boys—but I wasn't a bit surprised, as their distances are longer and their trails even worse than at the other end. At 3.30 Mr. Simpson joined us and gradually seven grown-ups arrived for the Service, two men, and five women; one of whom (Mrs. C., the Finn) had waded over three miles through mud and water often up to her knees. As it was the last Service before Good Friday, I tried to give a little address about the "Meaning of the Cross." But it was terribly bad.

Afterwards they stayed and talked as usual, and then we cleared up, and finally got home about 8.0. Of course, that was absurdly slow; but I think it must have been almost the worst Sunday in the year for travelling. A great part of the road was still covered with three foot of snow so rotten and slushy that you could neither ride over nor through it; so I had to take Coronach out into the bush and pick our way among the trees through marsh and bog with fallen boughs and stumps everywhere. And even where the road was possible the mud and slush were so slippery that we had to walk or slither nearly all the way.

On Monday I went down to the Flats for a little District Visiting, chiefly to find out what was frightening all the boys away from the Scouts. There is a large clan of Alexanders—six brothers and their wives, and about forty children.[91] I visited the wives first, i.e., Mrs. Will, Mrs. Fort [*sic*, i.e., Bert], Mrs. Ed, Mrs. Sam, [Mrs. Jim], and Mrs. Bob. They all came up in waggons from Saskatchewan last autumn, almost like the Children of Israel. I found the rumour which had reached me was quite true, i.e., that one of the halfbreed youths, Sandy Taylor, had told the Alexander boys that if they became Scouts they would *have* to be soldiers and go to war and be shot. Of course they believed him without question, and that is why the heroic little fellows all faded away from me and gave no reason!

Then I visited Mrs. J. the returned runaway wife and found her pretty happy and settled. Evidently her flight, though it lasted less than a week, had a wonderful effect upon the manners of Mr. J.

Then Mrs. Large who lives with her husband, brother-in-law and three children in the tiniest little shack with two minute bedrooms.[92]

But it wasn't too small to be turned into an Emergency Lying-in Hospital. For a Swedish woman, a total stranger, was being taken out by her husband to Pouce Coupé for the first baby. But they miscalculated the date or something. Anyhow, on their way to the river, they had to stop at the nearest house which was Mrs. Large's, and there the child was born two hours later! The Larges took the greatest care of them all for nearly a month, and when I arrived on Monday they were just driving off in a delightful high-wheeled, old-fashioned buggy, and were taking most tender farewells of their host and hostess. I do think Mrs. Large was a sport, don't you? She is a very highly strung Englishwoman with three very troublesome children and no room to move. Of course, there was no doctor to be had, and for a final inconvenience the poor Swedes couldn't speak a word of English!

Finally, I visited poor old Herbie Taylor, whose wife died suddenly a fortnight ago, and just a week after my last visit to her. He has always been very confiding to me, and was more so than ever this time, poor old fellow, being dreadfully cut up about it He has nine children, immensely tall boys and girls with black hair and eyes. I hadn't the heart to discuss Sandy and the Scouts, especially as he told me that the children were little comfort to him, as he couldn't manage them at all. But I tried to talk a little about the future life upon which he lovingly produced his marriage lines and carefully explained that they would be no further use to him now. I begged him to come to the little Service next Sunday, and he said he would, and I promised to have "Abide With Me." But, alas! he never came.

Riding home was rather lovely. A very strong wind all night had made the road much better, and it was delightful, instead of the unbroken monotony of snow, to see natural and varied colours again.

Not that the colouring is much to talk about so far—pitiful of course compared with April at Home—more like very high heathland in England at the end of a very hot autumn. The grass is faded yellow and the little poplars a sort of ghostly grey, but when the setting sun struck across it all, they were changed into pale silver trees on a pale gold ground and the effect was rather tender and lovely. Then, beyond, as always, was the long high line of the Peace River bank, looking deep blue and purple, but streaked with white, wherever a coulee ran down still full of snow.

On Tuesday I went down again, but to the school only, and was amused to find that the tide had turned, and *all* the boys wanted to be Scouts! However, I only took the three eldest, both boys and girls, and told the rest they should start after Easter. I feel I have muddled this school rather badly so far, and don't want to do it again.

On Wednesday was the first *Wolf-Cub* enrolment at Baldonnel,

Petter's school. Eight little boys had learned the Wolf-Cub Law and
Promise and professed to understand them perfectly. It's *so* hard to make
out whether they really understand at all, because they can't possibly
express an idea themselves, and just blankly agree when you explain
things to them. However, I enrolled them as solemnly as possible and do
hope that perhaps the meaning of it all will grow in their minds as time
goes on. Afterwards I rode on to dinner with the Simpsons, a slow
journey because their trail is quite atrocious just now, lots of deep snow
still wherever the bush is thick, and all the rest deep water and fallen
boughs and jagged tree stumps for Coronach to fall over. I arranged next
Sunday's Service with Mr. Simpson and persuaded him to give the
address as it obviously is his turn, and I particularly don't want to set up
as *the Preacher!*

Then back to the Scouts for Signalling, about which they are now
very keen in view of a wonderful Rally and competition to be held at
Miss Birley's on the Saturday after Easter.

At the end, we, and several other children and Petter all dispersed on
horses, and it looked so pretty, like a little Meet. There were the three
McDonalds on their ponies, the two little Finnish boys [Ohlands] on a
very fat brown one, and Johnny Simpson, fetched by his brother on a
very lean grey one. Then there was Maurice, the immense, French-
Canadian on his bony little Cayuse, and Erving, the nice American boy,
on the black mule. The two Simpson boys went ahead of us, looking
in their striped sweaters like little jockeys on tall black horses. Lastly
came Petter and I, she on my late-lamented Rama, who looked as if
dynamite wouldn't make him buck, and I on Coronach, feeling rather
like Charles I riding down Whitehall (you remember his horse!).

On Thursday I had to persuade the smallest Guide Leader to retire in
favour of a much older girl who joined the Company after it was started
and is more suitable in every way. Lucina Lohman, the little girl, took it
awfully well and readily agreed. She is a sweet little kid really; and no
trained English Guide could have been more generous about what I'm
sure must have been rather a knock, because she is tremendously keen.

On Friday Ritchie met me at school for the Enrolment of two more
Scouts and the first six Wolf-Cubs, and afterwards I explained about his
temporary withdrawal and told them about the Rally Competitions.
The Guide Company of Margaret Popham's school, Havergal, at
Toronto are giving a Union Jack which is to be the District Trophy, and
we have staked all on its arrival in Easter Week. Then I went off to dinner
with Mrs. Chiulli whose husband has had to go out to hospital. She is
such a nice old thing, so utterly out of place and European as to make me

much more home-sick than any of the English settlers. We had a very laborious Italian conversation, made more difficult by the discovery that there arc two quite different Italys—hers and mine—and the only object common to both is Mussolini. Finally, when all else failed, I was reduced to telling her about Rama's conduct exactly a fortnight ago. But not knowing the Italian for "buck" I tried to illustrate with my hand on the bed, and kicking up behind. Unluckily it was *just* too near the cooking stove and my heels caught a large pan of hot black grease, which flew up to the ceiling and then descended, like the "gentle rain from Heaven upon everything beneath"—but chiefly upon my hat, coat, gloves, rucksack and breeches. You never heard *anybody* laugh like Mrs. Chiulli laughed! It really was worth while.

Afterwards I visited the mother of the sporting little Guide, Lucina.[93] She is a nice woman who has been ill all the winter, and had two very bad operations at Pouce Coupé. She is not a bit out of the wood yet, and ought not to do any heavy work at all. But of course, having five young children, she has to. Then a little sit with Mrs. Millar who has a touch of pleurisy and is still very much pulled down, poor old thing; and lastly a short look in on Gladys, a girl I am rather sorry for. She is about sixteen, and is a "hired girl" at the store, i.e., general slavey to the storekeeper's wife. She has no mother and her father has just gone to prison for distilling moonshine, i.e., that is distilling and selling illegal liquor. (He was the man in the livery barn who asked me so suddenly one Sunday morning, what I earned). The poor girl is terribly shy now, and I think feels a sort of outcast. I want to try and get her to Sunday School.

On Saturday morning May had a rather pathetic emergency to deal with. The father of one of the little Baldonnel boys was tying up his son's horse in the barn. The horse took fright at something and suddenly jerked back hard when the man's thumb was in the halter rope. The thumb was caught somehow between the rope and the manger, and the horse pulled until it was *cut clean off*. There was no one in the house but the little boy, as the man's wife has deserted him; so he walked the three miles here and May dressed and bandaged his poor lacerated stump. Then he stayed to dinner with us; and I was amazed at his pluck and serenity. He managed his food with one hand and talked about things in general just as naturally as if it were an ordinary friendly visit. He has just come into the country and hasn't a soul to help him but the school-boy of ten years old. Wouldn't you make more fuss? *I* would, anyhow.

After dinner I took Coronach over to Mr. Birley to have his nails cut. Of course you know that horses' nails have to be cut. But I didn't. Mr. Birley did it with big pincers.

Week ending April 12, 1930.

There will be almost nothing to say about last week, partly because nothing happened, and partly because I've got a toothache which has completely swallowed up my memory.

Anyhow, Sunday was Taylor's Flats day, being the first in the month, and therefore Coronach's first long day out. We trundled over to Fort St. John first, starting about 9.30. There I had a better, but not yet fully revived, Sunday School, and tried to tell them about the events of Holy Week as far as the Betrayal. To all but one of the boys, almost the whole story seemed quite unknown. I showed them the pictures from Hole's book, which are most wonderfully helpful, especially as we have still got only two or three Testaments although I am expecting some more from Archdeacon Burgett at Edmonton. I find it almost overwhelmingly difficult to teach the Passion for the first time like this. It is so terribly hard to know what to leave out, and it's all so far too deep and tremendous. I suppose the children got some impression, but rather dread to think what.

Afterwards we trundled on the eleven miles to the Flats and got there just in time for 2.30 Sunday School. Mr. Simpson followed very soon after with the harmonium and hymn books in a waggon. Very few kids turned up. I don't know what is the matter with the Taylor's Flats children. They're dreadfully erratic and the boys especially seem quite indifferent. In fact, only two boys turned up—one, the youngest son of Herbie Taylor, a very dusky little halfbreed—and the other a queer interesting little boy called Ernest who ought to be called Oliver Twist.[94] He is an adopted child, and must have originated very far from here, for he is the most completely Dickens child I have ever seen—very pale, very refined and dignified and imperturbably grave. As it was the only School before Good Friday I took the Story of the Cross and was appalled at my inability to convey anything of what it means. How can it be taught? I don't know a bit. We learnt "There's a Green Hill Far Away" and sung it very feebly, and then Mr. Simpson and about eight or nine grown-ups arrived and we had a grown-up Service. Mr. Simpson gave a little address on the "First Word from the Cross," very simple and nervous, but I thought, good. Afterwards the usual friendly backchat all round, and then clear up and rather a long trail home—twenty miles all told—not cold but very slushy going.

On Monday afternoon I went over to the "City" as we usually call it, to take the bigger Scouts for signalling. They are a funny mixed bunch, and I am rather keen about them because Ritchie says they are hopeless, and will never get the spirit out of Scouting.

Their names are: Dave, aged seventeen, pure Italian, jolly, but conceited and rather irresponsible, *very* bouncing.

Johnny [Donis], aged fourteen. Also physically a man. American by birth, practically a grown-up farmer, fearfully quiet and inscrutable; not a boy at all.

Art, aged fourteen. Canadian-American. Tall and quite grown-up looking, but very shy and with an appalling stutter; a nice and gentle but *dreadfully* slow boy.

Cecil [Pickell] (pronounced out here Seasill!), Canadian, with enough Indian blood to give him coal black hair and eyes. A delightful looking boy, full of talk, not the least shy, most attractive and quite unreliable.

Hughie [Byrnes], aged twelve. A darling little fair-haired boy who might have come from an English slum (Yorkshire for preference). He has no mother and his father is in prison (the bootlegger), and he is the most delightful little boy in the school; desperately eager, full of fun and completely unself-conscious.

We worked hard at sending and receiving flag words and sentences and at last reached the stage of a certain keenness, when Dave had to go home to kill a pig; and then we all went home, but arranged to practise again on Friday.

I shall now have to skip nearly a week, as the intervening days have quite escaped me, and I'm now most terribly behind hand.

Week ending April 22.

Palm Sunday was a glorious hot day, at least the morning was, and there really was a *feel* of spring if not much look of it yet. At Fort St. John we took the events of Holy Week, but mainly those of Thursday. Archdeacon Burgett had sent me from Edmonton three dozen splendid little pocket Testaments; so for the first time all the children were able to read the account in St. Luke for themselves. They promised to come on Good Friday, but it is a great innovation and I doubt whether they all will.

Afterwards at East Fort St. John only the two little Birley boys turned up, rather disappointing for both them and me, as we live less than half a mile apart, and therefore needn't have trailed three and a half miles each way for the pleasure of meeting each other only! However, they rode their bicycles for the first time this year and were very pleased with themselves, although feeble people like you and me would have thought the road quite unfit for anything on wheels. We had a little lesson on Good Friday, and I showed them the Hole pictures and gave them each a tiny Testament. Before we started home a heavy snow storm had begun and was blowing hard against us. None of us had coats, because the morning had been so hot, so it was tiresome for me, but far worse for the boys. They dashed off very gaily into the teeth of it, but at the end of a mile I came up with little Frank, the younger one, aged ten, stuck at the bottom of a coulee, his bicycle absolutely clogged with snow and mud, and himself wet through and rather done in.

He is a game little boy and said he was quite all right; but when to test him I asked if he would like to swap over and ride Coronach, he accepted with such meek alacrity that I knew he was really near the end of his tether, and was glad to shove him up on the horse. It was, of course, no trouble whatever for me to push his little bicycle home; so I was rather vexed when I reached the house to find Mr. Birley had given the poor kid an awful strafing for agreeing to it. Mr. Birley really lives for those children and Frank is his favourite, but he is a terribly Spartan father, and seems to think it unpardonable ever to show them any tenderness.

On Monday we woke up again to a perfectly white world and still snowing steadily. As Miss House had planned a break-up "Do" for Thursday, I had arranged to take both Scouts and Guides on Monday. So we had a combined noon-hour practice in which the Guides beat the Scouts at Knots, Flag and Law, and then I went on to visit the Red Cross nurse who has just arrived, and has been given a little house about two and a half miles farther on. It was a nice ride there through the white silent bush, and all the mystery and stillness of winter seemed to have come back again, although of course, I knew it couldn't be for more than a day or two. I found Nurse Roberts getting into her house, which is at present furnished exclusively with a bed and stove. She is Miss Hasell's product, and seems a very cheerful, keen Englishwoman, trained at the London. I should think she will be most useful, anyhow for the next six or nine months until the Roman Catholic hospital is built, (if that doesn't fall through). But she is nearly eight miles to the West of us, so I don't think she will greatly diminish Miss Birley's emergency cases from farther East. Afterwards I went back to school for a signalling practice with the Senior Scouts and Guides, and as it was still snowing, we played an indoor game of each taking it in turns to signal something to be done or touched. The fierce rush at the end of each message was tremendous fun, and Miss House, the head teacher, joined in and got quite as excited as anybody.

On Tuesday the weather changed again and the snow began to turn once more into deep mud and streams and lakes of water. I went to Taylor's Flats as usual and would you believe it, the three leading boys who had been so keen last week *had melted away again!*

The girls turned up all right, but could give no account whatever of the boys. Neither could we find any clue to the cause of the new debacle until one told me of a capital story which Mrs. Anderson had read to them all in school the day before—about a Scout who had *rescued a baby from a burning house.* Do you think that perhaps those poor little fellows thought that after all Scouting might be *worse* than war? Out of the frying pan—!

The chief excitement at Baldonnel next day was the beginning of Uniforms—i.e., Scout hats for the four enrolled Scouts, and bright red neckerchiefs for all, including Cubs. They were thrilled about them and really looked rather jolly, although the rest of their bodies were so varied and incongruous—some in blue overalls, (the nicest thing),—some in shirts, and some in sweaters. Of course, they are only supposed to wear the neckerchiefs on Scout days, but Miss Petter has since told me that they have worn them every day so far, and they are rapidly becoming red rags! At the end of School I photographed them all on their ponies and do hope it will turn out a good group.

Then I visited Alice Leclerc, the Lone Guide, and her mother gave me the enclosed snapshot of the Horse-shoe on our first hike when Alice was enrolled. One Guide is missing, and you don't see the others very clearly, but it's good of me anyway isn't it? Only for pity's sake don't show it to anyone with strict ideas about Guide Uniform!

Thursday was a strange day, considered as Thursday in Holy Week. Miss House had invited Miss Birley and me and all the parents, to an At Home at Fort St. John School before it broke up for the ten days Easter holiday, and had also invited the Baldonnel boys to go over and play their first inter-school baseball match.

There was, of course, nothing to object to in that, but the rest of the programme was a complete surprise and rather a blow to me, especially as I had had no warning and therefore no chance to protest. Apparently [?] had offered two prizes of two dollars each for the two best essays, senior and junior, on "Easter," and the winners to read their essays and receive their prizes at this party. Of course, very few of them knew the main events of the Passion and Resurrection, so the plan was, that Miss House had quickly read them the whole story from some school "reader," a few days before, and the Seniors had all written down as much as they could remember. But Miss Richards, considering the subject too difficult for the Juniors, had read to them *The Life Story of the Coyote* (a small kind of Canadian wolf which lives round here). So the winning essays on these two subjects—i.e., the Crucifixion and Resurrection, and the life-history of the Coyote—were read out *on an absolutely equal footing,* to a roomful of applauding parents and school-mates, and both rewarded by money prizes, after which we all had a big blow-out tea and an exciting baseball match; all this on the eve of Good Friday.

What could I do? What would you have done? Of course I could do nothing; and the odd thing is that neither Mrs. C. or Miss House nor anyone else seemed to think it anything else but a perfectly ideal arrangement.

My only hope is to prevent it from ever happening again. After all this very unusual excitement, it was not surprising to get a pretty bad attendance on Good Friday, or that it was difficult enough to recover any atmosphere of awe and reverence for events which had been treated like that, the day before.

On the other hand, I was rather touched by one thing, although embarrassed too. It was only just Sunday School, yet the new Game Warden's wife, a rather smart lady just come up from Vancouver, and both the school teachers arrived as pupils, and joined in with the greatest interest and reverence. So possibly I was too sensitive and critical about the day before. I don't know.

Afterwards, that stupid old tooth which has been tuning up steadily for the last few weeks, started full orchestra, and it became clearer than ever that I must go out to the dentist as early as possible next week. So after a funny little informal meal with the two Perry boys and an early Easter visit to Mrs. Millar, I spent rather a grim afternoon trying to practise the "Te Deum" and hymns for Sunday afternoon and finding I was too hopeless at it. Therefore I decided to be reckless and hire Tommy to bring Mrs. Devlin, if she would come, and the rest of the day was spent in finding them and fixing that up, and trying to find some means of getting out myself on Monday.

It was a perfectly glorious day, as Good Friday always is; all the snow gone again and delicious hot sun. On the way home I branched off North and visited a nice Glasgow woman whom I have only called on once before. She has been out since girlhood, but never lost her lovely strong Scotch accent, and just before I left she proudly produced a plate of queer flat pallid scones with a strange little design on their backs and said, "Ye'll no leave without a Hot Cross Bun!" Last thing in the evening, when Mr. Birley had gone home and May to bed, I played all the Good Friday music on the gramophone, and was more than ever thankful for it.

That day exactly concluded six months up here, that is six calendar months. There's little enough to show for it, God knows; but He also knows what can be made of it still.

Most of Saturday I prepared for Sunday, and in the afternoon we had a fresh gale and blizzard and seemed likely to be in for a snow-bound Easter Day.

Easter Eve produced a stiff gale and another little snow storm, but Easter Day was lovely, almost but not quite as lovely as Good Friday always is. I had my own Service first as usual, then groomed Coronach as smart as possible, and then started for Fort St. John, taking for the first time my Bethlehem Crucifix most carefully wrapped up in two scarves. I had billed a Service instead of Sunday School and had spent most of Saturday trying to prepare it as it was too far for Mr. Simpson to come there as well as to Baldonnel. I got there in pretty good time, and some of the children brought "pussy-willows" for decoration, which, with the Crucifix and a big Nelson picture and the bright blue tablecloth, made the school look almost like a Cathedral! Later Mrs. Devlin arrived with two vases, and some of the little mauve-coloured wild anemones which are here called crocuses. They looked charming, and my only regret was her crowning production of a bright orange vase full of large paper chrysanthemums. The children turned up pretty well, but alas! hardly any grown-ups, that is, only the Game Warden's wife, who came on Good Friday, Miss Petter, who was staying with Roman Catholic friends at Charlie Lake, and had for once broken away from Mass, Miss House, the Fort St. John head teacher, who arrived half an hour late, and Mr. H., a queer, earnest, intellectual man who most people here regard as dotty on that account.

As this only made five grown-ups with Mrs. Devlin, and about twenty-five children, I switched off the Service, or rather watered it down to a children's Service with a lesson instead of an address. I didn't know in the least, how to do it, and did it very badly, but the singing anyhow went pretty well. We began with "There is a Green Hill Far Away," and went on to "Jesus Christ is Risen to-day," and "The Strife is O'er, the Battle Won," and these were the only really inspiring parts of the Service, I'm afraid.

It was strange that so few people cared to come to the Service—considering there was no other Service of any denomination except the Roman Catholic Mass.

At Baldonnel I had a nice little school of about seven boys, after which Mr. Simpson arrived for the Service. For this the children helped me to decorate the school with "pussy-willows," and the only flowers in bloom as yet—a sort of pale anemone. Finding that I really couldn't play the "Te Deum" or psalm properly, I had hired Tommy to drive out Mrs. Devlin and take her back again after the Service. It cost six dollars, i.e., 25/-, but seemed to be worth it on such an occasion. Thirteen grown-ups came, which wasn't bad really, although the four Anglican women whom we always rely on, were *all* absent! But what pleased me most was that May came, and Tommy, who had brought Mrs. Devlin, instead of going away and coming back for her as he did on Christmas Day, came to the Service and sang most heartily. I was horribly nervous of preaching before him and May.

Afterwards we gave everyone an Easter card from the lovely lot sent me from Home. Then the usual friendly back-chat, and finally Coronach and I trundled back to the house—pretty tired, chiefly on account of the more or less continuous toothache.

I had made my own plans for the next few days off, as I wanted to go out to the nearest reliably sober dentist who lives at Grande Prairie, 150 miles from here. But it was a difficult time to go anywhere because the river was not yet out (i.e., completely thawed), and so the ferry hadn't started and no cars could go from this side. However, after I was in bed on Sunday night, May came in and told me that she had heard that a man called F. was taking a party from the other side of the river in a boat, at 9 A.M., so if I could get across the river in time I might squeeze in. That was a great chance, so before 8.0 on Monday morning Tommy drove me and a tiny suitcase down to the river bank where I waited for old Charon (i.e., Herbie Taylor), to come over with his canoe.

You see, every year the river freezes from some time in November to about the third week in April, and this is therefore the very worst month for travelling because often the thaw is gradual and therefore very dangerous, as no one can quite tell when and where it ceases to be possible to cross the ice. Almost every year either horses or men are drowned in this game of last across. This year, three trappers coming home with all their furs crossed just too late, and were all drowned.

After a fortnight or so of this dangerous phase the exciting moment comes when the river is said to "Go out." That means that all the ice breaks up and suddenly begins to move and then for a few more days the river is chock full of ice floes tearing down the stream, and is impossible to cross except in Herbie's canoe, and only possible then if Herbie thinks so.

All this sounds very adventurous, but as a matter of fact, when I got there, there was hardly any ice left except along the banks, and we paddled across in the most peaceful way, with no dodging at all—in fact, it was almost as exciting as the Serpentine.

At the other side I found Mr. F., with a pretty full load of two Government officials with stacks of luggage and a Fort St. John woman going to see the doctor at Grande Prairie. He had borrowed a car, and hoped to reach Grande Prairie in the day if possible, that is, mud permitting. He said he could squeeze me in between the men but wasn't ready, so I walked up the Peace River Hill, rather a fine, gradual climb, three miles long, too much surrounded by trees for any good views, except at one point just before you reach the top. There the trees fall away for a few yards, and you can see for several miles up and down the valley of the Peace. It's really rather a good river, but half a mile wide at this point and winding in big curves between thickly wooded banks from 700 to 800 feet high. I waited there till the car arrived, having been hauled up the muddy hill by a team of horses, and then we started off and had really a very good day.

The mud and ruts were tremendous, and we seemed to be swinging and banging and bumping and skidding in a way that *must* smash up the axle and springs in half an hour at most. But it didn't, and we only really got stuck four or five times, when trying to cross really deep mud holes.

F. is such a nice cheerful man, always good-tempered and full of resource. Of course, he had ropes and chains, block and tackle, spades, and shovels, and with the aid of these and a great deal of levering with tree trunks and boughs we got out of all the holes except one; and for that one we ended by having to wait while F. went off to the nearest farm for a strong team of horses. Luckily we had got beyond the first twenty-three miles or so, which is all virgin bush with no clearance or dwelling to be seen, otherwise I don't know how we should have got out. But in all our struggles (and very dirty ones too), I was impressed by F.'s modesty and jocularity. His chief exclamation was "OH MAN!!" But when things looked really bad, and we seemed to be stuck for life, he would burst into his strongest oath, "OH, MAN-CHILD!!"

At about 10 P.M. we got to Hythe—the railway terminus, and forty-five miles short of Grande Prairie—and decided to stay the night. The hotel was quite full, but after a certain amount of shuffling and piling up, a room with *two* beds (great luxury) was created for Mrs. Large and me, while the men slept on extemporised beds in the dining-room.

Next morning (Tuesday) we started directly after breakfast and got to Grande Prairie about noon. This is a perfectly deadly part of the country; it has been settled up for twenty years or more, and is almost bare and flat like the very dullest parts of East Anglia *minus* all hedges, big trees, churches and old buildings. Think of living there! Grande Prairie is quite an ambitious little town of about 2,000 people.[95] It has a main street and an Anglican and a United Church and a high school. But more important for us, it has a barber and a perfectly sober dentist. I got my appointment with one for 1 o'clock, and then ran to the other and got my hair cut short enough to last six months! The dentist was excellent. He found a criminal wisdom tooth in the top left hand corner, pumped in a dose of Novocain and hauled the fellow out—and all in about five, rather intense, minutes. And he only charged one and a half dollars, (6/6), which seemed funny, considering it had cost £2. 10. 0 to get to him, not counting meals or bed on the way, and would cost at least as much to get back to Fort St. John.

I left him and ran out into the street with a thankful heart and a bloodful mouth and was immediately stopped by a newspaper reporter, who wanted to know every detail of my life—as a stranger in Grande Prairie! I escaped from him to fall into the clutches of another man who was a keen Churchman and said I must go at once and see Canon James, the Vicar.[96] So he bore me off to a little Mission House, where it really was rather lovely to talk for a few minutes to a thin, cultivated, middle-aged, tremendously keen parson. Fancy that being a rare phenomenon for the likes of you and me! He was so kind, and actually offered to have a little Service for me at once in the church, but to my immense regret, that wasn't possible, because F. had to start back at once to meet the bi-weekly train at Hythe. It was a great disappointment, but I was comforted by the resolve to stop at Pouce Coupé and see Mr. Proctor, the Colonial and Continental Church Society parson there.[97]

We raced back to Hythe and got there just in time to see the *train* come in, so exciting—the first train I had seen since *October 15th*. Then we pushed on to Pouce Coupé and stayed there in a very nice Hart Hotel. Next morning F. and Mrs. Large and a new cargo continued their journey home, but I stayed at Pouce Coupé for the purpose of seeing the schoolmaster who also runs Scouts, and Mr. Proctor.

First I found Mr. McC.,[98] and had a long talk, in which it transpired that we were working on diametrically opposite methods, i.e., he has a fine Town Committee and meeting hall, but no enrolled Scouts, and I have no Committee or meeting place but about thirty enrolled Scouts and Cubs. I think (and hope) that we are both right for our own circumstances. Afterwards I learned that poor Mr. Proctor had just gone into hospital with congestion of the lungs. However, he said he'd like to see me, so in the afternoon I went and paid him a visit. But he was obviously feeling ill, poor man, and it really didn't seem fair to talk much shop with him at such a time. He seemed nice and keen, and is evidently a good organiser; and he told me he had the Bishop's [Bishop Rix] promise of an ordained priest to come North of the river this summer for eighteen months at least. I said the sooner the better or the United Church will sweep the board—and we left it at that.

After that I was pounced upon by two Government officials' wives who wanted to talk about Guides. Next day I was swept off for the night to a charming English couple living six miles out along a perfectly *appalling* road. They are called Tuck and are the most completely English people I have met so far, quite undamaged in voice and manner and the woman very refined. It was nice being with them, but I walked back to Pouce Coupé next day in order not to lose the chance of a lift home before Sunday. This chance didn't actually come till Saturday morning, and when it did, cost another thirteen dollars (£2. 12. 6), but the hotel was very nice and restful, and except for a still aching jaw, the whole time was quite a pleasant little change. In my mouth, it seemed that the widow and orphans were still making lamentations and not attempting to get used to their bereavement; I didn't know what to do to comfort them, but was at last reduced to aspirin most nights while they were feeling it so deeply.

Meanwhile I wrote a fair number of letters to the strains of a perfectly non-stop hotel gramophone. And on Friday afternoon a funny little homesteader just arrived, who had been watching me write for most of the day, suddenly said: "My Golly, you do keep some feller busy reading!"!!

On Friday evening a nice, queer little Government official turned up and invited me to hear *his* gramophone. He has a little house quite full of classical records, a very amazing thing to find, out here. I was thrilled, and should have enjoyed it immensely, but the little man had just bought the whole of Stainer's "Crucifixion" and insisted on playing it right through. So there was no time for Bach or Beethoven, or anyone else; and what was worse was that as he changed every record he paused to explain to he how much finer and more uplifting this music really was than the "Messiah"!

On Saturday morning F. appeared again and I was glad to join his party and be sure of getting home before Sunday. But as the widow and orphans were still unconsoled, I visited, before starting, the dentist at Pouce Coupé whose sobriety is said to be only intermittent, and found him in a lucid interval. He said the last man had done his job well, and there was nothing left to do, but a bad wisdom tooth often haunted the spot for days or even weeks after extraction. So now I know, at least, that it isn't mourners in the jaw! but just the old fellow's ghost and I call him Banquo because he comes at night especially and loves to trouble feasts:

"Never shake those gory fangs at me"!

Our journey back had a few tight places involving levers and tackle, and one requiring horses again, after eight men on a rope had failed, and finally we had to be hauled by a tractor *down* Peace River Hill. But the river was out and the ferry was in, and I got back here about 7 P.M. to make, as usual, the twofold surprising discovery.

(1) That nothing had happened.
(2) That I hadn't been missed.

On the other hand the MAIL was in, and interfered most shamefully with preparations for next day's Sunday Schools.

I am going to end this week on Sunday and probably the next few weeks also, as it really is more convenient for lots of reasons although of course entirely unorthodox. But the mail goes out on Monday morning, so it really does seem the most sensible point to end the week, doesn't it?

It was quite nice to get back here from Pouce Coupé; and certainly that little trip convinced me of the great superiority of the North side of the river. On the other side you find, first about twenty-five miles of almost unbroken and impenetrable bush, and then very tame open prairie country all pretty well cleared and cultivated. Pouce Coupé itself has a charming view of low wooded hills to the South; but otherwise there is hardly any distance and no sign at all of the Peace River itself. But our side seems to be quite dominated by the river. From every little eminence you can see the long blue line of its banks and everywhere else the country is cut up by steep winding coulees and creeks running down to it. Then we have got bush and prairie nicely mixed up almost like English woods and fields; although it's not nearly hilly enough to get some wide distant view. Above all, practically everyone up here is a genuine homesteader with almost everything to make, whereas to the South there are a good many officials and middlemen and society is already getting almost sophisticated.

On Sunday (April 27), I began very badly. May's clock loses, and my watch gains. So we always check the time whenever we go in to Fort St. John. But we had no occasion to go in, and I, not realising this, went by her clock and for the first time was LATE for Sunday School. And worse than that the darling children whose ideas of time are always chaotic and are seldom less than half an hour late *or early* chose that morning all to be fearfully early. Then as I didn't come when they expected (there is no clock at the school), someone announced that I hadn't got back from Grande Prairie and *they all went home again,* telling Mrs. Devlin on the way that there was no Sunday School!

So when I turned up I only found two little boys, ten minutes late like myself, and everyone else scattered beyond recall. Wasn't that a GOOD LESSON?

I put the smallest boy behind me on Coronach and we all went on the extra mile to the town to find any children we could. But, alas! they had all gone off to a baseball match (which accounts for much), and we only roped in two more boys for a little lesson on St. Thomas. The only bright spot in the while episode was Georgie Kelly's rapture in riding behind me on Coronach. His people are *very* poor and he is one of the very few children who have no pony—so he told me as I took him home, and Bobby, aged ten, ran alongside—that it was the best ride he had ever had in his life!

At Baldonnel there were seven or eight boys, which is the normal average for that little School. The road is quite dry now except for just one or two mud holes and at *last* the country is beginning to show some signs of spring. Of course, there are no leaves or flowers yet, but there are soft, downy "pussy-willows" everywhere and under the long coarse dead prairie grass there is a pale haze of tender green. Also quite a lot of birds are making a noise and if you look closely at the millions of chetif,[99] little poplars, you can see their leaf-buds really are swelling.

On Monday I went to the Fort St. John Scouts, to make final preparations for next Saturday's Rally, on Wednesday and Thursday did the same with the Baldonnel Scouts and the Guides, and on Tuesday enrolled the first patrol of Guides at Taylor's Flats. *All* the children asked me how they were to come, as their distances ranged from four to eight miles. I said I had no idea but it was up to them to come somehow—and, of course, they did.

On Friday I rode over to dinner with Mrs. McDonald who wanted to hand over the Sunday School by Post because it has become too much for her. I hadn't been out to see her since that snowy ride in January. It's a very pretty way along a vague winding trail, through largely untouched bush and small prairies. The last part is on the top of steadily rising ground and you get a fine view on your right, of the banks of the Peace, and to your left of its tributary the North Pine River.

Mrs. McDonald is very soon going to add to her family, which after nine years interval and with all the necessary strain of this new life, is rather a burdensome prospect; so I promised to relieve her of the Sunday School by Post, and shall of course try to find someone else to take it on. She has been doing the Northern half. It means sending out nearly 300 magazines and correcting and returning such answers as the children send in. It's not a big job, but too much for her just now. And not the least tiresome part is lugging the whole lot five miles to a Post Office, on horseback—as I very well know.

Our meal was fried eggs as usual just now, this being the egg season. It's rather amusing how the staple diet runs strictly according to natural home-grown supply. Thus it was nearly all eggs, when I got here in the autumn, but a few chickens were thrown in because we were killing the cockerels. Then Mr. Birley killed a cow, and we ate beef consistently from November till sometime in February. Then May's pigs were killed and she made bacon and ham, and we ate pork till nearly the end of April. Now that is finished and the staple is ham and eggs, or bacon and eggs, anyway eggs for the rest of the summer.

Saturday was the day of the Rally. It started rather cold and wet which was most agitating and there was a biting wind most of the day, but very little rain. The faithful Ritchie turned up at 9.30 A.M. to help in the preparations which consisted mainly in hiding a Treasure and laying out a trail, consisting of most ingenious maps and clues, all worked out by Ritchie.

Meanwhile the angelic May prepared a wonderful feast consisting of:

> a) Little sausages called weenies to be finish-cooked over camp-fires,
> b) Brown rolls and butter,
> c) Scones and iced cakes,
> d) Jelly and whipped cream.

All these, knocked up by herself in the intervals of running the house and farm, seeding the garden and hatching a lot of little chickens.

Just as we were in the grand final throes, a buggy drove up with the new United Church student [Mr. Lester] just arrived for the summer, who wanted to consult with me about mutual policy.

We were as kind to him as the crisis permitted. May gave him eggs and bacon; and I gave him a free hand with Fort St. John adults, but told him that all the children were convinced Anglicans! He was very nice and tactful and went away as soon as possible. The children were due at 2.30, but, of course, most of them arrived before 2.30 just as a sharp shower was beginning. Most of them came on horseback, some in waggons and two loads came in cars. They were all *very* early except one Patrol Leader and one Guide who arrived half an hour late.

Of course, the grand total was absurdly small, i.e., forty-four actually out of a possible fifty. Fancy a *Rally* of forty-four Scouts and Guides. Doesn't it seem absurd? Still it was the largest Muster there has ever been up here; and with the exception of four girls and two boys, included every available youth and maiden between ten and sixteen years old, within a radius of about twenty miles (Oh—No, except the Taylor's Flats boys).

This was the *Programme:*
Inspection
Knot Relay Race
Whispered Message Relay   } Junior Scouts
Ball-throwing Relay   } and Cubs
Signalling Competition   } Senior Scouts
Tenderfoot Knowledge Race   } and Guides
First Aid Competition
(had to be left out—no time)

————

Fire-lighting and Cocoa-making Race
Camp Fire Feast

————

Treasure Hunt

————

Final Rally
 Prizes and District Flag presented
 Cheers for Miss Birley
 Scout Law
 National Anthem

The Inspection was just a form to show them that appearance mattered. Their appearance certainly was very varied. About sixteen of the boys have now got hats, and about the same number belts. All have got neckerchiefs because May and I gave them—green for Fort St. John and red for Baldonnel. All have badges and shoulder knots (except those who have lost them!). Most had shirts which were nominally khaki. No one had shorts, a good many had breeches, but most had blue or khaki overall trousers!

The Taylor's Flats Guides have no uniform at all so far except pale blue shoulder knots; but the Fort St. John Guides were magnificent in home-made blue frocks and bright yellow ties and shoulder knots and real Guide hats and belts.

We had a lovely place for the Rally—a big field about 100 yards behind May's house, bounded on three sides by little woods, splendid view right down the coulee and away to the high river bank, and the distant hills. Everything of course took much longer than we expected but there was no hitch, and no vestige of dispute. Ritchie helped splendidly and so did Ethel House, the Fort St. John school marm, also Petter, only she chiefly helped May with the victuals.

The fire-lighting was so pretty. I gave each of the seven patrols a site on a big mound in the middle of the field; and there was frightful excitement as they raced to produce the first *drinkable* cup of cocoa over the seven little camp fires. The Guides won that easily, and then they all toasted their weenies and feasted, and then we had a tremendous inspection of "first out"—as the least carelessness that way can burn up half the country-side.

Then I told them all a foolish little story introducing the Treasure Hunt; and off they went baying like a little pack of hounds in every direction. That was the success of the day. Ritchie laid a splendid trail; and we had buried the treasure together under a spruce right down in the coulee by the waterside. For about half an hour they all ranged round the field and through the woods and up and down the hillsides, shouting to each other in a frenzy of excitement; and then the *Wolves* got it. The

Treasure consisted of a box containing a sort of lucky dip assortment of presents and Easter Eggs for each member of the Patrol. And one Wolf said to me afterwards, "Why Miss Storrs there's more than two dollars worth of stuff in our Treasure!" Meanwhile we had also hidden seven little boxes of minor Treasure round the edges of the wood, so I hastily deflected the other Patrols in that direction and in the end I think they all found something. Then we had a Final Rally on the hill-top; and I had to present the District Union Jack to *the Guides* who had won three events quite clearly, while the Scout-troops had each only won two. I think the boys were a little disgusted, but it did them no harm; and I must now write and tell Margaret Popham's kind little Company which was so generous in giving the Flag.

We finished at 7.30 and everybody *gradually* melted away. May seemed delighted about it all, and I was awfully thankful especially because there had been perfect good humour throughout. Mr. Birley was pleased too, I think (although he wouldn't acknowledge it), because Douglas had signalled splendidly, and easily won that event for his Troop. Poor Douglas had been dreaming about it for nights beforehand, and being a very highly-strung boy, we had feared he would lose his head when it came to the point, but he didn't, the least bit.

A lot of washing up and very late to bed.

Sunday, May 4.

May had a bad headache and stayed in bed. Profiting by last week's disaster I went out early to catch Coronach in the field, but the little beggar for the first time refused to come up to his breakfast, and I couldn't find him. Luckily Mr. Birley has two extra horses, so I carried the saddle over to him, and he mounted me on Buster, who as a matter of fact is the first horse I rode in this country. He is a tall bony, black horse with a *very* ugly face, and unpleasant expression. In fact, if Rama's grandmother was a volcano and Coronach's a pincushion, I think Buster's must have been a *camel!* However, he is strong and active, doesn't buck, and only shies about as much as they all do, so I was lucky. I really expected almost nobody at Sunday School after the excitement and fatigue of yesterday and was quite pleased that twenty-four turned up, and no one was apparently over-tired or worse for wear.

After that the ten miles on to the Flats, marked by one or two biggish side-springs, but otherwise placid enough. Fifteen children turned up there, and seven or eight grown-ups. They are the oddest children, ignorant and inexpressive to the last degree compared with whom the Fort St. John kids are prodigies of zeal and intelligence. After School Mr. Simpson appeared and we had a little monthly Service. I tried to speak on "Blessed are they that have not seen and yet have believed."

Only about eight people came; but never mind. There weren't any more in the Upper Room.

Home late and pretty tired, but just alive enough to write last week's diary.

May 15.

About last week the less said the better. It was dominated by Banquo, who shook his gory lock at me with increasing regularity every afternoon, evening and night. For the first three days I tried a very little idle life, pottering round in the house with my own washing, etc., and helping May to plant the garden. But after Wednesday night, May persuaded me to try a plan of three days in bed, and tied my head up in cotton wool till I looked like *half* of a very nice Nun. She was *so* kind and even managed two or three times a day between house-work, cooking, stable cleaning, chicken hatching, garden planting, and sowing, and stray first-aiding, to run in and play me a gramophone record.

But even that, and the Nun's trappings and a lot of Ovaltine, and aspirin failed to lay the Ghost; and I had to cave in and send S.O.S. messages for both Sunday Schools.

On Sunday Tommy blew in and said that he was going out next day to Grande Prairie with a mother and two little boys and should he call for me. I said no—because I felt better and wanted to avoid the expense and waste of time. But finally we agreed that if I had a really bad night, I should walk to Baldonnel corner by 9.30 next morning and wait till he came by.

So that's what happened on Monday. It came on to rain pretty hard before I reached the corner and Tommy didn't arrive till 10.30 so I had a nice little wait, but otherwise everything went according to plan (or schedule). The rain made the road horribly greasy, and poor Tommy had a nasty time on the hills, especially the steep winding Peace River Hill which is between two and three miles long and was deep, greasy mud nearly all the way. After that, however, it cleared up and the road got steadily better till we reached Grande Prairie, about 8.45 P.M.

Directly we reached Grande Prairie Tommy took Mrs. Mikkleson[100] and the little boys to the hospital for immediate treatment.

while I went to arrange things at the hotel. Then I had an inspiration and rushed round again to see Canon James, the Vicar. He is a nice, quiet, friendly, delightfully English little man, and produced a nice, hearty, red-haired wife, (also very English). He readily promised me a Celebration next morning, which was of course, the object of my visit.

Then I returned to the hotel, just as Tommy brought back Mrs. Mikkleson and her two poor babies both roaring like little bulls. I tried to help her a little to quiet them down, and prepare for the night, but it wasn't much of a night *she* had, poor thing.

Next morning I took duty while she went out to get some breakfast, and then just before 9 o'clock, rushed round to the little English church. It was exactly seven months since my last Celebration with Lillian Swanzy in Edmonton Cathedral.

Afterwards a quick breakfast in a cafe and then out to the hospital which stands right outside the little town. I had to wait a bit for Dr. O'Brien, a charming elderly army surgeon with snow-white hair.[101] But when he did come, he pommelled me with true military vigour, found some swollen glands pressing on a nerve, and told me to come back in two hours and have them out.

So I ran back to the town, found Tommy and Mrs. Mikkleson, told them I couldn't come back with them (a great nuisance), wrote to May, paid the hotel bill and returned at top speed to the hospital, smoking hot for the sacrifice.

They did it under gas, and I woke up in a clean little public ward, apparently *full* of yelling babies. I will spare you fruity details of a surgical ward, which you know well enough already. Both the nurses and patients are awfully nice and friendly and the whole management is wonderfully good and efficient. Of course, you pay highly for them, as apparently no Canadian hospitals have any voluntary support, and the cheapest rate appears to be four dollars (16/6) a day, plus doctor's fees. This comes fearfully heavily on many settlers and if some member of a family gets a really long illness—I can't think how they manage it. However, for me it's nothing, as I'm healing up very quick and am actually allowed to leave to-night (Thursday), and sleep in the hotel, with a view to starting home to-morrow. That's not quite so easy as it sounds, because nothing runs from here to Fort St. John. But I shall take a train to-morrow evening to Hythe (forty miles), and there am pretty sure to find something for Pouce Coupé anyhow.

My neck is very stiff and sore of course, and I feel very like Charles I, *half an hour after*. But O'Brien says May can take out the stitches, and the dressings can come off in a week. So *long before* you get this the incident will be ancient history, and I hope Banquo's ghost laid for ever.

(I'll probably finish this and post it from Pouce Coupé.)

Friday, 2.30.
In the train—for Hythe. (N.B. in a real TRAIN!*)*

On second thoughts I'll post this at Hythe, then it goes straight back to Edmonton in the train and gains a whole mail.

Another little bout with the dentist this morning—Banquo having returned in the new form of a splintered jaw! Kind Mrs. Tuck gave me brandy and milk and let me lie on her bed till time to catch the train. All's well now and a fine hot day. This rather sweet telegram came from the Scouts this morning:

Miss M. Storrs—Care Hospital—Grande Prairie, Alta.

Dear Miss Storrs, we are very sorry that you are ill and wish you a speedy recovery stop you are missed among us and we sincerely hope that you will soon return.

The Fort St. John Boy Scouts.

Wednesday, May 25.

I think I posted the last from Grande Prairie about last Friday. That is an awful little town and I was thankful to escape from it, though the hospital is really very good. Dr. O'Brien is very swift and definite in his methods and deeply interested in Jerusalem. He happened to find out in his first interview that I had been there, and simply couldn't let go the subject afterwards. So even after I was on the operating table while shaving my neck and sterilising his instruments, he pelted me with questions about conditions there now. And after the bag was over my nose, and I felt the nurse tying up my wrists and the spinning suffocation began, I could hear his voice getting farther and farther away still enquiring—"AND WHO ARE THE MOST TO BLAME, the Arabs or the Jews!—and who are the most to bl. . . ."

Two days later, when I left, he asked whether I would give a lecture on Jerusalem in Grande Prairie. I was evasive, anyway for the time being; but it's nice to find anybody so keen about it up here.

The dentist amused me too, though in a different way altogether. He is a terribly conscientious and diffident man. Only after three quarters of an hour's struggle with my jawbone, did his Natural Man get uppermost for a moment. During a moment's interval between the rounds when we were both rather shattered I said, "Do you get many like this?" And he said: "If I got many of these I'd quit the business right away." He said it so fervently that I was quite cheered up.

I got by car and train as far as Rolla that night, and had to wait till the following evening for the last stage of the journey. Rolla is a perfectly awful little place consisting of two hotels, and two or three stores and a garage and a school, and a United Church plumped down quite naked, so to speak, on a treeless waste of prairie. All the same it is the second city in the [Peace River] Block, and looks down most loftily on Fort St. John. The only incident there was a Pentecostal evangelist. He was a smartly dressed, *very* melancholy looking young man who appeared opposite me at supper. After the usual preliminary skirmishing I asked him where he was going, and he replied:

"I am a Pentecostal evangelist, and I am going to Fort St. John because the people there are in darkness, and there is no Christian witness *of any kind.*"

Wasn't it awkward?! I didn't discuss it then, but afterwards felt it only fair to the poor young man to tell him that in this benighted area he would find already working:

1) A Roman priest,
2) A United Church student (just come),
3) An Anglican Sunday School teacher,

plus 4) An Anglican priest (also just arriving).

He was horrified, poor lad, and quite sensible enough to see that he really hadn't a chance. It seems that he had been sent forth from the Pentecostal Assembly at Edmonton with a few dollars and no instructions. At Hythe a man driving a truck (lorry) had told him of the benighted condition of Fort St. John and offered to take him there for a consideration. Of course, the fellow was lying just to get a passenger. The poor little evangelist had paid him all he had but one dollar, being confident of support by the starving souls at St. John. We asked him whether he knew of *any* Pentecostal family where he could be sure of a welcome and could make a start. He said not near Fort St. John, but at Swan Lake, twenty miles South of Pouce Coupé. A little discussion, and adjustment, and next morning he started back in the mail truck happily flying South to evangelise the Swans.

In two months or so I shall have to visit that lake in the Van. I wonder whether I shall meet him again and be packed off North!!

Fort St. John
Two weeks ending June 1, 1930.

I quite forgot to tell you about the Elks' parade at Grande Prairie. It was on Thursday evening after I came out of hospital. The Elks are the big Friendly Society out here like the Buffaloes at Home; and I was told they were to have a big meeting to be proceeded by a fine procession up and down the street. So of course, I hung about together with everybody else *not* an Elk, to see it, especially as it was supposed to be attended by Elks from Hythe and Pouce Coupé and Rolla, and even possibly from Fort St. John, 150 miles away, so I had faint hopes of spotting someone to take me home next day.

At 7.30 the procession formed up outside the Elks' Hall and then, led by its own brass band, moved solemnly down the street. It was the most ludicrous sight you can imagine. In front rode three people, a girl dressed up as a cowboy, a man dressed as a sailor, but with a black face, and one man in the official Elks' dress, which appears to consist of white flannel trousers, a bright purple blazer (rather pretty), and a high purple *fez* cap with a long white tassel. After them came the band which was entirely composed of black-faced men, (not real negroes), dressed in long purple *tail* coats and bright scarlet tall hats.

After them came all the leading citizens of Grande Prairie, Hythe and Pouce Coupé, looking awfully pleased with themselves in their Elks blazers and purple fezes, and long white tassels. They marched the whole length of the little main street twice with the greatest possible solemnity and then disappeared into the Elks' Hall for their Mystic Orgies. I recognised no one from Fort St. John, and was really rather thankful!

On Saturday I reached home at last, about 7 o'clock, and there found the Mission priest from Montreal and his young student chauffeur firmly awaiting me.[102] They have been sent from Montreal by a new Society called "The Fellowship of the West," which provides them with a car and pays all expenses for two months up here. They arrived on Thursday with their tent and camping outfit, and apparently [have] been haunting this house ever since and eating up most of poor May's food while waiting for my return.

The priest is a Mr. Guiton, born in Jersey, but obviously reared in Eastern Canada, and a nice friendly man in the middle thirties I imagine, and to my great delight, a tremendously keen Scoutmaster, one of those, in fact, who took over the Canadian Contingent to the Jamboree[103] last year. He had no plans for Sunday, and jumped at taking the two Sunday Schools, which May calmly handed to him over my head! It was a good idea really, because there was no time to attempt to arrange a Service, so that at least gave him two little openings to start with; and then we agreed that they should both come in to supper afterwards and have a more extensive Council of War.

So after all the hurry back I did *no* work on Sunday and felt a great fraud. But about 4.30 Mr. Guiton and the boy Dick (aged eighteen and about eight feet high), turned up again, and we went at it till late in the evening, only interrupted by a visit from the *United Church student,* who heard I had been ill and very kindly, though rather inopportunely, called to enquire. May was out with Tommy, but of course we kept him to supper; that is, I threw him into the arms of Mr. Guiton, set Dick to work at the kitchen fire, and ran out myself to the stable to snatch all possible eggs from under the hens to make a Re-Union Feast. It was a splendid thing, really, because he and Mr. Guiton made good friends and planned all their little Services carefully so as not to overlap and also arranged to report to each other, Anglican and United families as they visited. Then he departed and Guiton and I roughed out first his Church programme, involving Services at Fort St. John, Baldonnel, Taylor's Flats, Charlie Lake, Hudson Hope, and two or three little centres up in the Montney District North of us. Then we made Scout plans and he readily agreed to stay for the Camp at the beginning of July, and also to help me work up a little Display beforehand in order to raise some sort of Camp Fund. I gave him a letter to Mr. Ritchie who had been acting Scout Master at Fort St. John since the Rally on May 3rd, and he promised to talk the plans over with him, and to go with him to a special meeting at the school on Tuesday. I wanted him and Ritchie to do that without me, so as to give Ritchie full responsibility and Guiton a good opportunity of sizing Ritchie up.

So on Monday I still lay low and only did my washing and tidy-ups; but on Tuesday I was determined to go to the Flats, and start up the little Guides in their preparation for the Display. However, Coronach having jumped the fence and run away, it was fruitless to discuss with May any further the question as to whether my neck was fit for riding! So she, having lately bought a second hand Ford, offered to drive me to the top of the Flats Hill, and wait for me while I walked down to the school. It's a pretty long, steep hill, and a very narrow road; neither of us knew the car and May is very nervous, so we did that. I took the baby gramophone and a Country Dance record, and had a delightful hour starting the Guides on "Gathering Peascods," which they loved. We meant to dance outside but there was such a *biting* wind that we had to do it all along the fixed desks in the crowded little school-room. But that didn't matter, and the only occasional difficulty was that they got so fascinated by the tiny gramophone that they sometimes forgot to dance!

· Next day, Wednesday, Guiton and Dick were to pick me up and go to the Baldonnel Scouts; but to my surprise they arrived on foot, having for the *second* time in this trip wrecked their car, by driving fast and ignoring the pot-holes and mud-holes in the road. The first time they broke a spring and this time they stripped the gears, so I suppose they'll be more careful soon. It was pretty late so May hired me her car on strict condition that neither of them drove it, and thus, after all these months, I lapsed from stirrups to pedals again, a great come down.

The boys had been warned by a note to Jack [McDonald], the Leader, and they gave Mr. Guiton a fairly successful surprise reception, after which we all sat on the Council Rock (wood-stack), and he told them about the Jamboree, foreshadowed our own Camp and Display and ended with a game. After that we had a picnic lunch and I took him to visit one Anglican family till schooltime was over. Then we returned to hold a committee for their share of the Display—to consist chiefly of "Pyramids," First Aid, and a little play. It is all to end with a Camp Fire, for which nobody knows one single song at present. That is to be my share in the training, as Mr. Guiton can't sing a note.

He told us the result of his interview with Ritchie—very unsatisfactory. Ritchie took fright at our suggestions, said neither he, nor the bigger boys had time for the Display, etc. Guiton thinks he will never give enough time or trouble to the Troop. Anyway, they had no Tuesday meeting, so I arranged to go with him on Thursday, have it out with Ritchie myself, and then if necessary carry on without him.

So on Thursday I visited poor Ritchie in his shack, for the second time, tackled him about the job, and finally extracted from him his resignation. Poor lad, he has got a homestead (mostly thick bush), but hasn't touched it yet; and is trying to make a living out of photography, which is certainly pretty uncertain here. We parted good friends. He is still a Scout, and will come with us to Camp, if possible, though not of course as Scout Master.

Then Mr. Guiton, Dick, and I went to the school and more or less repeated yesterday's programme, only of course, the Guides were included, and Miss House, as usual, got very keen. At this school, instead of a little play, Mr. Guiton has promised to teach the boys one or two real Indian dances that were performed at the Jamboree. It will be rather a job to mobilise the clothing and head-dresses, but I expect we shall succeed and the boys are thrilled about it.

Meanwhile, since Tuesday, my stupid old neck had been swelling and turning wonderful colours while two of the soluble stitches dissolved, but the third would not. So at last May, who has no forceps or surgical scissors, persuaded me to go and see the new English Red Cross nurse. I went on to her, therefore, between the two Scout meetings, and she cut out the stitch, and said the wound had healed but was septic inside, and must be re-opened with three-hourly boracic foments. She pressed me to stay with her, and occupy one of the two spare beds (the other has a maternity case), but I declined politely but firmly, let her apply the first foment, and escaped just in time for the second Scout meeting. I am

afraid my appearance was rather a shock to the lads, the modest neck
bandage and pad having given way to a huge Toby ruff of cotton wool so
that I looked more than ever like Charles I in his coffin (you know his
head was bandaged on again).

Next day I took the Guides and tried to work out with them,
something showy for the Rally. But to start with we had to satisfy
ourselves with Country Dancing, which they took to very well. I got back
as early as possible to finish sorting, addressing and wrapping the three
hundred or so Sunday School magazines which I had rashly taken over
from Mrs. McDonald just before my own collapse!

On Saturday I meant to stay in all day to give the foments a better
chance. But the Roman Catholics were having a sort of Empire Day Fête
for their hospital that is to be; and it seemed too unfriendly and
Protestant not to go, so I extracted permission from May, and borrowed
her car again, and took Douglas for a treat. The Fête turned out to be
nothing but a fruit-booth, and ice-cream booth and a baseball match.
(But they really made their money by the dance which followed).

The match was against the combined neighbour cities Pouce Coupé
and Rolla—much like a match against Chatham and Gillingham, if
those two were fifty or sixty miles from Rochester. I had never seen
grown-up baseball before, so scrambled up the rickety erection of planks
called the Grand Stand, and sat watching it among the aristocracy of
Fort St. John. The match started three and a half hours late, and only
then after all the cars surrounding the field (and about twenty had
come), began to sound their horns, and made a perfect inferno, were the
players goaded into beginning.

You know baseball? It's almost exactly the same as rounders, only
played with a hard ball and greatest possible violence. The pitcher hurls
the ball with all his strength at the batter, and the catcher (equivalent of
wicket-keeper), is dressed in padded body armour and a sort of fencing
helmet. I suppose there is room for skill and strategy somewhere, but it's
not very evident to the outsider.

But what staggered me was the behaviour of the on-lookers. I had
really often heard about it from Father, but never quite believe it. Do you
know, from the very first ball, all those respectable citizens with whom I
was sitting, kept up a connonade of *insult* and *abuse* against the visiting
team which made me hot all over though I tried hard to realise that it was
nothing but an understood part of the game! Two of my nicest Guides
were close to me; and at every ball that was thrown they screamed out
remarks like these:

"Oh, look at the pitcher—he's cross-eyed."

"Ow, look at the catcher—he's balmy, send for a doctor."

"Oho, young man, you're very pretty, but you can't hit a ball. Why did
you come, anyway?"

It would have been quite futile to protest at the moment, as this is the accepted practice wherever American influence predominates; so I just remembered my promise to May, and was thankful to come away as soon as possible, and spent the rest of the evening practising to-morrow's hymns and chants on the harmonium, which I still play disgracefully.

Ever since Easter, by the way, the weather has been cold and dry, with little sunshine, a strong dry wind and frequent frosts at night. On two nights last week there were twenty degrees of frost, and this caused a good deal of anxiety as to whether the oats and wheat—both just appearing above the ground—were killed, as of course most of the early sown vegetables were killed. Mr. Birley thought the wheat would recover, and the oats might, *if* only it would rain. I decided to remind Mr. Guiton on Sunday to pray for rain, but there was no need.

On Saturday night the heavens opened, and it poured in torrents, and on Sunday, it was pouring still. The whole world seemed to be under water. May had promised me her car for Sunday School, but in the morning we saw the road was a sea of deep, slimy mud, quite impassable for a car without chains—and May had as yet no chains. So, as there was no horse either, I walked to Fort St. John and certainly it was the wettest, muddiest walk I've ever known. I had on my new sou'wester and high rubber boots, but might just as well have had nothing. The wet and mud penetrated everywhere from head to foot, and great cakes of mud accumulated on my boots till they seemed as big as snowshoes, and I could hardly lift them from the ground. It really was funny!

Of course, there were no children—I didn't expect any—only was so afraid of the bare possibility of one or two turning up wet to the skin, and finding no one there. So I only waited a very few minutes to ensure against that, and then came home again; a queer futile sort of Sunday morning, perhaps, but I'm beginning to learn some new forms of worship that are not even found in the Deposited Book.[104]

There was just time to change and have dinner and then Mr. Guiton and Dick arrived in their repaired and heavily chained car to take me to the Service at Baldonnel. They were staggered by the state of the road, as I suppose in Eastern Canada they are all either paved or built in some way or other, as at Home. We didn't expect anyone at Service, except possibly Mr. Simpson. But we took some dry wood, and made a fire, and tried to make the little school as "Churchy" as possible, and to my great joy at the last moment May and Tommy turned up, he having picked her up in his car. Mr. Simpson also arrived on foot, being pretty well water-logged, and so we had a queerer and tinier little Service than any he and I had held together in the winter. I was awfully sorry for Mr. Guiton but he didn't seem to mind a bit. He gave us a nice little address, and we had full Choral Evensong, though nobody could really sing in tune except Tommy, Mr. Simpson and me!

Guiton and Dick took me home afterwards, and we were just arranging for me to go back with them for the Fort St. John Service at 8.0 when May suddenly cut up rough and said she wouldn't give me *any more foments* if I went out again.

It was annoying because I did want to stand by them at this difficult beginning and also loved the Service for its own sake, and yet the flesh was so weak that I was really thankful. (In the end nobody turned up at all, so they had no Service that night.)

All this time we had been steadily fomenting, but my stupid old neck though swollen and discoloured and on and off pretty painful, wouldn't burst! So I stayed in bed all Monday, and only got up on Tuesday to do my washing and write a few letters. Meanwhile it went on pouring, and no cars attempted to run, and Petter reported that Guiton had not been again to school as we had planned. So I decided to go next day and start the boys with Camp-fire songs. But that evening both the neck and old Banquo in the jaw set up one of their duets with such vigour, that all unbeknown to me, May told Tommy (who had come out to see to an injured horse of his that lives here), to bring both Guiton and the nurse out with him next morning in time to stop me going!

I had no idea of this conspiracy, and was all dressed up ready at 10.30, with breeches and top boots for wading through the mud, when up rolled Tommy again with the conspirators. Guiton declared that he had always meant to get to the school today (?!) and Nurse Roberts calmly announced that she had come to *take me back with her!* Nurse Roberts is a very bright, strong, capable, determined and tremendously self-confident woman, and she never *dreamed* that I would refuse to go!

So May and Tommy both with strict neutrality watched the ensuing conflict and witnessed the final Treaty—i.e.:

1) Freedom: I could stay here.
2) Bondage: I was to lie flat on my back in bed till my neck had burst, drained, and healed again.

So now you know why this letter is written so badly and in pencil. It is written so to speak by a recumbent effigy.

No sooner had the enemy withdrawn than I began to carry out the terms imposed, and then we found that in the heat of conflict (or the cold of panic), my neck had burst!

I have gone back to early childish days and am quite enjoying them. At first I was awfully worried about the children—and the Van, because Price[105] was to arrive at Pouce Coupé last week. But all that has been lifted off my conscience in a most wonderful way.

First the rain has been so continuous that Mr. Guiton simply *couldn't* take the car anywhere after Sunday, so he has been *thankful* at both schools to work up and make friends and was equally eager to follow up with them in Sunday Schools today. In fact, my collapse has given him just the work he likes, when otherwise he would have been simply wasting his time until the road recovers. Of course, directly conditions do improve he will have to push out to the Montney and Hudson Hope; but by then I shall be all right too, so it all fits in perfectly.

Meanwhile, I was still worrying about Price and the Van (having accepted full responsibility for the Block, provided I worked North of the river first), and was determined whatever happened to be well as soon as the road should be passable again. But on Ascension Day Guiton brought me over a wire from Hasell, saying she has got another teacher and *won't want me at all.* This, you may remember, is what I tentatively suggested in the winter, but up to now Hasell has said it was quite impossible. At first, the wire disappointed me a little because I was rather looking forward to the new scenes and faces and generally new experiences of the Van. But now, I feel sure this is altogether for the best. If my two little disabilities clear up in a week or so—as I'm sure they will—I shall be able to get back whole-heartedly to the children and the Camps and backing up Mr. Guiton generally; while, if they do *not* I shall be, for the time, of no use anywhere, and should be a most trying companion in the Van, because dear little Banquo, like most other ghosts, is chiefly neuralgia, of course—somehow born of glands and the tooth, and aggravated by the splintered jaw. I've told you all about him at this absurd length, because if I kept back anything, I felt sure you would think I had kept back more. So don't jump to conclusions or think it's anything more than that, for Goodness Sake.

As a matter of fact, since Hasell's wire lifted the Van off my chest, I have thoroughly enjoyed this time as a kind of Retreat, reading real books (Curé D'Ars,[106] St. Augustine and Browning), and having lots of time to think.

Mr. Guiton is quite determined to get a permanent parson in here next spring, and says if nobody else can come, he will. We have also mutually planned for a little church in the City, and a Church Hall at Baldonnel (eight miles east), both to be built by the unknown Vicar next spring. But Guiton says he can raise practically all the money through his Fellowship of the West in Montreal.

If all this really looks like materialising (and we shall know before the end of this summer), and if the Bishop[107] will continue to give me some sort of recognition, I hope definitely to come back next spring with or without a companion, and build a little house, exactly half way between two centres on the perfectly lovely site which May has offered.

On Friday I meant to go to Baldonnel for the dinner-hour, to start the boys on Camp Fire songs, and then to go down to the Guides at Taylor's

Flats whom I have shamefully neglected. I was to take the car again, and was told there were no bad mud-holes as far as the Flats. An added excitement at Baldonnel was to be a baseball match against the Charlie Lake School, for which I was to take up some rolls and cakes made by May. So you can just imagine how *mad* I was to find the back tyre as flat as a pancake. Worse still, there was only half a jack to be found, i.e., the jack itself but no trace of a lever to work it. I ransacked the car and the garage and house—all no good—and all May said was "There isn't one so you can't go." I knew the dinner-hour was doomed, but determined to get to the Flats somehow. There was no horse to be had, and May said I wasn't to walk, and I had to confess there was some sense in it, at the time. So I set to work with the levers, i.e., logs and poles, and after *two hours and a half,* with a good deal of intermittent help from May (who strongly disapproved all the time), I got the old wheel changed and myself entirely covered with dust and black oil. Fancy taking all that time to change a wheel! Anyway I got to school in time for the beginning of the match, delivered the food, stopped a little while, and then went on to the Taylor's Flats Guides. These poor little beggars hadn't had a meeting for two or three weeks, and were feeling rather neglected. So we went hard at "Gathering Peascods" and then started to learn some Camp-fire songs—two rounds, "Campfires Burning" and "Are You Sleeping?", and three songs, "Annie Laurie," "Billy Boy," and "John Peel"—*all quite new to them.*

These two tiny days tuned up old Banquo again pretty badly at night, which was a great bore, and forced me to another real idle Saturday with nothing but the usual wash and iron, and a few household chores and a practice on the harmonium for tomorrow.

To-day, *Whitsunday,* I was nothing up—a hanger-on to Mr. Guiton who took three Services—Fort St. John in the morning, Baldonnel Sunday School and Service in the afternoon, and Taylor's Flats in the evening.

Week ending Saturday, June 7.

There's almost nothing to tell about this week, because it's almost *less* than nothing that I've done. It continued to pour all the first part of the week, and May wouldn't let me go anywhere. So I got up late and did odd jobs about the house and altogether felt and was dreadfully futile. However, by Thursday it had cleared up and twenty-four hours very strong wind had dried the road so much that I was able to take May's car and start off for dinner-hour with the Fort St. John Guides. The road was splendid for about a mile, and then quite suddenly, I ran into one of those dear little mud-holes and stuck fast—deeply bedded up to the axles in black sticky mire.

I tried to lever up the wheels, but only went in up to my knees, and soon gave that up. It was no use walking back to the Birleys because I knew he was out in the bush. So there was nothing for it but to walk along the road towards Fort St. John, and hope to meet a car or truck. So I went on about one and a half miles and of course there was no sign of a car anywhere.

But at last I saw a farmer on the horizon harrowing his field and just disappearing over a slope, so I pounded after him, and with grovelling apologies, asked him for help. He turned out to be the father of one of the Guides, and came along most willingly. But of course it was a slow business unlimbering the horses and walking them all the way back to the car, and when they did at last pull it out I was far too late for the dinner-hour at school. Wasn't that sickening? However, I went on to the town, to do lots of things that had to be done, and presently met Mr. Guiton who told me that he and the youth Dick H. had stuck in that same mud-hole *all last night,* and only got pulled out this morning— not so long before I went in!

However, I got the Guides after school, and taught them to dance "Gathering Peascods" for the Display which, it's dreadful to think, is only a fortnight ahead of us now. I took the baby gramophone as usual, and we danced outside the school, with the minimum of grace and skill, but the maximum of enjoyment.

Then I went on three miles to see Nurse Roberts. She is *most* vigorous and capable and very plucky, and keen on the job. She had that day three in-patients, a maternity case, and a little girl with whooping-cough, and a man who had just ridden thirty miles, after chopping off two fingers with an axe. He managed to bring one finger just joined to the hand still, and was frightfully pleased because Nurse has saved it for him.

Besides these [demands, she] had, of course, all sorts of calls outside, and fairly often spends all night in a waggon going across country to some fairly urgent case. When the Roman Catholics build their hospital (next spring probably) I suppose she will be superseded, but at present she is invaluable, and does for the North and West part of the district what May has always done for the East and South. But the difference is that she is financed and has two spare beds, whereas May has never had a penny of help, and only her own bed to turn out of, when needed—pretty frequently too.

May's car having sprung another leak since Friday (second-hand wheels!) I borrowed Mr. Birley's Buster and rode over to the Morning

Service. He is a ridiculous horse, *so* tall and black and bony with a face just like a giraffe, *not* pretty. He is rather fussy, *loathes* waiting to be mounted and shies very violently at cars, cows, and pigs. But he has a good fast trot which never slackens, so he really does get there quicker than either Coronach or Rama, and neither bucks nor falls down. Did I tell you that I had *laid down the keel of my own horse?* Well, anyhow I have, that is, I have acquired reins and a saddle, so now you see, apart from the bridle and the horse, my mount is complete. These little finishing touches can be added next year.

Alas for poor Mr. Guiton, only five grown-ups and five or six children came to the Morning Service. Apparently nearly everyone had gone off to one of those beastly baseball matches that are played every Sunday in the summer. I was *dreadfully* disappointed to think of this nice man coming so far, and being a Scout Master too, and then getting a worse congregation than Simpson and I in the depths of winter. Luckily he seemed quite cheerful about it, and not in the least disheartened. He preached so well, too; but it all made me more ashamed of their indifference and of my own failure to break it down.

Almost the same thing happened at Baldonnel this afternoon, where I had been pretty confident of a better turn-up. Six boys came to Sunday School, and Mr. Simpson and five women to Service. Of course, Tommy was out at Pouce Coupé, and May was nursing a sick boy at Fort St. John, and Petter, as usual, was away for the weekend. But there were, at least, four other families that could have come, or at least did come in the winter, not to speak of the other people who had professed to despise "Amateur Parsons" and want the Real Thing.

Of the five women, it turned out, that none were *confirmed* Anglicans, so they went away after the shortened Evensong, and Mr. Guiton, Mr. Simpson, Dick H. and I were left for Holy Communion together. It was about 5 o'clock, and therefore my first Evening Communion; but I think it meant so much to the four of us, that the bald school surroundings and cramped little desks seemed as solemn and beautiful as a cathedral.

Afterwards, Mr. Guiton was as cheerful and undisappointed as ever, which makes me like him very much; though what I can't bear to think of is the people all round who are missing the opportunity *now that it has come, and don't even care that they miss it.*

Of course, as he says, the sense of God, and the sense of need, have both got to build up from the bottom in most cases, and it will probably take years.

To-morrow we hope to go out to Pouce Coupé for a sort of Rural Deanery meeting with Mr. Proctor concerning the future policy of the Church for this side of the river.

Monday evening.

Had another big molar out this morning by a dentist visiting the local store—and believe I am *permanently* cured this time!

Bishop's Court, Rochester
July 16, 1930.

Readers of the Diaries may like to know that I have already received £89 for the East Fort St. John Church Hall Fund, and that I can count on further promises amounting to between £20 and £30. The Dean has promised the Cathedral collections on Sunday, August 10th, to this object. But it will be a tremendous help if everyone will make the need known to people who may be interested in it. You will see an allusion to the keenness shown to get such a hall built, in the Diary of June 29th; but it has not been possible as yet to let them know at Fort St. John that money is being collected in England for that object.[108]

ADELINE HARMER

Week ending June 15.

Last Sunday evening Mrs. Pickell suddenly arrived in a car to take May back to her boy Cecil who was ill with a pretty high temperature. So off May went at a moment's notice with the minimum of personal effects and the usual instructions "If I don't come back for a day or two, carry on."

In the moment of waiting, Mrs. Pickell mentioned that a dentist had arrived for a week and set up over Finch's store. So as this seemed to open up new possibilities for deliverance from my chronic Banquo, I asked her to make an appointment for me first thing next morning. Later in the evening Guiton and Dick looked in on their way home from Service at the Flats and readily agreed to come out and fetch me in time for the interview.

So on Monday I visited a funny little elderly man called Mr. Buggins in a funny little dark attic, and in a trice he pounced upon another large molar and said "I bet you anything it's this." So out it came soon after, and certainly the root looked black enough to poison an army. I thanked him effusively, and immediately afterwards was carried off by Guiton and Dick to a Church meeting with Mr. Proctor at Pouce Coupé.

Except for the steadily bleeding and pretty sore hole left by Buggins, I thoroughly enjoyed our eighty mile drive and lunch of sardines and biscuits in the bush. At Pouce Coupé we found Miss Price who was to have been my driver in the Van. She had been there five days and had more than another week to wait for her new companion, Miss Pratt, who had distinguished herself by missing the liner in England! Poor Price was so bored that she insisted on accompanying us to the Proctors' and taking a silent part in the long-winded and pretty deadly conference that followed.

Mr. Proctor, whom I now saw out of bed for the first time, seems to be a conscientious, practical, strenuous sort of man. I should think a man's man and good for his job. Mrs. Proctor is a rather pretty, very worried looking little lady, with a little boy of three and a half called David. They live in a nice house but very badly situated about half a mile from the road and quite three miles from Pouce Coupé. This is rather hard on a parson's wife with a baby; because of course he has to be out all over the district most days and many nights, leaving her quite alone with the baby and all the chores—water to fetch from the creek, wood to get in and chop, etc.—no means of getting supplies and no neighbours within reasonable distance. It's rather lonely, I think, and she looks as if it told upon her, but of course people make up their minds to that when they marry a pioneer parson. We had a long discussion of Fort St. John needs and prospects, all rather unsatisfactory because so entirely uncertain.

Apparently the resident priest who had undertaken to come in August for two years at least, has suddenly been prevented by family reasons and *can't come at all.* He was a volunteer, able to pay his own expenses. Now the Bishop has no one else and there is no money! Guiton has written to the Bishop and the Dean (of Montreal) and various friends about the need.[109] But as the railway between Hythe and Edmonton has just been cut by the rains and no trains are running, his letters can't have got out, and *meanwhile* he thinks the Dean has gone off for his holiday to the States. So everything is in hopeless uncertainty once more and we don't know what to say to anybody who cares to ask about the future plans of the Church up here. Mr. Proctor can never get up North of the river. His hands are quite full with the larger and more populous district to the South; and the people here are dead sick of visiting students, carpet-bagging parsons and women! All this we discussed in and out with Mr. Proctor but got very little further than the following entirely provincial plan:

IF an ordained man can be found, suitable and willing to come early next spring, and supported from without for three or five years at least—

Then we believe the people will help to build a little church at Fort St. John and a Church Hall at Baldonnel; and I have undertaken to come back with or without a companion, to work under him.

But if NOT???

Mrs. Proctor gave us supper at which the little boy David did much to change and clear the air by his *stupendous* appetite. He had had a good dinner at 3, and supper at 6; but he insisted on sitting down with us at 7 and eating more than anybody!

The hotel was pretty full, but Guiton and Dick shared a bed, and I shared with Price in the matter-of-course way everybody does out here when hotels are full. You're in luck if you doss down with somebody you've met before! Price is short and plump with red hair and an East Canadian accent (quite different from the West). She talks a great deal and laughs at everything. She is slow-moving but capable and self-confident and immensely good-natured. I think we should have been very happy together in the Van.

Next day we had to hang about and do nothing, because a mail was expected late, and both Mr. Proctor and Mr. Guiton hoped for letters which might throw light on our problems. So Price and I visited a few people we knew in Pouce Coupé, and in the afternoon Mr. Guiton and I paid a Scout and Guide visit to the school, after which I went to see a little Taylor's Flats boy who was in the hospital with an injured leg. In the evening we all trailed off to, what do you think? A whist drive! One of the many thousands got up by the Women's Auxiliary to pay off the debt on Church Halls. This was about eight miles off, at Dawson Creek, a tiny row of shanties which is expected before the end of this year to blow out into the new *railway terminus*. When that happens, Fort St. John will be only sixty miles from the train and we shall be suburban indeed! Luckily it can't come any farther this way on account of the big creeks and the river. The whist drive was rather fun, and only a little sobered for me by the blessed old neuralgia which Buggins seems to have roused to a fresh and fiendish activity. In fact it wiped out both nights for both Price and me so effectively that I weakly agreed to let Guiton take me on to Grande Prairie for an X-ray. This was the third visit and a hideous waste of time and petrol, but he was very determined, and as we were only ninety miles away it did seem a good chance.

The road was good and we reached Grande Prairie at 3 o'clock to find the whole town and both its doctors assembled at the Court House for a rather gruesome murder trial.[110] A prosperous farmer had suddenly disappeared two years ago; and shortly afterwards his son had sold the property and gone right away. *Six months ago* some dogs dug out from the farm manure heap *human bones!* It took six months to find the son, and bring him back for trial. The Court House was packed, so we had to wait outside till it adjourned at 4.30, and then followed Dr. O'Brien back to his office. He readily agreed to an immediate X-ray of my jaw and said it could be done at the hospital at once. But when he cheerfully rang up to warn them we learnt that *they had no films!* So that little journey was all for nothing, and O'Brien had nothing more to suggest; so back we went to Pouce Coupé and got there about 11 P.M.

On Thursday we came back to Fort St. John, a slightly anxious journey because rain had begun again and made the road pretty bad already. At the bottom of one steep hill we found a truck (lorry), buried up to the axles and a very helpless man and wife fluttering round it in the rain. So of course we all turned to and had the usual struggles with boughs and logs and much splashing in deep mud. Then we harnessed our car to the truck and got both engines going and the wheels racing furiously and everyone heaving, until at last when we were all mired from head to foot, the truck gradually emerged like a prehistoric reptile from the swamp. After that we didn't have much trouble apart from violent skidding which caused a few exciting moments on the Peace River Hill. We reached Fort St. John about 4.30; and as Price had discovered a good quarter of Dr. Buggins' tooth still in situ, we went straight to him to give him a chance to finish the good work. This gave more trouble than we had expected. In fact long before he got it out I began to understand why he left it in! However, at last he said there really was *no more;* so we all came back to this house, found May was still away nursing Cecil Pickell, so set to work to cook some eggs for supper.

By that time the rain had developed into torrents, so we pushed off Guiton and Dick as quickly as possible that they might get to their camp if it could be reached, and if not, to the hotel.

I had another beastly night, but put it down this time to Buggins' rather drastic excavations. It pelted all night and on Friday morning the deluge was still going strong. Guiton and Dick had promised to come and fetch me for Scouts and Guides Camp-fire practice. I didn't think they could possibly come so started in good time to walk; but had hardly gone half a mile before the car hove in sight, skidding and tacking from side to side rather like a Medway barge. We got to the school somehow, found only about a dozen children there, and had rather a jolly hour teaching them "Old Folks at Home," "John Peel," "Home Sweet Home," "Poor Old Joe," and a round. Their singing was at first too feeble for words, but before the end it got *almost* hearty.

I implored Guiton and Dick not to attempt to drive me back but they insisted, and sure enough after about a mile we skidded gently into a deep ditch, and climbed out of the car as quickly as possible while it canted over more and more at a fearful angle. Most luckily we were within half a mile of a farm, and owing to the pouring rain the farmer was at home. So within an hour Mr. Ohland and his horses had pulled them out; but long before that I broke away, and came home on my own, to prevent any further nonsense about bringing me back.

I found Price cleaning up the house most gallantly. It was too late to go out again; so when Petter came home (from school), we had a hilarious evening over intelligence tests and guessing games. The result of this was a real proper *nuit blanche,* so apart from house duties I lay low on Saturday morning while the deluge still continued. In the afternoon Mr. Lester, the United Church student, arrived on horseback and stayed for hours. Then Guiton and Dick walked over and arrived for supper *soaking wet.* Lastly, an elderly and very deaf admirer of Petter's arrived; and the little beggar having disgustingly hidden herself, I had to bawl at him for half an hour in an unsuccessful effort at consolation. Finally May came home and reported Cecil Pickell to be convalescent at last, a great relief, as he had had pretty bad pneumonia.

That night the furies got loose in my head and didn't leave off at all. So next morning, Trinity Sunday, May got into a real fuss; and came and sat upon me and said if I really meant to come back and work here, I *must* go Home now and get really well. I think she was really making rather heavy weather, and was inclined to resist. But she pointed out sweetly but remorselessly:

a. That I was no longer wanted for the Van.

b. That Guiton could easily take the Scouts Camp if the weather didn't make it impossible anyway. Also he could as easily take the Sunday Schools until he goes in July.

c. That this stupid little demon had been growing upon me steadily for about ten weeks and having eluded the only doctors and dentists up here, was not likely to retreat of its own accord within the next week or two, in which case I should be no use in the Scout Camp and quite unfit to take the Guides by myself

In other words, she made it clear that just now I am no use at all and had *much better be deported.* I was too weary to argue, so at last, with a good deal of shame and reluctance, agreed, and consented to allow Price to wire to her kind father at Quebec asking him to get me a berth on the first ship I could hope to catch.

After this they kept me in bed all day, where I had only occasional jags from the Foe, but felt the Eminent-Grand-Arch-Super-deluxe-Failure of the World.

June 18.

Since then it has gone on raining almost ceaselessly, and not only has the road become impassable to anything except horses, but we hear that the telegraph wires have been down and three railway bridges swept away since Saturday. So neither mail nor telegrams can come in or out, nor can my deportation take effect for another week at least!

Meanwhile I am being confined to barracks and am recovering with embarrassing rapidity. I've had no pain at all since Monday midnight and slept bang through last night with only one bromide. I do feel such a fraud and am trying hard to get out of the Deportation Compact, and Price and May are holding me to it with a solicitude that seems more sinister than sisterly! Therefore, if all the means of transport recover enough and I don't recover too much, Mr. Guiton will try to get us both out on Thursday, 26th, dropping Price at Pouce Coupé to join Pratt (who is at present stuck at Edmonton and quite cut off from us), and taking me on to Hythe. If the bridges are mended and the train running, and we don't stick in a mud-hole on the road and miss it, I ought to reach Edmonton on the 18th and Montreal about July 2. After that of course all this very provisional certainty fades away, as we hear that sardine tins are *nothing* to liners at this time of year. Nevertheless, if it has to be by flying or swimming the Bad Penny will get back somehow.

June 21.
Codicil to be read first.

Since writing the enclosed, everything has altered; and I am not after all starting Home for another month at least!

You see, first of all the rain has continued almost without a break for ten days; and the road is so destroyed that nobody can get away from here for another week at least.

And secondly, I have entirely and completely and finally recovered.

I have left the last page or two in the letter, although they are out of date, because I don't quite know where to cut them off.

But don't forget that's all ancient history and from henceforth

There will be no more moaning at the bar.

I must obviously wait another month or six weeks and try to run the promised Camps, if and when the weather ever makes it possible.

The Guides are very keen about it and I can't disappoint them without reason, although it will certainly have to wait till nearly the end of July.

Another great reason is that within the next few weeks Mr. Guiton hopes to have an interview which will settle more or less definitely whether or not there will be a resident parson here in the future.

Upon that, of course, depend all my little plans. So I shall hope to know before coming Home whether to travel light and leave most of my junk up here for future use or whether to bring away every blessed thing and go on the dole once more.

Diary of a Sort to June 29.

I can't write a decent diary just now because since the rain everything has been so held up that even the days seem to have been washed into each other with no clear outlines and nothing to record.

You remember we brought up Price from Pouce Coupé last Thursday week. She is to drive the Caravan with the unknown Miss Pratt, who missed her ship and has not arrived so far—in fact could not arrive for nearly another week. Therefore Guiton and I persuaded Price to come back with us in order to study the road and hills she would have to drive over, and Guiton undertook to get her back to Pouce Coupé on the following Tuesday. Unluckily, the new rain-spell began that very day (June 12), as we were returning.

This is the *25th* and she hasn't been able to get back yet. They had hoped to go to-morrow, but a fresh downpour last night makes it most unlikely. Besides the total collapse of the road, three railway bridges were washed away and the telegraph line broken down, so for over a week all communication with the outside world was cut. It actually took Mr. Guiton seven or eight days to get a telegram through to Edmonton!

Poor Price was in a great stew about Pratt, who was first held up at Edmonton by the railway collapse; then at Hythe by the road collapse; and now we imagine she has got to Pouce Coupé, but know nothing for certain!

My bad week-end followed, and unluckily included Trinity Sunday, though as Guiton was prevented by the state of the road from going out to take Service at the Montney, he was glad to take Sunday School for me instead, so that was all to the good, really. On Tuesday (Barnabas), I recovered so suddenly and completely that no one would believe it. And May, who had decided on Sunday that I was fit for nothing but immediate deportation, was naturally disgusted. In fact, if the road had been open, she would have shipped me off that very week, and Price actually telegraphed to her father at Quebec to try and get a passage. But her telegram suffered the fate of all the rest.

So from Tuesday to Friday I lived a life of absurd convalescence—
perfectly well but not allowed to do anything except pack. While all the
time it went on raining, and the thought of Home got more and more
thrilling, and the certainty grew clearer and clearer that I had no right to
go.

On Friday I told May, and then had a long interview with Mr. Guiton,
reviving the little Camp plans which had been allowed to lapse. We
agreed that if the weather should recover and at least twelve boys able to
come, he should take them (somewhere as yet unsettled), before the
middle of July when he has to go. And I should go too, to mother the
little ones, because most of them will be under twelve. Then I called a
meeting of the Guides for yesterday (Tuesday), to find out whether they
still wanted a Camp also. And as it seems they do, we agreed to prepare
for one in the third or fourth week in July. Then I went to Mrs. Millar
and arranged to move over and stay with her for a week or two, partly to
be in the middle of things for making arrangements and partly to give
May a rest. She has had boarders and visitors and patients sprawling over
her for nine months without a break, and I suspect she would like her
house to herself for a bit. Petter's term is just finishing and she goes back
to Vancouver, and will probably leave with Price at the first
opportunity. So May really will soon be able to sing

"Peace, Perfect Peace, with Loved Ones Far Away. . ."
—though maybe she'd sing it with more confidence if I were a little
farther!

As a matter of fact last week-end was a bad one for her, as the continued
damp or something brought on a ferocious attack of sciatica, and for
three or four days she lay in acute pain, compared to which mine had
been a pleasant Sunday afternoon.

On Sunday it actually cleared up and was *boiling* hot. Guiton and
Dick walked over to Baldonnel for the afternoon Service and I walked
over to join them there. It was to have been a lantern service, but the road
being impassable for anything but feet, we *might* have carried the
lantern slides, but couldn't make any light without the car battery. So
that had to be postponed and we had Evensong instead, with ten
children, nine grown-ups and a baby—not so bad, considering.
Afterwards Mr. Simpson only stayed for the Holy Communion, when
we prayed especially for the future work of the Church up here. Then
Mr. Guiton trudged on through another three miles of appalling gluey
mire to hold an Evening Service at the Flats. I longed to go too, but
simply didn't dare, for dread of the mingled fury and triumph which a
new collapse would arouse in everybody, but especially May. I am going
to be absurdly cautious for the next week or so, because the slightest new
twinge that got known about would be more than my life was worth!

Mr. Guiton had, of course, no lantern, and no harmonium, and expected no congregation, so you can imagine his amazement when thirty-five people turned up at the Flats! They quite crowded out the school, and most of them had to stand. Nobody has ever had such a multitude up here, and we don't suppose it will ever happen again.

Little Mr. Simpson is awfully keen to carry on in the future *whether a parson comes or not*. He says he and his friends will haul the logs and build a Church Hall in Baldonnel for Church and Sunday School on Sundays and general community purposes in the week, and if I come back he and his sons will haul the logs for *my* house and do most of the building for me! It's very touching of him to be so keen, but I think he is far too optimistic about his neighbours' co-operation, and am not at all sure really of the practicability of carrying on next year if no parson comes.

We are now full in the mosquito season, and in spite of the rain they are in great form. Everybody walking along the road has a little halo of them singing round his head, and especially if you stand still, they settle upon you by the dozen. Of course the house is wired, but even so they queue up outside the door and pour through every time it is opened. Last night May killed thirty-six indoors before going to bed, and I wrestled with nine in bed between 4 and 5.30 yesterday morning. To be quite honest, although fearfully annoying, I don't think their bite is nearly so virulent and poisonous as those in Egypt or Palestine. *But if I say that here,* although nobody present has been to the Near East, they all burst into such a storm of patriotic resentment that you'd think I had offered Canada a mortal insult!!

On Monday it was still fine and very hot (two whole days), luckily because it was Petter's little break-up party for the Baldonnel school-children. She asked me to help, so I walked over with Mrs. Birley, and from 1.30 to 5.30 the fun was fast and furious. Petter organised the individual and I the team races, and they were all great fun. About seven mothers came besides Mr. Simpson, Mr. Guiton and Dick. We made a sort of Camp-fire and damped it down with weeds and grass to smoke away the mosquitoes. Then we all sat round in a Horseshoe and ate cakes and ice-cream provided by the mothers. It was a very sweet little party and made me long for Camp. At the end I taught them "Are You Sleeping, Brother John?" and they sang it with moderate success.

Yesterday (Tuesday), was cloudy and tempestuous again, but the road seemed to be drying well, so Price's hopes for departure on Thursday rose high, and Mr. Guiton promises to take Petter too.

I had a Guide Meeting to make preliminary plans for Camp, and also started to find out how many boys could come. It's all very difficult and tentative—first because of the ghastly weather, and then because many fathers need, or *say* they need, their sons to work for them all the holidays; thirdly, because at this time of year nobody has any money. They all offer food instead; but when you ask *what* food? they become very vague, because there is no meat except bacon, eggs are getting scarce and all vegetables have been ruined by the rain! If we ever do pull it off (which is still doubtful), I think we shall live on a sort of offertory of loaves and bits of bacon, all collected and taken out at the start. We haven't even chosen a site yet. There are two suggested—one at Charlie Lake, and one by the Peace River—but so far it has been quite impossible to go and see either.

On Tuesday evening after supper Guiton and I explored through the bush down to the top of the river bank. It was awfully rough and swampy, up to the knees in places, but the view from the edge is very fine, an 800 foot steep slope down to the river, and then it winds in great curves between high hills covered with bush. Right below us about three miles to the West was a tiny group of derelict buildings. That is the old Hudson Bay trading post—first built in 1805 and called Fort St. John. It is that little tumbledown house with a barn or two that is named so absurdly large on all the maps of Canada, because it is the oldest named settlement in British Columbia.

On the way back we heard heavy crashing through the trees and bush and presently came upon fresh foot-prints of moose, both large and small, apparently a moose mother and baby—but we never caught up with them. On the other hand we found two complete moose skeletons.

On Tuesday night, being the end of Midsummer Day, the glass fell to one degree above freezing, and it snowed heavily. But I must say the snow soon melted, and on Wednesday morning it was raining hard again. Everybody says this is by far the worst summer since one year at the beginning of the War (when only about two people were here). I'm sure I hope so, for up to the present as you would say it has been *literally* "a Wash Out." Amongst other misfortunes, May had thirty-six young chickens and several baby turkeys *drowned* by the rain.

On Thursday, in spite of some fresh rain (written 29th), Guiton and Dick set off with Price and Petter to try and get to Pouce Coupé. We had heard nothing yet and Guiton has not come back, but we presume they got through all right and he is staying a day or two.

I don't think May really wanted me to come away, but it will give her a rest to be quite alone for a bit. I shall probably go back in a week to prepare our revised plan of two modest little Camps in succession on Mr. Birley's land. Yesterday morning we had a violent thunderstorm followed by heavy rain till about three, when a boiling heat succeeded. Coronach having still run away, and the road being impossible for a car I packed the rucksack and two other little sacks and had a proper sweltering walk. The mud was so deep and sticky that it kept oozing in over the tops of my long rubber boots and several times very nearly pulled them off. Other parts of the trail had turned into knee-deep swamps with lots of submerged logs and tree-stumps to add to the fun; and a devoted little horde of attendant mosquitoes followed all the way. It was only five and a half miles, and it took me two and a half hours; wasn't that absurd? I shall never dare tell May, who regards me as the arch-snail of the world as it is!

Sunday School today was badly attended. I'm afraid school holidays are bound to have a demoralising effect. But I hope to have one more next Sunday and after that to concentrate on the handful of boys and girls in Camp for the rest of the time. Meanwhile Mr. Guiton hopes to pull off an epoch-making interview with some important friend whom he is to meet at Hythe next week. That is supposed to decide whether all this is to be just a flash in the pan, or a prelude to some real Church life. So before I leave here—with luck about July 25—I hope to know whether it's for a few months only or perhaps for ever.

Fort St. John
July 11.

I can't make this a diary because the last fortnight is entirely dominated by the terrible trouble which has come upon us near the end of it and wiped out all possible interest in what went before.

Last Tuesday, the day after I went to Camp with Mr. Ritchie and ten Scouts, May and Mr. Birley went out in her car to Pouce Coupé to finish the grave of a brother who died here about two years ago. They had planned the expedition for weeks and been held up by the weather until this week, which is glorious. I thought very little about them and was quite absorbed in the excitement of the Camp which was going splendidly, when the blow fell upon us. About 9 on Wednesday evening, we had just finished supper when Cecil Anderson appeared (husband of Mabel Anderson, the school-teacher, who was with me as female companion). He told us that a telegram had come to say that a fearful accident had happened to the car, and May was lying at Pouce Coupé between life and death. Apparently through some error of judgment, in a narrow place they had just backed too near the edge of a steep bank and slipped over, the car rolling 100 feet down and turning completely over three times. Mr. Birley was miraculously unhurt. But May was crushed under the collapsed car, most, if not all, of her ribs broken, and no one knows the extent of internal injury because she is too completely broken, bruised and swollen to be touched, and too dangerously ill for chloroform. It's all especially dreadful because she has had two previous bad accidents—one a fall from a horse which paralysed her for three months, and the other an overturned car which injured her back a second time—ever since which she has been very nervous of cars and only gone out with people she trusted, like Tommy and Mr. Birley. And another dreadful thing is that Tommy saw it happen and both he and Mr. Birley are distracted with grief—Mr. Birley because he was driving, Tommy because he had just overhauled the car and thinks he *might* have made the brakes tighter. It all happened sixty miles away of course, but Tommy had to rush back for something to Fort St. John yesterday and he came in to tell me about it.

He says she is conscious, and in terrible pain, can just speak in a whisper and asked him to tell me. For three days and nights now there has been no change. She is not seeing anyone except Tommy and Mr. Birley and there is nothing to do but wait.

I left the Camp with Mr. Ritchie for two nights and went to see Mrs. Birley and settled the Andersons into May's house to take care of poor Rowdy and the cats and chickens. It all looked so pathetic because the summer has come at last and the garden (the only one anywhere up here), is full of poppies and pansies and sweet williams. The country also is beautiful at last, covered with wild roses, wild lupins and honeysuckle and all the things that May used to tell me about, to prove it was really nice. I longed to stay in the house and at [least] do that much for her. But the Andersons can do it every bit as well, and it was obviously my job to go on with the Camps. So I came back here to the little boys, who go home tomorrow, when the Guides come and stay till next Thursday. It has been a terribly amateurish, but I think very happy little Camp, at least for the boys, and they have been wonderfully good. But, of course, the bottom is knocked out of both of them for me, and all I'm aware of is nine miles of rough road from the nearest telegraph office, and no other way of learning from day to day whether she is alive or dead. Possibly you think I needn't have carried on the Camps. Of course I wouldn't if she wanted me, but the one thing she would hate would be for me to disappoint the children.

I am awfully perplexed, too, about going Home. As things are at present, I must leave Hythe on the 25th, i.e., today fortnight, and up to Tuesday evening I thought of nothing but that! But now the bottom seems knocked out of that too—not of coming Home of course, but the date. It seems so miserable to leave just when she may be beginning to creep back to life. And yet the passage is booked and I have already changed twice, and of course May won't need me. Still, I can't bear to go away before she is safely round the corner.

Sunday. Last night one of the fathers [Mr. Neilson] who brought three Guides from Taylor's Flats said the latest telegram said "General improvement." He is telegraph operator down there, so it's sure to be official, and not just one of the many rumours, so I am more thankful than I can say, and feel almost light-hearted again. This sounds as if she must be going to live anyway, and only leaves anxiety about her back. In any case recovery must be fearfully slow, and I do wonder when she will be able to stand the journey home. It's a pretty racketty road at the best of times.

I think she would be so *mad* with me if I postponed my departure again, that I hardly dare do it. But [I] shall try instead, if I can possibly get through with striking Camp and getting everyone and everything home on Thursday, and doing all my packing too, and one or two unavoidable farewells, and go straight to Pouce Coupé on either Friday or Saturday next (18th and 19th), and stay in the hotel there till the Thursday following (24th), when I am obliged to go on to the train if I stick to the shop on August 1st. By that means I shall get four or five days near May and see how she is really getting on. Luckily she has a sister[111] who is at present visiting in England but presumably Mr. Birley has sent for her and she ought to be here in about a fortnight.

The boys' Camp was dreadfully amateurish but happy, I think, and the boys though terribly *dull* compared to little Cockney boys were wonderfully good and sweet.

Only seven girls could come after all, which is very disappointing and they are a dull lot too, compared with English Guides. I don't know why but it seems to come out more in Camp. Also they are very lazy and unimaginative about Camp duties and have to be shown and kept up to every blessed thing. And of course they don't know a single song to sing at Camp-fire or a hymn at Prayers except the one or two we have learned at Sunday School. So altogether it's a heavy little Camp. But more likely it's all my fault because I'm worried and anxious. It's a perfectly lovely place and ideal for camping, except for swarms of mosquitoes, and marauding hordes of sheep who break into the tents whenever our backs are turned and devour everything they can find—shoes, books, salt, bread. We have had to build a high platform between trees for our stores, and the next thing we expect is that the sheep will climb the trees. There's an old ram who joins us for every meal and Prayers and everything else. And if for a moment we fail in civility to him, he just backs a few steps and *charges!* It's boiling, blazing hot now, and the children don't want to do anything but bathe. I have to ration them strictly to three times a day, and keep an iron control of their manoeuvres.

Now I must stop and ride nine miles each way to post this, rather a bore being quite so far from anything—bread, stores, post, etc., especially as the sheep ate all our bread last night.

Pouce Coupé
July 21, 1930.

Before we went to Camp I wrote to the kind Archdeacon at Edmonton and he booked my passage and everything else for August 1st. It was terribly exciting and very hard to really think of anything else. However I had a busy week preparing for the two little Camps—busy because the necessary lack of communications makes any sort of organisation, however slight, very laborious. When there's no such thing as daily post or delivered telegrams, let alone telephones, every sort of message has to be taken by yourself on a borrowed horse if you want to make sure of its arrival. Transport is the same. It's such a job to get anything or anybody anywhere, and you find yourself longing for a bus or a carrier or *anything* that regularly goes anywhere, instead of endlessly trying to wheedle help from trucks and waggons and never being sure of anything. Equipment is the same. No one has anything to *spare*. It took days of visiting to find and borrow three or four leaky tents—chiefly without poles or pegs—and as for spare pots or pans, bowls or spades, buckets or axes, there seems to be a world-shortage of them all!

On Saturday evening I heard of a truck kept by a young Scandinavian who *might* take boys and all to Charlie Lake for nothing. He lived fourteen miles East and no one quite knew where, so I had a longish ride and rather a job to find him, but to my joy he agreed, so the problem of boys and tents was solved at the last moment.

That Sunday (July 6), was Mr. Guiton's final appearance. He came back from Grande Prairie the night before bringing Mr. Naylor[112]—another Big Bug from Montreal—and together they announced the good news that *Montreal is going to father Fort St. John.* The Bishop agrees, and they propose to put in a layman for the winter and a priest next spring, and also to put up two church buildings. On Sunday we had two nice little Services, the second one at Baldonnel being the long-deferred Lantern Service. Afterwards Guiton and Co. went on to Taylor's Flats and I went home to make final preparations for next morning.

Monday was cloudy and cold, a typical bad start, also two boys failed to turn up (whether from panic or parents I don't know), so we were reduced to ten besides Mr. Ritchie and Mrs. Anderson who came to keep me company. We camped in a rough pasture belonging to a farmer called S[owden][113] living on the East bank of Charlie Lake and about nine miles North West of Fort St. John. It certainly was a lovely place, a big field sloping in big terraces down to the lake, and surrounded on all sides by bush. So there was heaps of wood and water lying to hand. I won't tell you all the details of Camp, they are so dull; but everything worked out perfectly except for the continual raid of sheep, pigs and calves upon our stores. These domestic animals were more trying and determined than any moose or bears could be. They three times raided and once utterly destroyed the store tent and ate all our salt, bread, cookies, bacon and beans, besides mucking up almost everything else.

The only other drawback was dead bodies. A sheep died in the bush close to us, and as the weather was boiling hot, I had to collect a few picked heroes and burn it very quickly. Then we found a body of a horse calmly left in the bush by the Sowdens who seem to have no idea of burying anything. He was too deep in the bush to burn and too far gone to pull out, so Ritchie and I had to rush in and bury him as well as we could with one spade with a broken handle.

The lake was perfect for bathing, very shallow for a long distance out, There was not a *single* water tight boat upon it though it's ten miles long and two or three wide. Doesn't that seem extraordinary? But then, of course, there are only two or three farms. However, the boys collected big logs and made a fine rough raft upon which we all cruised blissfully round the shores of the lake, but I refused to let them push out into the middle. The boys were really *wonderfully* good and no trouble at all. Indeed it seems to me that they are much more and not less obedient than English boys. Of course they were rather lazy over Camp duties; but that is partly because they work so hard at home doing much the same sort of chores, hauling water and chopping wood and washing dishes, that these occupations have not the same thrill for them that they have for most English children.

At Camp-fire that night I told the boys about May, who has been ripping to all of them, and asked them to pray for her, which we did every night and morning while the Camp lasted. On Saturday the girls came and brought the news of "Distinct improvement" which was wonderful after the suspense.

Then the boys departed and I carried on with the Guides for another five days, which seemed rather like five weeks. I couldn't help still worrying about May, and getting a sort of pent up exasperation at their indifference and an open exasperation at their table manners! However, it was quite happy really, and I think they all enjoyed it, especially bathing two or three times a day. It was blazing hot all the time and that made them rather lethargic, especially as the only weak point in our otherwise ideal camping ground was shade!

On Thursday we had a huge clear-up and then had to wait about all day for two fathers to come with cars and take the children home. I got back finally about 8 P.M. pretty tired and blacker than Hell's mouth.

There was no more news of May, but next morning a letter came up from Mr. Birley saying [she was] out of danger at last but [had] five fractures and great weakness still. Also a letter came from Hasell asking me to join Price after all in September for the Montney and Hudson Hope. This was pretty disturbing as my passage was already booked by Archdeacon Burgett and I was especially keen to get back before Ritchie left. Still, I had previously offered to do this for Hasell, that is, after she had fired me from the main Van job; and for that and various reasons I didn't want to back out now.

However, September was so far ahead, and the other jobs so much at an end for the present that I determined to go out to Pouce Coupé packed for final departure, and find out there whether by staying I could help May or not. So I spent all Friday riding round and finishing up in Fort St. John and saying good-bye to people in Baldonnel. Mrs. Birley lent me a delightful mare I hadn't ridden before, called Lady, and we had a splendid day—except when I attempted a short cut to Baldonnel and nearly foundered Lady in two most ghastly swamps! She was terrified, poor dear, and I had to dismount and drag her through the worst of it, both of us sinking over our knees in horrid sucking black mud. I had hoped to get off to Pouce Coupé on Saturday but could get no transport. Then Tommy said he would take me on Sunday morning and Mrs. Birley said she would come too.

So on Saturday I had one more splendid ride on Lady—this time with Freddy, Mrs. Birley's brother, down to the original old Fort St. John, the Hudson Bay Post on the river—to see her father and mother. Mr. Beaton[114] had lived there forty years and is by far the oldest inhabitant of the country. He was the original Hudson Bay Factor [*sic*], who came to trade with the Indians of whom there were thousands here in those days. He married one too, and old Mrs. Beaton, although married to a Scotchman for forty years and the mother of nine sons and two daughters, can still only speak Cree Indian. Freddy took me down what is called the "Short Cut" to their home. It certainly is only about four miles instead of eight but as it is nearly all a trackless route down a hill like the side of a house, you have to dismount and drag the horse nearly all the way, and he alternately dragging back with fear or threatening to fall upon you on account of inadequate brakes. At the lower part the bush was so dense that it was just like impenetrable jungle, so that I had to shut my eyes and duck my head and blindly trust to Lady following Freddy.

You would love Freddy's appearance. He is twenty-one and a

halfbreed of course, but a very fair one. Only he speaks broken English like Mrs. Birley and all the Beatons because they were brought up by old Beaton as almost pure Indians in order to keep the Indian trade!

He wears fur riding chaps on his legs (which must be terribly hot but look delightful), a little moose-hide coat covered with bright coloured bead-work, and a gaudy pink and red silk handkerchief round his neck. But the crowning feature is his hat-band. Round the usual immense cowboy hat runs a blue silk ribbon bearing in large white letters this pathetic appeal: "Single, Willing to be Married." Hatbands like these are the latest fashion among the smart young men of Fort St. John, and Freddy is a typical Peace River fop.

The old fort is a little group of derelict trading buildings right down by the river, in a remote and lovely bit of country once thickly peopled with Indians (up to this century), but now entirely deserted except by the Beaton family—all overgrown with dense bush and inhabited only by moose and deer. But just now every vacant corner is aflame with brilliant wild flowers, especially wild roses, big blue hare-bells, wild delphinium, and a tall bright salmon and rose flower called Indian paintbrush. Of course all the country is full of them now, but none so full as this remote, deserted corner, which was the centre of life here in the days when there was no road and no farming, but only Indians and fur traders, and the river the only highway.

We had dinner with the Beatons, eggs and bacon as usual at this time of year. Mr. Beaton is very attractive with a strong Scotch accent and an old-country dignity rather wonderful considering that he has been out here far longer than anybody else. But then, you see, he has lived entirely alone with his own family or among Indians, so is not the least Canadianized, still less Americanized as are so many of the new-comers.

He told me there were no white men but thousands of Indians all round Fort St. John until about twenty years ago. Then came one or two more white traders and trappers, and then measles and scarlet fever which wiped out whole tribes of Indians. He tried to help them but it was no good. Directly they caught the disease they crawled out of their teepees, drank the cold water of the river and crawled back and died. They were too frightened to bury each other, so all that was done by him. In a few years the survivors had dwindled to a few hundreds and retreated further and further North, till now there are very few pure Indians within fifty miles, though there are numbers of halfbreeds.

But the real object of my visit was Mrs. Beaton because she, poor dear, has had for *two years* on and off, exactly the same facial neuralgia that I had for three *months* and made so much fuss about. Mrs. Birley had told her about me, and she was thrilled at the prospect of meeting a fellow-sufferer. So I'm afraid my obviously complete recovery and rude health were rather a disappointment to the poor old lady, and it was difficult to soften the blow. However, we compared symptoms at some length (poor Mr. Beaton and Freddy having to act as interpreters as Mrs. Beaton only talks Cree), and although she owned that the pain had gone away for the time being, she insisted that it would come back with the first cold wind, and added with grim satisfaction, "So will yours!"

I admired all her treasures in the stupid blatant way you have to with people whose language you can't talk; and when we came away she offered to make me a pair of beaded mocassins if I would send her a pair of *strong flat candlesticks*. I said "One for each foot," and she thought that the joke of the century. So we ended well.

We came home by the waggon road—eight miles instead of four. But the day was so boiling that I was quite satisfied with towing Lady for three miles down a precipitous path and not the least anxious to haul her up again. So we came back by an easier road, and at last I began to realize the beauty of the country, anyway at this time of year. The great steep hills rolling down to the river, the ever widening distances as we climbed them, the unturned fresh green everywhere and the millions of roses and paintbrush, bluebells and larkspur making every open space a sort of cloud of pink and blue above the green. It really was lovely. Even the stupid little poplars looked bright and jolly and the tall dark spruce trees made a splendid contrast, standing like the solemn cypresses in an old landscape painting. But the finest thing of all was the sky. It always is up here. Partly because we are on a 2200 foot plateau, it seems so vast, partly because it is crystal clear, and the endlessly changing clouds are so sharply and beautifully outlined that they seem to be painted by some wonderful Old Master. Anyway, I was beginning to fall in love with the country and it was funny not to know whether or not I was really leaving it next day. But anyhow I was glad to be coming back next year.

Meanwhile, Freddy gossiped on about broncho-riding which is his passion, and told me various wonderful exploits with buck-jumpers, and of the prizes he had won at several annual Stampedes; also about his winter trapping farther North with his brother—a horrible pursuit, I think, but a strange, hard, utterly lonely sort of life.

I packed in a frenzied way all the evening, sorting all my endless possessions into three categories:

     a. Book-box, hold-all and big trunk to stay in May's garage.

     b. Small trunk for England.

     c. Suite-case for Pouce Coupé and the railway journey.

I packed like this in stubborn obstinacy, but not in confident excitement, because I knew that everything must depend on May's real condition and prospects. If she really needed me I must stay and also agree to work for Hasell in September, so as to give a reasonable colour to the staying, in May's eyes.

Plates 1 and 2. The portrait on the left was made before Monica Storrs left England. On the right is an early photograph of her in the North Peace. On the back she has written: *"Is it grisly bear or Eskimo—/ or only apostolic Mo?/With shrinking form and face of woe/Alone amid the parky snow/at 25 or more below?"*

Plate 3. Fort St. John, c. 1928. The photograph looks down Main Street, showing Finch's store, the Dinner Plate Cafe, Titus rooming house, and Bowes and Herron Garage.

Plate 4. May Birley during World War I when she served in France and was decorated with the *Croix de Guerre*.

Plate 5. Kenneth Birley at Fort Vermilion in 1912. At that time he worked for Revillon Frères.

Plate 6. Douglas and Frank Birley, the two eldest of Kenneth and Mary Birley's three sons.

Plate 7. The interior of May Birley's house.

Plate 8. Pouce Coupe, c. 1935. When Monica first saw it she described it as "a cross between a soldiers' permanent camp during the War, and a home for lost bathing machines." This photograph apparently has been made from two others.

Plate 9. The rally held at May Birley's on 3 May 1930. The grand total of forty-four "was the largest Muster there has ever been up here; and with the exception of four girls and two boys, included every available youth and maiden between ten and sixteen years old, within a radius of about twenty miles." Only the Fort St. John guides had complete uniforms.

Plate 10. Four children off to Taylor School.

Plate 11. Brother Wolf on Charlie Lake, the site of the camps.

Plate 12. Letitia Petter, back row left, with her students at Baldonnel in 1932.

Plate 13. Scout troop raising the flag at camp. Included are Bert LeClerc, Doug Birley, Neil Kirkpatrick, Frank Birley, Austin Hadland, Joe Brooks, Ernie Brooks, Jim Ogilvie, Owen Pickell, Cecil Pickell.

Plate 15. *Back row*: Father Luc Beuglet, O.M.I., who arrived in Fort St. John shortly after Monica in 1929, and Billy Cooper. *Front*: Doreen Cooper, Dolores and Richard Soman, Lawrence Lohman.

Plate 14. Donella Chiulli and Lucy Lohman in 1930.

Plate 16. A Brownie Enrolment at Fish Creek in 1932. Monica Storrs is in the back row, left, with Lillian Taylor and Miss Hasell. The Brownies, left to right, are Hilda Large, May Taylor, Alene Darnall, Margaret Middleton, and Betty Darnall.

Plate 17. Lawrence and Dave Chiulli with Lawrence's furs in front of the Chiulli home.

Plate 18. Anton Framst getting in the hay in 1930.

Plate 19. Eden Robinson with the first tractor on Bear Flat.

Plate 20. Providence Hospital, Fort St. John, opened in September, 1931.

Plate 21. Hudson's Hope, 1929.

Plate 22. Logs being hauled to build the Church Hall barn at Baldonnel.

Plate 23. Ferry crossing the Peace at Taylor Flat.

Plate 24. George and Lila Maginnis and their four-month old daughter, Dorothy, camping in the Spring of 1930. They had a cabin built by fall.

Plate 25. St. Martin's Church, Fort St. John.

Plate 26. Monica making her district visits.

Plate 27. Church Hall at Baldonnel.

Plate 28. Roy Cuthbert and Tony Flatt, at the time when Tony first came to live at the Abbey.

Plate 29. Adeline Harmer, Monica's friend from Rochester who came to join her as her first "Companion of the Peace."

Plate 30. Monica Storrs outside her home, "The Abbey."

On Sunday morning Tommy brought Mrs. Birley and me and the three little boys to Pouce Coupé, she to see May for the first time, the children to go to some special picnic given by the Elks, and I to be guided by circumstances.

Mr. Birley brought me straight to the hospital and asked me if I would read to May as much as possible, and, When must I go? I said I needn't go at all if I could help them, and he said "Sure. You can help."

Directly I saw May it all seemed to be settled. She is out of danger but unable to move an inch and helpless even to use her hands, and in more or less continual pain. Mr. Birley has got her a special night nurse, and himself been with her the whole of every day feeding her through a tube. Now he has gone home for a day or two to attend to the farm, and I am left in charge. There is not much to do but feed her and read to her, readjust the pillows and knock flies and mosquitoes off her face.

The hospital is very tiny and fearfully noisy, being full of newborn babies and pervaded by a terrible jazz gramophone. It's very expensive too, like all hospitals out here, so May is pining to escape from it somehow and get back home. This *may* be possible by the end of next week, but of course she will not be able to look after herself for some weeks after that. So what was there but to throw in my lot with them and help all I can, first here and then back at Fort St. John, till the end of August? I don't think anyone could do anything else, do you?

Pouce Coupé
Extracts from letter written July 28, 1930.

I am thrilled about the Knight's Place meeting;[115] how amazing to find £50 like that. But do you really think the rest will be forthcoming too? It seems almost too much to expect, but it would be lovely if Rochester should really father that little Church Hall. Baldonnel is the centre nearest us. It has only a school, a post-office, and a little store just opened. But the land is settled up pretty well all round, and there is quite a little group of Anglicans. The hall would have to be available for ordinary social purposes in the week, but the East end would be partitioned off as a tiny permanent sanctuary, and opened on Sundays. We have already agreed on the site—a little bit of uncleared land at the one cross-road in the middle of the district—the place where I had that Guide meeting and enrolment in the snow.

Mr. Simpson has also produced some logs for my house and is prepared to build it at any time. But I simply can't take that final plunge till I come back in the spring.

There's no diary to send you because there is simply *nothing* to record since I wrote last Monday. I am living at the hotel here, which is luckily as nice as possible, and kept by the nicest old couple, Mr. and Mrs. Hart. They are so kind and hospitable that you really feel like honoured guests although you have to pay through the nose for the privilege.

The rest of Pouce Coupé is dreary enough. It's the capital of the Peace River Block and therefore *very* important, with a population getting on for 200 and about forty queer little wooden buildings, chiefly garages, cafes and Government offices. The best part is the view from this hotel which is really charming. It stands on a high natural terrace and looks across the little valley of the Pouce Coupé River to a wider valley between two ridges of thickly wooded, low hills, which approach each other just on the horizon and seem to make a broad gateway out into the real world.

The hospital is only about five minutes walk away. It has a little men's ward, a little women's ward and a tiny private ward where May is. She is distinctly better, and can now lie more comfortably and lift her left hand to her face and even read to herself. So I just sit with her for half or most of the day, as she feels inclined, help with the feeding and pillows and other odd jobs too small to require a nurse. Between times I have meals at the hotel and talk to the queer people who drift in and out, walk a bit and read a bit and write a bit—a terribly desultory life. My greatest treat is to listen to the gramophone of a funny kind little man called Mr. F.[116] He is a clerk in the Government office, and has a tiny house *entirely full of gramophone records*. And the wonderful thing is that they are practically all classical and beautifully chosen. Practically all day he is at work, but the house is open and he has given me a standing invitation to go in and play the gramophone at any time—so you bet I do, about twice a day.

On Saturday night the Sunday School Caravan came in from serving the district round Swan Lake. It contained Miss Price, the driver from Quebec, and a dear little Miss Hope Littlewood, who was put in by Hasell instead of me. But being a school teacher, it has *just* transpired that she must go back to her school at the end of August. I mean to try and put my back into it when the time comes and make up all I can for an ineffective winter and a very slack summer. I shall probably have just a fortnight more in Fort St. John before Price joins me on August 29th and I shall spend that time partly in doing what I can for May, partly in clearing up a few of the innumerable odd ends I have left there, and partly in preparing for the last lap. We shall try to have three final Sunday Schools or Services in Fort St. John district on the 31st, and start off together on September 1. Do please pray for that last lap, that Price and I may work well together, and be able to do some real service for our Lord.

You would be amused at some of the people in this hotel. There is such a blissful equality between all parties concerned. The waitress for instance, a pretty young woman called Mar*ie*, said to me yesterday when I came in for supper, "Hello, Honey, you eating again? You'll be getting too fat!!" And the call-boy, a tall solemn looking young man with a son of five, gave me another surprise. I had written on the calling card 7 o'clock, but yesterday didn't come down to breakfast till 8.30. So later in the morning, Charlie, who was dusting the hotel lounge, stopped and said: "Miss Storrs, I'm sure mad with you. What's the good of me calling you at 7 if you don't get up?"!!

Don't imagine this is rude. It's just friendly!

Pouce Coupé
Extract from letter written August 3.

The doctor says May may try to sit up for a few minutes next Tuesday—that will be exactly four weeks from the accident—and hope to go home in about a fortnight, i.e., somewhere round August 16. Mr. Birley came again yesterday and stayed till this afternoon, and he says he will try to come one day next week to see how May sits up. Luckily the Sunday School Van is careering round here just now, and keeps putting into port at Pouce Coupé; luckily, because Price is a great favourite with May and makes an occasional change of companion. I find I am terribly dull just now, because you see, we have talked over most anterior subjects long ago, I am doing nothing, *nothing* happens in Pouce Coupé, and we get hardly any news of the outside world!!!

One morning I had a rather nice little walk through the bush. It's hilly and rather beautiful round here, and the close bush is so dense that once off the road you can hardly shove along at all, and can only see the way by getting up as high as possible. But I must say the wild flowers are heavenly. They are all big and showy, and make the fields and open bush seem almost like herbaceous borders with wild roses, larkspur, willow-herb, golden-rod, Indian paintbrush, wild sage, Michaelmas daisies and enormous purple thistles.

The elections[117] caused a mild excitement last Monday, but terribly tame after the delightful tortures we used to work ourselves up to at Home. I had no vote because I have been only ten months and not twelve in the country, but was rather glad because I can see no difference between the parties whatever.

Today we had such an awfully nice Service—Matins and Celebration. It was in the perfectly frightful Community Hall, left very dirty from the

last dance, and there was nothing on the Table but a white cloth and a
flagon of wine and the cup. But there were more than a dozen people, all
grown up and all apparently Anglican (except one Presbyterian I had in
tow), and they all really joined in the Service and sang capitally too. And
we were actually ten Communicants, by far the biggest number I have
seen since I came, and the whole Service seemed wonderful. Mr. Proctor
is a really nice, reverent, earnest man, who works tremendously hard,
and seems to get on well with the people.

Afterwards I wondered rather anxiously what my little Presbyterian
would say, and half waited for the usual criticisms about "formality"
and "impossible to understand." So you can imagine my joy when she
said, "I really believe I should get to like your Service best. It gives the
people such a big share in the worship and prayers and there is no time to
look about and fidget." Wasn't that delightful? Especially as she is a
Taylor's Flats woman and will therefore belong to *our* parish when we
get a priest.

By the time you get this I hope and trust we shall have got poor May
home again. Then Mrs. Paling, her greatest friend, will desert her
husband for a fortnight to come and really take charge. I shall remain as
bottle-washer and also to try to put in a penn'orth of real parish visiting
to make up a little for the summer's neglect. Then on September 1 Price
and I shall start off together over the hills and far away. I am really rather
looking forward to that at last. Price is plump, kind, efficient and
tremendously dominant, so if I don't murder her we ought to get on fine.

Pouce Coupé
From letter written August 3.

. . . May is gaining strength steadily but very slowly. She was very
achey and depressed all the first part of the week, had a fierce headache
for two days, and wearisome neuritis in arms and shoulders after that.
But this cleared off more or less later, and for the last two or three days
she has been far more comfy and cheerful, though not able to feed herself
yet.

She likes to be read to in small doses; so we are now slowly and fitfully
reading Masefield's Captain Margaret,[118] not an ideal book, there is
not much choice, however. I am actually contemplating the introduction of Cross Word Puzzles—in fact, am really only deterred from the
fatal step by the difficulty of finding one! When I do find one I mean

to try it on, and see whether May snaps my nose off, as she quite likely will—and I almost hope it.

Unluckily I didn't bring any real good books here, only short stores for reading aloud. But I went to see Mr. Proctor (who hasn't many either), and he lent me Papini's *Life of Christ* and Headlam's *Doctrine of the Church*,[119] so I shan't absolutely starve that way. Papini is a queer fellow. Have you read him? An Italian who was an atheist writer and is now a passionately keen convert; rather tiresome at times, but quite worth reading.

The nearest attempt to an event that did happen to me was a violent knock at my door at about 2.30 a.m. on Friday night. I came partially out of the deepest abyss of sleep and thought it was a drunken man. But as it went on I woke up a little more and cautiously opened the door. There stood a Fort St. John woman, mother of one of the Guides. She said, "Oh Miss Storrs, we were driving Mrs. G. home after a trip to Grande Prairie, and she feels ill and can't go on. But we want to go on and get home in the morning. So can she come into your bed?"

I was a little bit dazed, being still only half awake, not knowing Mrs. G. very well, and having no idea what was the matter with her! But of course I had to say "Sure. Bring her right here," and tried vaguely to tidy up the room and clear a little space, while the poor lady was hauled in and shot up on the bed, accompanied by a large glass of gin as restorative!

At first I had a moment's terror that drink was the trouble, but that was quite a mistake. It was a sort of temporary nervous collapse and to my great relief she didn't want the gin at all. She is the Game Warden's wife and quite a nice, refined woman and stayed here till this morning when her husband arrived and took her home. She soon got well. There wasn't much the matter.

Diary sent with letter dated August 18, 1930.

All the ingenuity in the world couldn't produce anything to tell you about last week. Isn't that dreadful? And doesn't that give me away? The weather was glorious and May got pretty steadily stronger, and I did nothing whatever except potter between the hotel and the hospital, read a little, write a little, talk a little and swim a little every day.

May sat up twice a day for an hour or more at a time, and walked to the verandah and back, but paid for this speeding up by a good deal of exhaustion and various odd new pains, now chiefly muscular, I think. However, it was definitely settled that she should go home next Monday, the 18th, that Mr. Birley and Tommy should fetch her together (in case of any trouble with the car), and that I should go on ahead this week-end with the Naylors.

Mr. Naylor is New Testament professor at the Theological College at [Montreal] and great friend to Mr. Guiton. In fact, they are the twin pillars of the Fellowship of the West. He is a charming man and I think well suited to this kind of job in spite of his professorship which certainly no one would suspect. He wears a very old khaki shirt and breeches, with sleeves rolled up and no hat; all of which would be ludicrously affected in England, but quite sensible and fitting here. It's tremendously hot and at any time when the trail becomes impassable, he must leave his car, and mend a bridge or wade a creek, or ride or walk or camp anywhere and sleep with anyone. So that I think nothing but a white enamelled cast iron dog collar would stand the strain. Nevertheless, for the avoidance of all contention, I will add that on Sundays and really cold week-days he does appear in a Norfolk jacket, black stock an' all and looks by comparison a little ridiculous!

Well, we did nothing more at Pouce Coupé and I came back with the Naylors on Friday afternoon, it being arranged that Tommy and Mr. Birley should go down on Sunday and bring May back today (Monday).

I spent Saturday morning in Fort St. John finding a new place for Mr. Naylor's Service, as the school was being repaired, and trying to beat him up a congregation. I secured a nice empty shack, which will, however, be occupied again next week; but also discovered that most of the men were away for one reason or another, and that the three leading ladies of the town were up the river on an annual trip. Mr. Naylor, meanwhile, went to a new district across the North Pine, and found some families including babies for baptism, while Mrs. Naylor with the car took Nurse Roberts up to the Montney to try and arrange about sending a poor little blind girl away to a special school. I had no horse, so after beating up Fort St. John not very successfully (and being greeted everywhere by ironical surprise about my short visit to England!), I walked back to May's and found Mrs. Paling already arrived.

Yesterday I had hoped to borrow a Birley horse but they were all out grazing and couldn't be found, so I walked in to Fort St. John and had a little Sunday School in the shack before Mr. Naylor's Service at 11. Alas! Alas! only six women and a big boy turned up for that, *very* disappointing for him and humiliating for me. Of course, the Fort St. John grown-ups have never yet come to anything held by anybody (except a political meeting), but it is baffling when one is friends with them all, and the children are pretty good, to find the grown-ups so stolidly indifferent. Of course there are not many of them in the town itself (about twenty-four men and women), and the three leaders of each were away, as well as the keenest of the Scouts. But four of the Guides who were in Camp could have come, and only one did, which makes me realise something of the meaning of failure.

Afterwards Mr. Naylor went off to baptise a baby and I started back, had a hasty meal with Mrs. Paling, induced her and Mrs. Birley to mobilise in time to be picked up by the Naylors for the afternoon Service and went on myself to East Fort St. John. The school was filthy after a political meeting, but there was just time for a rough sweep up before the Naylors arrived, bringing Mrs. Birley and Mrs. Paling and little Harold, while Frank followed proudly on his bicycle. I really did expect a congregation there, as it is our warmest corner, where the H's, C's, C's and S's all profess to care, and S's, M's and F's[120] all come occasionally. But of course there had been no time to visit on purpose, and I suppose this was an unexpected Service, anyway, *nobody* but Mr. Simpson came! It really was too bad for poor Mr. Naylor because Simpson and I have always had a decent little turn up, at least never less than six or seven grown-ups. Mr. Naylor was very good and uncomplaining. However, I thought it all well worth while because we had the Holy Communion, and Mrs. Paling communicated, her first chance for ten years. Afterwards I went with the Naylors to visit the McDonalds and see whether they would like their new baby baptised. They were in an *awful* muddle as usual, and did want it, but *not then*. "Because you see, Mr. Naylor, we're not fixed up at all. If you would come next week Bill and I will fix ourselves and the kids and the house and get Baby *nicely* fixed too." After huge family discussions, Mr. Naylor agreed to that, because he is going to the Hope this week and will be back here chiefly for baptisms next Sunday before he starts back for [?].

Afterwards Mr. Simpson persuaded us in to supper, and finally the Naylors went on to their last Service at Taylor's Flats and I walked home, intending to write letters. But alas! it was too dark, and we are out of lamp-oil, so they will be short and few this week even if I do catch the mail.

N.B. Mr. Naylor has agreed with me not to be really the least disheartened about this place but to bear in mind that it is not a *parochial* but straight *missionary* job for whomever comes, i.e., there is no Church at all to build on, but everything has to be from the very start. He has no news yet for the future, but *may* hear before he leaves next Monday. I hope so because I also leave for the Hudson Hope trail with Price on September 1. We go up on foot, and come down in a boat, if we're lucky.

There is nothing at all to tell you, so it won't take long. We've had an awfully happy week and May is getting better every day. She walks once round the garden each morning, and then sits out in the sun till the evening; isn't that splendid? Of course she gets very tired from time to time, but no real set-back, and she is in splendid spirits. Mrs. Paling is charming and looks after her wonderfully. I am only tweenie,[121] allowed to give her her breakfast and help her dress, wash the breakfast dishes and sweep and dust a bit before going out for the day. My outings have been very uneventful, chiefly trying to visit most of the families in Fort St. John and the East end, to get the Sunday School by Post roll complete, and beat up for a final Service in all three centres next Sunday when the Van comes. Incidentally also, I had to find a place for Mr. Naylor's Lantern Service tonight and do a bit of beating up for that, while he was off walking up to the Hope. It has been good exercise, because Mr. Birley's horses were lost all last week, so I had a chance to get my legs into some sort of trim, very necessary after last month's slacking at Pouce.

Every evening I try to collect and bring home a quart of milk or so and a little cream because May has to be fed up, and Mr. Birley's cow has stopped payment. Most of the people are awfully fond of her and grateful for some past nursing she has done for them, so they seldom let me pay for the milk, and yesterday one of the women gave me a fine young chicken too, all ready plucked. I was grateful for that because it all mounts up on a five mile walk home. It's pretty hot still, but lovely I think; the country really looks delightful now that the crops are ripe. There are big stretches of yellow wheat and grey-green shimmering oats surrounded by dark green bush and rough open land covered with golden red and purple Michaelmas daisies. All the colours are very brilliant in the strong sun, and from every high point you see the distant hills and the long Peace River bank intensely blue. Only, unluckily, you hardly ever see the mountains now because they are lost in the summer haze. So it's more a foreground of beauty now compared with the background beauty of winter.

Yesterday I went down to the river with Mrs. Naylor to meet Mr. Naylor who floated down the sixty-five miles from Hudson Hope all by himself on a very small raft. Wasn't that fun? He sat in a box in the middle of the raft and had one long paddle to steer with. It took him about ten hours and he said the only real difficulty was to get to shore when he wanted to, because, of course, the current was determined to take him another two or three hundred miles. I was so jealous of him, and long to come down from the Hope that way next week, but doubt whether Price will agree to it.

The harvest is pretty well ready, and cutting begins this week. I do wish I could help with the stooking, but fear I must spend the first part of this week finishing the Sunday School round up, and the last part getting ready for Price and the Van. She is due on Friday or Saturday. On Sunday we hope to hold three final Services—at the Flats, Baldonnel and St. John. Then on Monday, September 1, we abandon the Van and leg it by the old pack trail up to Hudson Hope. I don't know how long that will take but am looking forward to it immensely, and shall not hurry it more than we can possibly help. We shall try to do all the visiting on the way up, so as to come down in a boat if there should happen to be one. After that, probably a week or nine days later, we shall take up the Van again and cruise round the Montney district due North of here. I am rather looking forward to that too, though the road and hills are pretty tough and we shall probably break down every odd day or two.

How long that will take we have even less idea, because it's impossible to get any sort of list of the settlers up there, though it seems that a big lot have gone in this year, largely squatters. But I mean to get down *somehow* by October 6, so as to join Christopher[122] at Edmonton on the 9th, or at latest, on the 11th. And then, if funds permit, I mean to be quite reckless and go with him to Vancouver and see him off from there on the 15th. It's rather a wild-cat scheme, and may not be possible; but I do hope it will because it would give us six days and a wonderful trip together, instead of about three days only in that perfectly deadly Edmonton.

Mr. Birley found his horses yesterday, a great comfort as he needs them badly for the harvest, and good luck for me, because he has lent me Buster for the next few days. I rode over this morning for Sunday School and am going again this evening for the Lantern Service which is to be held in a shed belonging to a Syrian store-keeper. It's really his warehouse and is almost full of sacks of flour and rolls of barbed wire. I had a lively hour yesterday trying to combine these with a few boards and ginger beer cases to bring forth pews. It made me long more than ever for some permanent building, and not to be reduced to these makeshifts, which are all very well in their way, but not helpful to anything like worship.

It's perfectly wonderful news about the Knights' Place meeting and its results. The people here are willing enough to help with labour but they have almost *no* cash. And, moreover, they are mostly not keen enough to give what they could. You see, the old timers, who have made a little bit, have been so long without any sort of Church, that they have got quite indifferent, while the newcomers are having a hard struggle to get going at all. Therefore we have to regard this as a real missionary job for the

present; and that is why I am so *tremendously* thankful for this splendid
help from Home, and am longing to see that Church Hall built. It will
have to be available for social things in the week, like a parish hall. But I
shall hold out strong for a little permanent sanctuary to be partitioned
off at the end. Wouldn't it be a wonderful thing to have an altar there all
the time; and a little place actually built and standing there on purpose
for prayer?

Fort St. John
Week ending September 1.

This week has been delightful all through and I have thoroughly
enjoyed it. Last Sunday morning Mr. Birley lent me Buster again (he had
been away for a week with the work-horses and just been found), so I
rode over to Fort St. John and had a dear little Sunday School, chiefly of
younger children whom I tried to tell about the Ascension and
Whitsunday and the new Unseen Presence of Christ.

Then a marvellously peaceful afternoon in the garden with May,
waiting for Mr. Naylor to pick me up for the McDonald baptism, and
shamelessly relieved because he never came! Afterwards I discovered that
his car had broken down for the hundredth time, and he had spent the
day on horseback. After supper I rode again to Fort St. John for the
Lantern Service which was to be in the little warehouse belonging to one
of the stores. When I arrived there was a sprinkling of people at the door
but no Mr. Naylor. He had borrowed a horse in the morning and gone
across the North Pine River. I was afraid of the congregation melting
away if he delayed much longer and still more frightened of having to
take the Service myself without preparation if he didn't come at all. So I
made a great business of getting ready, collecting the lantern and slides
and a barrel to stand them on, fussing with the sheet and borrowing a
lamp and generally trying to employ everyone as much as possible.
Mercifully he was sighted at last, and actually arrived about 8.45 (only
three-quarters of an hour late, which is not serious here). Then to our
great joy the door kept opening and all the odds and ends and loafers of
Fort St. John dropped in, so that the little shack was quite full of about
twenty children and twenty grown-ups—the largest number of adults we
have ever mustered in that hard-boiled little settlement. Mr. Naylor
showed a lot of really beautiful slides taken from Hole's *Life of Christ*
and gave a nice simple account all woven into a sort of address. We sang
three hymns and finished at about 11. It was certainly the best Service we
have yet had at Fort St. John and I was so thankful.

Someone offered me a lift home in a car, so as it was pretty late and Buster is very nervous especially at night, I left him in a livery barn and arranged to walk over in the morning for a sort of conference with Mr. Naylor and a United Church Superintendent[123] who was coming up to see him.

This conference was a wash-out as far as I was concerned, because Mr. Naylor forgot he had told me to come, and went off to the little Red Cross nurse's house three miles away and met Mr. Rodgers there without letting me know. So when I got into Fort St. John at 10 A.M., no one knew where he was. I waited until 4.30 and then collected Buster and rode home, feeling strongly inclined to *leave the Church of England!*

On Tuesday I had twelve hours out, and rode all round Taylor's Flats looking up mothers and children and putting in a huge visit to a nice little woman who is going to hold the Guides together till I come back. She's not a Guider and knows very little about them; but I gave her a lot of books and she promised to have a good, long, informal sort of meeting at her house at least once a month.

Buster was very good all day. He is like a large, clumsy, black camel, awfully bumpy and rough in his paces, but quite well-intentioned and *wonderfully* good for a congested liver, if only I had had one.

On Wednesday I rounded up East Fort St. John and went to the more distant people—seven, eight and eleven miles away. It's a lovely trail right off the road and high up on a sort of table-land from which you look across the Pine on the North and the Peace on the South, both their banks steep and dark, and the country beyond flooded with sunlight. It was so lovely that I came to the conclusion that this would be an ideal country to live in *if only* where the beastly little town of Fort St. John is, we could just plant Rochester instead. On the way home I met the Naylors on their way out of the country, the car having at last been mended. We had a friendly farewell, in the course of which I told him about my grievance about Monday, and rubbed it in pretty hard, because I was so afraid of feeling cross with him afterwards if I didn't. He confessed frankly that he'd forgotten all about me; and I told him that many people had left the Church of England for less, and we parted the best of friends. Wasn't it lucky I met him?

After that I returned Buster to the Birleys and spent the rest of the week round about the house with May and Mrs. Paling. But on Friday, to the general excitement, May's sister Nina returned from England. Mr. Birley drove down to Hythe and brought her home. She is older than May, about forty-four, I should think, and much more quiet and self-contained. She brought a trunk entirely full of marvellous presents for the family and the house; so Mrs. Birley and the three boys all came over for the afternoon and there was great rejoicing.

On Saturday evening Price arrived with the Van, bringing back Petter ready for school which begins again next week. It was a cold, wet night so May wouldn't let Price and me sleep in the Van, and we all six dossed down very happily in the sitting-room, kitchen and three little bedrooms. On Sunday Price and I had three Sunday Schools, morning, afternoon and evening. The children turned up pretty well and we took their photographs after each School. At Baldonnel we also had a little Mothers' Service, and seven mothers came, which is nearly all there are; so we were very happy. But my greatest satisfaction was at Fort St. John where Mrs. Brown[124] and Mrs. Devlin actually volunteered to keep on Sunday School together till I come back. They are both nice women, one a Presbyterian and the other an Anglican; but these children know so little that there will be no difficulty, and I am really thankful to think they will do it.

On Sunday night I slept in the Van with Price for the first time. It's really very comfortable when you *are* in bed, though a bit confined for dressing and undressing. But of course that doesn't matter in reasonably fine and warm weather. Of course by day it is chock full of every sort of junk; and I think the only real trial will be turning all this out at night and packing it all back every morning!

The Northern Lights are getting perfectly lovely again and it is almost impossible to stop looking at them and go to bed. They are great streams and waves of pearly light always moving and changing shape and generally stretching right across the sky, sometimes like a fan, sometimes like a huge wavy ostrich feather, and sometimes like a waterfall, but never the same for five minutes together.

Monday (September 1), we observed as a holiday for Price because she has had a pretty stiff six weeks already. We spent it washing, packing and stooking, i.e., in the morning I washed and she stooked oats for Mr. Birley, who is now cutting his crops; and in the afternoon she washed and I stooked from 2 to 6, a hot job and very scratchy, but a nice change from visiting and Sunday Schools. I should like to stay on another week and help him, but that's not what we're here for, and anyway a neighbour is coming today who will do it about ten times better and quicker than Price and me. For this and all other odd jobs about the house and garden I wear, like May does, blue men's overalls, or rather overnaughts, for there need be and generally is nothing underneath.

In the evening we sorted out pictures and books and cards to take up the pack trail to Hudson Hope.

Today (Tuesday the 2nd), is perfectly lovely and we are just mobilized for the start. Our packs are rather full, so if we get too weary we shall have to lay a little trail of prayer cards and sacred pictures to lighten the ship and at the same time hope they may help someone coming after.

We don't know how long the walk will take or how we shall get back, so if I miss the next mail you'll know the reason why.

Hudson Hope
September 8, 1930.

We have had a delightful week with no real hitch anywhere. We left Fort St. John at 2 o'clock last Tuesday, and got a man to drive us the first five miles or so in the Van, and then take it back for an overhaul. The graded road runs for about three miles past Fort St. John and after that the wagon trail is not too rough or steep till you come to a tremendous hill called Tea Creek, where we left the Van and took to our legs. Our packs were fairly heavy, having a complete change each, and a good lot of Sunday School cards, pictures, tracts and hymn papers. Also, as I was walking in jodhpurs, I put in a dress for Sunday. It was pretty hot, what we should call a heat wave at Home, so one of us carried an army water bottle, and the other a Kodak, and we streamed fairly profusely.

Tea Creek is the first of the big creeks running into the Peace between Fort St. John and the Hope. It sounds so small and domestic, but really is a tremendous wide and deep gorge with steep green walls and great hangers of pale poplar and dark spruce. But this time of year only a tiny little muddy stream trickles down it, like a degenerate heir living on the fame and wealth of his ancestors.

On the other side we followed the trail across about five miles of lovely high open country with splendid views of the river till we came to the first farm belonging to people called H. They are Americans. The father is rather what is here called a Tough, and the mother rather a sick woman, at present out of the country. I wanted to see the daughter, Hattie, who is on the Sunday School by Post. She is seventeen and has just got married, but is still living at home till her husband can build a house on his homestead. She had another girl staying with her, and they were very welcoming and gave us tea. I put the other girl on the Sunday School by Post, and tried to stir them both up to answer the questions, and gave them each a prayer-card and promised to send them Testaments. That is roughly what we try to do at each revisit when there are boys and girls.

After that the trail wound along quite close to the river another three miles and brought us at 7.30 or so to people called Flatt,[125] with whom we had hoped to sleep. They are a charming youngish couple, both English and educated. Mr. Flatt was at one time in a bank at Cairo, and during the War served in Palestine, where he was for a time in the same Division with Christopher. They have got two tiny boys, and were most welcoming, but alas! their tiny house was *chock full* as two men had come to help with the harvest, and another to help build a new house, so there was not a blanket, or an inch of floor space left! They were very worried about it, but gave us a fine supper, and then Mr. Flatt said he would start us on the seven miles trail through the bush to the next place which was a Stopping House and bound to have room. So we started at 8.30 and he pretended that he was only coming 100 yards or so. But directly we were well away announced his intention of going with us right through to the cultivation because he said the bush was very rough and the trail very faint, and we might easily lose it in the dark. We protested at first but afterwards were more than thankful, for it certainly was the roughest, darkest walk I've ever had, and we should certainly have lost the way, not to speak of getting mudded to the knees in two or three dear little swamps. All the way he talked delightfully about Egypt and Palestine, just punctuating his conversation with little remarks like, "Look out, now, steep drop on the left . . . look out, big log there . . . wait a minute, deep mud here . . . whatever you do, don't slip." I felt awfully like the second part of *Pilgrim's Progress,* and didn't despise it half so much as I always have before! Our progress was further complicated by Price's *heel* which kept coming off, and had to be tied on every few minutes, first with elastic, then with string, and finally with a pocket handkerchief. Finally, in crossing a swamp, she lost her *hat* and it had to be abandoned in the darkness. We reached the Freers'[126] first field at about midnight, and there parted with Mr. Greatheart or Lob, whom he really reminded me of more, as he led us through the dark enchanted wood. It was really rather awful to think of him trailing all that way back again through the night in the midst of his heaviest harvesting days. But he made nothing of it, and said he was only so ashamed and disappointed at not being able to keep us.

After that we had another mile across stubble fields and between hundreds of ghostly stooks. Once I charged straight upon a barbed wire fence, and was nearly impaled, but otherwise had no more trouble, and at last found the Freers' house wrapped in sleep. The dog rushed at us, as they always do, but he was quite harmless; and poor Mrs. Freer woke up and proceeded to make us up a bed by the weird light of a very dim electric torch held in the hand with the blanket. She said they were out of lamp oil and had no candles, but we didn't mind that in the joy of finding a real bed and falling into it.

Next morning we woke up awfully late, long after Mr. Freer and the eldest boys had gone to the fields, but Mrs. Freer had a big breakfast waiting for us and we ate it talking to her while she cleaned up and the eldest daughter did the washing, and the two youngest boys did the chores. Mrs. Freer is American and remarkably dark and handsome and dignified; but the children are flaxen-haired like Scandinavians, so I suppose their father is that type. We were immensely impressed at the way the eldest daughter was making underclothes and even quite pretty cotton frocks out of *old flour sacks!* Four of these scrubbed hard with home-made soap to get the maker's name, etc. out of them, and then dyed again, pink or blue, make quite a tidy dress, costing *nothing at all*, and she says they wear splendidly. The great industry of the women and children at this time of year is picking and bottling wild berries. They get hundreds of quarts of wild strawberries, raspberries, blueberries, cranberries and saskatoons,[127] and bottle enough to supply themselves with abundant fruit until next summer, also at no cost at all. Mrs. Freer was just sealing up her last cranberries and we admired her huge supply.

After that we had the usual Sunday School business with the available children, and then came away, Mrs. Freer refusing to take any money from us, which was awfully nice of her considering that theirs is a real Stopping House, and we couldn't really do anything for the children. There has been a little school there up to this term, but the only other family went away and the Freers can only produce five of the six children of school age required, so the school has been closed until a new family comes.

From there we only had three miles of very beautiful trail before we came to a marvellously neat and well-built farm where we found a delightful elderly woman called Mrs. Robinson.[128] She comes from Ontario and was once a school-teacher. She is about sixty-nine and quite cultivated and full of fun, such a *joy* to meet some one like that. We asked her how she liked living twenty-five miles of rough waggon trail from the nearest shop, and whether she didn't miss Ontario, and she said "Not a bit. I haven't been to a store for *nine* years. But I like it much better here. You *don't have to keep up with Mrs. Jones.*" She made us stay to dinner and was splendid company. Her husband and two sons, Allan and Eden, were out hunting cattle in the bush, so she said she was quite glad of company, especially women. After that we had a pretty long nine miles to the Half-way River—in fact it seemed endless, and what with the boiling heat and the ups and downs, and the pretty attentive mosquitoes, poor Price's feet (which are very dainty and much too small for her body), nearly petered out altogether. At last, from a beautiful high point, we saw far away on a flat close to the river, a big pale patch, and knew it for harvest fields again. Beyond them was a steep blue ridge running at right angles to the river which we guessed to be the banks of Half-way River coming down to join the Peace. After that there was still about four miles, chiefly of very long and steep descents which tried poor Price's toes very sadly. At last we got down to the harvest fields but saw no house anywhere. And then, just as it was getting dark, a figure appeared on a horse. It drew nearer and called us, and to our joy it turned out to be a little Englishwoman called Mrs. G. who had met Price at Pouce Coupé. We asked rather tremblingly whether the Tompkins,[129] who owned this farm, could put us up, and if not?— She said: "Follow the trail and I'll ride on and fix it up." We followed thankfully, and after another mile reached the farm buildings and a good-sized log house.

Then we found that the blessed Mrs. G. had prepared for our arrival, so there was none of the pause that might have been expected. It turned out that Mr. and Mrs. Tompkins were away at Edmonton, and Mr. and Mrs. G. had been left in charge of the family. They owned that the house was *pretty full*, but immediately proceeded to make room for us by turning out of their own room. The house had a living room, a little kitchen and three bedrooms, or rather one small and one large made into two by a partition. In the small one Price and I were thankful to be inserted. In one of the others were the Tompkins' daughter, the hired girl and Mrs. G., together with two little twins of three. In the living room were two elderly men, harvest workers, sharing a small sofa and already in bed. In a bunk house outside were another harvester and Mr. G. And in the third bedroom were the Tompkins' *four* sons, another little boy who lives with them, *another* big boy working on the telegraph, and the unfortunate young schoolmaster, just arrived from Victoria and condemned to live and sleep in a room with his entire school. Eighteen people altogether, and where Mr. and Mrs. Tompkins sleep when they *are* at home I never could discover.

The gallant G's got up supper and were so kind; and I must say I did admire Mrs. G., obviously not long out of a snug little suburban home at Forest Gate and yet taking it all so naturally and full of fun. Her husband has been out much longer, but they are both new arrivals here, and waiting to go up to their homestead in the spring. They will be almost the first settlers in another new district on the Half-way River, where there is at present practically nobody at all.

Price was so worn about the feet next morning that she had breakfast in bed and we idled about vaguely helping Mrs. G. until 12, when all the others rushed in for dinner, i.e., the schoolmaster, the five small boys and the one schoolgirl, the three men and Fred the telegraph boy, and we all sat down together, plus of course, Mary, the hired girl from Kentucky. It was great fun, such a squash and everyone so good-humoured about it. One of the harvesters was an Australian by birth, and we had a great time wrangling about the superior climates of all our native countries. Afterwards, by the schoolmaster's invitation, I went up with him and the children to see the school, and he allowed me twenty minutes or so to talk Sunday School with them, and give them prayer cards and little Scripture books. After that I rushed back, had a little talk with the G.'s about Church prospects, they are good Anglicans, and gave the hired Mary a little book or two. Then Fred put us across the Half-way River in a wonderfully leaky boat, and we started on a puny seven miles walk to our next stopping place.

That was entirely through bush, and horribly full of mosquitoes who ought to be over by now, but don't seem to have found it out just there. Anyway they fairly swarmed round us, and attended chiefly to Price's stockinged legs and my thinly shirted back.

We reached the next place about 6 and found a complete contrast to the last, as usual. Mr. Ardill is the son of an Irish Canon, and Mrs. Ardill is a highly educated and most charming Dutch woman. They live on a lovely little hill looking up and down the river, and their log house is shaped like a long low railway carriage, divided into three—kitchen, living-room, and bed-room. There are four children ranging from three to ten, all beautifully brought up and most sweet and friendly.[130] Mrs. Ardill was most welcoming and very apologetic at our having to sleep on the sitting room floor, as the family of six naturally filled the bedroom, and the living room sofa was already dedicated to a neighbour who was helping with the harvest, and his wife. Mr. Ardill was out hunting cattle, so we soon had supper, and then washed up and went out with the children to "help them" (courtesy term), to feed the pigs, milk the cows and water the horses. It was perfectly wonderful to see this little boy and girl of ten and nine managing all the animals in the evening darkness with greater skill and less fuss than I make over cleaning my teeth. Finally Mr. Ardill came in, *not* having found his cattle. Then he had supper, and after a rather long talky-talk we started going to bed. The neighbour and his wife (called D)[131] slung a rug across the end of the sofa to hide us from them. Mrs. Ardill brought us chair cushions and blankets. We all washed by turns in the kitchen and so to bed.

(A sudden chance to get this off, so I must leave it here to be continued in our next).

Fort St. John
September 10, 1930.

I hope my last volume reached you, the one scrawled in pencil and all about our little walk. I gave it to the mining engineer who brought us down in the boat, and he said he couldn't possibly forget to post it at Edmonton, but you never know. Anyhow that left off at the Ardills, and I will go on from there.

We left the Ardills at about 10 o'clock on Friday, after the usual seance with the children. They live too far from any school, but Mrs. Ardill takes correspondence classes for them in ordinary lessons, and she also promised to help them with the Sunday School magazine lesson too.

The next reach was to be either seventeen miles to the Mc-

Dougalls¹³² or twenty-one miles to the Hope itself, according to our speed and luck. It was to be pretty well all through bush with only one known family to visit on the way, and we were in high hopes of seeing a bear at last, or at least a moose, as there are lots about all along the trail. But alas! I may as well confess that we were disappointed after all. Price says *I* talk too much which is obviously absurd, but whether her voice drove them away or our fairy footsteps or whatever the cause, we never saw any game bigger than squirrels or fiercer than mosquitoes—wasn't it sickening?

After five or six miles we came across two nice young American brothers in the middle of the bush clearing a bit and building a cabin. They had two horses and an adorable foal, and two of the usual anonymous but delightfully friendly Canadian dogs. They were very welcoming and asked us to stay for a cup of tea, so we sat on the logs while they boiled water over a little campfire and then threw in a handful of tea. They invited us to some beans also, but that was dinner and we didn't want it so soon, so we gracefully declined and went on as soon as possible after photographing them and offering the elder a pocket St. John. He was so nice and said: "Thank you, I would like it but you may be short of them, and we have got a Bible here and we do read it. I'm rather keen on these things myself." After that I should have liked to have talked to him further, but we had a good way to go and didn't want to delay, especially as it was growing cloudy.

About five miles brought us to a shallow river bed and in crossing that close to the mouth we met two more men who offered us a lift in the mail-boat all the way to the Hope. We refused that, but on Price's feet making a little protest, we agreed that they should take us as far as the next family four miles farther up. They had pulled ashore for dinner and made us join them, and we had great fun frying bacon and eating it out of the pan with our fingers like Arabs, and dipping our mugs into the common pail of tea. They were two very interesting men, one a little Scotchman from Aberdeen who was wounded pretty badly in the War and now lives at the Hope, partly trapping and surveying and partly writing books; the other a tall, rather aggressive looking Englishman whom we afterwards learnt to be the son of a parson and nephew of General T. They were called Jimmy R.¹³³ and Charlie T. and had perfectly educated English voices under their good rough backwoodsman disguise. The mail boat is a flat open boat about twenty feet long driven by a "kicker" or tiny portable engine. It made an awful noise, but we quite enjoyed the lazy four miles for a change. At the next creek they put us off again because there was certainly one family there, possible two. We found a very reserved little mother lately come in from the States to join *her* mother—a Canadian. The older woman was out, having been sent for suddenly to act midwife to a neighbour. Apparently the poor neighbour's baby had arrived quite unexpectedly when she was all alone in the house except for a child of two. By a merciful chance a man was walking along the trail, and passed near enough to hear her cry. He found out what was wrong and then ran five miles to the next house to get Mrs. Robinson.[134]

We enrolled three new children there, and then went on to find another new family from Kentucky. By the time we found them it was pouring with rain, and we were glad to get into a house. It wasn't a very good house certainly, just one large room full of double beds, and while talking to the mother we had to move about as unostentatiously as possible to avoid the biggest leaks in the roof. It was a strange family with a strong dash of negro blood I'm sure. There were about seven large, adolescent sons, all apparently the same age. They were *very* dark, and collapsed into hysterical giggles whenever we addressed them. Their mother told us that the youngest were named Elma, Thelma and Delma!! When I said we were Sunday School teachers she replied: "Oh, there's no need here; their father is a BISHOP!" I tried to express polite gratification when she pointed proudly to the wall (which was neatly covered with old newspapers), and there, sure enough, was a framed certificate saying:

THIS IS TO CERTIFY THAT CHARLIE R. IS A BISHOP
IN THE CHURCH OF THE FOLLOWERS OF GOD.

Unluckily the Bishop was out, so we never saw him; but she said that he was disappointed in his new sphere of influence, and was trying his utmost to get the whole family back to Kentucky. I don't know what his form of religion really is. But apparently the one neighbouring family is not very responsive to his ministrations; and if his sons are chips off the old block, I'm not altogether surprised.

After that we went on through rain which got heavier and heavier till at last we were so wet that when we had to wade through a creek it made no appreciable difference; but when we reached the McDougalls' house, we were ashamed to approach the door.

So you can imagine our delight when it was opened by a little plump old English lady who might be a Nanny or a housekeeper in some Old Country house—and she said, "Oh dear me! Come in at once and take off all your clothes!" So there we stayed for two nights till it stopped raining, while she treated us like long-lost daughters home at last. She came from Yorkshire thirty-six years ago and has never been back. She has five sons who were all away, and two daughters—both married; so although Mr. McDougall is a most agreeable old fellow, she seems to be a bit lonely. In fact she kept saying, with reference to every extra household duty, "No, I won't do one unnecessary thing to *spoil the visit.*"

Sunday morning the rain stopped and we walked the last little bit to

Hudson Hope and got there about 12. It's a pretty little place, really almost like a small Swiss or Austrian village, with a green in the middle, a school, hotel, store and half a dozen other little houses grouped round it. On one side are tall hills stretching away to the real mountains and on the other a big drop to the river. We went straight to the bran-new little hotel and had dinner at a long table with about twenty Canadian Pacific Railway surveyors[135] all just in from three months work in the bush, and struck awkwardly dumb by our presence. The funny thing was that we ate to the strains of Schubert's "Unfinished Symphony," played on a perfectly beautiful gramophone which had been lent to the hotel keeper by some passing prospector when he went off into the mountains. We looked through the records and found beside the Schubert, Stainer's "Crucifixion" and about fifty jazz foxtrots. Evidently he is a man of remarkable tastes!

Afterwards we ran round and collected all the available children for Sunday School. There are seven of them—five boys and two little girls—and they *all* came at 4 o'clock. There were no hymn books, so we wrote out the hymns on the blackboard and had quite a nice little Service. Afterwards we visited the half-dozen or so women and invited them to an Evening Service. Then supper with one of the ladies, then back to the school to write out three more hymns and hang up a borrowed lamp before 8 o'clock. Finally, nine people rolled up to the Service, including two unexpected men. We had a sort of little Mission Service and gave a few Gospels and little books afterwards. They all sang wonderfully keenly, considering we had no instrument and no books, and only my sprawling handwriting on the board in a wavering light. It was a very tiny Service and I gave a very confused and blundering address, but somehow it felt very well worth while altogether. It's curious that the people up there as well as along the trail are practically all Anglicans, compared to the very few *real* Anglicans down here. When we get our resident priest, I hope he *will* go up the trail and hold a Service at least once a fortnight.

Above Hudson Hope the river passes through a deep canyon and drops over 200 feet, so that for fourteen miles it is not navigable, and any boat has to be hauled on a waggon over a rough trail called the Portage. Twenty miles above the top of the Portage is another family called Beattie[136] and I desperately wanted to get them, not the less because I heard that the father is strongly anti-religious. There are three ways of reaching them:

1. Riding all the way—thirty-four miles.
2. Riding over the Portage and going on by boat.
3. Walking all the way and sleeping in an empty cabin half way.

We couldn't hear of a boat, so Number two went out. Price said her feet wouldn't go any farther, so Number three went out, and every available saddle horse was away with hunting or surveying parties, so Number one went out! I was *dreadfully* disappointed and could hardly even be nice to poor Price, who, I suppose, was really tired and couldn't see that we were missing the best bit of all.

However, I couldn't walk off and leave her, as it must have taken four days at least. So I had to swallow my disgust and try to find a way of getting down to Fort St. John again by boat if possible, as we had visited everybody within reach and held the little Sunday School and Service, and there was really no more to do at the Hope. After wandering round and inquiring of everybody, we heard that a mining engineer had just come across the mountains and was going down in a kicker boat some time on Tuesday. We were also told that he was an Englishman with a moustache and large feet, so most of Monday morning I looked for him round and round the village. When found, he readily agreed to take us, but said we must be ready to start at any moment from 4 that afternoon, and take a coat each and a blanket between us in case we should have to camp out in the night. So we borrowed coats and a blanket and at 7 P.M. said goodbye to Hudson Hope.

The boat was like the mail boat, and besides the owner who ran it and the mining engineer who had hired it and ourselves there were three other men, all similarly bound for Taylor's Flats. The river is terrifically shallow just now but very swift, so that with current plus kicker, we buzzed down at a great rate and after a glorious sunset over the hills it soon got quite cold. Then the moon rose and it was perfectly lovely till about 11 o'clock. Then it got misty and the channel hard to see. So after we had run on to one gravel bar the men decided to go ashore and camp till dawn. So we pulled in and made a campfire and the usual tea while we warmed ourselves. Then they put some canvas on the ground for P. and me and we rolled in our blanket by the first fire, while the men went a little further off and made another for themselves. It was a little hard and a little cold, but the moon came out again and gleamed on the water and we heard strange noises in the bush behind us and hoped again and again that it was a bear or a moose—until suddenly the men started talking again and we woke up to find the dawn had come.

We piled back into the boat and started again at 5.30. It was perfectly lovely going down between the tall banks and the changing hills while the daylight grew and the mists came up and wandered away over the trees and up the coulees—almost exactly like Scotland, at least the little bit of Scotland that I know. Just before 8 the sun came out and soon after that we arrived at Taylor's Flats—journey's end. There is a Stopping House by the ferry, so we poured in and had a huge breakfast,[137] and after that we all scattered in different directions.

Price and I shouldered packs again and walked up the familiar road with fourteen miles to go and fetch the Van at Fort St. John, but with strong hopes of a lift on the way. Sure enough, after seven miles a car came up behind us and the journey to all intents and purposes was over. We picked up the old Van and last week's mail and drove back to May's. She seemed wonderfully well and rather horrified at our getting home so soon.

After reading a marvellous mail, I scrambled into men's overalls and spent a long afternoon stooking wheat for Mr. Birley. It's a fairly hot job and very scratchy to the hands and arms, but it's rather fun, except when the devil gets into some sheaves and they *will* fall down.

Price and I slept in the Van again, and during the night it began to rain and has continued ever since. It's now Wednesday afternoon and tomorrow, if the rain stops, and the road is passable, we hope to start off to the Montney. This will be a good contrast to the trail anyway, a wide rough country with lots of creeks and one big river, the North Pine, no definite road or itinerary, but numbers of new families settled everywhere. If fine, it should be splendid; if wet, rather fiendish. And four weeks today I hope to be in the train for Edmonton.

St. Andrew's Van
Muddy Trail, Fort St. John
September 19.

This last week has been confusing but rather delightful. We were terribly delayed in starting with the Van by two days of pouring rain which utterly destroyed the road as usual, and also, of course, horribly delayed the harvest. On Wednesday, the day after our return from Hudson Hope, it was still hot and fine, so I washed in the morning and stooked wheat in the afternoon. But all Thursday it pelted, and we actually stayed in and mended and wrote letters. But as May's house was pretty full with herself and sister, Petter, and Mr. and Mrs. Paling, (three single bedrooms), we not only slept in the Van as usual, but tried to be very conscientious about washing and dressing in the garage, and cooking our meals outside. This last was rather a job, owing to the soaking wood, and I'm afraid we fell every morning to the temptation of breakfast in the house.

On Saturday the road seemed dry enough at last and we started off for the Montney district which lies North of Fort St. John. Last year it only had one school and now it has just got *five*, so you can see how the population is increasing. We stopped for the weekend at a very beautifully placed farm looking right across the valley of the North Pine. The man was away freighting, but the woman gave us a delightful welcome, and didn't let us have a single meal outside while we were there. We found that one of the new schools, i.e., Fish Creek School, was to start on Monday as the teacher had just arrived. I asked whether a little opening Service on Sunday would be possible and Mrs. Darnall[138] approved. So we dashed round the remaining families concerned—only four—(two of them from England), and they all approved and so did the teacher [Miss Barbara H. Bernard], a nice girl lodging with one of them. There remained two little boys living about two miles across the creek, so after supper I walked over to tell them, and had a funny time losing my way in the dark. The hired man started me off on a waggon-trail, but I thought I could improve upon it by taking what looked like a footpath, but was really just a cattle track down to the creek. So at the bottom I had to wade and was faced on the other side by a vertical bank of about 100 feet covered with dense bush. At the top it was just more bush and no trail at all; so I wandered vaguely Westward in the gathering dusk until my Guardian Angel suddenly traced two faint parallel lines upon the long coarse grass and I clung to them thankfully. You see a one-line track in this country is quite unreliable, as nine times out of ten it is merely made by horses or cattle; but two parallel lines must be made by a waggon and therefore must lead somewhere. They were so faint that I lost them several times, but reached the farm at last and found everyone in bed. But kind Mrs. W. woke up and promised to tell the boys, and put me on to the real trail back which I followed most conscientiously, and resisted all further temptations to stray.

Next day being Sunday we had the little Service in the new school, such a darling little neat log shack about twenty by fourteen feet. All the children came, i.e., ten, and two fathers and two mothers and the teacher. I made it a sort of Sunday School, and we had lots of hymns. The parents afterwards said they would like Sunday School to go on somehow, and the teacher said she would think about it! She seems a very nice girl. At the end we photographed everybody and just after I snapped and said "Thank you," one of the fathers said: "*There now*, and I hadn't got my teeth in." Of course I took another, with a special warning to everyone to get their teeth in first.

That evening the hired man at our farm shot a bear and before we left on Monday we ate some of his shoulder for dinner—quite good too, like stewed beef.

After that we started off for a district East of the Montney Creek which involved two very steep muddy hills, and showed the engine to be pulling very badly. In fact she failed just before the top of the second, and

Price had an awful job to get her up. In the evening we camped with
another very nice family, the father a Canadian, the mother a Londoner
from Clapham.[139] She welcomed us most touchingly and her little boy
Jimmie followed us about like a dog and *clamoured* to be allowed to
sleep with us in the Van! In the morning a little friend came to play with
him, and I had a tiny Bible lesson with the two, gave them books and
pictures, and lent Mrs. Lea the *People's Life of Christ*. Poor woman, her
little girl of seven went blind this year through an accident, and has just
come out to a Blind School at Vancouver. Mrs. Lea feels it terribly.

After that we visited three or four families in that district (which hasn't
yet got any school), and found one family still living in a small tent
which they have occupied since May. Then the engine once more
showed signs of heart trouble and Price said we must go back to Fort St.
John and have it seen to before we got too far away. I was very cross and
wanted to walk on; but there were miles of unknown trail ahead and no
known stopping-place, so in the end I had to eat humble pie and go back
with her. Only I made her drop me three miles out so that I could visit a
halfbreed family we had heard of. Their home was buried in the bush
and when I did find the little shack there was only a full-blooded squaw
nursing her baby. I shook hands with her and asked whether she had any
other children, but all the English she knew was "Bill," and he was
nowhere to be seen, so that was rather a fruitless visit. When I got back to
Price I found the usual discussion going on about "compression" and
"distribution." They did something to stimulate St. Andrew [the Van] a
bit, and then to my deeper rage she said we must go back to Birleys to fill
up from our own barrel of petrol. By the time we had filled up it was too
dark so we slept there, and that night and all next day it poured and
poured again!

So on Wednesday I took to my legs once more and looked up two new
families who had just come into the district. They were so nice and
welcoming and all at home on account of the pelting rain.

(Must stop this and post and start away).

Indian Creek
Mid-Winter, i.e., September 23, 1930.
(To be posted at Whiskey Creek).

I left off last time in the rain and am writing this in the snow—all
rather tragic for the farmers who simply can*not* get in their crops. Last
Thursday opened fine and lovely, but the road was far too slushy to

attempt a start with the Van, so I decided to have a day across the North Pine. I knew there was anyhow one family there, but there is no road or bridge. So you have to walk or ride to the river and either ford it or get over in a boat.

Price didn't want to go because she doesn't ride and I had the offer of a horse from the Perrys who live three miles from May. (The Birley horses are now all engaged). So I started at 8 o'clock, wearing my long rubber boots and waded through three miles of long dripping prairie grass to the Perrys. There was the first snag. All their horses were out grazing and nobody quite knew where. One of the six brothers immediately started out to find them, but it was nearly 11 before he brought one back for me, a grey mare called Belle. It was sickening to wait so long at the start, but I helped the two sisters to wash up the family breakfast, and made better friends with them. They are expecting their parents up from Alberta and the brothers are busy building a fine, new log house with an upper floor to welcome them.

Meanwhile they themselves have all been sleeping in a tent and living, cooking and eating in a small one-room shack which is also the girls' bedroom. Directly Belle arrived, I started off, rather thrilled at the thought of fording the North Pine at last and visiting the other side which has always looked a sort of Promised Land from different high points round Fort St. John.

It was three miles to the crossing, the first part just high prairie, but the last mile or more a steep greasy descent down the 800 foot bank of the river. That was nasty, slippery riding but perfectly lovely otherwise, like a Scotch glen, the trees and all the banks glowing with autumn colours. But at the bottom, where I expected to ford the river in state, I found to my great disgust a swift rushing torrent, pretty wide and obviously deep.

Luckily Mrs. Birley's sister lives just the other side, and her brother Freddy Beaton acts as a sort of informal Charon. I saw him and shouted across "Can I ford?" and he shouted back "No." Presently he put out in a little boat, half full of water like all the boats here, and came over for me. I wanted to make the horse swim, but he said she might get injured by the rocks, or might refuse to swim at all and run away into the bush. So, as she wasn't mine, I didn't take the risk, but tied her regretfully to a tree by the water and came over without her. It was fun crossing. We poled laboriously up one side of the stream, then pushed out into the main current and paddled hard to keep straight while the water swept us down to a tiny sandy beach on the other side.

Mrs. Mikkleson who lives there is the halfbreed lady whom I went with to Grande Prairie in June when she took her two tiny boys to the hospital. I found her busy with the washing and we had the usual long friendly chatty delay till dinner at about 1. The baby was unaccustomed to strangers and yelled most of the time, and the elder boy aged about three did every naughty thing he could think of to mark the occasion, so it was rather a restless visit. Mrs. Mikkleson was very welcoming. She lives at present in almost complete isolation, but she looks forward optimistically to the day when there will be a bridge across the Pine and graded roads both sides and "all kinds of cars go by." That day may come, but I doubt if she will see it. She had never been up the big hill behind her and had no idea where anybody lived on the top, so at 2 I broke away and climbed the steep waggon trail for 800 feet. It was pretty stiff and took forty minutes exactly, with lovely views up and down the river whenever you paused to puff.

At the top was just rolling "parkland" as it is officially called, rather beautiful because so high and apparently empty, quite untroubled by roads except the one rough waggon-trail. After about a mile I found a shack, and in it a charming oldish man pleasantly called [Harry] Ambrose. He told me there was only one English-speaking family and they were one and a half miles away. I was so thankful as I expected them to be at least five or six. The way on to them was nearly all through quite thick bush, and I had new hopes of seeing a bear, but no luck as usual. Instead, I found in a clearing, a one-room shack, a dear little family, and a mother born in the *Isle of Thanet* [Mrs. Framst].[140] She was so nice and pleased, because she really has no neighbours at all, at least no woman. But she was quite cheerful and hopeful, and looked forward to a new house which her husband (a Dane I think), was building. I had a little Sunday School with the four very sweet little children and then they gave me tea and I came away quite regretfully. The kind father appeared just as I was leaving and politely lent me his horse to ride as far as Mr. Ambrose, for which I was grateful because I wanted to cross the river again before dark. Apparently the only other family was three miles farther on and *quite* Russian; so I had to abandon them though not without shame.

The wind got up and the rain began again on my way back, but I reached the river about 5.30, found Freddy Beaton again to put me across, and poor Belle still waiting on the other side. She was full of beans to get home, so we reached the Perrys about 7, just as they were going to have supper. Of course they made me join them, so I shared their meal of potatoes and turnips and wild strawberries and finally got back to May's at about nine.

All that week the Northern Lights had been wonderful after dark. But that night they were perfectly amazing and we could hardly go to bed. They seemed to run all over the sky like gigantic plumes and waves and waterfalls continually rippling and moving and waving and unfolding and breaking out into fringes of rose and green and mauve. You never saw anything so extraordinary and mysterious, but the people here say, "My! Ain't they *pretty!*"

On Friday it was fine at last and a good strong wind blowing, so we decided to give it to the late afternoon to dry the road and then to start again for the Montney, and go as far as we possibly could. This time all went well, and although there is no road up the Montney but only a waggon trail, most of it was tolerably dry and none of the mud-and-water-holes were *quite* bad enough to stop the Van. The Montney is a sort of wide moorland about thirty miles North and South by ten East and West. It is rather beautiful and rolling, and is watered by three big creeks and various little coulees all running into the North Pine. The first eight miles by four is an Indian Reserve and quite uninhabited except for a handful of Indian tents. But after we had crossed that we began to see one or two scattered shacks, the first one we reached being the Montney Post Office, fourteen miles from Fort St. John. There we found a tremendous welcome, because it turned out that Mrs. Long was alone with her little boy, Mr. Long being away in Fort St. John.[141] We asked if we might camp outside her house, and she implored us to come and sleep inside and keep her company. So as it was a bitterly cold and windy night we yielded and brought in our bedding from the Van and laid it on her floor.

Hold-up Creek[142]
Michaelmas Eve, (September 29).

No nonsense about pens up here. I am spending the night with a halfbreed lady who runs a little store at the end of all things. That's not quite true either, because I hope to ride twelve miles through the bush tomorrow to the next house where lives a solitary widow with six children.

I told you how we got to Montney Prairie last Friday week and slept with the Postmaster's wife, Mrs. Long. She was such a kind, welcoming little woman and really thrilled to have us. Her husband, known as "Shorty Long," is chiefly a job carpenter and earns what he can by helping to build other people's houses in any part of the country. So he is constantly away and she and her little boy of six get rather lonely. They are obviously very poor but being a Post Office their shack has two rooms, i.e., the Office-kitchen-livingroom and the bedroom. She insisted on our going inside for supper and breakfast, so we retaliated by taking in our supplies and forcing her to share with us—soup, tinned

fish and bottled fruit—I think the biggest supper she has had for years. It
was mail-day, so various stray men looked in for their letters, and mostly
stayed sitting on wooden boxes and sharing a bit of supper for luck. Next
morning was lovely, and we had a very interesting day visiting all the
families we could reach from there and inviting the children and grown-
ups to a Sunday School and Service next day. We found most of them
still living in one-room shacks, and some still in tents, but nearly all had
a better house or an extra room in process of building. What they put up
with quite cheerfully is really wonderful. We found the school
teacher,[143] for instance, lodging in a one-room shack with a man and his
wife and two boys, under a roof which was leaking almost everywhere,
and every time it rained, soaked all their clothes and furniture. The
obvious question is, "Why not mend it?" and the answer is, "No time."
You see, nearly all these people have only been up here a few months,
and have every blessed thing to do to get their farms started at all, and
everything else is so urgent if they are to make a living at all that the last
thing to be attended to is their own house.

We had supper again with Mrs. Long but refused to sleep inside a
second night, as it really is against Hasell's principles and ours. Mrs.
Long's chief inconvenience is lack of water. She has to carry her buckets
over half a mile for every drop, and the result was there was none to wash
in the first evening.

On Sunday morning we visited some more, and then went straight to
the new school for Sunday School. It is a dear little plain log building
like the rest but less finished than Fish Creek, having no desks but only
one little improvised bench about a foot high. We hastily made two more
of logs and boards and then had the Sunday School. There were ten
children, nearly all very small and unable to read, so we had a very
simple sort of lesson and tried to teach them to sing "Jesus Loves Me,
This I Know," and then gave them the usual little books and cards. I was
rather touched by one little girl to whom I had explained the picture of
our Lord and all the children. She ran to show it to her mother and just
explained quite simply, "Look Mummy—He liked them *all*."

Afterwards, to our great surprise, *sixteen* people came to the grown-up
Service and joined in delightfully. Before it was over a big storm of rain
began and a freezing wind, but we managed to take the usual farewell
photograph of the congregation before starting off for Indian Creek.[144]

That was only fourteen miles, but awful going through deep mud and
we were wondering where on earth to try and camp, when a blessed
chance guided us to a widow lady called Mrs. J.[145] She was a perfect
angel, made us go in to supper, offered us her bed and generally treated
us as long-lost daughters. Of course we refused the bed and slept in the
Van and were rather amused to wake up and find a world of deep snow

and plenty more still driving in the wind. This lasted for the next two days, so we abandoned the Van by day for fear of sticking in a drift and visited all the Indian Creek families on our legs, quite fun in a district so innocent of roads or any other landmark and only the very vaguest of snowy trails to find and follow, and these sort of directions:

"Go straight North West (in a sunless blizzard), for about a mile, then turn North East and go till you come to a *fence*. Follow that down for three-quarters of a mile and then strike due North and go through some *bush* till you come out on some *breaking*. Cross the breaking in a Westerly direction and go on till you come to a *shack*. But before you reach the shack strike North West again until you see a field of *oats*. Angle across that field toward the West and you will come to a *stream* which is quite shallow if you hit it at the right spot (we never seemed to!), and right the other side you'll see a pig pasture and beyond that you'll find two trails. Follow the *faint* one and that will being you straight across a deep coulee and up to Stimpsons'[146] farm."

I am very sorry to say that Price is about *twenty* times better than I am at remembering and following these directions. In fact she is a regular sleuth-hound and fools me at every turn which was annoying at first, but one of the many little things you soon get used to. Only I couldn't resist a malicious consolation at her greater tendency to fall over snags hidden in the snow! Wasn't it beastly of me?

We had two very full days mushing about in the snow and visited almost every house, including, of course, the school. It was pretty cold in the Van at night as there were about 22 degrees of frost, and our tin walls seemed to invite them in. But the angelic Mrs. J. made us have breakfast and supper indoors so there was no hardship at all. On the third morning it had ceased to snow and the ground underneath was frozen hard enough to run the Van, so we seized the chance of getting on to Rose Prairie before a thaw should turn the trail into an impassable bog.

Rose Prairie is another new School District in the Montney, higher and much less bushy than Indian Creek, but otherwise much the same. It was originally called Whiskey Creek, but the British Columbia Government, in allowing a school, changed the name, which amused everybody rather!

On the way we passed a little store, and as I had no gloves and my hands seemed to know it, I tried to buy some. The man had none to sell, but he said "Wait a minute," and running to his little inner room, came back with an old pair of woollen mitts of his own which he insisted on giving me, as well as a prairie chicken which he had just shot and thought we might be able to cook for supper. Wasn't it decent of him?

At Rose Prairie we heard of another woman whose husband was away and presumably lonely. So we called to ask if we might camp with her, and found her in a small one-room shack with three tiny children. She said, "I'm afraid I've only got one bed but you're welcome to share it, and I've got no bread or milk, but lots of potatoes to offer you." Of course we explained about sleeping in the Van, and having brought our food, and only asked for the luxury of cooking and eating it indoors as it was dark and cold. Of course she agreed to that and we brought in a lot of tinned soup and stuff and a whole loaf given us by Mrs. J., and made her and her tiny boy and girl have a real supper, which I'm afraid they hadn't had for ages. Mrs. M. is a pretty little Scotchwoman of twenty-six who came out with her parents when she was four. She and her husband and babies came up to the Montney last year with hardly any savings, and have been living from hand to mouth ever since. Now he has gone away South to look for harvest work and she and the children are living on two meals a day based on vegetables from their little garden. She was most refined and full of fun and we had two nights there cooking inordinately large breakfasts and suppers and doing all we could unobtrusively to stoke her up especially in view of the lean little four months baby she was nursing. You can imagine what an excitement the prairie chicken was on the second night. I never saw anyone more sweet and plucky than Mrs. M. She made nothing at all of her obvious privations, and hated even my getting water for her from the creek, though she owned it sometimes made her side ache having to go half a mile for every pailful, especially on washing days.

She was full of ingenuity, always making something out of nothing, and not only clothes but *toys* for the children. She showed me a really splendid rag-doll she had made and dressed quite beautifully, without even *scissors*. She had done all the cutting with a disused razor blade of her husband's! He, alas, is an agnostic but she isn't. So she was glad to have prayers with us each morning and promised to carry on with the children. I think in spite of all her gaiety and resourcefulness she had really been feeling pretty lonely and depressed. Anyhow, when we left on Friday morning she said quite simply, "You folks have pulled me out of a deep hole."

We found much the same conditions at Rose Prairie as at Indian Creek. Most of the people had been in less than a year and were living in one-room shacks. A few families were still living in the tiny tents they had occupied since they came in this spring. Of course they intended to build houses and some had them nearly built. But the necessity of getting on with the farm work before the winter is so urgent if they are to live at all, that the house is quite a minor consideration, and has to take its chance after clearing and breaking land, planting vegetables, etc. They were all wonderfully welcoming, and wanted to give us food, however cramped their space and short their victuals and leaky their roofs.

I had a good meeting with the children at school, but, as at Indian Creek, didn't attempt a grown-up Service, because we had no Sunday [School], and also because a nice United Church student [Mr. Lester] had been holding Services for them all this summer.

For those two days the frost held hard and was very lovely; wide rolling country all crisp and clear, the green spruces still heavy with snow and the little poplars with their yellow leaves still on, all sparkling with hoar frost. The nights were pretty parky, especially the all-over wash on the front seat of the Van, and we woke up to find hoar frost in our hair. But on Friday the thaw came with a rush, and we fled before it to try and reach our last centre called the Hold-up before the trail was too rotten. We ran about fourteen miles (chiefly on low gear), and then at a house about seven miles short of the Hold-up realized that the Van simply couldn't go any further without getting fatally bogged.

So Price went to the house to ask if we might camp there and I walked on to visit two houses about a mile up a side trail. One of these gave me supper and I got back to find that Price was practically a member of the B. family, and was doing most of their chores with her usual firmness and efficiency. This was a well-to-do family with two or three rooms and lots of food. They are keen United Church people, but welcomed us as "all the same thing." The mother is very devout in the best sense of Methodist piety. Early in the night the rain began, and for the next thirty-six hours it poured and poured. So in the morning we abandoned the Van, took knapsacks and an iron ration of Sunday School books and pictures, and set off in waterproofs and rubber boots for the Hold-up. There were various families to find on the way and the going was so heavy that we didn't reach the first Hold-up house till after five. The mother there is a keen Anglican and has a good house of three or four rooms, so we had some hopes of getting in there for the night. But it turned out that besides her own husband and nine children, she had two more newcomer families staying there, i.e., nine extra people, making twenty in all. So we didn't even stay for supper (though asked), but hurried on in search of rather less crowded beds. The Hold-up valley seemed to be one continuous swamp, and we plunged and splashed along for another hour or more with the water nearly over our boots, looking for the T.'s house, because this seemed our best chance. But on the way we found one other family and invited the children to a Sunday School tomorrow.

At last we reached the T.'s, and found them still living in a one-room shack as Mr. T. and a couple of friends were building, but had not yet finished, a good new house. Luckily Mrs. T. only has one tiny baby, and although the school teacher boards with them,[147] she was mercifully away for the night. So Mr. T. promptly invited us into their tiny home which we nearly flooded with our dripping clothes, and said, "I'll go and sleep with a bachelor, you folks can sleep in our bed, and my wife can have the neighbour's." We protested rather feebly, but there was really no alternative, so in a few minutes we sat down to supper with them, i.e., Price and me, the two men helping with the building—one of these is a German—Mr. T., a Yankee, and Mrs. T., a very pretty, refined girl from Norfolk. The night plans went off splendidly, as the men melted away to some bachelor's shack, and we three had a capital time, plus the perfectly sweet little baby. Next morning we had our little Matins under difficulties as the men turned up for breakfast at 8, and in a one-room shack there's a lot to be done before that. Mr. T. is unluckily a professed atheist but Mrs. T. is an Anglican as far as her present surroundings permit. She is so pretty and refined and a little reserved that I fear she must be a little lonely in that swampy valley twenty-seven miles North of Fort St. John and with no English woman of any sort within reach. Still she's got her husband and baby, and the prospect very soon of a three-roomed house, so I think she is really happy, apart from a half-conscious spiritual starvation.

After helping her a little with the house and baby, we mobilised again and visited the two or three remaining very small and very scattered homes. At the end of the valley we found a little store kept by a halfbreed lady called Mrs. Slyman,[148] whose husband, a *Moslem from Syria*, was down at Fort St. John. I arranged to come back and sleep with her after Sunday School in order to visit one more family the next day. This family lives by the Blueberry River, thirteen miles farther on through thick bush and everyone (specially Price), was so *determined* that I couldn't go that if there had been no other motive in the world, I must have gone somewhere.

So, through Mrs. Slyman, I got the promise of a horse from an old Yankee. Then Price got into a stew about my going alone (she doesn't ride), so we were in the middle of *that* argument when we spotted an Indian camp a few hundred yards away. I said, "Let's see if they are going back North tomorrow." So Mrs. Slyman came with us as interpreter. It was a squalid little camp, as all the Indians of our district are pretty debased, more or less like Gypsies, and speak hardly any English. They don't do any sort of work, but only hunt bear and moose and barter their meat with the white men for vegetables and butter. I grinned at the women and children and gave them some chocolate, while Mrs. Slyman found out from the men that they *might* start back tomorrow at 10 if it was fine. So I said I might go with them if they started early enough, and Price had to be satisfied with that.

Then we almost waded the two and a half miles back to the Hold-up School and had a terrific struggle with soaking wood to start a fire and warm it up as it was a wet and biting cold day. Also, all the chinking had come out between the logs, so the wind fairly whistled through them. We got everything ready and then had our first real disappointment, for only *one* girl came! She was the fifteen year old daughter of a rather disreputable mother and she waited with us for two whole hours but nobody else came. Certainly it was a foul day and you couldn't walk a yard without being soaked from heat to foot, and none of these children have rubber boots or waterproofs, and none lived nearer than a mile away. So we sang a lot of hymns with Valma and read the Bible and had some prayers, and gave her a book and a prayer card to go on with. She longs to be a Guide, and I must try and arrange something for her. After that Price and I separated—she to trudge back to the Van at the B.'s place and I to spend the night with Mrs. Slyman. She is such a nice woman, most clean and refined, but being a halfbreed, had no education (they do now of course), and could not read or write one word. She was pleased to have me, being genuinely *nervous* at night—a very unusual thing out here. She made me a bed on the floor and I slept very well in spite of an almost deafening stampede of mice which echoed through my dreams almost like cavalry charges.

Next morning I said, "Do you like to have *quite* so many mice?" "No, I don't." "What about a cat?" "I can't get one." (Fancy that!)

Monday was fine and cold—no move on the part of the Indians. Mr. Long brought me round his heavy, young grey mare called "Fanny Rooseveldt." Still no move on the part of the Indians, so I gave them up, and taking a knapsack with pyjamas, prayer-cards and chocolate bars, started off on the North Trail for the Blueberry River. I soon found out why all the men had been a little discouraging. The whole blessed thirteen miles was deep, *deep* clinging mud, only varied by deeper water or more treacherous muskeg (bog). Poor Fanny hated it and I'm sure I don't wonder and she certainly had a filthy time of it. Added to that the heavy snow and rain had brought down or bent over *hundreds* of trees, blocking the narrow trail every few yards. So that almost all the way we were either ducking under, forcing through, or climbing over barriers. And of course every blessed tree we ducked under discharged all its rain or snow down my neck.

The bush itself was rather wonderful, some of it only poplar, but chiefly deep, sombre spruce, very thick and close-growing, and the ground (but not the trail), still covered with snow. Of course the sun couldn't penetrate it a bit, so it was very dark and bitterly cold and rather uncanny. Going as hard as I could push Fanny, it took us a good four hours to get through, and then you can't think what bliss it was to come out to open country again and to see the Blueberry hills ahead. It seemed just like the Promised Land and after a mile more of lovely open slopes and valleys we came to the top of the high river bank, and down a steep hill to the solitary shack near the water.

I found a sort of coloured hired-man first, and then Mrs. Rodgers

herself.[149] She is a good looking young middle-aged widow who has
been there since last autumn. She has had great trouble, first her
husband died, and then this summer her baby boy was drowned in the
river. She told me all about it, and was, I think, glad to have a woman to
talk to as apparently she never sees one now. The shack was *very* small
and she had five more children, so I didn't see how I could sleep there,
and decided to start back at 8.30 so as to be sure of getting past the bush
before sundown. To my great delight Mrs. Rodgers said she was
Anglican and wanted to bring up her children real Anglicans too. She
was delighted to have them on the Sunday School by Post, and agreed to
a little Sunday School class at once. So she called in the three little boys
and one little girl (the eldest boy was unluckily out), and we immediately
had a very informal little Bible Class all sitting on the one bench
together. The children were awfully keen and not a bit shy, and we sang
three hymns in all, together, most lustily, and ended with some prayers,
during which they were wonderfully reverent and sweet.

Unluckily my time was awfully short, so I gave them all the books and
pictures while Mrs. Rodgers fried up a big dish of potatoes which we had
for dinner. I had a few sweet biscuits for the kids and also a chocolate bar
each, which caused *fearful* excitement because apparently they had not
seen them since came to the Blueberry. Mrs. Rodgers had no
Testament, so I gave her my little one and also a tiny book for mourners
and then most sadly had to come away. The happiness of this visit far
more than made up for the washed-out Sunday School disappointment
yesterday, and I was deeply thankful about it.

The ride back, though it took another full four hours, seemed like a
pleasure trip. There was only one disappointment. I saw neither moose
nor bear, and had felt pretty sure of one or the other. However, as the
hired man had remarked, "If your horse smells a bear he'll likely go crazy
with fear," the disappointment on the return journey was not quite so
bitter as before. Poor Fanny was really very good and gallant. Of course
she loathed the deep mud and muskeg, and kept trying to start aside into
the bush to improve her footing, without any regard as to whether my
body or head could follow. So before the end I had a stronger fellow
feeling with Absalom than ever before.[150] We got in just before sundown,
and I spent the rest of the evening sleepily talking to Mrs. Slyman, and as
early as 8.30 was ready to defy the mice.

On Tuesday I left Mrs. Slyman and do hope her husband joined her
that evening as she does so hate being alone. I walked the eight miles to
the B.'s and found Price ready to start off in the Van *back to Fort St.
John*.

The trail had had two days to dry up a little but was still pretty fierce.
Poor Price had to drive in bottom gear for about half the distance and

we had two bad sticks in the mud, the second one requiring a team of horses which mercifully came along just at the point of despair. Price certainly drove awfully well, and was clever to get us back to May's about 9 o'clock. But the engine was pulling so badly that we agreed that it should go into dock next day while I borrowed a horse to finish up the job round Charlie Lake.

Wednesday was a gorgeous day and I raised another horse (my twelfth), a charming grey colt, and spent the whole day visiting all the people round Charlie Lake with one last school visit. Charlie Lake was looking lovely like everywhere else just now, surrounded by the gold and bronze, and red and bright yellow trees.

So I was riding home in the gloaming, blissfully feeling the job finished, and out to Pouce Coupé on Friday—when I was suddenly hailed by a strange man in the darkness who turned out to be . . .

The Bishop of the Diocese![151]

C.P.R. Train, crossing the Rockies
(Posted October 11).

One more try to get this finished however late it may arrive, because it is the only diary I have attempted to keep. Last edition left off at meeting the Bishop quite unexpectedly late in the evening of Wednesday, October 1. I'm sorry to say it was more of a jar than a joy to see him just then, because we had made every plan to start for Pouce Coupé on Friday and it was clear that this would stop it. He said Mr. Pickell had just brought him in, that he is going straight to Taylor's Flats for the night, and off first thing in the morning to the mail boat to Hudson Hope, that he would be back by Saturday night, and be glad if I would bill him three Services for Sunday and arrange transportation.

I knew Price would kick hard against any delay in our departure because she believed it would be all we could do anyway to put the Van away for the winter and be sure of Wednesday's train. So we had rather an earnest discussion that night when camping for the second and last time with the Rodgers. But eventually Price agreed that we really could not turn tail at such a moment, and so we planned to prepare all we could beforehand, and not to bolt till Sunday night or Monday morning.

So all Thursday we billed and boomed the Bishop as hard as possible, and tried to raise a fever of expectation in all three centres (Fort St. John, Baldonnel and Taylor's Flats). Dear May was very scornful as usual, and thought I was a fool, but then she always does, so I take little notice of that. Price played up well, and the people seemed responsive. Practically none of them have ever seen the Bishop, and indeed hardly any are really Episcopalian, but all were prepared to welcome him as a mild excitement; and there was as usual real enthusiasm in the charming Brown family—who are devout Presbyterians!

On Friday we planned to wash all the Van pots and pans and other junk, and I meant to make up my reports for Hasell and even send out all the Sunday School magazines, but another call-off came to try poor Price's patience. We had to go in early to Fort St. John for something and there we learnt a very sad thing—that up in Rose Prairie where we were last week, a tiny boy of three years had wandered into the bush and been lost for forty-eight hours.[152] All the men out there had been searching for him ever since his disappearance and were quite exhausted, so the mail man had ridden in to ask for help. Nearly all *our* men were widely scattered on their farms trying to stack their grain, so only seven were actually in the settlement and these immediately volunteered, and some looked inquiringly at the Van. But Price was very firm. She said the engine was not in fit condition to make that trail again anyway, least of all with a bunch of men on board, and I *knew* she was right but was none the less miserable for that.

At last someone produced a truck; and then they wanted more volunteers to comb the bush so we went off to the school and collected the three Scout leaders with their dogs, while Price had the bright idea of asking Dr. Brown. He agreed at once and said he would take his car and any extras. But there were no extras, and that only made eleven and so I couldn't bear it any longer, and asked whether I might go with them. Of course this was letting poor Price down again, but she was very good about it and agreed to go on with the Van-cleaning without me. Dr. Brown said we must take bed-rolls as goodness knew when we should be back. So I rolled up a sleeping bag and a pocket-comb and a washrag and borrowed the Postmaster's wife's breeches and off we went. The truck had already started a good while, but Dr. Brown drove terrifically fast, charged the mud holes, banged over ruts, jumped the big tree stumps, and soon caught it up. Then we stuck twice in the mud, but not badly, and got out pretty easily both times, though neatly plastered all over ourselves. All the time we wondered whether the child could *possibly* be still alive, or whether a beast (bear or coyote), had got it, and thought about the poor mother.

We had gone about twenty miles and had only about five more to go, when we saw Mr. Devlin, the policeman, riding towards us. He waved his hat and shouted, "He's found!"

When we came up he told us that one of the men had found him an hour before, only about three miles from home, but in *deep* bush, that

his clothes were torn, but there was no injury and he was *perfectly well*—
just fancy, after being lost in the bush for two days and two nights
without food or shelter—and a hard frost the second night! What about
Guardian Angels?

Dr. Brown asked lots of questions to see if he was needed, but the
answers convinced him that he wasn't. The child had had some warm
milk and a warm bath and had gone to sleep quite happily with his
mother. Apparently what saved him was being such a baby and having
no imagination. If he had been five or seven it would have been much
worse—as it was, all he said when the men found him was, "Mummy's
gone."

I should love to have gone on, and given thanks with her but Dr.
Brown, finding he wasn't needed, naturally wanted to get back to work.
So we turned straight round and took all the afternoon getting home,
including one good stick of over an hour in thick mud up to the axles.
Dear May was rather scornful again, and I suppose it might be called a
wasted day. But we couldn't possibly know that beforehand, and
anyway, I was so thankful about the boy that nothing else mattered at
all.

Next morning I tried to make up for it with reports and packing and
the rest of it; and in the afternoon we went into Fort St. John to make
finally sure of the Bishop's transport, and also to collect two or three
men to meet him at lunch in the hotel between the Services. That was our
last evening at the Birleys and rather spoilt for Price by anxiety about the
weather, and for me by having to get off all the Sunday School
magazines, which completely filled up the time—such a prosy
professional finish and no chance of any sort of farewell talk.

On Sunday morning we finally weighed anchor directly after
breakfast, said a last goodbye to the Birleys and drove complete with
baggage to Fort St. John for the first Service.

There Mr. Pickell handed me a wire from the Bishop saying: "Boat
broken down. Cannot reach Fort St. John. Arriving at Taylor's Flats
afternoon. Will take two later Services."!!!

There was nothing for it but to call off the luncheon-party, call the
people in town and then hurry to school and face any who should have
come early.

At this point, of course, the Peace River diary breaks off. Monica went
with Christopher to Vancouver, to see him off to Australia.
She then returned across Canada to Montreal and so to England to

*resume her life at "Home," to relax and to restore her strength. But if not
active on the frontier of the Peace, she was engaged within five months
in preparations for her return to take up the work begun, this time on her
own, and from her own base. She had grown to love Peace River and was
committed to the work she had started there. How much the North Peace
had become Monica's, with the support of her circle in England, was
shown by the return of Adeline Harmer, her closest friend, with her.*

In the train for Pouce Coupé
May 9, 1931.

We reached Montreal last Saturday evening at 7.30 and at 10.30
boarded the Montreal train, and got an upper bunk in a pretty full
tourist coach. The journey lasted exactly three days and three nights and
was all too short for us: we did enjoy it so much. We were pledged to Mrs.
Harmer[153] to have one meal a day in the dining car but cooked the other
three from an immense supply on the coke stove in the tiny kitchen at the
end of the coach. Our companions were plentiful and friendly and
included one family of four children. These were awfully good
considering the long confinement, and we could hardly object to their
playing hide and seek and having wrestling matches for a few hours each
day.

The country was first all bush, rocks and lakes and then all prairie—
pretty monotonous but that saved you the trouble of looking at it more
than once or twice an hour and in some parts, but not all, there was a
shimmer of pale green leaves among the endless little white poplars.

We reached Edmonton at 10.40 on Tuesday night and found the
faithful Archdeacon Burgett waiting for us. I must say he is a perfect
fairy godfather. He took us straight back to stay at the delightful Mission
House where he lives, and did absolutely everything for us until we left
on the very last train yesterday (Friday) afternoon.

This allowed us exactly two and a half days in which to lay in all our
furniture and tools. I thought it would be heaps of time but actually it
turned out to be sharp work. Edmonton seems to be almost entirely
composed of furniture shops, either new or second hand, and every piece
of waste land seems to be sown with old stoves, old beds and old cars for
sale. The Archdeacon went with us everywhere, introduced us to various
dealers, got us special terms, and took an impassioned interest in
everything, sitting on all the chairs and lying on all the beds with the
utmost earnestness. It was awfully hard to steer between luxury and

squalor and to combine the simplicity of a Mission among settlers with the necessities of a probable guest-house as well as a home for two others besides myself. In the end I'm afraid I fell into luxury and extravagance, although I did reject at least four out of every five suggested "essentials." But it really is extraordinary what a lot it seems to take to start a home, however small, absolutely from zero.

Well, anyway, I spent £60 and this is what we got for it.

(1) Two stoves, i.e., a cooker and a heater.

(2) Four beds, one of which acts as a sofa in the living room, and three of which are expandable so at any moment we can accommodate four guests without beginning to use the floor.

(3) Two tables, i.e., a very grand dining table, round like King Arthur's, and a small kitchen table. I had intended to make the latter, but came to the conclusion that it would be rather hard on whoever does the cooking.

(4) A second hand refrigerator, which I grudge horribly, but believe to be worth while.

(5) Three wicker garden chairs.

(6) Four little wooden chairs for the oratory.

(7) Thirty-four square yards of linoleum, the sort which looks exactly like plain polished wood.

(8) Three little floor mats.

(9) Two door mats.

(10) Three wall mirrors, of the sort called "shock glass." The Archdeacon thought these would be most satisfactory "because each time you see your slightly distorted face in them you can say, 'I am better looking *even* than that really.'"

(11) Endless kitchen things from zinc baths and water buckets, kettle and saucepans and flour bin, down to the tin-opener.

(12) Carpentering tools for making everything else—axe, saw, hammer, plane and smaller oddments.

(13) Gardening tools, the usual.

(14) A tent and a portable mosquito net.

It's a huge lot, isn't it and yet I don't think there is anything we could well leave out and of course there are no drawers or cupboards or washing stands or book cases. That's where the tools come in—we hope.

At lunch time on Thursday, to my great surprise, Mr. Simpson (the Fort St. John layreader), rang up. He and a group of other men from the North were on their way to act as witnesses in a murder trial at Jasper. You remember there was a double murder last summer across the North Pine River? Well they have just arrested a man for it and Mr. Simpson is one of the few people who met him and I think gave him hospitality on his way out of the country. He was a stranger and a foreigner and said he was looking for land. And not till three weeks later were the murdered bodies discovered. There is apparently no direct evidence and probably not enough to convict.[154] Poor Mr. Simpson has had a pretty hard and discouraging year with a poor crop and no market and of course no holiday, so it's an ill murder that does nobody any good.

He was going on to Jasper by the night train so the Archdeacon asked him to supper and we had half an hour's talk about the plans for my HOUSE which Mr. Simpson is to build (if he ever gets back from the trial), but I think I shall need all that time to look round and settle on the site. Mr. Simpson has got all the logs dovetailed and fitted together temporarily, so when all is settled, they have only got to be taken down and put together somewhere else.

Yesterday morning the Archdeacon celebrated the Holy Communion in the Mission Chapel as usual on Fridays. It was a wonderful thing to be able to have that Service on the last morning.

Yesterday we clinched and paid up everything and collected a few flower seeds (to start the garden)—lots of vegetable seeds to be got up here—and finally our most kind friend drove us to the station, complete with suitcases, and hat-box, gramophone, tent and TREE, and saw us off on this last lap, exactly one month from the moment we left Liverpool.

Only twenty-six hours in this wonderful old swaying, rocking train and at 6.30 to-night we shall be at POUCE COUPE.

We reached Pouce Coupé at 6.30 on Saturday, the 9th. It was rather fun coming along the last sixty miles that had just been laid, going twenty miles an hour over the new line and feeling vaguely adventurous about it. It was almost exciting being at Pouce Coupé again, the place where I had been so anxious last September and was now so perfectly hopeful and happy with Adeline. Everyone was most welcoming and we had quite a lively Sunday. First we visited the Anglican Sunday School held by a most faithful little Government official. Then, since there was no Service of our own in the morning, we went to the United Church where a young student held forth with great eloquence upon "motherhood." In the afternoon we called upon various friends and had an immense talk about Brownies with the second school teacher who is tremendously keen and begged us to come and see hers at school next morning. In the evening we went to the Anglican Service in the Community Hall (no church there yet), and saw Mr. Proctor and his wife, both just the same but enriched (?) by the arrival of a baby daughter.

On Monday morning we went to the school and found a very sweet party of Brownies in uniform who danced for us and simply adored. being taught a new game by Adeline. Then had to go into the big school-room and I had to make an impromptu speech about nothing at all to the Scouts and Guides, of which the only merit was that it interrupted lessons for a few minutes. One day we hope to arrange a big joint camp or rally but of course the sixty-five miles between us does make it rather difficult to do anything on a large scale.

Mr. Simmons, the school master, seems to devote all his spare time to the Scouts. He lives in a log shack right in the bush about two miles from school and he pressed us to go and see it. So in the afternoon when school was over we joined him and he led us in triumph to his house. The short cut is across the new railway bridge which spans the Pouce Coupé River. It's a high wooden trestle bridge over a gorge about 100 feet deep and 150 yards across. It was just a single railway track, of course, with no sides and six inches or so between the planks so you had to watch your feet and be careful not to be blown over by the very blustering wind. Adeline and I were both secretly rather fussed about the other. The shack was very well built and outside a good model for mine. One room inside, of course, but nothing but boxes for shelves and tables and chairs. He made us some lemonade and then led us all the way back over the bridge again.

At the hotel we found Tommy arrived so after supper we started on the last lap with a fine evening and good road. There was no event on the way except that we saw a bear in the bush quite close to the road which was luck for Adeline, and finally about 10.30 P.M. we reached the old ferry again, crossed the Peace and entered our own parish again. At 11 we arrived at Journey's End and found May in bed but awake and Nina (her sister), waiting to receive us. They both seemed so warm and welcoming that it was almost like coming home, and by the time we fell into Petter's deserted bed it all seemed so natural that but for Adeline's presence I could hardly realize that I had been away.

Tuesday was a glorious summer day. We had hardly had breakfast and hadn't had Matins or begun to unpack when in strolled Miss Muriel Haslam, who had walked over from Fort St. John to see us, and I suppose, learn the worst at once. You know, she is the girl whom Miss Hasell sent in last winter to carry on in my absence. She had written to me two or three times—awfully nice letters—and I had asked her if she would like to stay and join forces with us. So you see we were both dark horses to each other and I believe we shall get on together. Haslam is tall and very fair with corn-coloured hair—and looks and speaks un-mistakeably English. We had a good preliminary talk sitting in the sun

on the wood pile and worked out a sort of interim programme for the
next few weeks, i.e., until the men come up from Montreal. It's quite
clear that Haslam has done and is doing splendidly at Fort St. John. She
has pretty well concentrated all her time at the centre and has made first
rate progress with the Sunday School, Scouts and Guides there, besides
starting a little Prayer Meeting and Girls' Bible Class. So we agreed she
should carry on with them all for as long as she can stay and that I should
go to each in turn once with her to speak to the children and show there
is no rivalry between us. This sounds absurd but you know it's just the
sort of idea we have to be on the look out for. Meanwhile, Adeline and I
are to revive the doings at Baldonnel and Taylor's Flats and also get out
to other schools and centres whenever we can. There's lots to do for us all
and I cannot be too thankful that Haslam is so excellent and can stay.

We started by walking back with her to Fort St. John to her Prayer
Meeting which took place in the Postmistress's house. Only two other
women came but apparently there are two or three who often do. We
prayed sitting down and Haslam led by giving us heads of Intercession
spaced with good long pauses. We prayed for the needs of the place and
people in trouble or illness and it was very simple and very nice. We hope
to join forces for this as often as we can.

That evening I talked over sites for the house with May. It appears that
the first site she offered me has become impracticable since Mr. Birley
has decided to break and cultivate the field between it and the road. It's
disappointing to me because it's far the loveliest position I've seen. She
took us to see another place about a quarter mile farther on, nearer to the
road, very convenient for the work, being almost exactly four miles from
each school and very pretty—but NO VIEW. It's a very good offer. She says
I can have all the land I want there and for as long as I like, but she won't
sell right out or take any rent. There's a slew [slough] pretty handy where
we could sink a well and it's only about eight minutes walk from the
coulee and about ten from May. In fact every prospect pleases—except
the view and only my stupid obstinate longing to see the river or the
mountains or the sunset goes on giving trouble.

May is quite wonderfully better and far more active than I dared to
hope. She can do almost everything she used to do except anything heavy
with the right arm or anything delicate with the right hand. But even so,
both these are far better than they were, thanks to that visit to the Grande
Prairie hospital and the little operation she had there. May says we must
stay here till the house is well started and since the site is not yet chosen
and Mr. Simpson, the builder, is still at the murder trial at Prince
George, it almost looks as though we shall be here well into July.

On Wednesday we joined Miss Haslam again at Fort St. John for the
Brownies which she has started there and is running admirably, and on

Thursday we joined her again for the Guides. The Company has increased to fifteen. She asked me to enroll the latest Tenderfoot and to present two second class badges. After that there was a Campfire and each Patrol gave a short entertainment got up especially for our benefit. It all seemed very much alive and really far better than months ago when I left them. We are planning a joint Rally of Scouts and Guides to welcome Mr. Guiton and Mr. Wolfendale[155] and to be on June 13 if possible. It will be very like the one held here last May—awfully primitive but a chance for friendly competition and an opportunity for the two parsons to meet a good many of the children and their parents.

Oh, I forgot to tell you that I have bought a CAR. It's Tommy's old one, a very old, old Ford called Elijah. It's very cheap, of course, and I paid the first instalment and took possession on Ascension Day. The screens have entirely gone and just at present all the tyres are quite dead, but Tommy is going to replace these with three middle-aged and two quite new ones. So when they come we shall be sound in the legs and Tommy swears that all the vital organs are as sound as a bell. Moreover he has promised to look after its health for me all this summer so I don't think I've done too badly.

On Friday we went out to Baldonnel School and Adeline took the Cubs while I took the Scouts. Another day she will take Brownies while I take Guides. They are all very backward compared to those in the city and we shall have our work cut out to make them put up any show at the Rally. Afterwards we went to visit some of the mothers and incidentally found far more bad health than I ever have before. We had to go back twice to one family and drive May in a completely different direction to help a woman who had nearly cut her arm off with a cream separator that broke and flew to pieces. So you see, Elijah is beginning to earn his keep even while he is both down at heel and flatfooted.

One other visit we paid on Friday was to Mrs. Simpson. She was awfully welcoming and full of talk, and out on her field what do you think we found? MY HOUSE. That is, the shell of it, all the logs dovetailed and fitted together, a perfect skeleton of an oblong shack waiting to be taken to pieces and put together somewhere, like a puzzle. There were no doors or windows cut, of course. It was just like a very primitive fortress but I was determined to get in. So we wandered round till we found a place where the ground fell away about six inches below the bottom log. Adeline crawled under first, just like a snake. I followed and stuck at the shoulders (so humiliating), scratched at the ground to make it an inch lower and squeezed into our stronghold. It seemed very strange and small, bare and hard to realize as a future home. But anyway we shall have either to find more logs and add another room or buy enough lumber to make one in the roof. I don't know yet which it will be. While we were inside the gap seemed to close up a bit, for coming out was harder than ever. But Mrs. Simpson laughed so much to see me pinned under the threshhold of my own house that it was well worth the mud we took away with us.

Almost nothing happened last week so it won't take long to tell about it. All Sunday it rained hard and was as cold as you could wish. The road was very greasy and two of Elijah's tyres were quite flat so we decided to use our legs until either the new ones arrived or the road dried up. So this Sunday we tried the experiment of morning Sunday School at Baldonnel, i.e., 10.30, but the attendance was not good and I am inclined to think the afternoon is better after all. I started a new book of lessons on the Church and Catechism called the *Sign of Faith,* while Adeline took the little ones at the other end of the room, round the stove. We walked home through rather heavy mud, after dinner had to use Elijah after all to take May over to the woman whose arm had been so terribly cut by a bursting separator. Having delivered May we did not dare take the car out again, so walked over to Fort St. John to be in time for Haslam's little afternoon Service—at least that was our intention. But being delayed in starting and the mud very heavy, we were twenty minutes late and found to our disgust that only one other woman having turned up, Haslam had abandoned the Service and locked up the tiny shanty she uses for a Chapel. We went round to see her at Mrs. Millar's feeling rather aggrieved, as twenty minutes late is NOTHING in this country. But Haslam was so apologetic and gave us such nice tea that in the end we forgave her, stayed an hour talking, and walked home only just in time to hold our own Evensong before supper. We like Haslam very much. She is terribly capable and her genuine efficiency leaves me rather faint. But she is perfectly modest and unimportant about it and very easy to make plans with. She has undoubtedly got a splendid hold on the Fort St. John children and I am still in hopes that she will stay on and live with me after the summer. But she is not able to decide anything beyond September as yet. On Sunday evening I played Mr. Birley all my new Church records—anthems and hymns. He seemed to enjoy them very much and said, "It's a funny thing but I sure like Church music."

On Monday we walked out to Fort St. John once more to visit the Scouts with Miss Haslam, tell them about Mr. Guiton and the coming Rally and endorse her carrying on with them until Mr. Wolfendale can take over. She has never dealt with boys before but she is running them admirably.

On Tuesday we had the Baldonnel Guides and Adeline the Brownies. They are a tiny little party about eleven in all but awfully sweet and tremendously keen to do well at the Rally, a hope which certainly seems to require a miracle as they are miles behind the Guides at Fort St. John. Afterwards we visited more families at that end and got delightful welcomes from them all. They *are* nice people, awfully hard up as regards cash—in fact practically cashless—but quite cheerful and most hospitable. Everybody trades by direct barter, exchanging eggs, butter, chickens, pigs, horses for whatever they want. But even that process is rather at a standstill now because everyone has too much of the same thing and the stores are refusing to be paid in unlimited eggs instead of dollars. One poor man took fourteen dozen eggs and tried to exchange them for groceries but the storekeeper would not give him a pinch of salt for the lot, so he had to take them all home again. There's heaps of milk and cream now too, and people would love to export it if only to Pouce Coupé, but the cost of getting it out sixty miles would be far more than it's worth, so that's no good either. I long for them to make cheese with it, if only for home consumption. But nobody seems to know how to and alas! I don't either.

Wednesday was Baldonnel Scouts and Adeline took the Wolf Cubs. She has never touched Cubs before but that's no matter: they seemed to be very happy and so did she. We pegged away at signalling and bandaging and they're not too bad, really, and great fun. After that another round of visiting, cross country and off the beaten track for me, a hot day and everything looking very fresh and lovely. I can't make out whether Adeline likes this country or not. It's rather monotonous and not a bit exciting but I must say I am getting very fond of it myself. Coming home we tried a short cut, which led us through several swamps and thickets, making us very late and entirely destroyed one of my stockings but gave us several fine new views and was quite worth it.

All this time my house has been held up, (a) for lack of a site; (b) for lack of a builder, that's all. On Thursday, therefore, having no children for once, Adeline and I went off to have a look at the one available homestead which might possibly do. It lies about three miles South of Fort St. John Post Office and about four miles West of here. I had to find one particular little halfbreed boy to take us, his home being the nearest to it, i.e., about a mile away with a big coulee between.

The homestead lies along the level top of one of the steep hills dropping to the river and the view from it is quite lovely. I fell utterly in love with it—the beauty of the steep fall, the green foreground and the blue background and the river wandering away into the distance—and would give my eyes for it—and could have it for two dollars (8s.4d.). But alas! there's the job to think of. It's about one and a half miles from the nearest decent trail and a pretty steep hill to it, which no car could negotiate in winter. So it would enormously waste both time and fuel in getting anywhere, and nobody could ever drop in on us. If only we were Premonstratensian Monks[156] it would be the Heaven-sent site but as things are I fear it is more like a temptation of the devil. So really and truly I believe I shall close with May's kind offer; though it has practically no view, it is geographically almost perfect. So I am gradually making up my mind to be sensible and accept a small viewless corner of someone else's land instead of a glorious freehold of my own.

After this rather depressing expedition we went off to visit Mrs. Anderson, you remember last year's teacher at Taylor's Flats. She is now living on her own homestead about a mile from here and has Petter for her lodger. She was most welcoming and kept us both for supper in her little shack twenty by fourteen feet. Petter came in from school and told us all about her wonderful plans for a visit to England next holidays. She is actually going to stay with her uncle, Sir Ernest Petter, who stood as Independent Conservative for St. George's division of Westminster. Isn't that a funny coincidence?

By that mail I heard from Mr. Simpson that the murder trial had not yet begun and he had no idea when he would be back—so would I find another builder. Therefore, after Guides again on Friday we set off to hunt a builder and had a most unsuccessful time. Late in the evening we went to look for Karl Anderson,[157] a Swede, who is said to be very good. We found his homestead away in the North Pine but he was off building for someone else at Charlie Lake. So there, I'll have to chase him on Monday. Meanwhile I saw a nice old Frenchman who has some extra logs and arranged to buy them from him directly. My Site and Builder are both finally achieved. We had supper that night with Mrs. Simpson and little Johnny. She comes from South Wales and is always longing for it again—though I think if she were [back there] she might be longing for the blessings of [the] Peace.

On Saturday morning Miss Haslam sent me a note asking me to take Fort St. John Sunday School for her as she had a chance to go to Pouce Coupé to see a friend who has just arrived there to drive the Caravan. So I spent most of that day, on and off, preparing for that School in the morning and this one, plus grown-ups' Service in the afternoon. Incidentally, we also paid a long visit to Dr. Brown's family (whose father is one of the absent witnesses). And at last got the new tyres fitted on to Tommy's old car which is now the *exact opposite* of Nebuchadnezzar's image[158]—being entirely disreputable in hood and body but beautifully shod about the feet.

It's a great comfort to have it sound and ready and I think the engine is good. But all the same we shall have to run it as sparingly as the job allows because, what with the cost of petrol and oil up here, and the roughness of the trails, I find the expense of actual running is about four times what the same distance would be at Home. Adeline drives most of the time. It's a funny contrast to her Austin and the Kentish roads but she makes a good job of it and only winks when we sink axle deep in a mud hole or an unexpected bump shoots us into the air like a rocket.

The acacia is going strong and so far is watered every day after the morning's wash.

Week ending May 30, 1931.

Last week was full of ups and downs but it ended in a blaze of glory.

Sunday was Whit Sunday and a perfectly glorious morning. We went to take the Fort St. John Sunday School for Miss Haslam, and I was glad of the chance, because although I am delighted that she is carrying on this school (and much more successfully than I ever did), still it was nice to take these children once more. Of course, having the car made it perfectly simple too, and we did not have to leave here till nearly 10.30. Haslam has got the children into perfect order and they turned up well and in good time. We started with a short singing practice and learned a new hymn—"Our Blest Redeemer." The lesson was, of course, a gift of the Holy Spirit, an entirely new subject to most of these children. Haslam has inaugurated a Birthday Roll and each child whose birthday falls during the week before receives a tiny present from the Sunday School. A little girl called Etta was ill last Sunday so Haslam left me a little sacred story book for her and she had the additional glories of choosing the last hymn and carrying the collecting bag. I think this is a very innocent form of bribery and mean to imitate it slavishly at Baldonnel and Taylor's.

At the end of School it was pouring, so we loaded up the car twice and dropped a few of the most unsuitably clad females near their homes before coming back to dinner. Afterwards it cleared up again and we had a good Sunday School at Baldonnel followed by a grown-up Service. About ten women turned up to that and two men which wasn't bad and I was awfully glad, though a bit embarrassed, to see May and Tommy. We took the gramophone and Adeline played some voluntaries before and after the Service, chiefly "He Shall Feed His Flock," and "O Rest in the Lord." They sounded lovely and really did seem to supply a little of the atmosphere that is bound to be lacking in these bare little schools. After Service we had the usual *conversazione* and didn't get home till supper-time.

Oh, I forgot to tell you one rather typical little incident at Sunday School. Four of the boys turned up too early and drifted off half a mile down the road to watch the men play baseball. I arrived just in time to see their backs. I didn't bother much till five minutes after starting time when it seemed clear that the little beggars weren't coming back. So I said to Jack, the patrol leader who has taken a fit of wonderful cleanliness and helpfulness: "Well, Jack, what about those four?" "Sure," said Jack, "I'll round up the guys." So he jumped on his horse and galloped off and five minutes later came back in triumph with the four little deserters in tow. They looked awfully sheepish so I said nothing till after School, then called them alone and asked What It Meant? They all got more sheepish still and one said "Sure we meant to come back in time but got excited and forgot."

I started Monday with our domestic washing while Adeline went with the car to fetch Mrs. O. so that May might dress her arm. She lives three and a half miles off, rather a boring walk. After that we went off to Charlie Lake in search of a builder for my house, Mr. Simpson being still held up, together with twenty-seven of the leading citizens, so there really are no amateur builders left free enough to take it on. So we are reduced to a choice between the two or three professional carpenters who are all foreigners, and, I'm afraid, dreadfully expensive. Karl Anderson was building a large addition to a house belonging to people called Powell.[159] Mr. Powell runs a little lumber mill by the lake. They have a living room and two little bedrooms and eight children living at home and six extra men to meals, so it really seems a good idea to add a room or two.

We interrupted Karl at his work to ask when he could take on another job. It began to pour so he climbed down off the roof and cowered with us under a beam to discuss it, making all his calculations very slowly with a stump of a pencil on a handy plank. He sat and thought for what seemed like hours, after I had given him my plan, and at last produced some sort of rough estimate of costs together with a most complicated list of all the materials which I must supply. We've got the logs already, that is most of them; so all that is required is lumber and shingles for the door and floors and the little stable. Yet apparently these necessitate thousands and thousands of feet of timber of every size and shape. You'd think we were collecting materials to build the whole of the Spanish Armada. After that, combined with an immense visit to Mrs. Powell, we drove back to Fort St. John to put in an appearance at the baseball match got up in aid of the hospital. Directly we arrived, another builder appeared and asked to "put in a tender" for my house. I like this grand expression, but his estimate was even higher, so after that we drove home a little chastened in spirit. The truth is that if you build your own house of your own materials found on your own land, a house is wonderfully cheap. But if you are a helpless and landless female, dependent on bought materials and bought labour, it's quite a different business.

Anyway, it decided one thing—I could not build so expensive a house on borrowed land, so the Site Hunt began all over again. After an interval of Guides and Brownies at Baldonnel, Adeline and I drove round for an hour or more looking at possibilities, then picked up May and went off for one more look at the Beautiful Homestead. She was enchanted with it but agreed that *for the Job* it was too remote and stiffened me in my sorrowful resolution not to take it.

On Wednesday we had the Scouts and Cubs and discovered that the boys' baseball match against Fort St. John next Saturday had been changed to Sunday because they could be taken that day on a truck. I hate baseball matches on Sunday anyway because they excite the boys so much that they can't think of anything else; but it was too late to protest about this, so all I could do was to make it a point of honour that they should come to Sunday School first at 10.30.

That afternoon was dedicated to a solemn tea-party in our honour. Adeline and I put on our best Sunday clothes but found we were not half smart enough, for the little shack where they live till their new house is built, was cram-full of ladies in full garden party dress. They really did look awfully nice and made us feel fearfully frumpy, except that they were all so very friendly, and I slowly came to realise that it was all intended to be an act of corporate welcome to Adeline and me. Wasn't it nice of them? We ate endless cake and fruit and cream from 3 to 5, but I did manage to poke in just a little about Mr. Guiton and Mr. Wolfendale coming and the Church Hall to be built and I really think they are getting quite keen and expectant.

Next morning we had an inspiration about the Site or thought we had, so we called Mrs. Crawford,[160] but she was away.

After that, Guides and Brownies at Baldonnel. The Guides were perfectly thrilled because I took them some old hats and uniforms sent me by Margaret Popham's late company at Havergal College, Toronto. There were just enough to outfit the six of them and you would have enjoyed their delight. They found the names of various original owners inside the hats and tunics and jumped at the idea of writing a letter of thanks to every name they could find and giving them to me to address.

After that we went down to the Flats and started visiting Mrs. Mikkleson who lives right down on the ferry. There we found a complete and unmistakable Englishwoman called Mrs. Jones.[161] She married a Canadian during the war and has lived ever since forty-seven miles the further side of Hudson Hope. The nearest family to them on that side is twelve miles away and on the other side there is no family at all. She has no children and has only once been away. That was eight years ago when she started on a visit to England but on arrival at Moose Jaw heard her husband was ill and went straight back. She is just going Home to see her people. But her husband can't leave the farm so she has to leave him alone for several months. She begged us to visit him if we go up the trail. But I'm afraid we shall not get so far. It's nearly 120 miles from here. She had come down the river in some boat and landed at the ferry that morning in hopes of getting lift on to Pouce Coupé in time for tomorrow morning's train. So she was sitting with her trunk outside the Mikklesons when we came, looking like a ship-wrecked sailor on a desert island. It seemed an unlucky day as nothing had gone by, but just as the problem was becoming actue, suddenly a car flashed past us and stopped at the water's edge. It was easy enough to catch it and there was Tommy, quite glad to pick up another passenger, so Mrs. Jones was rescued and I do hope the same luck will follow her all the way Home.

After that, more visits and then we went to Taylor's Flats school for the first time since my return. The six Guides were tremendously welcoming and so was the new teacher who let them out half an hour early to meet me, while Adeline had seven little girls thirsting to be Brownies. We had a preliminary pow-wow with them, announced Sunday School next Sunday evening and Service afterwards, and finally got home to find visitors. One of them was the Red Cross nurse who has married a man at Rose Prairie and had come South in a waggon to meet him in his return from the trail, with the rest of the Fort St. John witnesses.[162]

She was very full of another shooting outrage which had just happened a few miles away West of us. Apparently a man and girl stole a car somewhere to the South and a lot of other stuff with it, came up here, wanted to cover their traces, went to a lonely house which they knew to be empty, took out some of the wooden wall, put the car inside and screwed up the wall again. Then they tried to get away on horses but our local policeman had notice of it and somehow tracked them down. He accosted the man who, without any warning, shot at him at close range but marvellously only hit his ear. The policeman fired too but I suppose he was a bit stunned, for apparently he missed altogether and the man got away into the bush and escaped.[163] The girl was caught and taken down to Pouce Coupé and she is only sixteen, poor child.

While Mrs. Young was talking, I had another inspiration re: Site. Supposing Mrs. Crawford failed, there is a narrow strip of land running round the head of the same coulee, between the coulee and the trail we follow to Fort St. John School. The land belongs to Mr. Holland,[164] school-master at Rose Prairie, and he has never used or even fenced it so he can't want it very much. I wrote him a note and gave it to Mrs. Young and begged her to give it to Mr. Holland if and when her husband should get back and they both got home. Then we set off to try our luck first with Mrs. Crawford. She was most welcoming and would make me a definite answer tomorrow. Then we learned Jim Young had got back and returned with his wife to Rose Prairie so Mr. Holland would get the note, unless they forgot it.

Meanwhile, Mrs. Crawford added another possibility by saying that a cemetery was to be started close to the Beautiful Homestead and a proper road made to it. Of course this revived all my old passions; so accepting some very stale doughnuts, Adeline and I set out to explore again, i.e., to find out on foot how near it would be possible to bring the place if a direct road were really made to within half a mile of the homestead. It gave us a most glorious walk anyway, first through thick bush and then across scattered woodlands with lovely glades full of blue and white violets, and finally out on the high, windy bluffs that stand out like cliffs above the river. These bluffs are covered with wild sage and thyme that make them look quite grey in the distance but smell delicious when you walk upon them. They are divided from each other by the coulees which are not much like the combes of North Devon but much bigger and deeper and not so thickly wooded. Eight hundred feet immediately below us were the little white buildings of the original trading post of Fort St. John, now deserted, and there the river takes a tremendous curve to the South so you can see it wandering among the hills for miles and miles, both up and down stream. All round the grey bluffs are hills covered with thick bush rolling away indefinitely to the faint line of mountains in the West. And except for the old trading post and one shack both far below us, no sign of human habitation anywhere. We sat there and ate the doughnuts and calculated once more all the pros and cons. If the cemetery really was made near us (and there are only two graves waiting to be moved), and if the road really should be cut and graded to within half a mile of us, we should still be two miles from the nearest house, three from Fort St. John and nine from Baldonnel. Almost I decided to change my vocation (if anyone can change their own), and to found a new Order of Nuns Contemplative of the Peace. And then we took an oath not to think of it again any more and you will say high time, too.

On Saturday morning we heard that the little H. baby was rather badly ill and his mother wanted to take him to the doctor, but her husband was away on business with the horses. So Adeline took the car and went over to fetch them while I went off for the fateful interview with Mrs. Crawford. She was awfully kind and had come to the conclusion that her land was not the best place for us. "Well, I think you had better try somewhere else." We parted excellent friends and I went off to look at two other sites. Then I walked home and on the way met Mr. Perry arriving on a rather tired horse. We got in at 2.30 and kind May gave us some cold pork and heated up the coffee. Mr. Perry talked and I listened languidly enough, feeling rather baffled, when in rushed Adeline saying, "I met Mr. Holland in the city and brought him here." Then off she went again to take the baby and its mother home.

Mr. Holland was very grave and courteous. We started in with rather a vague and dreamy conversation in which he expressed strong sympathy with my plans but remained entirely non-committal about selling. After the same sort of thing in the morning, I was just beginning to despair, when he suddenly said, *"Would you care to walk over the land?"*

Of course Adeline came too, and we all walked about the strip peacefully conversing. Then he suddenly said, "You could build a house here . . . the view might be better here . . . You would get the most shelter here. There should be water somewhere below us now. You might get a well dug here." At last I managed to pin him down and finally, after a good many marches and counter marches, he suddenly offered me the whole strip of *25.7 acres for 100 dollars, i.e., £20*, half to be paid next week and the other half within the year.

After that things went fast enough. We traced out the limits—or rather he did—and then went straight off to sign the agreement in the presence of Mr. Thorsen, who is the notary public of these parts.

Mr. Thorsen is a perfectly speechless Dane who keeps a store at Grand Haven, a place two and a half miles from Fort St. John, which consists merely of two houses and the store itself.[165] Nobody ever seems to go there and he sits on the counter all day long wrapped in contemplation like a Scandinavian Buddha. When Mr. Holland explained his business he nodded, pointed to ink and paper, and relapsed into his trance. Mr. Holland wrote out two whole sheets of description of himself, myself and the land. We all signed. Adeline witness. I paid him a deposit of *one dollar* (borrowed from Adeline). We decided to celebrate the deal by a fifty cent supper at the hotel. We begged Thorsen to come too, but he smiled silently and shook his head, so we left the notary public sitting on the counter.

Twenty-five acres—a funny strip half a mile long and of varying width—two and a half miles by a good road to Fort St. John (only one and a half to the school), two and a half to May, five and a half to Baldonnel. It could not really be more central for the job taken as a whole. The road, which is an excellent trail but not a highway, runs all along the back or North side of us and the coulee lies in front. It's a splendid big coulee, dropping steeply beneath us, widening out into a valley full of trees, and running straight South into the unseen Peace which flows only just out of sight, 900 feet below.

Last Sunday was complicated by a baseball match between the two schools. I had arranged for Sunday School at 10.30 to be followed by a picnic lunch at the school. At the very last moment we learned that after all no truck was available, so to prevent bitter disappointment, I promised to take the team over in Elijah in two trips. However, Mr. Birley offered his car if Adeline would drive it and so make one trip only necessary each way. It was a boiling day. We had a good Sunday School, bigger than usual on account of the match, and four girls brought lunch, too, in hopes of going over to see it. The boys were quite good in School but far too excited to eat anything and at about 12 they all started standing anxiously around as if there was not a moment to be lost. Finally we squeezed in the extra girls, besides picking up May and the two young Birleys, and drove off in triumph with seven in Adeline's car and nine in mine. Of course we were far too early at Fort St. John even if they had started punctually but as they think nothing of starting at least an hour late it was rather trying. Indeed, there was no sign of Johnny, the St. John's Captain, till well after 3 and as Miss Haslam's little Service was at 3.30 we saw practically nothing of the match. She held it in the tiny shanty she has bought and made into a sort of little chapel. Only three other women came, one a Presbyterian, the other two United Church. The little Service was very nice. It took the form of a study of a chapter from St. Luke together with Intercessions and two or three hymns. Afterwards we returned and found the match over and Baldonnel beaten as they usually are. We gave them a consolation prize of ice-creams at the tiny [Chinese] restaurant[166] and then filled up the two cars and trundled back to Baldonnel.

After that, Adeline and I returned for a quick supper with May and then went off to Taylor's Flats for an evening Sunday School and Service. The children turned up pretty well, headed by the six Guides. It's a funny little crowd down there, about twenty children, mostly small girls, very shy and apparently entirely ignorant. Adeline as usual took all the ones who couldn't read outside to the woodpile and there heroically taught them something till I was ready. I took the story of Whit Sunday and something about the work of the Holy Spirit and tried to teach a couple of hymns. Nearly all these children belong to six brethren called Alexander and their two sisters, so they are all either brethren or first cousins and nearly all Alexanders. Apparently they are a sort of patriarchal clan with the most extraordinary herd instincts. At first all the brothers and their two married sisters lived in Ontario. One day one brother said he was going to move to Saskatchewan; upon which all the others picked up their homes and families and moved too. Then last [year] another brother said he was coming up to Peace River and exactly the same thing happened again. This autumn I believe they all intend to move again but this time only a few miles farther North. You can hardly wonder that the children are curious and backward and all most baffingly alike. After the Sunday School, a few mothers drifted in and we had a short Service, finishing in the dusk at about 10 o'clock. Then we agreed to have Sunday School for the rest of the term every Sunday at 3 and drove home in the gloaming.

On Monday morning I had intended to go back to my new bought land and get on with the plans for building. But quite early Erving Foster came riding over to say his brother Herman, who had come back from Grande Prairie on Saturday, was taken worse and seemed to be dying. They wanted May, so I immediately drove her up to their house, while Adeline undertook to turn out our room and do the family washing. The Fosters are about seven miles from here, three of them on the road and the other four a pretty good trail. You remember a fortnight ago we found the second son so wasted and ill and helped them through the Church Fund to go out to Grande Prairie and see Dr. O'Brien, Dr. Brown being for three weeks away at the murder trial. Dr. O'Brien found neither tuberculosis nor pernicious anaemia and sent him home after a few days with no definite diagnosis. After that he got rapidly worse and became delirious. When May and I got there he was unconscious and certainly seemed to be at death's door. Mercifully for May, Dr. Brown arrived about an hour after we did and took the responsibility from her. But try as he could he was unable to get at the bottom of the poor boy's illness. He took every sort of test and tried everything but was clearly mystified. Finally he had to go to an urgent baby-case but promised to come back tomorrow. May offered to stay for the day and I promised to come back for her in the evening.

For the rest of the day I chased builders and bought more logs for the house and finally got caught in drenching rain. Next morning we took May up again. It had rained all night and the road was like lard. We put Tommy's chains on the car and slithered through. There was no change in Herman's condition. All the family was bewildered and miserable but wonderfully sweet and self-controlled. Mr. Foster is a slightly deaf, middle-aged man who seemed specially pitiful because he had nothing to do and yet had to keep wandering in and out making suggestions which everyone sorrowfully knew to be no use. The oldest boy, Clarke, a very good looking man of about twenty-three, was equally bewildered but less helpless. He and I washed up an accumulation of supper and breakfast things and peeled potatoes and tried to talk in low tones in the little kitchen next door to the living room where his dying brother lay.

Outside was Erving, the charming school-boy of thirteen. He was kept home lest he should be wanted so I was glad to have brought up a Scout hand-book and signalling flag to help him while away the hours and distract his thoughts a little. Then there was Aubrey, the tiny brother of four, a perfectly sweet little boy, with the friendliest manners, who wanted to talk and play with May and me all the time and was entirely unconscious, even when he ran in and up to the bed, of all that was going on. But the finest member of the family was the mother. Mrs. Foster is an American, born of Norwegian parents. She is dark and very handsome and distinguished looking, and obviously the leading spirit of the household. Herman was her most beloved son—apparently they had always had the closest possible affinity; even Clarke, the elder brother, told me that. She had never had to deal with serious illness before and had never seen anyone dying or dead and now she knew that Herman was dying. I got her to come outside while May and the doctor were watching him and we talked it over together. Then we went in and had some prayers by the bedside and she was perfectly brave and controlled and entirely determined to trust God, either way. I never saw anything more beautiful than her simplicity and courage and consideration for others all through the week.

Tuesday was just like Monday, only with two sets of Guides and different errands in the middle of the day. In the evening there was no change, except that the pulse was weaker, and on Wednesday, an hour before our evening visit, he died. The doctor had just arrived and was perfectly splendid. First he kept all the family and prayed with them; and then he turned them all out and prepared for the burial. Adeline and I arrived just as he was leaving, and after he had gone, when we came out of the darkened room into the brilliant sunshine, Mrs. Foster asked me to take the funeral. I was amazed and rather averse, feeling it should be taken by a man and that failing a priest, the doctor was the one to do it. I put this as strongly as possible and begged her to talk it over with her husband and Clarke. But she said they had talked it over and were quite settled.

I objected all I could without unkindness but finally agreed to hold a Service in the house on Saturday afternoon and at the burial [in] Herman's own field about half a mile away. Then Mrs. Foster and I made the room as beautiful as we could with a white wooden Cross and a few wild flowers, while Adeline took care of little Aubrey and Clarke borrowed the car to go and find a carpenter to make the coffin.

Friday seemed to be full of small preparations. I don't remember much of it. But we helped the Scouts to make a wreath of spruce and Adeline made a Cross of moss and pansies. Then I had been commissioned by Mrs. Foster to buy something to cover the coffin because she hated the thought of its rough unstained boards. It wasn't easy to find anything suitable at Fort St. John but at last we did fine some lavender-grey linen and took it up to her and she thought it perfect.

Adeline was marvellous all the time, keeping the car in order (no joke at present as it needs a lot of attention), keeping me in order, underpinning everybody and doing all the essential things, while I was getting the credit.

Saturday was a blazing day, between 80 and 90 in the shade and perfectly still. At 1, Adeline drove us once more to the Fosters' home. I had planned all the details with the family on Friday, so we didn't have to go specially early and as the funeral was to be in their own house we didn't expect many people. So we were rather surprised all along the trail to overtake waggons full of women and about sixty men waiting outside. Luckily it is a big house with a specially large living room as well as a bedroom and kitchen. The Fosters brought in planks, logs, motor cushions and eventually about seventy, chiefly men, were somehow squeezed into the room, besides those standing in the kitchen and doorways and outside. It was rather a wonderful congregation for this country. I began with a two minute introduction about the Christian view of death (because Herman was a Christian), and then took the Service, slightly modified, from the Revised Prayer Book. Probably hardly any there except Mr. Birley and May had ever been to a funeral and probably most of them thought I was making it up. We sang three hymns, chosen by Mrs. Foster, "Jesu, Lover of My Soul," "Nearer My God to Thee," and "Safe in the Arms of Jesus." Hardly anyone could sing and there were not nearly enough books, but we did our best and the gallant little brother, Erving, played the accompaniment splendidly though he was crying silently all the time.

Afterwards they had to have the dreadful custom of walking past and taking a last look at the face of the departed before the coffin was screwed down; then there was one awful moment when Mr. Foster couldn't find the screw-driver. And then we formed a long procession and walked across the rough pasture land covered with wild roses just bursting into flower, to the solitary grave under a group of black poplars on a high slope looking Eastward across the Pine. Except for Adeline's Cross of moss and pansies there were no natural flowers because there are none yet in the very few gardens here and the wild flowers even are hardly out, but there was the Scouts' spruce wreath and a good many bright paper flowers which looked much better than you would imagine possible. After the Committal we sang "Abide With Me." On the way home one of the LeClerc boys came up and said that his mother, who has lived and worked on one lung for twelve years, had had a severe haemorrhage [and it was important] to prevent another which might be fatal. It seemed pretty urgent so [we] were glad to be able to lend him a car at once and walk home, Adeline and I, quietly together. I had meant on Saturday to do all sorts of things about logs and building plans but did none of them. Haslam came to settle details for the little Scouts and Guides Rally next week. She is really an awfully nice girl.

Herman was just twenty-one and he died on the same day as her [Miss Haslam's] father, exactly twenty-one years ago.

Week ending June 13, 1931.

Last Sunday was quite uneventful, a most lovely day, and the air already full of the faint scent of wild roses which are now bursting out everywhere. They grow very low, running all over the ground everywhere, especially on the sides of the coulees and are a delightful, bright pink. There was a good turn up for Sunday School and as everybody's minds, even the children's, were still very full of Herman's death, death being so very rare up here where almost everyone is young and healthy, I took for subject something on the lines of the Gospel of the Hereafter and for [a] hymn we tried to learn "There is a Land of Pure Delight." Erving arrived late and sat at the back and wept a little, very quietly, but he was all ready to play the organ after the lesson was over and did it splendidly. He *is* a nice boy. Afterwards he waited behind to ask "Would you mind if Aubrey came to Sunday School with me? He's only four but he wants to come and I can easily bring him along on my horse." I agreed, a little dubiously, because four is rather young and four miles is rather far to bring such a little boy hanging on behind a fairly rough horse. But it was difficult to refuse Erving anything that day.

At the Taylor's Flats School which is much more primitive, we had a lesson on the Bible and chiefly practised finding our way about the New Testament preparatory to reading it together.

After supper Tommy appeared with his car and for something to do we all went to view my land. This is a ceaseless pleasure to me, about which Adeline is very ironical, but *she* hasn't yet tasted the intoxication of having Real Estate of your own. We found all the Simpson logs had arrived and some of the extra ones from LeClerc. The latter are of jack pine and by far the best logs and quite suddenly we all jumped to the same idea—to use the Simpson logs for the barn which is to be part stable and part garage, and to try to get enough LeClerc logs to complete the house all of jack pine, which is far more durable. Mr. Simpson came home last week and was to start digging the cellar on Monday when I should have to break the news to him.

So first thing on Monday we went once more six miles East to the

LeClercs and began by visiting poor Mrs. LeClerc who had a bad haemorrhage last Friday and is in a pretty bad way. We took her some papers and sat with her for a bit. There is very little to be done except try to take her mind off the tedium of having to lie still. She is a tremendously active, hardworking woman who has slaved all her life for her farm and family of eight, and to be inactive now seems a real purgatory to her. And yet her husband says she ought not even to read as much as she is doing.

Then we had to negotiate with Mr. LeClerc about the logs and find out whether he could produce and would sell a further twenty-two at twenty-four feet, and twenty-two at eighteen feet and what they would cost. After endless measurements and discussions we found he was short of twenty-four's but his eldest son Art had "a swell bunch of twenty-four's" which he might be willing to sell me, and if I could find and get his consent, the next brother, Alphonse, would haul me the lot at an inclusive price of a dollar apiece.

So, after spending the noon with the little Baldonnel Guides and Brownies, who were frightfully excited about next Saturday's Rally, we went off to look for Art and finally found him twelve miles away at Fort St. John. He said he had cut and hauled the logs to build his own barn but finding himself without horses or money he was quite prepared to part with the logs for any ready cash. Finally we had to tell Alphonse and break it to Mr. Simpson that his spruce logs were degraded from the house to the barn.

We found him and his entirely silent son B. waiting to dig the cellar directly I should tell them exactly where and how large it was to be. Luckily I had my plans made and having decided on a cellar ten feet square by six feet deep, it only remained to indicate exactly where in my twenty-five acres this dungeon was to be dug. Then we had to chase Fonse, who was half way home with his team of four horses, and break to him the good news of forty-four more logs to be hauled in the next day or two.

I have told you all this at rather weary length merely as a sort of instance of house-building methods here, that is, for helpless people like me who cannot fell and haul and trim and build their own logs.

On Tuesday came the long-desired rain, heavy and steady, splendid for the fields, fatal for the roads. We started with a sad tragedy by losing the mail. It went off an hour earlier than usual and the mud made us slower than usual. After that blow we took the Scouts and Cubs at Baldonnel, having decided to take some of the children each day this week as their only hope for the Rally on Saturday. Then we pounded across heavy, muddy tracks and through deep water to visit three families that we hadn't reached before.

And when we got back to the car I made quite an interesting discovery. I had possessed the car for nearly a month and all that time thought it was a grey car. This afternoon it had stood in pouring rain for three or four hours and behold, it was a GREEN car, just like our old Buick at Rochester. Isn't that nice? It still leans heavily on the port side till it can be spared for a rather drastic operation for bolts in its back spring. So meantime, we beg all passengers to sit and lean as far as possible to the right. It consumes the most awful amount of petrol and oil that you can possibly imagine: simply devours them both in gulps at every mile and as petrol is 2/3 a gallon and oil 2/ a quart it's getting to be a problem with us as with everyone else who owns a car up here, whether we shall have to lay it by pretty soon.

Of course it is the road and trails that make this huge consumption and the only solution is to fall back on horses as soon as possible. Practically all the farmers have laid up their cars for the same reason. But one enterprising family has turned theirs into a carriage and we met them last week driving to the funeral in an old Ford touring car drawn by a team of strong farm horses. Wasn't it a good idea? They had all the comfort of the springs and cushions with *no* expenses of oil and gas, a perfect two-horse power car, and very cheering to see, even at a funeral.[167]

I must tell you the only comment I heard about that Service. Adeline and I were walking home rather overwhelmed by it, when we met Mrs. Birley. She was obviously moved too and full of genuine sympathy so you must not misunderstand her for saying "Oh my, WHAT a Funeral! It was Sure Dandy."

On Tuesday night Mr. Birley calculated with me the amount of sawn timber we should require for the roof and partitions and doors of the barn and it was almost as appalling as the requirements for the house, but I decided to go down to the saw mill at the river and order it at once.

So on Wednesday, as it was still pelting, we put on the chains and took the trail four miles round to avoid one hill which gets practically impossible on rainy days, took the Guides again and then waddled and slithered as far as the top of the hill where we left the car and walked down. About half a mile down we found two cars stranded. It was a party of American men coming up to find land. The steepness and mud had stopped the car and they had been too short of petrol to start again. We told them to take a bucket and walk up the hill to our car and take as much gas as they needed and then they could leave some for us at the little store at Baldonnel. At the bottom we found two more loads of new settlers, one containing a mother and a very small baby who had driven all the way from Edmonton and seemed awfully tired. They didn't attempt the hill but were starting to camp in a tiny, tiny tent at the side of the road. Poor woman, She's got a good way farther to go, for this is part of a new rush to some fresh land that has been surveyed and thrown open for settlement thirty or forty miles North of there.

I found Mr. Hoffstrom[168] and we sat on a pile of lumber which was steaming in the sun, for the rain had stopped, calculating on planks at our side about rafters, two by fours, two by sixes, etc. It's rather fun, really, and all an endless revelation of the complexities that make up something like a roof. At last I got back across the river and found Adeline. Soon after that the heavens opened again and torrents fell upon us so that we had quite a struggle to walk up the hill and were deeply thankful that we hadn't taken the car down. As it was, the drive at the end was fairly uneventful. Twice the chains broke and twice we slithered into the ditch, but managed to get home intact at 10 o'clock, rather tired and very ready for supper.

On Thursday we put in two visits to the school in a determined effort to polish up the signalling and first aid, both of which appeared to be deplorable.

Next morning, Friday, Mr. Guiton and a great big Scout youth called Charlie Clarke came. They had been buying horses near Pouce [Coupé] and brought up three of which I rather hope to succeed to at least one and possibly two at the end of the summer. Wolfendale and his mate, a student called Whatmore, were held up over some car business but would be up in a day or two. We planned three Services for Sunday and the angel Adeline posted off with the notices to the respective schools. Then we went into the church site question and settled where to build both in Fort St. John and Baldonnel, so it wasn't an idle day.

Saturday was the day of the Rally and dawned cold, drizzling and threatening. Just before 2 o'clock, our scheduled time, the rain began. Upon that I became desperate and decided to transfer the whole party, somehow, to the Community Hall at Fort St. John. We started by cramming ten Brownies into the car with Adeline and me. On the way we met Dr. Brown bringing his four children and shouted to him to pick up as many more as he could. There were two more cars which we commandeered in the same way. Adeline made two more trips with Elijah, bringing about ten each time, about a dozen more who had horses rode and at last, within an hour, the whole sixty, besides mothers and hangers on, were transferred to the Hall—and immediately the rain stopped. Outside the Hall is a splendid baseball ground so we used that and the programme went off splendidly. After the inspection we had a signalling race won by Fort St. John Guides and First Aid won, to my astonishment, by my Baldonnel Scouts, and Book-balancing Race for Cubs organised by Adeline won by the Baldonnel Cubs and finally a Tenderfoot test race for [the] conqueror, won by—MY Scouts. Then we made a big Horseshoe, Mr. Guiton made a nice little speech and presented the District Flag. The Brownies made their Grand Salute, the Cubs their Grand Howl, the Scouts and Guides said the Law and after a prayer and the National Anthem we all dismissed, and Adeline surpassed herself by driving home a carload of thirteen including four grown-ups and all their picnic tackle. English five-seaters please note.

Week ending June 20, 1931.

Last Sunday was our first with a full staff and certainly for the present it is very full indeed. First there is Mr. Guiton, the Priest and Officer Commanding of the party. Next, Mr. Wolfendale, the newly ordained Deacon who is to be our permanent Missioner. He is English, aged thirty-two but looks younger, has lived in Canada since the war, first at lumber work then as a Lay Reader in Northern Ontario so he knows quite a lot about Canadian life. Then there is the Divinity student called Whatmore, working with Wolfendale, and an enormous Boy Scout called Charlie, aged about seventeen, with Mr. Guiton. They have brought up a good car and three horses bought at Pouce Coupé so they can get about freely whatever the roads are like. On Sunday morning, Guiton functioned first at Fort St. John, and in the afternoon at Baldonnel took the bigger boys. Afterwards, he took the grown-ups' Service which rolled up to fifteen adults apart from any of ourselves, the best we have had so far. May came and Mr. Birley too. After supper we took Mr. Guiton down to the Flats and repeated the programme there— Sunday School first at 6.30 and Service at 7.30. To the latter nobody came till 8, when first seven or eight grown-up girls arrived, and ten minutes later five young men came in a waggon from the lumber mill across the river. It was a cautious and obviously unchurchy congregation but Guiton seemed quite pleased and hopeful and made it the simplest possible Service. We got home about 10 as usual, and as usual at this time of year, there was broad daylight still.

On Monday morning I rushed first to my estate and interviewed Karl, the carpenter who is at last at work there. I started him on the barn first which will take four or five days to build, and makes a home for the Church horses if they want to save expense. Then on to town for a conference with Mr. Guiton and a very important act—the purchase of the Fort St. John church site. We decided on a nice high acre on a North and South road just about 200 yards from the main road which would be a very noisy and dusty place. There is a fine open view all round and the church, when built, will stand just behind and above the settlement as it is at present. The land belonged to the Postmaster who sold it to us for £10 and promised to return £5 to the Church Funds. In the afternoon we went off to do the same thing at Baldonnel, i.e., Guiton, Wolfendale, and I. The saintly Adeline did our washing all the morning and spring cleaned our room and in the afternoon wrote letters to make sure of catching the mail. We went off to Baldonnel which is exactly three miles due East of this house and found the owner of the land busy harrowing a field. He immediately tied up his team and came along with us to visit a notary in whose presence the land could be legally bought. On the way we discovered that although the poor owner has proved up his homestead and received his title, he had not registered it and therefore it could not be legally transferred to another owner. Guiton asked why he had failed to do this and he said "Because it costs twelve dollars more than I have got. I haven't had a cent for months now but when you pay for the site I'll be able to get the whole place registered at last."

Isn't that strange to think of and yet it is quite true that a good many of the people here haven't got any actual money at all. They could not sell their crops last year so they just live on what the land produces and do without anything else. Unluckily the land does not produce false teeth, and the owner, who had had all his own pulled out by a wandering dentist last summer just before the big slump, is now completely toothless. I do feel that if I were a real Christian I would offer him mine but alas! I have not done it yet. The notary has lived for four years in a one-roomed shack. He is a good farmer and a clever man and knows more law than anyone else in this part. He drew up a deed of sale, Guiton and the owner and he signed it and I presented the cheque out of the Home Grown Money given last winter. So the site is ours.

Next day, Tuesday, having heard that Mrs. Foster was ill, Adeline and I drove over to the city and had our first ride with Guiton on the new Church horses. We rode the two smaller horses—"Brick," who is quite a good little dark chestnut, and "Nigger," who is really a Cayuse (Indian pony), so docile that he never requires a bit or a bridle but you just direct him with the halter rope. These two, if they survive the summer and develop no obvious faults, will be offered to me on easy terms by Guiton and Company when they leave. Adeline rode Nigger and steered him perfectly with a rope attached to his nose. I rode Brick whose name I shall change immediately if I do buy him. They go well together and appear both willing and gentle, which are two virtues not generally combined in the horses here. It was about eight and a half miles to the Fosters and half way there another sudden storm broke upon us, soaking us all to the skin again, rather a bore, but June is the rainy month here and this is nothing to what it was like last year. The Fosters were so sweet to us, snatched off our wet shirts to dry them and lent us each a big man's shirt to sit in. Mrs. Foster was up and about but obviously dreadfully pulled down and exhausted. She was so brave and cheerful during Herman's illness and death and now the reaction is clear. What she ought to have is a complete change of surroundings even for a few days, but she has, of course, no money and also nowhere to go. That is the difficulty with women here who have sorrow to bear and are run down. I hope to get as many as possible to my house when it is ready. Even a different type of house for a few days may help, not to speak of freedom from the monotonous round of chores for a large family.

About five miles from home we had to branch off North to avoid a swamp and in a few minutes succeeded in getting lost in the bush. It really was quite ridiculous. We picked up trail after trail but they all seemed to lead nowhere. Guiton and I even differed over the points of the compass because the sun seemed to have set all round the sky, and Adeline wisely withheld her opinion. After about an hour of trotting round in spirals, we suddenly heard a dog barking and by following the sound came at length to a house, and to my great delight, were greeted and directed by little Hughie Byrnes. It then turned out that we had been going more or less parallel with the right trail, but two miles North of it. We all felt dreadful fools to get lost within five miles of Fort St. John. We reached the metropolis at 9 and having had no supper, were pretty hungry, so we got a quick meal at the hotel and then Adeline and I had to buy some provisions for tomorrow before starting home in the car. The four men were coming over to clear the Baldonnel site and we were to provide dinner for them. We bought a loaf and some butter and cheese, tinned sausages and tinned tomatoes. By that time it was 10 and had started to rain again but the road seemed good and with only five miles we didn't stop to put on the chains. Alas, as we drove Eastward the rain and the road got much worse. It turned quite dark and about a mile from May's gate, in trying to make room for an approaching car, we slid quietly and firmly into a deep, muddy ditch. Two of the men sat tight in their cosy saloon but the colonial official whom I had met before, jumped out into the mud and helped me haul and heave Elijah while poor Adeline grappled with the works. It was no good: she sank deeper and deeper and at last we had to abandon ship and walk home. The other car had moved on so we thanked Mr. West fervently, buried our bread and tins under Elijah's seats and took to the boats. But two minutes later the enemy car came back, having evidently been compelled to turn round by the chivalrous Mr. West. May said afterwards what could you expect of Pouce Coupé (this is just the wild free Highlander's contempt for over-civilized lowlanders).

It poured all that night and all next day too so we did not attempt to rescue Elijah but on Wednesday Tommy arrived with a big chain and pulled the derelict home. Then Guiton and Whatmore and Company turned up, armed with axes for the clearing operations. First they stopped to bale out May's cellar which was two or three feet deep in water for the third time since yesterday morning, and then they drove on to the newly acquired Church land and Adeline and I, having hastily collected pots and pans, followed them. It was no joke trying to make a camp fire as the place was still more or less under water but eventually we got a fire going. The Church land consists of two acres lying exactly at the corner where I enrolled the first Guides in the snow eighteen months ago. The ground is practically all bush at present so we decided on an area on its Southern frontage and the men set to work to clear a bay of about 150 foot radius. They are all four good axemen, so by the end of the day they had felled enough trees and cut enough undergrowth to make a charming semi-circular glade, with the straight side racing the road and due South, and a fine shelter of trees from all the other sides. It really did look very pretty and is quite big enough already for the actual building.

The dinner was quite a success and Adeline and I felt ourselves wonderful campers, although everything except the potatoes had come quite unorthodoxly out of cans. When it was all cleared up we had to hurry off five and a half miles to my land to see how things were going there. Unluckily we found Mr. Simpson had knocked up and he was lying on a mattress on Mrs. Kelly's floor looking very miserable. I asked whether he felt up to eight miles of very bumpy drive and he said yes so fervently that there was nothing for it but to wrap him up and make him as comfortable as possible while Adeline steered us through deep canals and heavy ruts and mud holes, back to the care of Mrs. Simpson. We went on to look for another man to take his place. He was the usual tall, shy Scandinavian and was delighted to come for two dollars a day. I said, "If you come now I'll give you a lift for five miles so you'll only have to walk two and a half." He said "Sure. Let me run and get my things. I will make very quickly." As he was to live on the spot in Anderson's tent, I imagined him to be collecting pyjamas and a sponge but five minutes later he appeared ready for a stay of any length of time—and all his luggage was an axe, a hammer and a saw. I couldn't help wondering if only we Church workers set out for a new job with needs and equipment as simple as that perhaps *our* building would be quicker.

On Thursday we had another morning at the church site, the men trimming and piling their felled trees and making huge heaps of brush wood to be burnt. We supplied dinner again and afterwards held a short conference about actual building plans. We decided regretfully that both churches should be of lumber and not of logs. I

God's Galloping Girl

won't tell you all the reasons but the chief one is that for memorial buildings lumber is more suitable because, given decent care and regular painting, it lasts far longer. We decided on their general dimensions and plans and to get immediate estimates from two good carpenters who are free at present. At 4 Adeline and I went down to the Flats for the Guides and Brownies and interviewed one of the carpenters.

The Flats is a wonderful place for producing hitches. You remember last year how coy and erratic the boys were over Scouts and how finally I had to abandon them for the time being. Since then the six eldest girls have been Guides and Adeline is just starting Brownies. Well, last Thursday only four Guides were there and I got a message that two had been removed by their father on account of some obscure quarrel among the parents. They are pretty, attractive girls, just reaching the critical age. I do want to keep them in the Guides and must tackle the father next week if I can get him alone.

On Saturday as usual we visited the Estate and supervised operations. Questions always seem to be arising, especially with home-brewed plans, which need immediate settlement. Also things are wanted, like nails and building paper or the width of the stable door is disputed. And "If you have the roof as steep as that you will need another 1000 shingles." It's rather fun learning architecture from hour to hour at the expense of your own house. Later, another Swede came to discuss fencing my little property. He calculated that my twenty-five acres will need 300 fence posts. He suggested 1½ or 2d each, and considering that he has to choose, cut, sharpen and haul them about fourteen miles, I magnanimously promised him 2d each. But he said, "If later anyone thinks it is too much please tell me." I am to get the wire and help him put it up. So you see I really am learning something. Also Adeline and I are responsible for chinking both house and barn, that is filling in the cracks between the logs with home-made cement and moss.

Haslam and the young Fort St. John school master [G.M. Neal] came to spend the day at the Birleys but we didn't see much of them because May, Adeline and I spent the afternoon at a funny little baseball match between the Baldonnel boys and the Flats. May took some cakes and we cocoa and sugar and one of the mothers, milk, so we could make a little feast for the teams. In the evening we had a gramophone concert and played lots of new records. The young master is passionately fond of music and would, I think, have liked to stop and listen all night. Haslam is a remarkable person and I do most sincerely hope she may decide to stay or to come back here.

Short and inglorious week ending June 27.

There is practically nothing to tell about last week because it was ignominiously cut short on Wednesday by a real super boil on the leg and the rest of the week was spent ingloriously in bed, being formented and otherwise spoilt by Adeline.

On Sunday for the first time we had morning Celebration at Fort St. John. Mr. Guiton took it, of course, and in the tiny shack which Haslam bought in the winter for Church purposes. It is a lumber building about fourteen by sixteen in size. Now two of the men, i.e., Wolfendale and Whatmore, are living in it, sleeping in bed rolls on the floor which they put away in the day. Before we could have Service they had to stow away every sign of having slept there, and turn it into a Chapel. So they asked us not to come till 9.15. There were the four men and Haslam. It was our first United Service and we hope to repeat it every Sunday while Guiton is here. Afterwards Adeline and I and Wolf. and What. went straight on to Baldonnel, leaving Guiton and Charlie with Haslam in the city. We felt it a great chance to turn the men on to the children and to get Wolf. known to them all, whatever his future policy may be about them. So he and What. took a very simple Service, while Adeline and I contented ourselves with being officious with the register, organ and flowers. One little girl brought two clean baking powder tins for vases. They look quite decent and will carry us on till the charming blue ones given by the Messengers arrive in my freight. Incidentally, my freight has arrived. It came by river and is lying down at the old Hudson Bay Post until I can do something about fetching it. But it is twelve miles off, down a fairly precipitous hill, so I am obliged to leave it till: (a) I am fit for the road; (b) the road is fit for the car; (c) the barn is ready roofed for the freight.

The two men turned up again for the afternoon Service and we joined them with materials for a wayside supper afterwards. Wolf. took the Service, well I thought. He read very clearly, took the prayers very slowly and feelingly, which is what people here like, and gave a very nice little address. He seems to know quite clearly what he is after, is first rate at all kinds of manual work (which carries more weight here than any kind of scholarship), and has a perfectly *enormous* singing voice which causes the tiniest gathering of practically silent women to sound like a packed congregation of Welsh miners.

Mr. and Mrs. Foster were both at the Service, besides Erving and little Aubrey. They came in the waggon drawn by two big mules. It was the first time for Mr. Foster. They were all so reverent and attentive and it's wonderful to see how this great sorrow has drawn them nearer to God. Afterwards I took them to look at the newly cleared church site and they were very keen and said they had no money but were ready and would be glad to do any work or hauling that might help. Then Adeline and I loaded up the car with organ and hymn books and other Church furniture ready for the Flats and we all had a very pleasant campfire supper in the bush on the way there. We had brought hard boiled eggs and cheese and they had brought tea and sugar, but by a trifling oversight, neither had brought bread. However that did not matter much, as May had given us a marvellous tart of rhubarb and dried apricots which, when Wolf. saw it, caused him to exclaim, "Not Deep Pie! I haven't tasted Deep Pie for eleven years." We made him eat nearly half the treasure and he was quite awe-struck about it. Afterwards I was impressed with the masterful rapidity with which he washed up everything in a little muddy water and got everything clean and packed up again in two minutes, a small detail but valuable in this sort of life.

The Flats Sunday School is erratic as usual, late and straggling in arrival, vague and fearfully shy. The main hope seems to be the small group of older girls of whom six are Guides. Violet and Joyce are withdrawn temporarily by their father but still come to School and I am hoping to train Violet to be organist, as Erving is at Baldonnel.

The two men conducted a similar sort of children's Service and then, after the usual awful delay and uncertainty, thirteen grown-ups trickled in, including the two nice newcomers I had found in the tent last week; all the older children stayed and we had quite a good little Mission Evensong. We even embarked on quite a new hymn, "Thou Didst Leave Thy Throne, and Thy Kingly Crown," which I can't play a bit. But with the Rev. Wolf. there, what the organ does is quite immaterial. He turns it into a Handel Festival anyway.

The main event of Monday was an expedition on Charlie Lake to look for a new camp site for Guides and Scouts next month. Tommy took us in his newly bought boat, for which he had borrowed Mr. Birley's kicker, a tiny, portable petrol engine complete with propeller, and you can take it anywhere in a car and attach it to any boat in a few minutes. The boats here are a sort of scow, large, heavy, and nearly flat-bottomed, too heavy for rowing. All the Church team came, the four men, besides Tommy, May, Adeline and me. Unluckily, the kicker was in a bad mood, suffering from a severe cold and could not breathe freely. Every few minutes it choked and stopped dead and finally two miles from the start it died altogether. Luckily we had four paddles and a pole so pushed on and landed on a bit of land (eighty acres), which May has just bought from the King for two dollars. At present it is all solid bush and the trees so dense and so choked with undergrowth that you could hardly push through. So we regained the boat (Tommy and the Wolf had been trying to operate on the kicker), and pushed out towards the middle and scanned the ten miles of shore but it all looked the same to the East. On the West side we saw what looked like open spaces but had to abandon it till another day.

This expedition may seem to have been a failure but anyway it did one good thing: it produced in Tommy a real respect for Wolf., both as waterman and mechanic, and started a friendship between them.

By Tuesday morning the road had dried up and Adeline took the chains off with my hearty (passive) concurrence. It was Guide Day but first we had to go and see how the old Manor house was progressing, and we forgot all about two deep sloughs on the road. Up to now they have been canals which look formidable but are not much trouble, really. Lots of the trails turn into canals after heavy rain with water a foot or two deep for fifty yards or more at a stretch. But the car runs through quite happily. The windscreen becomes opaque with muddy water and you get splashed all over but it's really rather fun. Later, as the water sinks, things look better but are really worse as they often leave nice little bogs. We got out at last with the help of two kind men, a shovel and a lot of bush which we cut and laid in piles across the mud.

The only unlucky part was that I was in full Guide Uniform and this is just about the worst clothing that could be designed for mud-hole wear.

At last we got to the house which is now eight feet high and complete with partitions, but as it has no openings, it looks like a very formidable ancient Canadian fortress, rather grim and forbidding. The mud-hole left us no time to enjoy it but only to settle the height of the living room, eight feet, and of the other two downstairs rooms (chapel and bedroom), seven feet six inches each. Then we flew off to Guides but had to go round four miles to avoid repeating the former trouble. After the Guides we ate our sandwiches in a sheltered bit of bush and went on to see Mr. Simpson who, we found, had been pretty bad with ptomaine poisoning. We found him better and as clean and neat in their leaky shack as if he were in a hospital ward. We departed, promising to try to procure for him quinine cachets and shin of beef. Then on to the Flats for Guides and Brownies, after which I tried to see Mr. Neilson about Violet but alas, he was away on the job of mending the telegraph wire. After that we were actually coming home to supper and were very proud of it being only 7 o'clock when we saw nice, plump, Finnish Mrs. Ohland standing in the road. She talks at a tremendous pace and without any stops like a legal document. "Oh Miss Storrs and Miss Harmer if you *was* going to Fort St. John would you take me to Dr. Brown he said he would sure pull my teeth if they got too bad and they have sure got too bad now and I don't know how to make out with them so I wondered if—but of course not if you're not going to Fort St. John."

Having some memory still of the same sort of feelings this time last year, I said we were sure going and in she jumped and talked all the way of the fine little pig she intends to give "you ladies so soon as your house is built." Poor Dr. Brown is not a dentist and hates drawing teeth but in default of anyone else he has to do it for people who lack the time or money to go the sixty miles to Dawson Creek where the sometimes sober expert is to be found. We left Mrs. Ohland with him and went off to get the shin of beef, besides a few other commissions from people who had said, "If you happen to be going to the city . . . ." Finally I noticed, among a bunch of guys gossiping on the steps of the store, a certain fat farmer who has the reputation of having been in a previous existence, a barber. It seemed rather a chance as Mrs. Ohland wasn't ready so I called him boldly away from his friends and asked if he would cut my hair at once. "Sure," said Mr. B., "Where can we do it?" "Sure I don't know." Then I thought of Mrs. Millar's porch, "But what about scissors and a comb?" "Oh I've got them in my pocket, I never knows when I won't need them." So off we went—and Adeline says I shan't need another cut till I start homeward in 1933. After that we returned for our patient and found rather a crisis. The teeth had broken up, the gums injured, and Dr. Brown in great agitation said she ought to go out to the dentist at the Creek as quickly as possible. It was rather a poser, past 8 o'clock and a high wind and evident rain coming on and almost certainly nobody going out tonight. Our car is open and very cold. Moreover, the boil on my leg had been getting steadily worse for a week and I doubted whether I could survive another 120 miles of these roads in the next twenty-four hours. Guiton and Company were not to be found. At last Mrs. Ohland saved the situation by saying she'd rather wait till tomorrow anyway. So I wrote an S.O.S. to Mr. Guiton and left it for him at the hotel. Adeline drove Mrs. Ohland back to her family and we all got home to supper at about 10—just before the storm broke.

It poured all that night and most of the next day but sure enough at 9 the faithful Wolf. and What. appeared, their car stocked with axes, shovels, chains, ropes, food and bedding, just to report that they were going at once for Mrs. Ohland and were prepared for any emergency.

I had got up by then but was feeling pretty bad with the boil, and on learning that the rescue was safe in other hands was only too thankful to be chivvied back to bed by May and Adeline for the rest of the week.

It's a bore of course, but a well-timed bore. The Rally and the school term are over. The clergy have come and we shared the first Sunday with them. The Camps are not due for another fortnight. Both the church sites are chosen and cleared and they don't need my help to start building although as regards the Baldonnel plan, Guiton is most kind and consults me all the time. The only thing that gets really hung up is the house which I simply dare not allow to grow up without me.

Week ending July 4.

Last week I was in bed till Wednesday, nursing Job. Really, between the clergy, Adeline and Haslam there was hardly room for me out of bed. So Adeline and they carried on throughout Sunday and on the other days she did endless visiting and transporting and messages in the intervals of supplying me with blazing foments and hearty meals. Guiton was awfully good and looked in almost every day to report progress. And more nobly still he accepted without a murmur a drastically altered plan for the Baldonnel Church which I presented to him from my bed of suffering to supplant his own (plan, not bed). He was so good about it that I have had awful qualms since. It's an awful responsibility to plan *every* detail for a Church Hall with *exact* dimensions while lying flat on your back in bed. You see, there are two conflicting ideals to be harmonized, i.e., the ideal Community Hall big enough for *everyone* in the district to gather for dances, school concerts, etc., and the ideal of a really reverent and devotional little church which will suggest worship on Sundays and where a small congregation of a dozen or so will not feel cold and lost. The present plan may produce an odd looking building but I think it is the best for combining the two purposes, with priority to the church. But I shall not be happy till I see it built and I dare not even send you the plan yet, till I have seen a little how it is going to work out.

Guiton made his own plan for Fort St. John which is a simpler matter, being a church only. He has hired a first-rate carpenter by the day as foreman and under him are working Wolf. and one or two volunteers. They have been at it a week now and their church is already a fine building looking rather like a smaller Netley Abbey all in wood. But a Swede has contracted for Baldonnel and starts work sometime this week. He had to collect his lumber and let the site dry out a bit. Apparently the Baldonnel Church is to be trusted almost entirely to my planning, for after Service on Sunday the Swede [Hoffstrom] rushed at me and said, "How high? I have the length and the breadth but you never gave me the height or the pitch of the roof or the shape of the ceiling." No more I did. Wasn't it careless? I appealed to Wolf. but all he said was, "Oh no. I'm doing the other church. This one is your business." What the outside will be like I tremble to think because none of us can draw and none of the carpenters have ever built a church so we just have to plunge in.

On Wednesday I rose up and spent a heavenly day sitting in the garden like an old lady, and on Thursday too, for that matter. It was frightfully idle but delightful too, and boiling hot. The Birleys went out to Dawson Creek to seek their brother's grave, the same expedition as the one last year when they had the accident. I think she was rather nervous at making exactly the same trip with Mr. Birley again. But of course she never showed it. They stayed away that night and all the time I was a bit nervous and really thankful to see them safe home.

On Friday I returned to duty after ten days' idleness. Before we were up, Slim appeared, having bicycled over nine miles of muddy and rutty trail to go with us to my estate and mark out the fencing lines. We gave him breakfast and started off the the two and one half miles to my land. But just before reaching it we plunged axle deep into a treacherous mud hole. For over an hour we dug out mud and cut down trees for levers and strewed branches in the ruts and tried both backwards and forwards, Adeline at the wheel, Slim levering up from behind, and me hauling on a rope in front. But nothing would make Eliza budge.[169] So at last we had to go off and look for horses and were lucky enough to meet a man coming home with his team. He hitched them up and after a little plunging and slipping they hauled Eliza out to firm land as if she had been a child's toy. Isn't it absurd that these cars are called fifteen or eighteen horse power? You can hear the real horses snorting with contempt.

At last we reached the domain, and then found it wasn't half so easy to line out the fence as we had expected. The East to West line is easy enough because it simply has to run sixty-six feet South of the opposite fence, leaving the intervening space for what is called "Road Allowance." But the two North and South lines are all mixed up with the configuration of the land and the indenture of the big coulee which bounds me on the South. We had great fun looking for survey marks and taking sights and I had a busy time trying to mask my invincible ignorance from Slim.

Then we concentrated on the baronial hall where we found Karl and Harry and Benny straining at the leash to begin again. The great ceremony which I couldn't miss was the hauling up of the two top logs. They are tremendously heavy and it is wonderful how they haul them up to the top of the eleven-foot walls. They do it with skids, i.e., huge, long sloping poles laid up against the walls. The log is rolled up to the foot and then everyone pulls on a long rope—and up she goes. Then there is the hewing and fitting of the ends till they all dovetail perfectly, entirely done with axes and fine, strong, primitive craftmanship. Still of course without a roof, windows or door the house still looks like a fortress. Tomorrow the roof will begin to go up and then at last we shall get a dim idea of what she is going to look like and whether my proportions are possible—or all quite wrong. Meanwhile the combined garage and stable barn is quite finished and waiting for horses, car or freight and I must say it is a dear little building. If the house turns out a failure we can always live in the barn. Next week, when the suspense is over and we know the worst, I will take and send you photographs of both. By the way, you can't think how delicious the jack pine logs smell in the sun. It's a perfect joy to be near them.

Saturday morning we spent at the house again, varied by occasional diversions to the fence. Once Slim rushed at me and said "Where exactly will you have the gate? And which way will it open?"

But our great excitement was, of course, seeing the rafters go up. This was the climax after another awful series of problems. "How high do you want the peak to be?" "Sixteen feet." Awful pause. "And how deep the eaves?" "Two feet." Another awful pause and then, "Right. Where [is] the chimney to come out?"

At 1 we joined Guiton and Charlie to go and find a camp site on the West side of the lake. We went as far as the car could go, then left it and walked on along an old waggon trail for another mile. Finally we decided on a pretty nice bit of rough, open land sloping down to the water. The Scouts will be able to clear up the dead fall before the Guides come. It's rather a remote place but there is a little store two miles off and they will keep horses at the camp and the car as near as it can be got. It was agreed that Guiton [and] Charlie should take the boys from Wednesday 8th to Tuesday 14th, Adeline, Haslam and I to join them for the week end and the Guides' Camp to follow immediately from the 14th [to the] 20th.

So we trailed back to collect tents, equipment, and children's names and to make out the usual notices and lists of kit required. Because, as you can see, there was no time to be lost. Preparations like these we used to make for weeks beforehand in England and fill up endless forms in triplicate, saying, for instance, whether the water was "Government tested." Would you say Charlie Lake is Government tested??

Week ending July 11.

The end of last week was shadowed for everyone by a very sad accident almost on the anniversary of May's last year, but far more pitiful in its results. You remember Mrs. Chiulli? The nice Italian woman who could speak no English and whom I used to visit and talk about? She was the one whose pan full of grease I kicked up into the air when trying to illustrate how Rama had kicked me off. Well, she and her only daughter, a nice schoolgirl [Donella], wanted to go to the annual sports at Dawson Creek and the eldest son, Steve, was taking them in their dreadful ramshackle car. No one knows whether the brakes failed but anyway at the beginning of the Flats hill he seems to have lost control and developed a fearful speed and round a bend he met a team and waggon, lost his head, ran over the edge, jumped a fence, turned a somersault in the field below. He himself escaped with hardly a scratch but his mother and sister were killed on the spot. The funeral was on Saturday morning in the Roman Church and of course everybody went. I felt I must because the girl had been one of my Guides and the mother a real, welcoming friend. So after our Celebration Adeline and What. went off in the Church car to take the Baldonnel Sunday School and I was to follow in ours for the afternoon. May suddenly announced she would like to come too so she drove over with us and came to the Celebration also. At 10 Adeline and What. departed and the rest of us went to the Roman Catholic Church, which I had not ever been in before. It's a biggish church, rather bleak and barn-like as all big buildings are here. It was quite full. Four-fifths of us were not Romans and most of us, of course, didn't know a single word of Latin.

After it was over, we met What., speeding back in someone else's car with the news that he and Adeline had barely gone two miles when the wheel had come off their car, luckily not without due warning in the form of smoke and smell. They were six miles from Sunday School with fifteen minutes to get there so he had walked back to get help and Adeline to the Birleys, feeling rightly it would be very little use to arrive at Sunday School nearly two hours late. Mercifully old Eliza was in good form and able to replace the younger, smarter, but far less reliable Church car for the rest of the day. So after a hasty dinner we collected Wolf. and What. and went off to the Baldonnel Service, at which my function has now changed into that of organist, very much *faute de mieux*. The Rector (as we call Wolf.), had been hard at it building Fort St. John [Church] all the week. He is a very gentle and friendly person with three distinct sides to him: the fellow worker, courteous and companionable, with great reasonableness and consideration in all discussions. Then the side of manual skill which is a great asset, and finally the ministerial side; his sermons are simple and earnest, with a touch of the Church Army[170] about them. We all had a campfire supper afterwards and then proceeded to the Flats as usual. Down there there seems to be a plague of petty quarrels just now which has for the time being entirely spoilt both Guides and Scouts. Certainly the devil does seem to be specially active at the Flats. The net result was a Sunday School of three or four and a group of youths and girls to the Service, but no grown-ups except the man who is building Baldonnel Church. He is anxious for a little church at the Flats and offered to give land and supply the lumber very cheaply, but we haven't come to that yet.

Do pray for Taylor's Flats. It is a beautiful little district in spite of its name: a fertile plain about ten miles in area. There are about a dozen families and a few bachelors, but they all seem strangely limp and lifeless except in the matter of quarrels. We got back at ten and I had just snatched the opportunity of starting to cut Adeline's hair (which was awfully long), when a car drove up with four visitors. Rather hard on May, wasn't it? 10.15 P.M But she took it awfully well and produced the usual tea, besides showing them round the garden [in the late summer light].

Next morning, having lent Eliza to the clergy last night, we walked to my estate and had the usual impassioned discussion. You have to fence here with barbed wire. It's beastly, I think, but there is nothing else that will keep your own cattle and horses at home or prevent other people's wandering animals from eating your crops. Just now there is a wire famine. At last on Monday I succeeded in buying two eighty-pound rolls to go on with, which will be enough for one strand round a pasture of about seven acres. At one place the ground is cut by a sharp little ravine with sheer sides and a drop of about 150 feet. So we had to climb up and down selecting the best pasture line. At the very bottom Slim said he had found a *spring*. Great excitement as [this] might solve the water problem. He said it was "Beautiful water—the sweetest I have tasted about here." I scrambled down and under some rocks we did find a very small pool of pretty muddy water. Slim filled a little pail and we both drank. It didn't strike me as very remarkable water but it certainly had no unseemly taste (beyond a little mud which does not count), and it was rather romantic as being my own. Only we don't know yet whether it is a real spring or just a seeping. Also, for the house it will be useless unless we could tap it higher up, because it would really be too steep a haul. Still, it may do for the horses until the dam which we shall have to make, fills up with melted snow next spring and it would be something to solve *their* problem. While this was going on, suddenly a truck arrived with all the purchases we made at Edmonton. It was very exciting, unloading and stowing them in the barn. But it was a little sobering to have to pay £13 for their freight from Edmonton.

After that a sort of Church and Camp Committee with Guiton, and a long talk with an old man called Munro on the cost of a possible brick chimney. Most people are content with the ordinary iron stove pipe and I meant to do the same for it's wonderful how few fires there are. But I'm putting a good deal of money and trouble into this little house and want to leave it intact to my successor: so I finally agreed to lash out and have a

Real Brick Chimney at a cost of about £6.10. It is really cheaper than I expected and does seem worth while.

In Fort St. John we met again the Pouce Coupé school teacher and arranged for a joint Brownie Revel and Weekend to be held on my land at the beginning of September. We think it will be splendid for the little girls though of course it depends on many things [such as] whether she will get the necessary transport for hers of sixty miles each way. On our way we visited two families whose boys we knew wanted to come to Camp and were apparently prevented by poverty. The first was Hughie Byrnes. He lives as chore boy with some people who are very kind to him but alas, said they were too busy and could not spare him. Poor Hughie said nothing all through the conversation but stood at the door and stared and stared at us. He was the life and soul of the camp last year. But of course there was nothing for it but to say, "Better luck next year Hughie," to which cheap comfort he made no reply but only went on staring till we had gone. Then we went to the home of Jackie who was longing to come and his mother wanted him to, but like so many, there was no cash. We said we would take him for as many potatoes and loaves as she could send with him and this was fixed up in no time, to everyone's delight.

Tuesday was the day before the Scouts' Camp so most of it was spent in borrowing a waggon, arranging with parents and getting kit lists round, all of which would have been unnecessary but for the collapse of last week's Sunday School. In the evening, after a Guide Camp Committee, we went to the house which is at last getting quite human with the doors and windows cut out and the roof shingled. Also the Fort St. John church (St. Martin's) is getting on marvellously. The men often work till 10 at night. Incidentally, Mr. Simpson told me his little boy John was eating his heart out about Camp because he is only nine and we had put the age limit at ten and a half. Later in the evening Guiton said, as he had only fourteen boys, he would take Johnnie IF I could get him. Next morning from 8 the blessed Adeline did our washing and other chores while I rushed over to Baldonnel to get the boys off. One was missing so I drove off as hard as possible to fetch Johnnie. It was 9 o'clock but he and his mother were both still asleep in bed. They woke up at once and in twenty minutes we had Johnnie dressed and his kit collected. There was no time for breakfast but anyway he was far too excited to want any. Two miles from camp the trail became impossible so we carried everything on to this site which is more romantic if less convenient than last year. There's any amount of wood and water, pretty safe bathing and complete detachment from ordinary life—and not a cowbell or a cock crow or even a distant dog bark to be heard. We stopped for a sandwich lunch and incidentally I agreed with Guiton who departs for good on

Saturday, for the purchase of two of the Church horses for £12.

This is the letter which I should have got off last Monday. On Saturday, 11th, Adeline and I went to the boys' Camp to share their last two days and look round a bit for the Guides, who were to come directly the Scouts left. We had the usual scrum getting off, packing bed-rolls and mugs and plates and trying to think of all the odd things that might be needed. On the way, of course, I had to go to the house for a thorough seance there, in anticipation of nearly a week's absence. It was even more of a seance than I had expected because all my huge swarms of workmen were there and all clamouring for something to be settled. Slim was, as usual, on the warpath about fencing wire, of which there has been an acute famine. I have only been able to get him odd rolls which apparently he eats for breakfast and is always hungry for more. Meanwhile the two little horses have broken through Mrs. Crawford's old fence which bounds me on the South and in the language of this country, "Beat it." However, as everybody's horses are always roaming about in droves and being recaptured at intervals, we don't take that too much to heart until we actually begin to need them. Then there was Karl firing off ceaseless questions at short range. This time they were chiefly about the beautiful series of book shelves he was making in the living room (which being, of course, a combination of kitchen, refectory, cloister, study and extra bedroom is to be called the Common Room). Then there was old Munro who was building the extravagant brick chimney and also going to do the chinking for me. We had hoped to do it ourselves but the house having grown larger than I first meant it to be and being in a pretty exposed place I decided to have it done by rather more experienced hands and with cement rather than mud. The mud cracks and falls out nearly every year but the cement (which can now be got from Pouce Coupé), if well put in, is supposed to last twenty years. So old Munro was on the war path for brick lime, sand and a bag of cement all of which had to be procured somehow, and meanwhile, I kept him and Mr. Simpson happy as possible mudding up the barn. All these men have to be paid two dollars a day plus their food at Mrs. Kelly's and I shall have had three of them for a month, besides Slim a few days for fencing. It is an expensive way of doing things but only by taking no part in the Camps could we have saved anything. As it is, we shall have all the log-peeling and painting and no end of rough carpentry to do directly the men are out.

We finally got to the Scouts' Camp about supper time, having on the way said good-bye to Mr. Guiton and Charlie, who were just going back to Montreal. Mr. Guiton has certainly done a splendid job here in pulling everything together and getting both churches started. He still longs to come back and if they can ever raise the money for two men here, I'm pretty sure he will insist on being the second.

There were only fourteen boys, all perfectly good and radiantly happy, in and out of the lake all day and of course, like all these western people, entirely self-reliant and capable in all matters of physical requirement. Only we were amused at their meals which consisted entirely of canned food—pork and beans, sausages, tinned fruits, even cornflakes for breakfast—awfully good but rather shocking to the more austere and laborious ideal of a Guide Camp.

On Saturday night Mr. Wolfendale came out to Campfire and surprised us all by blossoming into a first rate music hall artist. He is quite a good comic actor and taught the boys several uplifting choruses like "Sister Susie Sewing Shirts for Soldiers," which they simply adored and got to make quite a noise about, though you would hardly call it singing. He gave a nice little talk at the end and taught two sacred choruses too, of the ejaculatory sort, which he said would stay in our minds all our lives. But I must say that what actually rose to our lips for the rest of that week-end was "Sister Susie."

On Sunday morning Mr. Whatmore took a nice little simple Service and in the afternoon Mr. Pickell and Tommy arrived in their kicker-boats and took the boys for a little trip on the lake. All day it was grilling hot, but just after supper the rain began in earnest and we had to retreat into one immense tent, the sort that a large family had lived in entirely for two or three summers. It was torn and rather leaky but so big that you could avoid the leaks, so we had our evening sing-song inside and it was most happy and successful. We ended up with hymns and a very informal Service, and went to bed, still in pouring rain. It pelted all night, steadily and remorselessly, and Adeline and I listened to it as it destroyed the last vestige of passable trail. At 7 we had a hurried consultation with Mr. Whatmore, left him to keep the boys asleep as long as possible while we went off to look for a waggon. We walked two miles to the store, found the store keeper away, on to a man called Johnny whom we found still asleep in his shack (everybody sleeps here when it rains to make up for the overlong summer days). He told us the way to the only man who had a waggon, who was also asleep, but woke up more completely and promised to bring his waggon within two hours and take all the kit and boys, riding in turns, into Fort St. John for four dollars. We got back to Camp and found them all just going to have breakfast (so easy had it been to keep them asleep) so we were in luck all round. After breakfast the usual scramble of packing kit. Everything was so soaking that we decided to delay the Guides' Camp till Tuesday to give the ground twenty-four hours to dry up again. We shut up all the tents and hid the remaining food as well as possible, and all came away in a procession.

Next morning we all got off finally from Fort St. John in another waggon and trundled slowly but cheerfully along the nine miles to Camp again. We had arranged that I should be Commandant and Haslam Quarter Master. Adeline, whose first camp it was, took on all First Aid responsibility and eventually acted as Sanitary Engineer and General-in-Command of every unforeseen emergency and odd jobs, especially those connected with daring sallies for food when supplies ran out.

The first thing we found was that somebody's wandering cows had found their way to the Camp, ripped open the big tent, eaten what they could and trampled the rest.

I won't tell you all about every day but I must tell you that it was the best and easiest and happiest Guide Camp I have ever known yet. The place couldn't have been better. In fact, we got more and more in love with the place every day. It was a rough bench of open land twenty-five to thirty feet above the lake with heavy bush to the West and North and rough scrub to the South. All our tents stood in a row along the top of the bench with just room in front for the Horseshoe and flagstaff. A little way below that again, on the slope to the water, we had our meals (in the hot sun which was hot enough but never fatal). From the tents we looked due East across the lake and from the Campfire which we made on a tiny bluff a few yards to the left, we could see right up and down the lake as well, and watch the last red glow reflected on it almost up to midnight. We reached the water down a rather steep bank at the foot of which the boys had made a clearing in the willows where we kept an old boat lent us by May, a heavy flat-bottomed old scow, capable of holding about eighteen people and equally difficult to propel or capsize, a perfect boat for my purpose.

The approach to this Paradise is along the old trail to Hudson Hope. It is pretty rough and only fit for a waggon. In dry weather, however, you can get a car with care within ten minutes walk of the Camp, so at that point we left Eliza parked.

Of course the whole ground is gloriously rough and not the least like an English field or even common. It is nearly waist-high now with a great tangle of willow herb, goldenrod and wild roses, and hidden underneath, there are innumerable fallen or burnt trees and branches known as snags, over which, as you can hardly ever see them, you fall pretty freely. The nearest farm is nearly two miles off and all round us is primeval bush with no fence or habitation of any kind.

Only twelve girls came in the end, which was a little disappointing, but we have to get used to small numbers and the usual heavy falling off of people we were sure of (rather like a GDA [Girls' Diocesan Association] week in this way). The three little patrols were told to choose their own names and the result was three awfully good names: the Tiger Lilies, Mermaids and Chipmunks—a darling little animal like a small and rather Cockney squirrel. He has got a splendid tail which never ceases to point to the zenith whatever the angle of his body, so that gave a good motto straight away. Everybody was so good and happy that it was peaceful almost to dullness. Adeline and Haslam and I slept in very close quarters under one tiny mosquito net (the mosquitoes were like the hosts of Midian,[171] especially inside the tents), which was a great help towards mutual acquaintance. We washed blissfully in the lake, *au naturel,* and were awfully happy. In fact, the only small disturbance was early in the second morning when the ominous sound of cowbells slowly penetrated my dreams. Before I was awake, Haslam had jumped into her gum boots and gone off to meet them and drive them away. Adeline and I groaned gratefully and we all went to sleep again. A little later the bells began again, and this time I heard them first. Adeline was jammed so tight between us that she was practically walled off from all sounds. I crawled out of the net and jumping into my boots, rushed off to meet the foe and teach them a lesson. I decided to drive them right back to the shack on the edge of their farm. It was delightful herding cows in the early morning and I was thoroughly enjoying it when the fiends started to double back at a wide and pretty deep mudhole. I made a plunge to stop them, the mud held my boots tight, they came off and I fell on my back in the mire. After that we arrived without further trouble and I roused the man and confided the cows to him.

The next day it was necessary to come into Fort St. John to buy bread. In the town we found and had supper with Miss Gibson and Miss Mortimer, the two Caravaners just back from a fortnight in the Montney. They are most charming people and we look forward to seeing them in our house when they come down the trail at the end of this month. It is wonderful how much ground they have covered on foot in the Montney, as they could hardly use the Van at all and both said it is too heavy a vessel for that muddy and almost roadless country. They agreed that a light car and tent would be better and for the most outlying parts, horses and a packhorse best of all.

The rest of the time was just bathing and meals, one good supper hike into the thick bush, one trip in the kicker boat, one good stunt night for which the Tiger Lilies rigged up a splendid stage in the bush for the three Patrol plays (a huge joy and excitement), and lots of dancing and singing round the Campfire before our last hymn and prayers each night.

On Sunday morning we had the Service in the boat, which was the only cool place, and rather lovely and suitable. We sang quite a lot of hymns and without knowing it had some extra congregation, for Mr. Finch, the Harrod of Fort St. John, and his new-wedded wife were having a Sunday trip in their boat just out of sight, and afterwards they told me they had stopped and listened and heard every word. In the afternoon we all reverted to the boat again, and Haslam read aloud some letters from a friend visiting Palestine, after which we pushed off and went for a very slow and solemn cruise in the old ark, using poles and paddles fashioned by Adeline and me the day before. The poles were just young spruce trees trimmed and peeled, but you never saw such wonderful stone-age paddles.

After supper we had a Campfire Service and ended with a special little ceremony adapted from the torch-lighting one sometimes used in England. We made a specially big and glowing fire to represent the Love of God, from which each Guide lit a torch to represent one of the Laws. Two of the little recruits lit theirs as Good Turns. We Guiders lit ours for the Threefold Promise and the last little girl, aged ten, lit hers for the Brownie smile. After that we laid on the fire a big white Cross to symbolize the Love of Christ and as it flamed up, sang "There Is A Green Hill Far Away." After that, each of us in turn gave back our torch to join the Cross in the fire, to represent the offering of ourselves to Our Lord, and after a few Thanksgivings as the flames sprang up and gave us new light we sang "Praise My Soul The King of Heaven." I don't know how much it meant to the Guides. Of course you never can. But they had all shared in making the torches and the oldest leader had made the Cross so anyhow the little ceremony was very much their own. The torches were very uncertain in their flame while we were singing. They kept flickering and going out so that first one and then another had to light again from her neighbour or else dip again into the fire. At first that worried me, until suddenly I realised that here was quite unconsciously the truest symbolism of all.

Next morning at 7 we had our last bathe, then the usual business of striking Camp which lasted till nearly noon. Then the winning patrol, Chipmunks, hoisted the flag for the last time and held it while we sang the National Anthem and "Praise God from Whom All Blessings Flow." Then we all trailed home in the waggon. It was Adeline's first camp but you would think it was the twenty-first. She grasped everything at once, underpinned every department and, of course, undertook and carried through every specially hot, dirty or tedious job. After three months of extreme caution, Haslam and we dropped surnames into the last Campfire. I think she was happy about it all too. We all feel sure we shall be able to pull together in the future. Adeline and I had two more nights in May's home and left her last Wednesday to move into OUR OWN NEW HOME.

Week ending July 25: HOME LIFE.

We were rather sad to leave May after nine weeks of great happiness with her. She gave us some eggs and a bit of bacon and some lettuces and radishes and wheatmeal for porridge, so, as we already had a loaf left over from camp, and some sugar and very inferior coffee, our house-keeping for the first two or three days was simple and very cheap, which was a satisfaction to our Lady Housekeeper, Miss Adeline Harmer.

We have now been here five days—the most delightful I have spent in this country so far. We are taking a complete holiday from all public works (except Sunday Services), and are entirely absorbed in our home. We sleep in the big loft bedroom which rises from three feet at the sides to eight feet in the middle, wash at a hastily improvised table we made the first night, and cook and eat our meals in a patch of bush about thirty yards away. Up to Saturday the men were still here finishing off the house. Twice we had to take the car down to the river and fill it with sand for the chinking; all one day we spent making a door; and all Saturday we worked as a united team on making a porch for the house, among other things sawing up twenty-four fat logs into exact lengths for the wall. Karl has developed into a perfect treasure. He works steadily from 7 A.M to 9 P.M. and only stops when I tell him to. Also he has abandoned all ideas of his own and is like a sort of silent and immensely skilful and powerful Genie, harnessed to my will.

On Saturday night we drove them home as far as Baldonnel. Then Muriel Haslam, who had been helping with the porch and log peeling, stayed for the night and we had great fun rigging up a bed in the perfectly empty house. She is coming to live with us in the second week of August and is quite keen about it now, though I don't think she was at first.

Now that the men are out we can get to working oiling the floors, staining all the white woodwork, and peeling and rubbing down the logs. That will take several days, I expect, so we shall not get the stoves or any furniture in till after August 1st. And meantime, Mr. Colpitts,[172] another neighbour, is coming to break me four or five acres for next year's crop and a bit round the house for garden, with his plough.

Our milk and bread we get most luxuriously from our neighbour Mrs. Kelly, who lives only 500 yards North of us, and our water we fetch up each morning from the so-called spring at the bottom of the coulee. It is well over 100 feet down and a pretty rough steep climb, so we can only get one bucket a day each and with care, can make that do, but still hope some day to achieve a well. So far alas, the barn is much the better looking building of the two, being naturally lower and plastered with mud. Just now the house looks ugly, chiefly on account of the white lines of cement and the white wood of the roof and eaves and window frames. But the former is supposed to tone down very soon and the latter I shall stain or paint as soon as I get the time and money. Neither at present available for any purpose but just getting in. We mean to put a plain white wooden Cross over the porch and to find a name for the house which will depersonalize it from me and somehow express its purpose. But this name has not emerged yet. Meanwhile we are intensely happy in it and it is above all a wonderful delight to have Adeline as my first Companion of the Peace.

Week ending July 27.

We have [had] another enchanting week of purely worldly enjoyment of our Property. I really am rather ashamed about it but there is no use in hiding the fact that I am deeply in love with this little estate. Just at the start you can't quite realise the sort of intoxicating delight in starting a home where there has been literally nothing at all. Naturally everyone here has done or is doing it and they all take it for granted. But to Adeline and me it comes quite differently. I once thought I could never be happy in a house that wasn't Norman, but you know, quite as wonderful as inheriting the walls and traditions of centuries is to acquire a bit of nameless, untouched bush and start everything from the very bottom. To have to settle every single detail and collect every bit of material is such fearful fun that it is hard not to feel yourself a creator even when, like me, you haven't the skill to do more than the fool-proof jobs yourself.

The porch was built on Saturday week. It is nine feet wide and seven feet long and is a sort of Corinthian portico in logs. Karl did the real building but Adeline and Muriel and I measured and sawed and fitted in the logs and it was completed by 9 o'clock. A porch here is a very real part of the house. Sometimes in the summer you sleep in it. Always you stack the day's supply of fire wood in it and it also keeps all the big or dirty things like oil cans, gardening tools and rubber boots. The chief difficulty is to prevent it from getting quite silted up so that no one can get in or out of the front door.

On Sunday we joined forces with Messrs. Wolf. and What. for Baldonnel and Flats Sunday School and Services. This is only a pro-tem. plan till after the Bishop's visit and consecration of the churches on August 23rd. From that date we shall all spread out and work in different places on Sunday. Both the Services last Sunday were typical. Hardly anyone present at the beginning, the usual trickle as it went on and quite a large influx just as we had finished. In both cases Mr. Wolfendale, with great presence of mind, immediately announced a new hymn and improvised a complete Epilogue for the sake of the late comers, who were always in perfect time by their clocks. Muriel joined us for the evening.

On Monday we had a new kind of enjoyment. For the first time we woke up without any men about the place and were able to have a splendid, all over wash in cold water outside the house. Having as yet no furniture and no means of heating water except at the campfire in the bush, a big wash indoors is difficult and not much fun. But outside in the sunshine, looking over the coulee, it is glorious. We have two kinds of water at present: First Class water fetched in buckets from the bottom of the coulee; it lives in a sort of crock and may NEVER be used for washing. The second class comes from the Kelly's dam a quarter mile off on the level. Sometimes Mr. Kelly hauls us a barrel full. Sometimes we fetch it in pails. It is pretty green and scummy and not so good for drinking but it is soft and splendid for washing.

We meant to devote Monday entirely to the mail but as usual that was just a dream. First Karl came to make partitions and feed boxes and hitching posts and we had to discuss all the details. It was a glorious day and after our usual campfire dinner we really were settling down to write when a car drove in with one of the officials from Pouce Coupé, who brought an English lady to see us. She was a Miss Kemble, a great Empire traveller. She was doing Canada and had found her way to Fort St. John for a few days sketching. Before we had said five words Mr. West had darted off in his car to fetch another lady. Adeline and I were a little bewildered and so I think, was Miss Kemble, until we all hit on the scheme of log peeling. This is a splendid employment for visitors and as far as I can see, it will last for years because there are over one hundred biggish logs in this house, all covered with very thick, rough bark. We shall leave it all on outside but inside shall peel gradually. Otherwise the worms do it for you more gradually and with a continual and uncontrollable mess. But so far we are only doing the living room. So after a few preliminary civilities we produced a chisel and a small hatchet (the King's School present), and pressed them into Miss Kemble's hands and she became perfectly happy.

But very soon after, back came Mr. West with the next lady. This time he was very important indeed and introduced her in quite awe-struck

tones as "Miss Penrose, the Government Waterfinder." Miss Penrose
was another Englishwoman, dressed most beautifully in smart English
breeches and riding boots, but in her belt were stuck her hazel rod and
various lengths and twists of wire so we knew she meant business and got
rather excited. At last I plucked up courage and asked whether she could
find a spring for us. We all stood at a respectful distance watching, and I
must say it was perfectly thrilling. First she walked vaguely about with
her hands outstretched a little, as if blindfold. Then, suddenly, she
stopped and took one of the wire coils from her belt. She walked in a
curiously meandering path and suddenly made straight for the patch of
bush directly behind the house. Before reaching it she stopped and called
out, "I must have a man with an axe." Karl rushed forward and cleared a
path for her with such enthusiasm that I thought my poor little bush
would soon be all cut down. But at last she came to a little black poplar,
commanded him to cut her a path all round it, circled round several
times, then made endless strange bowings to it with a long heavy wire,
then straightened up, walked back to us and said, "Exactly under the
middle of that tree you will find all the water you need for domestic
purposes." I asked breathlessly how much, thinking of our bucket a day
and she said, "The usual requirement is fifty gallons a head per day.
Would that be enough?" Fifty GALLONS . . .! Adeline and I could only
laugh rather like imbeciles till I remembered to ask "How deep?"
"Probably 100 to 150 feet." We got her some tea. Then Mr. West carried
her off in triumph to some more dry settlers.

Meanwhile Miss Kemble was to remain at the hotel at Fort St. John. It
did seem rather dreary so I had a hasty consultation with Adeline, then
asked Miss Kemble if she would care to camp here and take completely
potluck with us. She accepted with rapture. Indeed it was quite
touching, considering what we had to offer—a completely unfurnished
house, no bedding, very little food and [this] to be cooked and eaten
outside. We arranged to call for her next morning and we started letters
again, but soon Mr. Wolfendale arrived with various Church matters to
discuss. He was great fun and in tremendous spirits. A little while after
he left, another car drove up and a strange man got out and came to the
porch. I went up to greet him and he said, "Oh I'm a stranger and I just
saw this cute little house and wanted to look at it nearer." Luckily his
curiosity was soon satisfied. Then May arrived with Tommy and had to
have a look round of course. But before she left, she almost threw two
parcels at Adeline saying, "I must have the cans back and the chicken is
seven years old and died yesterday of rheumatism." When she had gone
we found a tin of wild strawberries just gathered and the rheumatic fowl
beautifully trussed and boiled. Soon after, another car to take Karl home
and finally Mr. Colpitts and his plough slowly lumbered up in a

waggon, arrived to break my land for next year's crop. Adeline and I went to sleep saying, "Fifty gallons a head. Under that tree. BUT at least a HUNDRED feet down. How can it be done???"

End of Diary for week ending July 27.

At 4.30 that day we decided to go down to the Old Post by the river where my freight had been waiting for two or three weeks and see what could be done about getting it up. The actual distance is about ten miles. We lost the way several times and finally got down to the river about 6 o'clock. There we found a most welcoming family called McLeod. The old man showed me five or six immense packing cases and I had to confess that the only thing that could possibly haul them up the hill was a waggon. It was wonderful, though, to see them and I longed to open one at once and look at some of the things from home.

The McLeods were quite excited by visitors, as apparently they hardly ever see anyone.[173] The Old Post is a lovely place close to the river, surrounded by bush and backed by hills: the sort of place that charabancs[174] would visit in England and where you would find lots of notices of Teas and Minerals. Here, however, it is entirely remote and secluded, rather too much so to please the McLeods who have six children isolated from any school. If only another family would settle there they could have a school. But Mrs. McLeod's only neighbour, one and a half miles off, is Mrs. Beaton who can speak no English. So we spread out our visit a bit. I resolved to go down and hold a Sunday School for them as soon as possible.

About 7 we started back and Adeline drove majestically up the long steep narrow trail across rickety little bridges of poles and through deep, muddy pits. We got to the top and began to hear the first call for supper when, in dodging among trees, we ran into a slough and stuck fast. That was a maddening hole. After an hour we had to confess ourselves beaten and look for help. We didn't the least know where we were but followed the trail till it came to a house and there found one of the Fort St. John Guides. But both parents were out looking for a cow and she was minding the baby and anyway they had no horses. She directed us to another house about half a mile farther on and eventually we found it, at about 10 o'clock. We did hate coming to ask for help at that hour but luckily the little boy greeted us gaily and turned out to be one of the Fort St. John Sunday School. He took us to find his parents. You can't think how kind they were. The man said, "The horses are out but I guess I can catch them" and the mother said, "Meantime you must come in and have a cup of tea." The funny thing is that we found we had both been feeling guilty about the other. The fact is that I had called upon her on my first real round in October, 1929 and found her and her husband both on the roof shingling their house. They were obviously awfully busy so I hadn't dismounted but had a few words and left them, meaning to come again but alas, the plot had thickened so much that I never did come again. So you can imagine my relief when she said, "I'm ever so glad you came. Jim and me have been feeling ever so bad about it because we didn't come off the roof that day and ask you in. We were sure you were offended and would never come again." Then she gave us some tea and cookies for which we were thankful, having had nothing since mid-day sandwiches. We discussed Sunday School and Tommy and then Mr. Kelly arrived with the team and they came to the place where Eliza was buried, about a mile off, and we all made great friends. Isn't it splendid how things turn out? If it hadn't been for the freight going wrong and the hidden slough we might have gone on indefinitely without getting to know the Kellys. Soon after 11 we were out of the swamp: just on midnight we got home.

On Thursday morning we had a very grand moment. I had paid Mr. Guiton the sixty dollars for the two horses and the time had come to take possession. We went to the livery barn, paid off their board and lodging and led them off the two and a half miles to their new home. The only sickening thing was that we couldn't ride them in state, because my leg isn't healed yet. So the long-suffering Adeline didn't either, but we walked along leading them as importantly as possible and tried to feel like trainers exercising Derby winners. It was a splendid moment when we opened the little wire gate and led them into the newly-fenced pasture. I don't think I have ever felt so important though it may be very different when we have to catch them.

On Friday morning I had told the Baldonnel Guides to meet at the school and get full particulars of kit, etc. The moment I left the house it began to pour so I arrived at school pretty well soaked and expected to find no Guides. But four awfully keen little girls turned up and we had a delightful time discussing plans and needs. It is interesting how one learns to adapt needs to possibilities in this country. For instance, when I reeled off the list to these VERY clean and refined little girls and included brush and comb, sponge, wash rag, soap, toothbrush, their jaws dropped and they all said, "I haven't got a brush." "I've never had a sponge." "I think I've got a tooth brush." But don't you imagine these are squalid children. They are just as clean as you and me. Soon after this, Adeline arrived with the car and sandwiches for luncheon which we ate in the school before going on to the Flats to see whether the air down there had cleared with regard to Camping. But Adeline broke it to me, Charlie had struck a specially big bump and injured Eliza's spring so that she was once more suffering from a heavy list to port and looked terribly drunk. We didn't like to drive her down the Flats hill so we walked down to visit one or two troublesome families there. Alas, no luck at all. No one for Camp and no definite reason but dark hints about other people. I am really afraid we may have to close down Guides and Sunday School for a bit till maybe they miss it and grow ashamed (as the boys already do about Scouts).

We started back at 4.30 because Eliza had to be set on an even keel that day before going into Camp. So we drove back to Fort St. John and on the way had the great glory of pulling George B. out of a muddy ditch. It was satisfactory because only a few days before he had pulled us out, so now we are quits.

The next day being Saturday we were to go out to the Scouts' Camp for the week-end and stay on for the Guides. So we started by packing furiously, then drove hastily to the city to meet and say good-bye to Mr. Guiton who, to everybody's regret, had to go back to Montreal. He was full of enthusiasm about the Camp and about the Church and about everything else, full of hope and a great desire to come back himself.

We had a farewell luncheon of sausages and ice cream and were all sincerely sorry to say good-bye. He has been such a keen and whole hearted friend to this place and has won respect and friendliness from everyone. I really hope he may one day be able to come back and work here for a good number of years.

When he had driven off with Tommy to Pouce Coupé, we picked up one extra boy and lots of extra food and tackle and started for the Camp.

(There is no diary in the surviving text for July 28 to August 7.)

Adeline's Diary ending August 17.

On Tuesday Miss Kemble came to take up her abode with us. She had been prepared to camp with the Van folk so we gave her our tent and she settled in. She worked like a Black, besides providing all kinds of food. She and Monica and I peeled logs and stained wood from morning to night. At intervals we cooked a large and hasty meal on a campfire. Mr. Colpitts also caught the horse Puck and fixed the kitchen stove. Before

the end of the week the Van workers came back. They are a nice pair.
They came to supper, camped on our ground and next day took Miss
Kemble off with them and Muriel also, who went to a Sunday School
Camp at Pouce Coupé.

August 8.

When I tell you that towards the end of the week we simply could not
remember what day it was—hoped it was Thursday and found to our
disappointment it was Friday—you will not expect daily details in this
diary. Muriel comes back on the 14th, and then the Guide official from
Vancouver comes to stay and then on the 21st the Bishop arrived (though
not to stay with us). Monica gets awfully worried at being so absorbed in
the house, but really the house itself ought to help the work here
tremendously and the care spent on it to make it suitable and beautiful
ought to count too. She has the Fra Angelico picture of the monks
welcoming Christ as a Stranger[175] in our little hall. She asked in to
dinner to-day a man to whom she had just lent her car so as to get his wife
to hospital. The baby was born within twenty minutes of the arrival at
the hospital. It is a great joy to her to be able to give hospitality to all and
sundry visitors. This man kept evidently trying to see how he could
repay her for the loan of her car, offered us vegetables and greater help
still, just picked up and carried upstairs a roll of linoleum which has
required the united strength of both of us to get from the car to the front
door.

We had feverishly prepared for Sunday School on Saturday afternoon
and evening. Sunday was a boiling day. At Baldonnel we found a
smallish Sunday School. The attitude of both children and parents to
Sunday things is very baffling. For no reason the regular comers quite
suddenly fail to appear; yet on the other hand, entirely new people may
stroll in to the grown-up Service. The real thing is that in the summer
they are berrying to provide fruit for the winter—every available person.

At the Flats, after an endless wait, only two small boys turned up but
for the Service we had by the end quite a nice little congregation.

We haven't attempted to do anything to our bedroom yet. Consequently our room has nothing in it except our washstand and a couple of
stools. A small boy is coming to live here, go to school and do the chores.
He and his father live six miles from the nearest school. His mother is
not with them and when the father has to work on the road Harvey
[Cheverton] has to be left completely alone for a week at a time. He is to
have the West bedroom upstairs.

August 17.

On Sunday, as usual, we became perfect ladies in cotton dresses, shaking off the chrysalis of filthy dark blue overalls. Monica first of all rode Puck to Fort St. John and took Muriel's Sunday School there. On Friday we were due at a Church meeting at Baldonnel to elect officers. The meeting began, as most do here, by no one arriving for ages and then a few women trickled in. Whenever Mr. Wolfendale had finished explaining something, some more folk came in and he had to begin again. The meeting was held in the Hall. The Secretary (Monica), was perched at a table on a keg of nails and the audience (self-segregated as to sexes), were seated along two enormous planks also upheld by nail kegs. Light was provided by our hurricane lamp which threw a yellowish light on a very small circle. When voting had to be done, two small pencils of Monica's and sheets torn out of a tiny note book of Mr. Wolfendale's provided the materials. Old Munro (the Scotsman who built our chimney and is now a devoted follower of Mr. Wolf. and comes regularly to Baldonnel Service), marched solemnly round with the lantern in one hand and Monica's hat in the other and collected the voting papers. He then marched off with the lantern, leaving us in almost pitch darkness while he and another scrutinised the votes. However, all were quite happy except Monica and me, who were remembering that Muriel was arriving at a perfectly strange house—for she had never seen it furnished—and we had omitted to leave out the matches. For the election of the People's Warden it is to be either Mr. Birley or Mr. Simpson. Should Mr. Birley refuse, he is to be asked to be a Trustee of the Hall part of the building for which there are to be six: Monica, Mrs. McDonald, Mrs. Simpson, Mr. Colpitts, Mr. Simpson or Mr. Birley and another man.

Our coming events are terribly thick as follows:

> Tuesday 18, Bee 9 gathering at Fort St. John of women to make hassocks, sew curtains, etc.
>
> Wednesday 19, Bee at Baldonnel, men to make fences, benches, etc.; women to sew curtains and provide meals.
>
> Thursday 20, Monica brings back Provincial Secretary of British Columbia Guides to stay with us.
>
> Friday 21,   12-3, picnic lunch for Guide Patrol Leaders and Seconds to meet her. Bishop arrives, also Rural Dean.
>
>   8 P.M., social gathering to meet him [the Bishop] in Baldonnel Church Hall.
>
> Saturday, 22, Bishop (and we don't know who else), to lunch with us.
>
> 3 P.M. BLESSING OF THIS HOUSE.
>
> Fort St. John ladies to tea afterwards here to meet Bishop.

Evening supper for men to meet Bishop in restaurant in town.
Sunday 23, 10., Children's Service.
>   10.30, Consecration of Fort St. John Church.
Ordination of Mr. Wolfendale.
>   2.30, Children's Service, Baldonnel.
>   3., Consecration of Church end of Hall.
>   7., Service, Taylor's Flats School. Bishop leaves.
Monday 24,3., Guides and Brownies meeting.
Miss Williams leaves.
Into all this hurly burly Cecilia[176] arrives, we imagine, tomorrow.

Tuesday 18, night.

Eventually we rolled home between 11 and half past and found Muriel established here, having borrowed matches from Tommy who brought her from Pouce Coupé.

On Saturday Monica has a long talk with Muriel about the division of work in the house, etc. Muriel is quite keen on being cook-housekeeper for the first month. It does not mean that one has to stay in and cook each meal but that she is responsible for any real cooking and for the food in general. She is very capable and has been quite a long time in Canada.

On Saturday we did a thing we've never done before. We sat round the lamp and read four unopened *Weekly Times*. We felt so grand until sleep overcame us and we rolled into bed.

August 17, 1931.

Once more I have left the diary to Adeline who has managed skilfully to combine it with doing all the household chores while Muriel and I have been out in opposite directions, beating the covers for next Sunday. We have now been here for over three weeks and the house is every day getting a little more human. For a fortnight we knocked off all outside duties (except, of course, Sundays), but for the last week we have lived a sort of half and half life and this week is to be a blaze of Public Events. For the first ten days the men were still in the house and we lived in our tent and cooked and fed at a campfire in our own tiny bit of bush. It was great fun, that part, especially as quite a lot of people dropped in for stray meals (chiefly strange men travelling up country), and had to put up with undercooked beans or burnt pork or whatever else was going. It is such a delight to be like Abraham and Sara on the plains of Mamre,[177] able to run out and welcome travellers, give them a little precious water to wash their feet, and kill and dress for them a fried egg and a few young potatoes. These strangers are always interesting, generally on their way to take up land in some newly surveyed area, where of course, we always promise to pay them a return visit one day. One of them, however, was an oldtimer called Wagner (English pronunciation), who lives fifty miles up the Halfway River pretty far from anybody and subsists entirely by his own rod and gun in the summer, while in winter he traps furs. He invited Adeline and me to go with him for a fortnight's trip in the bush in September. We both long to go but as a project it is not exactly in the line of business.

Of course it is much more delightful now we have a real table in a real house to invite them to, especially as there are no class distinctions to complicate hospitality, and no sort of fuss about food. Any guest just shares as a matter of course what we are having and if it's only bread and cheese they are perfectly satisfied and always expect to help to wash up afterwards. Mr. Colpitts also was a temporary boarder, that is during the five days in which he broke my land. You can't think what a solemn event that was. He only broke five acres in all but when walking round with him and driving stakes and pacing out what he called "The lands," I felt the Duke of Northumberland to be nowhere in it with me. And when the plough first cut in, and the black soil turned over, it caused quite a fool lump in my throat. When that was all done we had to decide what to break for next year's garden. It was really difficult to decide how much we can hope to cultivate. Finally we surrounded the house with a sort of square of thirty-five yards each way, like this, about five yards of grass all round the house. Then to the North, seventeen yards of breaking for vegetables and South, East and West, five yards for flowers. Of course we can do no more this year and the immediate result is only that the house sits in the middle of a tiny ploughed field; but we shall be able to cultivate it directly the frost goes out in the spring. In the meanwhile it acts as a fire guard to the house against any danger of fires from the bush.

Mr. Colpitts' plough was rather the worse for wear and once or twice I had to take it off in the car to the blacksmith. On one of these trips I noticed Eliza was steering rather badly and thought it was just old age affecting me in a new way, but after about three miles I really had to stop and look her over. And then I found the front right tyre had completely vanished so that we had been running gaily on the rim. Mr. Colpitts and

I walked back, tracking the rim through dust and mud along the road and across a rough prairie trail, where at last, two miles back, the escaped tyre was found nestling in deep bush quite a long way from the trail.

Just before Karl went I grew very dissatisfied with the upstairs room which was a large but exaggerated type of attic. As Muriel and Cecilia are going to sleep there I felt it must be improved, so suggested to Karl a dormer window. In the end he agreed, so we measured off the number of rafters to be cut and then I had to go to the city to fetch extra lumber, nails, galvanized iron and shingles. They had to be collected at different places and finally I was built into the car with fourteen-foot one by fours piled high and lashed on all round and drove back cautiously enough over the bumps, as I could scarcely see over the barricade. And it was harder still to climb out. Karl made the window in two days but just when he had cut open a huge gaping wound for it in the roof, the weather changed and we had twelve hours steady rain, which was a little disconcerting. However, we covered the hole as well as we could with ground sheets and moved all our junk to the far corner. Outside, I'm afraid, the window rather spoils the house, but inside, the effect is splendid and the room really transformed, with far more light and head-space and the best view in the house down to the coulee. Adeline and I sleep downstairs in a smaller room which I feel rather guilty in taking for myself, but it is the obvious one for guests and as we hope for quite a lot of these it gives me the chance of turning out and sleeping in the living room, which in houses that have separate bedrooms, is of course the owner's duty and privilege. I couldn't be always asking Cecilia or Muriel to do this for my guests. But it is a delight to do it oneself and we have a little narrow bed disguised as a sofa for the purpose.

A great agitation was the floor of the house. We started by staining it all as well as the shelves and doors and windows, with permanganate of potash, 2/ worth of which did the whole house and left a big bucketful over. But the flooring being of very poor and unequal quality, the result was dreadfully streaky and uneven, varying from yellow to black. After this we oiled it all over with boiling linseed oil and meant to leave it for two days to dry. But first Karl, making the windows upstairs, caused continual showers of sawdust to fall through the thin upstairs floor and cover the one below. Then the rainy day came and Karl and his assistant stumped up and downstairs with muddy boots and the mischief was complete. Adeline and I mean to have a grand scrub tomorrow and try to start it all over afresh. Upstairs we have laid a light oak linoleum bought at Edmonton. It looks rather nice and we got a little rug for each bedside from Edmonton, which is rather necessary in the winter.

The grand excitement, after getting in the four beds, the two tables and the cooking stove was the arrival of the English freight. We had a marvellous day unpacking the big case out in the barn and bringing in blankets and linen (we started sheets again that night), the Deanery brass coffee pot, Home spoons and forks, and above all, the whole of the china given by Pet.[178] We nearly came to blows arranging it all on the old Welsh dresser, but in the end, the effect was very good and we sat looking at it for a long time in speechless admiration.

The next event was finding the lovely crocus cretonne given by Lady Goodenough and cutting out window curtains, door curtains and curtains for the lower shelves of the dresser where the rolling pin and wooden spoon live. All these were hemmed by Mrs. Kelly, who has a machine, in rapturous gratitude for a pair of shoes which are too large for me. These curtains are all up now and look delightful and when we have got the books into the shelves the living room will be complete. After that we had two or three days intensive carpentering, put up a lot of shelves in the pantry (alias front hall, alias bathroom and guests' washing room, summer kitchen and summer dining room, size sixteen by six foot six), laid down a sort of floor in the cellar, which is just a pit, rather muddy at the bottom. Then we made a rather fine guests' washing stand of log ends and winny [?] edge which is complete with everything except an actual basin. These haven't arrived yet so the dish-pan flies backwards and forwards and has a very lively existence. But the greatest effort was our bedroom furniture, a hanging cupboard of poplar-poles and shiplap waiting for a cretonne mantel, another basin-less washing stand and an Old World wardrobe consisting of four long shelves on heavy corner posts, one spruce, one willow, the whole as solid as a Tudor cupboard—at least we hope so.

By this time we were longing to make a similar suite for Cecilia and Muriel, but didn't because it's such tremendous fun that I'm sure they would rather do it themselves. Also Muriel is apparently a fairly good carpenter and probably Cecilia too, whereas Adeline has had only two lessons at Richmond and all my previous carpentry was to hang a picture crooked.

But even before the living room was done we got the little Chapel fixed up and it seemed to come at once just right. It's a good sized room, eleven by nine, and its walls are of unpeeled logs. We made a table of shiplap on two big upright log-ends to fit Grandfather's old red frontal given me at Cornwallis. On it is the beautiful little Memlin tryptych of the Adoration given us by Lady Goodenough and above that, a big copy of Fra Angelico's Crucifixion.[179] In front of this is a sort of kneeling rail of more up-right logs and carefully planed shiplap and kneelers of two bedside mats. So the Chapel is really complete except for chairs. At present we have got four only and these live active and varied lives, like the dish-pan, but with this advantage that two or three of them always go to Prayers. We have slightly modified Matins and Evensong with Intercessions daily, directly after breakfast and about 10 P.M., taking it in turns to be Chaplain. And of course the Chapel is available always as a quiet place away from the cheerful racket of the living room-kitchen. On the whole the house is a success, I think, that is, moderately good on the outside but delightful inside—at least I think so but perhaps its mother is prejudiced. Karl has made us a beautiful plain Cross of white spruce which we have nailed to the pediment of the porch as the sign of the house.

Water is still the chief difficulty. Our waterhole is exhausted. The Kellys' dam is very low and too green and weedy even for washing. So last week we were at length reduced to buying water. A man called Jim has a tank on a waggon which he fills at Fish Creek about four miles away and hauls to his customers, at a pretty high rate. We bought four old petrol barrels at the garage. Adeline brought them home in the car and Jim filled them for two and a half dollars, i.e., 10/6. It's fairly good water but an awful price, and of course we try to catch every possible drop of rain water to eke it out. The simplest plan is to fasten a long plank of shiplap high up to the corner of the eave and then to slope it the whole length of the house to the barrel below. If you get it just under the eave all the way the rain is so innocent that most of it gets caught on this flat board and runs straight down into the barrel or bath tub or other vessel below.

At intervals all through the week we went to Fort St. John and Baldonnel to watch the progress of the churches. Mr. Wolf. and What. have built the former almost entirely unaided and it certainly is beautifully finished, both outside and in. Baldonnel, as you remember, has been built on a contract and on the while I think it is also a splendid building and worthy of the sacrifice it has meant to lots of people at Home. The blue cross and candlesticks from the Messengers arrived with my freight, also the lovely red hangings from Crayford[180] and quite a lot of altar linen. On Wednesday we are to have a Bee of men and women to hang the curtains and arrange the whole building for the Bishop's visit at the end of this week and the consecration on Sunday week. That will be a great series of events to come in the next letter and we will take a photograph. Don't expect it to look like a proper church. It doesn't a bit but it's simple and dignified and the Cross will make it clear.

PEACE COTTAGE, St. Bartholemew's Day,
August 24.

We have just come to the end of a perfect week and are all very happy

and thankful about it. Last Sunday (16th) Mr. Wolfendale took a day off
in which to prepare a little for his ordination, so Mr. Whatmore took all
the Services and we the usual Sunday School. Unluckily Mr. What. and
Adeline and I had weakly consented to go to supper with the McDonalds
between afternoon and Evensong, Mrs. McDonald having promised to
have it absolutely ready at 6 o'clock. It's a bit out of the way, being four
miles beyond Baldonnel, in the opposite direction to the Flats, and of
course the dear old thing wasn't nearly ready. We waited about and
played with the children but it wasn't till a quarter to 7 that supper
actually began, i.e., just about the time we had intended to leave. It was a
most excellent and elaborate meal but dreadfully confused and
pandemonic. All the older children wandered round and round asking
where were their places and their food and above all rose deafening
shouts from Billy, aged one. He sat in a little chair between his elder
brother and sister and every time he let out a yell his father and mother
called out in unison from opposite ends of the table, "Feed him, Jack!"
"Feed him, Helen!" Upon which Helen and Jack, without looking
round, mechanically and *simultaneously* held out sideways large
morsels of pork on the end of their knives, or saskatoon berries on their
forks. We broke away at last, very late, and rushed down to [the] Flats
feeling awfully guilty but trying to take comfort in the thought that for
the last three weeks practically nobody had been attending. Of course we
found the School fully assembled and about seven had come and gone.
Wasn't it sickening? We were very unhappy about it but took it as a
warning never to accept such invitations again.

Coming back I spent a good half hour in Baldonnel Church trying to
come to the best conclusion about lighting the little sanctuary. You see,
the builder and I are having a fearful tussle over South versus East
window. He wants the latter and I want the former so as to get direct
light from the front upon the altar and cross and the picture above them.
Because in this kind of building there is of course no sort of beauty
possible in the East window itself. On Monday morning I went to get a
better light on the subject and finally left an urgent message requesting
the South window. Then I went and visited a few people to tell them
about the Working Bee on Wednesday. This involved a large dinner
with the Fosters and an expedition to capture Karl to make him frame
some pictures. He had already jibbed but it was quite clear that the big
hall part was going to look awfully bare for the opening unless a few
pictures were hung. So I persuaded him to stop building his own
chicken house and come down to the church with me. Karl started by
looking out pieces of Balm of Gilead (black poplar), which is much the
best for the purpose. We had no glass, but he collected enough decent
wood to frame five pictures that were stiff enough to stand firm until the

glass comes. These were two charming Scotch water colours by Lady Darnley,[181] the large reproduction of a sea shore and a few trees, given by Phyllis Ponsonby, my own big photogravure of father—all these to go at the West end; and for the back of the altar above the red dorsal, a beautiful, big, carbon photograph of Thorvaldsen's "Statue of the Welcoming Christ,"[182] this given by Mrs. Harmer. Karl took all day making the five frames which wasn't surprising, considering he had to do it with ordinary building lumber, but he did it wonderfully well and only charged three dollars for the five.

After that, Monday has escaped me except borrowing a sewing machine from Mrs. Birley for the Fort St. John kneelers.

While I was running round all Monday, Adeline was doing wonders as Home Sister, more particularly scrubbing the whole floor and roasting a good sized leg of pork.

Did I tell you Muriel had settled in for good, I hope? We are getting very fond of Muriel. She is extraordinarily gentle and considerate and entirely sincere. Really her only fault is an amazing all round efficiency, i.e., at cooking, carpentering, motor driving and running repairs, poultry farming (when required), horse management, accounts, in fact all the things I can't do, even to Bible and Sunday School teaching. Naturally I can't help resenting this. Otherwise we should be quite good friends. On Tuesday we had a women's Bee at Fort St. John making curtains, kneelers, the former out of mulberry coloured plush from Eaton Square,[183] the latter of red felt filled with excelsior which is the ludicrous name for the fine shavings in which my freight was packed.

Wednesday was to be the Bee at Baldonnel, supposed to start at 11 and go on till finished. It was necessary to make some benches and we had no big lumber left so Eliza had another good job to do fetching twelve heavy planks two by eight inches by sixteen feet, which we lashed, as usual, along the sides and then crawled in over the top. We also had to take dinner for an unknown number and curtains and kneeler material for the women to work at, besides tools and stain, etc. People rolled up gradually in waggons and on horseback till at length we mobilized ten women, fourteen men and about the same number of children, including two or three infants in arms. This was really very good considering the harvest has just begun and all the men are fearfully busy in the fields.

The women brought three sewing machines and worked splendidly at curtains and hanging while the men made a fence and a big gate and long benches and the children cleared away piles of shavings. Everybody was delightfully friendly and happy. One family brought lots of house-plants for decoration. Another woman stained the frames and hung the pictures, while two more helped to arrange the lovely red dorsal and curtains sent by Crayford behind the altar. My only disappointment was that after all Hoffstrom had put in an East window and no South one. I had to bear it for the time but am still convinced that the effect is bad and shall bide my time to get it remedied. We had a big camp dinner all together and were a most happy party. Adeline and I bossed the female contingent while Mr. Wolfendale gave the men their jobs and they slaved at making the prayer desk and lectern between ceaseless interruptions. All the while we were looking out for Cecilia Goodenough, who we knew had reached Pouce Coupé and might therefore drive past at any moment in some truck or car. Every time I heard the sound of wheels I rushed out and hailed them, but it was never Cecilia. There were two other disappointments—first the three dozen chairs hadn't come from Edmonton and didn't look like coming; secondly the fifty-two yards of blue stuff I had ordered to make the two big pairs of curtains right across the hall did come, but were quite the wrong blue, lovely but far too light, like a drawing room, so we sadly agreed to send it back and make up one smaller pair temporarily out of a remnant sent me by Archdeacon Burgett. Mr. Hoffstrom turned up and I forgave him about the window because he was so delightful about the pictures. He went into raptures about the picture of Thorvaldsen's "Statue of Christ"—chiefly, I think, because it was Scandinavian and has written beneath it the Norwegian words for "Come unto ME."

It was a pretty blazing day and everyone got very thirsty which was a bore because we have no water except what we can fetch from C.'s dam nearly half a mile away. Still we fetched a bucket or two and even made tea later in the afternoon.

By about 8 o'clock everything was finished as far as possible, though we were still waiting and longing for Cecilia to bring the frontal. Gradually everyone trundled away except Adeline and me and Wolf. Then, we having sent the car home earlier with Muriel in case Cecilia should have got there somehow, set out to walk home and in the fifth mile got a lift for the last few hundred yards. We got in about 9.30 and found poor Muriel still standing like Patience on a monument waiting to dish up the roast pork. We fell upon it very famished, when Mrs. Kelly arrived to talk about curtains, and I felt my gratitude creaking under the strain. Soon after 10, when we had eaten most of the pork, Wolf. drove up still more famished, having worked on alone till it was too dark to see anything. We revived some pork for him and he was just going when at last Cecilia arrived. It was delightful to see her and she looked so well and happy and not a bit tired. After a little talk she produced an enormous wooden box and out of it, among many other things, the FRONTAL, made and given by Lady Goodenough. It is perfectly lovely, a rich, red satin brocade with deeper red velvet and super-frontal and orphreys on which are embroidered two panels of tall white lilies and one of deep purple passion flowers. We were all amazed at its beauty and also at the perfect workmanship put into small accessories—the silk veil, the marker, and the thing that hangs over the pulpit when you have one—in our case over the lectern. I used to know its name but have forgotten it. They were all quite exquisite and Brother Wolf. especially looked and evidently felt exactly like the Queen of Sheba.

I had written poor Cecilia three separate letters of commissions to Edmonton but she had wonderfully carried them all out in the few hours on Monday, even to bringing us long altar candles and three enamel washing bowls.

We talked and unpacked and admired and at last went to bed. It is delightful having Cecilia and seems to bring Home a thousand miles or more nearer all of a sudden.

On Thursday Muriel and I were booked to drive down to Dawson Creek with two car loads of our ladies to hear the Bishop of the Diocese address the Women's Auxiliary. I had not driven there before and was a little uncertain how Eliza and I should manage the long steep hills and hairpin bends. We took seven women between us—all fearfully excited by the expedition and no wonder since most of them had not crossed the river for at least two years. Muriel had the Clergy car, which is a saloon and in better general order, so, as the dust was terrific and the road awfully bumpy, her passengers were the luckiest. However, we had a good run. The hills were not bad and no more was Eliza. We had luncheon in the bush where Mrs. Simpson actually produced a roast chicken. We did the sixty miles in good time and had a very nice meeting, rather like a very dressy Mothers' Union gathering because of course, all these ladies, when they do come out, are ten times smarter than English Mothers' Union Enrolling Members. At the end an hour of bliss was allowed for walking up Dawson Creek and admiring its two stores and then we had a good drive back, a lovely sunset over the river and home about 10.30.

And now, alas, I am so tired that I can't write any more. But I will try again later this week and hope to find some one to take a letter out.

August 31, 1931.

Last week I ended the diary three days too soon, with the trip to Dawson Creek. The meeting was a fairly dull one to my jaded palate, but to our passengers it was all interesting—especially the tea at the end.

Bishop Rix had arrived the night before and was most welcoming and friendly to us. He is so kind and cordial and was in very good form though apparently still suffering from his bad accident last winter when, like May, he had five ribs broken and had to be in bed three months. After the meeting we paid a swift visit to the Dawson Creek Cooperative Stores and all bought something to remind us of the event. I bought a lock and some hinges for the church and also had the luck to see a fine, large, wooden butter bowl which I bought in case it might be useful for making a font. We had arranged to meet and bring with us Miss Williams, the Provincial Girl Guide Secretary for British Columbia. We had warned her that she would have to play second string to the Bishop which left her quite undaunted. She turned out to be a delightfully easy guest for any circumstances: she threw herself right into our festivities and worked like a Black at all the chores. She slept in my room as it is really the guest room, while Adeline moved to the little room upstairs to be occupied by the boy Harvey next term, and I slept on the disguised spare bed in the living room.

On Friday we had a little meeting for her of Guide Leaders and Seconds, who also saw Cecilia for the first time. They stayed till 4 and soon after that we all tidied up and having loaded Eliza with lamps, cups, sandwiches, cakes, frontal, candles and a large armchair lashed to the roof, we went over to Baldonnel for the first social to be held in the Hall to welcome the Bishop.

It was lucky we went early because there was plenty to do. Adeline and Muriel fetched buckets of water from the nearest dam a quarter of a mile off and lighted a campfire to make tea and coffee, while Cecilia and I unpacked the frontal and helped to assemble the altar which Mr. Wolfendale had made in Fort St. John and brought over in pieces in the car. He had also brought (and made) the Communion rails, all of which needed careful fixing up, and in the middle of it all the Bishop arrived with Canon and Mrs. Proctor—a little BEFORE time. So I had to switch off and talk to them with strenuous unconcern for a tantalizing half hour while the others finished the work in the Sanctuary. Of course the social was entirely in the Hall and didn't really affect the Chancel, which was hidden behind the blue curtains, but we didn't want to have any kind of opening ceremony till we knew that was really ready. We suffered agonies of uncertainty as to whether anyone would come and also of perplexity as to what would happen if and when they did, because a dance had been vetoed till after the Church Consecration of next Sunday and the people have no other idea of evening pleasure so far.

However, they did come—quite a lot, dribbling in by two and threes for well over an hour longer. Then at last we had a formal meeting—Mr. Wolfendale in the chair. Canon Proctor made a very comprehensive speech, the Bishop a very nice one, largely about our friends at Home and how they gave the Church Hall in memory of Father. Then I had to say a little in answer to all that and then we had refreshments all round. It was a dull meeting, as meetings go. But everyone was tremendously happy and friendly and delighted with the Hall which certainly is something to be proud of.

To begin with, it is much larger than any other building round here—fifty-four by twenty-six feet the actual Hall and Nave part—plus twelve by ten the little Sanctuary at the East end. The other end is a good platform, so on secular occasions we curtain off the Sanctuary and turn Westward and vice versa. Of course it is all (except the Sanctuary) entirely bare. All the money has been used up in providing a really fine building and now we have to set to work here to raise the funds for a cooking stove, two heaters (without which it would be an ice house in winter), paint enough for the inside and out, and a [word omitted]. [No] other luxuries. All I could contribute straight off were the five pictures framed by Karl. The large engraving of Father hangs right opposite the door (the main door), and is much admired.

Well, the meeting warmed up and got quite keen. We all discussed the wonderful things we were going to do and the Trustees called me into a corner where we planned the first dance, to be held next week. Then the Bishop went on with the Proctors to sleep at Fort St. John. We stopped to see everyone out and got back at midnight. On Saturday morning Cecilia and I hastened back to meet a nice Mrs. Rider,[184] who with her two daughters, had volunteered to help clear up. We all swept and tidied (luckily there was no mud to cope with), finished arranging the altar and put together three dozen chairs which had just arrived and been dumped in sections outside the door.

Meanwhile Adeline and Muriel and the faithful Miss Williams had been spring cleaning the house and preparing for the first luncheon and tea party. We joined them at 12 for a last strenuous hour—Muriel did the cooking, Miss Williams cleaned all the windows and the rest of us worked at top pressure trying to clean and tidy every hole and corner for the Bishop's inspection and the Fort St. John ladies coming to tea to meet him. At one sharp (rather too sharp again), he arrived with the Proctors, and we sat down, seven of us, to a banquet consisting chiefly of two fine chickens given us by May. Afterwards we sat outside and talked until about half a dozen Fort St. John ladies rolled up and then the Bishop held a little Service in the Chapel to dedicate the house. He robed in the guest room and was most awfully kind and really helpful. Then a few more ladies rolled up, each one dutifully bringing a cup or two by request, as we knew we had not enough and those we have are the main ornament of the room when left hanging on the nails. Then we had tea, and things trailed on happily enough till after 6 when the Bishop and the Proctors went back to Fort St. John for a supper party to meet the men.

Sunday was the great day when both churches were to be consecrated and Mr. Wolfendale ordained Priest. Fort St. John was in the morning. Muriel and I went on ahead of the rest for a preliminary Matins (required by the Prayer Book) at 9.30. At 10 the children arrived and had a very nice little special address from the Bishop. At 10.30 the real congregation rolled up and the main Service began. You would hardly believe it but I have never before been to the Consecration of a church. We all met outside and walked in singing "Onward Christian Soldiers." Then the two Church-wardens, Dr. Brown and Mr. Finch, presented their petition to the Bishop and the Service went on till it seemed to merge insensibly into the Ordination, which is, of course, so familiar and so beautiful. It brought back Rochester to me more vividly than anything else out here. And all the contrasts—the bare little bran-new wooden church, the music provided by my old portable harmonium and the one small priest ordained for this great scattered district—only seemed to make the memory more vivid and the fellowship stronger. I did wish all of you at Home could have been with us. Though perhaps it's because you really were with us that you seemed so near.

Coming out of church we had an orgy of mutual photography, from which it was quite a job to break away and rush home for a quick lunch. Before 2.30 we were at Baldonnel, getting the children ready, and a few minutes later, the Bishop arrived and spoke to them too. I forgot to say that all his addresses that day (five) were admirable but the best of all was a really marvellous Ordination address on the "Vision and Call of Isaiah."

At 3 o'clock the Baldonnel Service was due to begin and we had the usual awful qualms as to whether anybody would come. But we needn't have been afraid for that day anyhow, for to our great joy waggon after waggon trundled up till first the thirty-six chairs were filled, then the six long benches, and finally all the planks propped on nail kegs, and we counted ninety-eight not including babies. That doesn't sound many but it was wonderfully good for this kind of place where there was not a house in sight and nobody used to Church-going. They were awfully reverent too, and sang all the hymns far better than their children do, which shows that they still have them in the back of their memories even after many years without any sort of Service.

The Sanctuary did look lovely. I tried to photograph it afterwards for your benefit but there were too many people to talk to and I couldn't snatch enough time. Mr. Wolfendale taught the builder to make a sort of semi-Gothic Chancel arch which breaks the bald square lines of the building. The whole of the East wall, up to six feet, is covered with the perfectly lovely red curtains given by Crayford, above them the pictures of the "Welcoming Christ," and behind that Mr. Hoffstrom's heroic attempt at a Gothic East window which I had resisted nearly unto death but in vain. The altar itself is pretty large—five by three feet. On it is the fair linen sent me by Sister Maud and the perfectly glorious red frontal worked with lilies and passion flowers by Lady Goodenough and brought out just in time by Cecilia. I can't tell you how beautifully it glowed in the afternoon sun. It must be one of the loveliest things in Canada and to think of our having it up in this lost little corner of the world is amazing.

On the altar were the Messengers' blue cross and candlesticks and vases full of blue and white cornflowers. These looked lovely against the red background and harmonized quite perfectly with the splendid thick blue kneeler made for the altar rail by Mildred Bowyer. So you see the main colouring is bright red and soft, deepish blue and yet both seem to lead up quite naturally to the uncoloured picture of Our Lord which dominates the little Sanctuary and seems to call out the reverence of all who see it.

After the Service, another orgy of greeting and photography. When everyone had gone we mobilized a campfire supper behind the church for the Bishop and the Proctors and ourselves.

The Hall could not, of course, be other than dedicated as it is to be used for "profane purposes," but the Sanctuary was fully consecrated so that the full dress title of the whole building is now "The Memorial Hall and Church of St. John," Baldonnel.

After supper we all went on to Taylor's Flats, except poor Miss Williams who began to wilt a bit, so she got a lift home and spent a happy evening washing dishes for us. The Flats had the usual rather muddly Service chiefly composed of women and children. But the school was full and the Service went very well in spite of me at the overworked little travelling harmonium. Directly afterwards the Bishop had to return to Dawson, so we took our leave of him and saw him off before ourselves starting back for Fort St. John. We were quite sorry to lose the Bishop. He is most fatherly and considerate, besides being rather a fine, simple sort of preacher.

Most of Monday I had to chase round after Church-wardens and Trustees to get certain legal documents signed at the command of Canon Proctor. But also we had a Guide meeting for Miss Williams, to which the Brownies also came. She inspected them, addressed them, had games with them, and we finished up with a tea-making race followed by a feast below the brow of the coulee at the place where you can just see a glimpse of the river. She was pleased with them, I think, and told us that we are far and away the most Northerly company in British Columbia and, she thinks (but is not quite sure), all of Canada.

On Tuesday morning she left us and went down to Dawson, having first persuaded me on behalf of the Provincial Commissioner to become District Commissioner for the Peace River Block. I agreed rather reluctantly because this involves South of the river too, and the area is so huge. But I insisted that Cecilia should be officially appointed Secretary so that she can keep me straight, and this is also to be arranged.

That afternoon we in the House held our first CHAPTER. It couldn't deal with actual work because we hadn't yet been able to have the conference with Mr. Wolfendale which must be the basis of it. But we discussed general plans for the running and life of the House and arrived at a provisional scheme to be tried for a month at a time and revised at the monthly chapter when necessary.

Daily Time Table

6.45 Monica lights the fire and starts the breakfast.

7.30 (in winter, 8), Breakfast, before which no talking.

8.0 Matins with Intercessions and Thanksgivings, followed by Silence for reading and meditation till 9.

9 to 10 House work and chores outside.

10 Work of the day.

12.30 Lunch for anyone who is about.

6 Supper.

9 Evensong (very much modified), after which Harvey (the boy) to wash in the hall and go to bed: after which the Community follow suit.

The Chaplain in charge of prayers is to change once a week.

The housekeeper-cook once a month.

Each of us in normal circumstances is to be at home two days a week, on which days we are responsible for the routine housework and chores and have the title of Home Sister.

Muriel is housekeeper till the end of September.

Adeline is Officer Commanding Eliza until she leaves, with Cecilia as coadjutor and successor.

Cecilia and I are co-grooms.

We also had the following list of URGENT PUBLIC WORKS for the House be done as quickly as possible:

1. Get the heater put up and stove pipes bought and connected.
2. Clear out the garage so that Eliza can sometimes go to bed.
3. Clean out and furnish the little room upstairs for Harvey.

4. Make partitions between the two upstairs rooms.

5. Make two stools for the living room, one for the organist and a bench for the Chapel.

6. Make some sort of linen cupboard somewhere.

7. Earth up round the outside of the house and make shelves in the cellar.

8. Catch Robin (the runaway horse).

9. Collect old fence posts, logs, and telegraph posts for firewood.

10. Put up a clothes line.

11. Lamp hooks and book shelf in Chapel.

12. Make more kitchen shelves.

13. Various sewing jobs.

14. Collect vegetables and fruit from friends to bottle or store.

15. Plant trees near the house.

16. Collect two kittens promised by May.

On Wednesday we carried out some of these but there is a lot still to be done before the house is in full review order, if it ever will be. We did get the kittens though. They are a silvery grey and a black, called Michael and Lucifer. Michael is as far as we can discover, virtuous and he certainly is lovely. But he is dreadfully detached and self-contained, an angel. Lucifer has all the vices possible to kittens and is *quite* maddening, but he is so intimate and so ready to forgive after chastisement, that when not beating him we all love him the best.

On Wednesday evening Mr. Wolfendale picked me up to go to the first regular meeting of the Baldonnel governing body. This distinguished corporation consists in its entirety of the Priest in charge, two Church-wardens, three men Trustees, three women ditto (of whom I am one). But the Wardens and Trustees act separately in their own departments. Rather to my wrath they made me Secretary. Still, if you have to belong to bodies it is best to be either Chairman or Secretary, on the whole. We worked at constitutions and regulations for FOUR hours and had exciting discussions about non-Anglicans and other knotty problems till 12.15 A.M. All through, Mr. Wolfendale was admirably patient and tactful. The men were wonderfully keen and clear in their minds about the safe-guarding of the Sanctuary—the consecrated Chancel—from all possible desecration. I was quite surprised to find them so clear and strict about it. And when the question came up of possible non-Anglicans wanting to use the Hall for a Service they all said quite firmly, "Of course they can't use the East end. That's quite out of the question." And I was rather amused to find myself pleading for our separated brethren to be allowed from time to time to use the body of the Hall with their faces turned West to the platform.

It was a cold night and when we came out, was freezing. Brother Wolf.

was driving me home as well as the old Scotchman, Munro (who is the Sexton), when we ran over a rotten culvert which collapsed and our hind wheels fell into a dark hole with no bottom. It was quite a job to get out in the dark and with the wheels resting on nothing. But Brother Wolf. took it all very happily and after about half an hour of collecting poles and leverage we pulled her out and I got home about 1.15 to find Adeline AWAKE and the fire lighted—very wrong and spoiling.

Thursday was chiefly swallowed up by preparations for the first dance at Baldonnel to be held on Friday. There was Mrs. Simpson's old stove to be fitted in temporarily and stove pipes to get and fix and cups and supplies to get in—all duties of the women Trustees, as the music and the money collecting was the men's. Adeline and I did it and got back to supper, after which we all went out collecting old disused fence posts for fuel and came back in triumph with sixty in the car.

Friday was the day of the famous dance. We tried to catch up with carpentering jobs all day, except during part of the afternoon when we each prepared something to take for supper. You see the plans of these dances is that men pay fifty cents (2/) and women go free but take a box of sandwiches or cakes. Adeline made some good sandwiches; Cecilia and I tried our hands at cakes, but having no eggs, we couldn't somehow get them very lifey, and hastened to dissociate ourselves from our sad and anaemic offspring directly we reached the Hall.

Well, I won't tell you all about the dance. It was very full and very well behaved and I think a real success. Muriel didn't go because it is against her principles. But the rest of us went early, helped with the supper and a bit of hosting generally. Cecilia made a sort of debut because very few people had seen her before and she was a great success. Adeline they all know quite as well as me, and no one can believe she is really going away again. We rolled home thankfully at about 2.30 and overslept so that we didn't get breakfast till 8.30.

The main event of Saturday was the first General council with Mr. Wolfendale. He came to dinner and we did quite a lot of business, chiefly in the way of settling turns and places of Sunday School and Services and how we could best co-operate. Incidentally, he also committed to me a very big piece of investigation East and North of the North Pine. Two of us are to find out and visit all the Anglicans in this region (most of which can only be reached on horse-back) and send in a full report by September 15 for him to forward to Toronto. Meanwhile he will be on a similar grand tour up the Peace and Halfway rivers, a distance of anything up to 150 miles to the West.

At the very end we settled about next day's Services. Both at St. Martin (Fort St. John) and St. John's there are to be baptisms. So just as Bro. Wolf. was leaving I asked him, "Have you made a font?" "No, I haven't had time. You must make one!" Seven P.M. on Saturday night and a font to be made for Sunday! Then we remember the wooden butter bowl.

N.B. The lay brother called Harvey mentioned above is a boy called Harvey Cheverton who is coming to live with us when term begins so as to be able to go to school. He lives five miles from anywhere and has no mother or brother or sister. He is twelve years old and very poor. I do hope he will be happy and not feel like Oliver Twist or David Copperfield. In return for board and lodging he is to do certain chores, like getting in wood and cleaning out the stables. Possibly we may later have Erving Foster too.

Adeline's Diary to supplement Monica's of September 6.

Last Sunday was still rather a special Sunday so it is difficult to gauge how far the presence of the church is to be a definite call to worship to those who have hitherto not attended Service in the schools. Brother Wolf. had announced baptisms for that day. Of course neither church has a font, but Monica produced a wooden mixing bowl which Muriel scrubbed till it became a lovely colour and Monica got a tall log and chiselled out the top and stood the bowl in it and it looked just like a Norman font—of wood instead of stone.

Muriel took a girl to a confirmation forty-eight miles away. She had been prepared by Canon Proctor at Dawson and just come up to work at Fort St. John, so Muriel seized the opportunity to taking three of the older girls in her Sunday School to see the confirmation.

Brother Wolf., accompanied by the grandmother of one of the babies, picked me up and we started the Service (half an hour late), having accumulated six babies by then. It was nice to see so many fathers there and also a grandfather who sang the hymns most lustily and when congratulated said, "Why, I used to be in the choir of St. Paul's, Hammersmith." The Sunday School children sat in front and we had the font near the Chancel. The babies were miraculously good. I think it was probably a good thing to have the mass movement of baptisms to begin with, but later single baptisms more carefully prepared for as regards godparents, etc. may have more significance. As it was, the numbers were smaller than was anticipated as one Swedish family (Lutherans) are considering the question anew, because of an absurd and persistent rumour that the Church of England is going over to Rome in TEN DAYS. Monica tackled the mother who is a great friend of ours but all she could get out of her was, "Well, I said to Mrs. F. whatever happens to the Church of England, MISS STORRS will never become a Catholic."

After Church, we were bidden to a feast at Mrs. Ohland's. She is a marvellous cook and we had a "sure dandy banquet," which was so good we could not refuse—turkey, jam and sauces and vegetables and ice creams the size of a small loaf and an enormous iced cake. Shamefully replete, we went back to Fort St. John for the Service and baptism there. Here again was a good congregation. We walked home and started to send out the Sunday School by Post magazines for the Peace River Block as a whole. Monica left us at it when she went off with Mr. What. for the Sunday School Service at Taylor's Flats and when she returned, between 10 and 11, we were still at it and they had to turn to and help also. However, we got those South of the river done in time for Monday's mails.

On Monday we took the washing tub full of them and helped the Postmaster to sort and stamp them. We found the Victoria League[185] books had arrived, so got the car loaded up with the packing cases and Monica and I came home to unload them—a task beyond the strength of women—when who should spring out of the bush but Slim who did it all. Since then he has been working for us, banking up the house with sods and sawing the most enormous logs.

The rest of the day we spent getting the room ready for Harvey. In the evening he arrived. He is just twelve but like all boys here, enormous, with a gruff voice, but fearfully shy. They are frightfully poor and his luggage consisted of exactly one blanket, but his father had fitted him out with new overalls and new, squeaky boots. He is a nice, grave, quiet boy, but goodness—how slow. He chops the wood for us, cleans the stable, etc. We may also have Erving Foster to share Harvey's room. There is great talk of a High School for older children here. However, the schoolmaster told us yesterday that it is to be a kind of senior school, taking his top grade and higher still and that a certain disused shack is to be hauled two and a half miles to the school land so that both are side by side and can share certain equipment.

The next day or two were spent in making shelves for the cellar, planting a forest of eighteen inch spruces round the house and protecting them from prevailing winds, etc. Brother Wolf. was prevented from starting on his tour by the funeral of a daughter of old Mrs. Millar. She died from appendicitis at Pouce Coupé six weeks after her second child was born. Monica and Muriel went to the funeral.

On Wednesday the Roman Catholic hospital was opened. It is said to be marvellously well equipped. It is run by Sisters of Providence and Dr. Brown approves it very highly. It will probably set free our Red Cross nurse to do district nursing more especially. We stood outside the hospital in the whirling dust and listened to speeches from practically everyone, led off by the Roman Catholic Bishop (endless, in broken French).[186]

That night Monica had another Trustees' meeting at Baldonnel, this time only till midnight. Next day when we went past, a bunch of men were cleaning and tidying all round, the two Church-wardens, two Trustees, the caretaker and another man.

On Thursday Cecilia and I went on an unsuccessful vegetable hunt. So many people have well stocked gardens and have asked us to take what we want only unfortunately they were all out. We went to Taylor's [Flats] to put up a notice and found to our relief that they have adopted the same time as us, instead of being an hour behind.

On arriving home, we found quite a tea party, Mr. and Mrs. Birley, May and Slim. We always make our visitors choose their cup from the dresser.

On Friday Monica and Cecilia were due at Braeside,[187] but first Eliza had to do some hauling—this time broken telegraph posts from the West end of the land to add to our fuel. Then they went off and Muriel and I had a domestic day, mostly washing.

Next day was a day of replenishing. Old Jim arrived with a tank of water to fill up our four barrels which we had emptied and cleaned for the occasion. He is a nice old chap and made us ransack the house for any receptacle. We left Muriel one mixing bowl and forgot to fill the three tea pots. Otherwise—bar cups—everything in the house was full.

I returned from a journey to the city to dinner and ironing and before long the Fort St. John teacher dropped in. He is very fond of music so I ironed to the strains of a Beethoven symphony and darned stockings appropriately to Schubert's "Unfinished." To our surprise Monica and Cecilia returned by supper, having cut their visits short in order to take someone to the dentist. So, after the schoolmaster went, the family settled down to a peaceful evening of preparing Sunday School lessons (the Godly ones), and mending stockings (the Godless one), until we rolled into bed about midnight, to be awakened at dawn by strange horses drinking the precious water from the barrels.

Monica's Diary for week ending September 6.

Last week we nearly completed the furnishing of the house. Cecilia and Muriel finished off their room with a delightful hanging cupboard and shelves covered with the cretonne bought with Petronella at Broadstairs. Adeline and Cecilia spent a long day with a lamp in the little cellar, just like miners, putting up shelves and making bins for potatoes and other vegetables when we get them. Then we hastily knocked up a suite for Harvey's room, consisting of a washing table, towel rail, and shelves. Finally, we made a lamp bracket and bookshelf for the Chapel and four plain benches on upright log ends to solve the seating problem and save us from having to drag backwards and forwards our four bought chairs.

The Chapel is now complete and really just what I wanted it to be—all rough logs but nearly finished—log walls, altar, desks, and benches. The only ornament is grandfather's red frontal from Cornwallis, the two twisted brass candlesticks, the lovely Van Eyck (Memline?) "Adoration" given me by Lady Goodenough standing on the table (it is a tryptych) and above it, the big "Crucifixion" by Fra Angelico which I got in Venice. Also, on the North wall just above the kneeling rail, is Phillipino's "Angel Adoring"[188] which the Rochester Girls' Diocesan Association gave me in 1920: but nothing more. On the South side there is a good window looking straight out down the coulee. The actual size of the Chapel is exactly the same as our bedroom, i.e., eleven by eight feet, quite a good size really. The whole house has turned out delightful and to my thinking lovely, so that it is a constant joy to us all: and I am full of thankfulness—for you know my ignorance and how completely experimental it has been from start to finish.

Our next domestic excitement is caused by the usual water problem. It is at present out of the question to get a well dug or drilled to the depth which might be needed to find that spring promised me by Miss Penrose, the diviner. So the obvious thing is to get a dam scooped out to catch the melting snow and spring rains. This is everybody's stand-by who isn't lucky enough to live near a creek or spring. Our water hole at the bottom of the coulee has quite dried up now and though we can get drinking water from Mrs. Crawford's spring, it's a steep and tedious climb and would be no use for washing or for the horses. So I have decided to get a dam dug at once before any danger of frost. It won't help us till the spring, of course, so in the meantime I must pay to get water hauled until the snow comes to our rescue. The hauling costs ten shillings a waggon-full, enough if eked out by a certain amount of rainwater to last a month. So it isn't very expensive, so long as you do hardly any household washing and can water your horses somewhere else.

I had a great time with Slim, prospecting for the dam. It is of course nothing in reality but an artificial pond about six feet deep and about sixty feet in diameter. After much tramping about and discussion we agreed upon a slight hollow surrounded by scrubby bush about fifty yards from the house. Slim is going to clear it and a friend of his is coming with a team of horses to scoop it out. I have to borrow for his use a big iron scraper called a Fresher [Fresneau], from the road foreman, if he will lend it. Close to the dam and connected with it by a trench, you have to dig a dry well about twelve feet. The water runs into that from the dam, gets filtered as it runs, and being much deeper, remains liquid all through the winter when the surface of the dam is frozen hard. So now you know.

On Friday Cecilia and I went off in the car to start exploring the district East of Baldonnel. There was no one there last summer but now there are quite a lot of families and TWO new schools to be opened this month under the awful suburban names of "Braeside" and "Peace View." We hope to arrange a monthly Sunday School in each of them. The people were most welcoming and pleased with the idea at Braeside. They are all hard up and almost entirely without cash, but they pressed us to stay for coffee and loaded us with vegetables when we left. One middle aged woman called Mrs. Davis[189] was entirely English: born near Birmingham and at one time a school teacher. She was doubly welcoming and talked and talked with the almost breathless flow of people who live pretty nearly off the map.

Afterwards we went to the Palings, a long promised visit, not possible before. They live at the end of a trail which is for ten or eleven months of the year quite impassable for a car. They are fourteen miles from the nearest store and Mr. Paling rides up now and then to do any unavoidable shopping. I had met him on Wednesday and he said, "The trail is perfect now. You can actually get a car to the top of the hill." It is an awfully rough trail with a constant series of mudholes and sloughs just now dry. But even so it was anxious work crossing them and I was generally guided by Cecilia walking in front like a Verger and picking out the driest route over each swamp. Finally we reached the top of a tremendously steep hill running down 700 or 800 feet to the Palings' flat above the river. We left Eliza at the top and walked down carrying our knapsacks and twelve new gramophone records to lend Mrs. Paling. On the flat we found Mr. Paling stacking a crop of rough oats with Mrs. Paling. She was tremendously welcoming, wouldn't let us help but carried us off in triumph to make the last descent to her home. Their tiny house is built on a gravel slip close to the river and you get to it by a steep little sheep-track dropping another 150 feet below the flat on which the actual farm is. It's a wonderfully beautiful little corner, right on the river bank, with the high hills straight up behind it and trees growing right down to the water and just turning bright gold. Straight in front of this little house is the broad flood of the Peace River about half a mile wide with its high banks on the other side covered as far as the eye could see with impenetrable bush and not a sound or sign of any other human habitation. All the farm work is, of course, up on the flat, i.e., 150 feet straight above the house, so he has to climb the hill at least three or four times a day, which adds a good deal to his single-handed farm work. They think of rebuilding their house at the top of the hill, but there is no water up there so they would have to carry up every drop which would be worse than the present job. It's all uphill work anyway and of course nothing is paying or prospering just now. But still they are very happy and cheerful and one of the most devoted couples I have ever seen. The house dates from the very first days of settlement when nobody knew where the main tide of settlers would flow in. So people just squatted along the river side because that was the only highway when there were no roads. The house is built of enormous fat logs, quite brown with use and smoke. Of course they gave us their bedroom and moved into the lean-to themselves. About 9 P.M. Mr. Paling finished his work and came down the hill for the last time. Then we had supper and afterwards a concert with the twelve new records we had brought them. Their gramophone is the one Mrs. D. gave me to bring out to Mrs. Paling and I really think it is the greatest treasure they possess. I couldn't get it to her for the first three months because the road was impassable, but in July Mr. Birley went down to them in a boat and took the present with him. First thing next morning we were awakened by the Christmas music from the "Messiah," put on by Mr. Paling, who a moment later brought us in a cup of tea each in bed—an absurd luxury I've never met in Canada before. Then he played us a selection till breakfast and Mrs. Paling says he always does, so that she is afraid he will wear out our records, especially the hymns. I said for goodness sake let him. They couldn't be better used, and it's splendid he loves the Church music best. We left them the St. Margaret's bells and Easter hymns and whenever we can get to see them again we will of course take some more. Directly after breakfast he had, of course, to go off to his crop. So we washed up with Mrs. Paling and then she joined us in our morning lesson and prayers. We left three new books with them (they are great readers), including Stanley Jones' *Christ of Every Road*,[190] which I hope may interest them perhaps. Finally Mrs. Paling walked up the hill with us, loaded our knapsacks with beans and onions and cauliflowers, and took us to the foot of the big hill where we compelled her to stop. On the top we found Eliza patiently waiting and had a good bumpy drive back to the crowded area of Braeside. We only had one bad stick and that was on a tiny bridge which had lost most of its logs at one end. So just as we were crossing, a great gulf appeared, and our back wheels sank into the void. We had nearly an hour of levering and hauling, rather fun if [it were] not delaying. Our last call that day was to a Mrs. F.[191] who proudly produced

nine children, six of them going to school, and then sorrowfully owned
up to a grinding toothache. She longed to go to Fort St. John (twenty
miles) for treatment, so we took her with us and delivered her ultimately
to her husband in the city (he works at the garage), to see what the doctor
could do for her in the absence of the dentist. Altogether, though
scattered, this seems a hopeful district and my hope for the future is,
while taking Baldonnel Sunday School every Sunday at 2.30, to put in a
circuit of four—Taylor, Braeside, Peace View and across the Pine for
monthly visitations. We got home on Saturday night just in time for
supper and then worked like Blacks to prepare for next day's Sunday
School.

North of the Pine
September 12, 1931.

I am starting this with great optimism on the off chance of getting it
into Fort St. John before the mail goes. We are twelve miles from there at
present, with the North Pine River between us, two tremendous hills,
muddy trails and nobody that I know of going.

Last Sunday Mr. Wolfendale was away walking up the trail to
Hudson Hope and taking Services where he could. So Brother What. was
in charge of us. He is a young student who hopes to be ordained in two
years. He is so handy and willing and courteous and such a perfect *gentil*
knight that I think he cannot fail to attract people to Our Lord.

We started the new regime of Service times—i.e., mornings at Taylor,
afternoons at Baldonnel, evening at Fort St. John. We think it will
sometimes be rather a chore in the darkest winter days to get to Taylor for
Sunday School at 10.30. The plan we are going to try is for Cecilia to take
the older children there and I the babies, and she is to start again those
Guides on a week day. At Baldonnel we reverse. I take the older children
and the Guides in the week and she tackles those babies. It is all
complicated further by the fact of four new schools about to be opened
all within possible if not exactly easy reach. These are *Braeside,* nine and
one half miles from us (i.e., about the same as Taylor); *Peace View,*
rather farther but I have not quite located it yet; and certainly one,
possibly two, schools across here where we are now, nine [miles] across
the Pine. We hope to reach each of these at intervals—say once a month
or once every two months, but how they are all to be fitted in is not at
present as the noon day clear. Also there are six schools in the Montney
district which we hope to reach at intervals for Sunday School and
Guides, not counting two (or possibly three) up the pack trail and one at

Fish Creek which Muriel is adding to her Metropolitan programme. Of course we can't hope to reach all of these on Sundays without a drastic reform of the calendar but we hope at least for a week day visit to each, once a quarter.

Just before Service began at Baldonnel and as I was pumping up Cordelia (the portable harmonium) who seems to have a bullet in her lung, Mrs. Kirkpatrick[192] stepped forward from the congregation and whispered, "I owe you still for Kenneth's Scout hat, but I haven't got the cash. Will you take this for it?" Then she pressed into my hand a very savoury smelling paper parcel containing a roast chicken still smoking hot. I smiled gratefully, secreted the parcel between Cordelia's feet and hastily started playing "New Every Morning," as Mr. What. came in for the Service.

On Monday Adeline and I meant to start across the Pine but it was a pouring wet morning and as we had to take our bedding and didn't know where we should sleep we decided to wait one day anyhow. Another difficulty was that I hadn't yet got back my little horse Robin who had first broken and then jumped Mrs. Crawford's (perfectly rotten) fence at last six weeks ago, having a very unloving preference for her 1000 acres and bunch of lively companions to my little pasture alone with Puck.

For this trip Brother Wolf. said I could have his horse, Miles. So Monday was partly occupied in going over to fetch him. He looks a fine work horse but is not at all bad to ride, especially longish distances. The chief drawback is that he is a little laborious to mount and dismount often and also about twice the size of dear little Puck whom he hates and despises and bullies whenever he gets the chance. Really this human pettiness is unworthy of a horse.

But the great excitement on Monday was the final digging of our POND. While Slim set to work to clear away the willows, I went off to borrow a big scraper and to bargain with a certain Mr. [Earl] Beggs who has four powerful horses to come and scoop it out to a depth of EIGHT feet. The reason it has to be so deep is that in the summer it evaporates and sinks a lot, while in the winter it freezes to a depth of about four feet, so either way you may get hardly any water left. A few yards from the pond, Slim is going to dig a well about ten feet deep and connect it with the pond by a trench. In this trench we shall put sand and gravel which we are to fetch up in the car from the river bed. This acts as a filter and so we shall achieve the most elaborate and scientific piece of waterworks in the district. Most people have a pond and some have a well. But only Mr. Birley has the two in combination and he has no sand or gravel filter. So I shall be immeasurably superior. Unless of course there is some little hitch and no water comes into the pond.

Apart from the need, we look forward to the pond as a great ornament to the estate and we have found in the bush quite a lot of little birches and planted them round the edge. Also Brother What. brought me twelve tiny little spruce trees which we have planted among the birches near the house. So now we are sheltered by a grove at least eighteen inches high and when I am ninety-three the general effect will be quite lovely.

On Monday night Brother What. came in and asked one of us to go up with him next day to play Cordelia at a funeral in the Montney. As I had visited the family last year I decided to go myself.

We also decided to have a meeting of the Women's Auxiliary in Fort St. John on Wednesday. So Adeline and Cecilia typed about thirty notices and invitations to tea and we shared them out for delivery next day. On Thursday first they had to take the letters to catch the mail at Baldonnel and as you might expect, Eliza would not budge. Her self-starter had sprung a leak somewhere and I had to summon Slim and all the vestals and together we pushed the old girl up and down the trail for about a mile before at last she spluttered into life, and by going all out, I just caught the mail.

Muriel took Miles that day and visited all round Fish Creek for her new Sunday School. Adeline and Cecilia took the car and the notes and I took Puck to the city, left him there and joined Brother What. for the funeral. We started at 10.30 and went in the car up the new graded road which runs straight North for fifteen miles. It's a wonderful road, quite good though very soft and all cut straight through the bush. And there is now a glorious mixture of dark spruce and pines and golden birch and poplars with crimson fire-weed and rose bushes covering the ground beneath them. All the way till the last mile there was not a house to be seen, and the trail off the road to the Philpotts' place runs through another mile or two of virgin bush. We arrived about noon and found the usual twenty or thirty men standing outside the house waiting while inside were fifteen or twenty women and little girls all busy comforting or rather harrowing the widow. Mrs. Philpotts is quite an elderly woman for this country—sixty-five I should say. She welcomed me very touchingly and told me how her husband had gone down with the horses to haul water from the creek three days before and did not come back. The boy had gone to look for him and found him lying on his back, stone dead, while the horses quietly grazed beside him. It was no accident—just heart failure. The eldest son is at Fort Nelson 300 miles North of here. He will hear in about a month's time when the next pack train rides up that trail. We waited nearly an hour more while neighbours slowly trundled up in waggons, each one saying that another was following a mile or so behind. At last we all crowded into another little shack alongside, where was the open coffin revealing the departed, pathetically dressed in his best suit, and also the harmonium waiting for me. The mourners and neighbours sat round on raised planks and Mr. What. took the Service. It was a little disconcerting playing the hymns, partly because nobody stood up for any part of the Service, and partly because, as is the custom here, none of the mourners took any active part or attempted to sing a note. So as we had four long hymns and hardly any of the neighbours sang either, it came rather heavily on Brother What. and me. But afterwards some of them thanked us for it and said it made all the difference having the music so I was thankful Brother What. had asked me. Then followed a rather trying procession back to the new church cemetery at Fort St. John. The coffin led the way in a truck and after it followed seven or eight old Ford cars, all of which had been laid up for a year or more on account of cost and were therefore in very bad trim. About every mile one of them broke down and held up the whole procession while everybody got out to go to the rescue. Then after twenty minutes or so of desperate efforts, the car was abandoned and its passengers distributed among the rest. This happened at regular intervals till the road was dotted with derelict cars and exactly two struggled into the city, absolutely bursting and covered with surviving passengers. Afterwards poor old Mrs. Philpotts wouldn't go away till the grave was quite filled in, so we got a chair for her and she sat there supervising with sorrowful dignity till the work was finished. Then I begged her to come to the Clergy's tiny shack and let me get her a cup of tea before her fifteen mile drive home. You see, it was after 4 and neither she nor anyone else had had any dinner. She agreed to come so I rushed on ahead to find in the shack no milk and no teapot. So I rushed on a quarter mile and borrowed both and was so glad because in the end she drank three cups and her daughters and grandchildren ate nearly the whole of a loaf.

This is the second grave in our little churchyard and both within the week. Isn't it a mercy that the church was built and all was ready just in time?

(Chance to catch the mail so this must go at once!)

St. Matthew's Day, September 19.

I believe my last diary ended abruptly with Tuesday because there was a sudden chance of getting it brought across the Pine. Wednesday was the meeting of the W.A. in Fort St. John. Of course you know all about the W.A. It is the Women's Auxiliary—that is the one great Women's Society in the Canadian Church. It is primarily missionary but also supports the local work and in fact, covers all the ground of women's work, except that it is chiefly "practical," i.e., organises silver teas *and* whist drives rather than Retreats or Quiet Days.

For most of the morning we were scrubbing up the house for so great an event. We had asked all the ladies of the city and suburbs (not Baldonnel) and had no idea how many would come but knew there would be enough at least to cause a cup crisis. So Adeline went off to borrow some, while Muriel made cakes and Cecilia and I started the clear up. Then Cecilia and Muriel went off to Guides somewhere and Adeline and I got down to scrubbing the floor. We weren't half ready when the first guests arrived. But as the party was called for 3 and they came at 1.30 we had a little excuse. After that the others trickled in for a space of about two hours until they rolled up the impressive total of sixteen. This caused not only a cup crisis but rather a seat crisis, too. We have four wooden chairs and three wicker ones, besides a small bed disguised as a sofa. These seated ten and for the rest we collected three homemade benches out of the Chapel. Everybody had first to go "all over the house" as it was our first party of any size. It doesn't really take very long to go all over a house of this size—three bedrooms, one living room, hall and Chapel—but we spun it out with discussions about log furniture and where to put the linen and how to improve the floor and all the wonderful qualities and uses of Old Country cretonnes, till the various conducted tours took about as long as they do round Hampton Court. After tea we had the meeting which was entirely business-like. They were very keen to form a branch of W.A. and after much discussion elected me President, Muriel Secretary, and fixed the annual subscription at two dollars and decided to meet on the first Thursday of every month at 2 P.M. in each other's houses. Thus the keel of our women's organisation is now laid down and it is for us to build it into the best ship we can. Of course hardly any of them are Church women yet, and several hardly ever come to Church. But at least it is a fellowship for the service of the Church and community and I hope it may grow into a fellowship of disciples too.

They trickled away gradually, as they had come, being dependent for the most part on husbands with cars and waggons, but by 7 we could make our supper off the uneaten sandwiches, together with the male part of our household. These are at present Harvey, who is getting a little less speechless but speaks when he does with such stiff jaws and motionless lips that you can hardly hear a word he says, and Slim who has insinuated himself into being an almost permanent hired man, and Mr. Beggs, a queer, silent little man who has brought four horses and a plough and a Fresneau, or road scraper, to start on the pond tomorrow. They sleep in the stable loft on the sheaves—as do all men visitors—but they eat with us, and the amount they eat is phenomenal. Harvey sleeps in the tiny attic next to Muriel and Cecilia and I think, in his strong, silent way, he eats the most of all.

Thursday was a glorious morning which was good luck for Adeline and me starting for our deferred tour across the Pine. My horse Robin being still at large, I was lucky to have Mr. Wolf.'s horse Miles, and we had a great time collecting food and bedding and Sunday School books

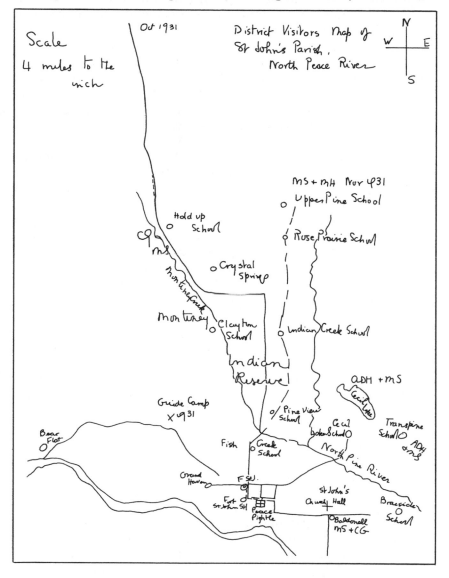

Map reproduced from the diary. The initials indicate where the Companions worked: Monica Storrs, Adeline D. Harmer, Cecilia Goodenough, Muriel Haslam.

and loading up for any emergency, because you see our hope was to find and camp in an empty shack.

Adeline rode Puck who was hung round with haversacks but didn't mind them at all. I rode Miles who is an immense bay about seventeen hands high and to all appearances a pure bred Clydesdale but comfortable in paces and most willing and gentle. Behind me was the bed roll for both of us consisting of the sleeping bag, rug and ground sheet and in front a small sack with tin cups and plates, and a tiny saucepan. It took us about one and a half hours to reach the long hill dropping about 800 feet and covered with dark spruce and golden poplars and some wild flowers still. The river was luckily quite slow, only three or four feet (unlike my only visit last year), so the horses splashed through without any great difficulty and we had great fun trying to photograph each other in mid-stream.

The first house on the other side was Mrs. Mikkleson. We ate our sandwiches with her and let the horses feed for an hour while we played with the little boys. Then we climbed the long hill and about 5 o'clock reached the house of Mrs. Framst, the woman from Kent whom I visited last year. She was most welcoming and made us stay to supper, also said she knew of an empty shack but it had no water or stove. Upon which another woman, Mrs. Copes (daughter to people in Baldonnel), immediately said we must go and stay with her—so we did.[193] She and her nice husband (an old Italian called Caesar) and a baby girl live in a two room shack only a mile from Mrs. Framst. The living room she carefully kept as such, pointing out what we might otherwise hardly have realized that the bedroom had "all kinds of room for four people." It was a nice little room, one half of it filled with a double bed and the other half just big enough for two people to lie on the floor. So there we spread the jaeger sleeping bag given me by Lily and had an excellent night, modestly screened from Mr. and Mrs. Copes by a cotton curtain quickly strung up on a wire. They were so kind to us and asked us to stay on the next night when there was to be a dance in the new school house. So all Friday we visited, finding our way up devious trails from house to house. The first we visited was one of the dreadfully poor ones, a small, one room cabin with a mother and three little boys and MILLIONS of flies. Poor thing, she could not afford screens to the door and window and had no fly papers so the table and food and everything else was quite black with flies. While I was there a man came to the door and was introduced. He found out what we were after and I invited him to a Service on Sunday but was a little baffled when he replied, "That's all very well but what I want to know is ARE YOU SAVED?" Unluckily I made the wrong answer, that is I said, "I hope so," and that fairly set him off. He was quite sure that if I was saved I must know the exact day and hour.

Otherwise, there was no hope for me at all and my venturing to speak to anyone about God was a blasphemy. Apparently a wandering preacher had been in this district, very strong on this doctrine, and had collected a few kindred spirits who carry it on and cheerfully believe all their nieghbours to be lost eternally.

When he had gone we stayed and read a little of the Gospels to Mrs. Budd and had a few prayers with her and it was quite clear she shared none of the hellfire views. After that we rode two miles East to the next family, delightful people called Kostick.[194] They had driven 1500 miles in a covered waggon—up from the States—taking three months over it, and they were still living in the waggon till their house was built. They consisted of a man, his wife, his sister, her husband and a little boy. They all lived, slept and cooked in the waggon which was pretty full of flies and fragrant with cooking. The men were out hunting a bear but the women begged us to stop and have dinner with them so we sat on one of the two beds and ate stewed bear with great enjoyment. Just as we finished, the men appeared, heralded by an immense dog. They looked so picturesque, two very Western men on horseback with guns, and leading a third horse, across whose saddle an immense black bear was lying, looking pathetically alive and helpless like a captive. But really of course, he was stone dead and a very fine specimen and weighing well over 400 pounds. We promised to come again and arranged to get the sister into Guides and the little boy on to the Sunday School by Post.

Then we visited two or three more scattered houses, two or three miles apart, surrounding a large, dull swampy expanse of water called Cecil Lake. On the North side of the lake we found the two most Northerly families arrived so far, a woman (with grown up sons) called Mrs. Pearce, and a family of halfbreeds whose English was very limited. We put the children rather optimistically on to the Sunday School by Post, gave a Testament to Mrs. Pearce and promised to try to hold a Service at her place one day as she lived at least six miles North of the school by a very rough trail. Coming back we found one more family of four living in a very leaky little tent. But like all the rest they were cheerfully confident of getting a house built before the winter came. It rained steadily all the way back and we got very cold and wet. We had each brought clean stockings and clean shirts and this was all the change we could make for the famous dance. Mr. Copes fetched Mrs. Budd and her three tiny boys (the youngest being eight months) and we joined them in the waggon, together with Mrs. Copes and Jessie, aged eight months too, and a little halfbreed girl. And of course there ran behind us a little foal, the child of one of the waggon team.

It was very dark and a fearfully rough trail. We kept lurching into deep ruts and after clinging to one another in each crisis we snatched a moment before the next one to count the children and feel the babies for broken bones. The school was about twenty feet square, well built but quite bare of forms, desks, stove or anything. We sat round the walls on planks balanced on piles of shingles "and were very happy." Nearly all the population was there within a radius of eight miles, i.e., about twelve women, twenty men and perhaps twenty children. The light was a petrol lantern which had to be pumped up pretty often, and the music was a violin and a guitar, rather good and brisk. Adeline and I made friends with everyone we could, danced with the children, and received an invitation to spend the week-end with a family called Kemp[195] at the East side of the district, i.e., eight miles from the Copes. About one o'clock we felt we had done our duty and need stay no longer, so we had an amusing walk home in the dark, Adeline, who is a far better owl than I am, groping ahead and calling out "Rut"—"Hole"—"Stump," for what seemed like several hours. The great joy of getting home ahead of the family was that we could heat some water and have a real wash. There is not much facility for that kind of thing in these houses—only one little basin of course and that in the living room. Everyone else seems to keep marvelously clean by occasionally washing hands and face, but Adeline and I, not being naturally clean, were thankful for an empty house and one good scrub all over.

About 4.30 the Copes family returned and poor Jessie, the baby, sounded a little peevish after her long revel. But they were soon all asleep and none of us woke till 9 next morning. When Adeline and I did wake up it was pouring with rain and we could hear Mr. Copes dressing and getting his breakfast. After he had done the chores he came back and got into bed again with his sleeping family and then we got up and stole out to get our breakfast. All the morning our host and hostess were sleeping peacefully and outside it was raining hard so after seeing to the horses and washing up we were able to write a letter or two. About 1 Mrs. Copes appeared and joined us in a search for dinner in a very leisurely manner. About 2 we started in on cold pork and salad and about 2.30 Mr. Copes appeared to join in so the meal got drawn out pretty well. At last it stopped raining so we decided it was time to move on to our next visit, the Kemps, so we packed up everything and rolled up the bedding and hung Miles and Puck round with haversacks and started off.

The Copes had never been to the Kemps and could only say that they lived roughly five miles East and two or three miles South. We lost our way completely towards the end and followed false trails for nearly an hour till at last we hit on the right one and got in just as the Kemps were giving us up. This family is the oldest established North of the Pine. They have been there nearly a year and a half and have reached the stage of having a real crop this year. They live in a good sized house of very rough logs with a large living room and two little bedrooms. I need hardly say the best of these was given to us. The mother and daughter occupied the other, a bachelor friend slept in the living room and the father and son went out into a tent. Our room was almost entirely occupied by a magnificent bed so there was no need for the sleeping bag. But there was no window of any kind and we couldn't draw the curtain from our doorway because it gave straight on to the sofa where the friend slept. So we crept into our den and dressed and undressed in pitch dark, just like bears in a cave. It ought to have been very stuffy of course but luckily the logs fitted so casually that there seemed plenty of ventilation and the funniest part was when we emerged in the morning from pitch darkness to bright sun, fully dressed but blinking like owls.

The Kemps are a charming family from the U.S.A. Mr. Kemp is a nearly middle-aged man, short and bright and very eager. At the age of fifty he has just taught himself the violin and so has his son and so has the lodger. They had bought two old fiddles somewhere before coming North and all spent every possible moment feeling their way about dance and song tunes—entirely by ear of course and so clever. On Sunday morning after breakfast I asked tentatively whether they could play any hymn tunes. First they all said no, but after a bit began one by one to pick out snatches of "Nearer My God to Thee," "Jesu Lover of My Soul," and various very strange and very racy tunes to other hymns, tunes which Mr. Kemp must have heard years ago in his boyhood in the States. Then they tried to learn one or two tunes from us, such as "O God Our Help" and "Abide with Me"—line by line. We sang and they played, but this was very uphill work and not awfully successful. However, before the end of the morning we had a programme of five hymns practised for the Sunday School, or Service or whatever it might turn out to be, which was to be held in their house that evening. At 1 Adeline and I started to ride back to the school for the first Sunday School, i.e., one for the East side of the district, and also to start Guides there, if possible. We were joined by the little Spence girls[196] who used to live at Baldonnel and went to Camp with us, but have just come to live here on their real homestead and go to the new school. They were delighted to see us again and arrived looking very sweet in Uniform and riding bareback on two big farm horses.

At the school there eventually rolled up six more girls, all of whom want to be Guides; one of these was English, one American and no fewer than four were Russians. We had a good talk about it, discussed the aims and a little of the Tenderfoot test and elected leaders who picked up two patrols. These will be the most Northerly patrols in British Columbia. They will belong to the 2nd Fort St. John (scattered) Company which has one patrol already at Baldonnel and another under Cecilia at

Taylor's Flats. After that the two or three remaining children rolled up for Sunday School and one or two mothers, including Mrs. Copes and Mrs. Framst, who is to be the teacher. The school is supposed to open tomorrow or Tuesday. It's an awful job getting things started in these inaccessible spots. After school one of the Russians asked whether we had any clothes to spare. She said she had six brothers and sisters and her parents had nothing to feed and clothe them with. I promised to go and see them but was cautious because we had been told they were a very begging family and no worse off than many others who never ask for anything. Then we rode back to the Kemps—six miles—and had supper and spent the intervening time writing out hymns as large as possible on the backs of trade calendars. No one knew who would come to this Sunday School as practically all the children had been in the afternoon so I really didn't know what to prepare for and hardly expected anyone beyond the Kemp family, who were all grown up but could scarcely escape. However, about 8 o'clock, a trickle of grown-ups began and by 8.30 when we began the Service there was only one child but four women and fourteen men. So of course we had a sort of little Mission Service by the light of one very dim lamp, the fiddlers struggling most gallantly with the hymns and Adeline and I taking it in turns to hold up the converted calendars where all might see.

It was rather a wonderful little Service, really. The people were so quiet and reverent, but I don't think any of them were Anglicans and it was rather a puzzle to know how to meet their needs. At the end I told them about Mr. Wolf., and how he hoped to come over and take Services once a month, so I do hope they will turn out at least as well for him.

We slept in our little cave again that night and next day visited out Eastward to the present limit of settlement. The last two women seemed specially appealing, one Mrs. Binnell, because she was so pretty and so desperately poor; the other, Mrs. Maginnis,[197] because of her isolation. She has one neighbour, Mrs. Birnell, [sic], two miles to the West, and to the East no one at all except twenty-four miles away at the Moose River where there is a man and his wife. To the North and the South there is no one. Her husband often has to go away for a week or more at a time to try to earn something, which leaves her entirely alone with her little girl of fifteen months and a boy of a few weeks. She said she wasn't at all nervous but it was sometimes rather lonesome. We stayed most of the afternoon, had tea, read a little of the Gospel and had some prayers before coming away at last. Next day, Tuesday, we hoped to get home again but had to visit one more family six miles North and didn't know how long we might be kept there. So we pulled out from the Kemps, really sorry to leave such kind people, but rather glad to let them all sleep in their proper beds again. Mr. Kemp is a natural pioneer. He said he would like to move on every few years taking up fresh homesteads, proving up and moving on again. But these sentiments were not apparently shared by Mrs. Kemp who had had more than enough of it already and even ventured to be a little bored at having nine roadless miles and an unbridged river between her and the nearest store.

It was Mr. Kemp who told us of one more woman and possibly two living on the Moose River twenty-four miles beyond Mrs. Maginnis. We must certainly try and visit them but decided not to do it this time. You see, Puck's feet are his weakest point and they have to be shod. We found he had cast a shoe and another was loose and I didn't feel it right to take him for two longish extra days like that. So we hope to visit the Moose River next month if all goes well.

Therefore we planned to cross the Pine that very afternoon if we could fit in three or four last families in time. The first was the Phillips (six miles North of the Kemps), very "superior" people from Vancouver who had only been here three or four months. We found a little group of three one-room shacks about 100 yards apart, Mr. and Mrs. Phillips, the parent birds, in one, Harry and his wife and two little boys in another, and the Phillips' daughter, married to a boy called Jack Earl, in a third. These latter were both candy-makers in Vancouver and are perfectly typical townees knowing nothing at all about farming but they are full of hope and fun, have just married and are making a honeymoon of discomfort and effort. But it was the mother who appealed to us most. Mr. Phillips is obviously a strong, hard man who lives for knocking about and trying new lands and new jobs. But Mrs. Phillips is a refined, middle-aged woman, obviously brought up to respectable, comfortable, fairly conventional conditions. When we first arrived she seemed cold and rather unwelcoming. In fact she even seemed to grudge our coming in though of course she said we must stay for dinner. We went into the small and roughly furnished shack and presently I asked the usual question about how she liked the country. To my surprise, instead of the almost invariable answer, "Oh I like it fine," she said nothing but went over to the stove with her back to me and as she stood there stirring the soup I saw that she was crying. Then I understood that all her coldness was just misery and shame at what seemed to be the squalor of her new home.

We stayed to dinner of course, sitting on upturned boxes and cutting the bacon with Adeline's Guide knife, while one of the sons was using the real kitchen knife to fit a door on to the shack. We reached no direct religion there because Mr. Phillips was a distinct non-conductor. But Mrs. Phillips grew more and more natural and friendly. In fact, she developed into a great wag, and when at last we rode away she stood at the door and called to us to come back again as soon as possible.

After that the Russian families of which the parents could hardly speak any English. But it was interesting to see their houses, in some ways more picturesque and homelike in their arrangement than the bald, utilitarian Canadian shack. Then one more family, a woman and three little girls quite lately arrived. That woman was awfully welcoming. Directly we came near the house she appeared at the door and when we asked, "May we come and see you?" she said, "Sure I'll be tickled to death." Her husband was away too and she was eager for company, though living temporarily in someone else's shack in obvious discomfort and great poverty. We had a cup of tea with her, gave her little girls pictures and cards and tried to teach them something about Our Lord. But their ignorance was pathetic. The eldest called her sister to show her one of the pictures and we were rather appalled to hear her explanation: "See Lois, that there is the Guy Lawgee healing the people." It sounded so dreadful but it was quite reverently meant—as far as reverence has any meaning for these little children. After that it was too late to cross the river so we spread our sleeping bag once more on the Copes' bedroom floor. The next morning we visited one last man and wife, a strange middle-aged couple who had trekked all this way from a good farm in Nova Scotia and seemed to be wondering why they had done it.[198]

After that we said good-bye for a month, led Miles and Puck down the long, steep hill all clothed in crimson and gold, forded the river [the Pine], climbed the 800 feet the other side and came out on to our own familiar and over-civilized plateau again. The graded road, the fences, the crops all round neatly stooked, looked so odd and conventional after the rough trails and the rare little clearings in the bush on the other side.

Last year when I crossed I found one woman. Now we counted twenty-four women and thirty or forty children. There is great poverty over there and besides desperate need of warm clothes for the winter, there is a complete dearth of books or toys. Any of these that people at Home like to send out in bundles and declare to be for FREE DISTRIBUTION TO SETTLERS, we shall hope to carry over month by month, so long as the river allows—and as many as Miles and Puck will carry.

Summary of weeks ending October 10.

The awful thing is that this is three weeks and I don't know how I can ever catch up. Adeline and I got back from the North Pine on the evening of September 10. It was quite exciting coming home even after the inside of a week, so I'm afraid I'm not really a good wanderer. Better still, after supper Mrs. Crawford's hired man [Mr. Shortt] brought back our little prodigal horse Robin, who had jumped the fence over two months ago. We were all enchanted to have him home again and the stable as full as is comfortable (Miles being so huge). We all felt more horsey than ever. In fact, I am fast becoming the old gentleman who invites his guest to come for a walk round the stables after every meal. But this glory was a little short-lived because Robin was more of an Odysseus than a Prodigal. I took him for a trial run in the evening and he was a bundle of nerves but quite good. However, next morning, when Muriel was mounting him, he seized one unguarded moment, discarded her gently but decidedly, and vanished. Cecilia and I went off on Miles and Puck and searched for him till dark but had no luck. Next day Adeline and I had the awful humiliation of calling on Mrs. Crawford because we were pretty sure he was on her land again. Finally she agreed to let us round up all her horses into the corral. So off we went and wandered for ages through bush and coulees and across fields and hillsides without seeing a single horse. Then suddenly we spotted one or two, then the whole bunch and the fun began. Miles and Puck got as excited as hunters and so did Adeline and I. It is almost everybody's constant occupation here, rounding up horses, but we had never done it and you can't think what fun it was. There were about twenty altogether and in the middle galloped Robin, all saddled and bridled, of course, just as he had jumped the gate yesterday. After about a mile and a half of tacking and steering and sudden plunges to the right and left we got them all into the corral and there, to our great admiration, the flightly little Robin allowed himself to be caught quite easily—by Mrs. Crawford.

Next day was Brownie day. That is to say, we had invited the Brown Owl from Pouce Coupé to bring up her Brownies to spend a day and night with us. Of course long before we were ready they arrived— thirteen little girls all in a perfect dither of excitement and Miss Bertrand their teacher, all in two cars. They brought sandwiches for luncheon, to which we added soup, so they sat eating and drinking at the top of the coulee until about the same number of Fort St. John and Baldonnel Brownies gradually rolled up to join them. It was a gloriously hot day and we spent a delirious afternoon, first playing games on our own land and then going for a short hike about a mile along the Eastern side of the coulee. This is Mrs. Crawford's land and is inhabited by her very precious Hereford cattle. She asked us not to frighten them because they were not used to seeing people. I said of course we would not, not realising how alarming thirty little chattering Brownies may appear to a Hereford cow. Evidently the poor beasts thought we were a marauding tribe for they fell into a complete panic and the bull, feeling it bad for his ladies to be so upset, began to follow us with resentment in his eye. This was beginning to unnerve the Brownies a bit, when Adeline did a splendid thing which I must tell you, though of course she mustn't know I have. She left us and went to meet the bull as he came glowering down the field: went straight up to him, took him by the nose, and began to scratch him under the chin. After a few minutes everything was explained between them. Brother Bull retired in perfect good humour and we finished our walk across his territory.

At the point over the river we danced and played singing games and each ate a cookie or two. Then we came back and had a high old time making a Campfire supper. After that we all squeezed into the little Chapel for prayers and then the Fort St. John Brownies went home. But our day was not nearly over, for the thirteen Pouce Coupé Brownies were to sleep in the loft over our barn and Adeline and I with them. They slept on the horses' oat sheaves, of course, and it seemed to take hours getting them all up the little ladder, sorting their blankets, finding their towels and gradually getting them settled down. Later on we took our sleeping bag and joined the happy party. But I can't say it was a very restful night. Every hour or so one or two Brownies woke up in a great state, being either cold, or homesick, or "sick of the stomach" (the latter was mercifully in each case a false alarm). I had matches and a lantern but didn't dare strike with so much straw all round and under us. So Adeline and I crawled round at intervals in the pitch dark, administering such coverings and counsel as seemed to be most needed. In the intervals when the Brownies were all asleep, the three horses woke up and apparently murdered each other in turns. I never heard such a noise of stamping and crashing and the whole barn shook and rocked till we thought it must fall down. At last there was a blessed lull when everyone seemed to be asleep above and the peace of exhaustion reigned below. Then I looked at my watch and it was time to GET UP.

It was Sunday morning and alas, the wind had gone round and it was cold and raining, so we all squeezed into the house for breakfast, sitting in a ring on the floor of the living room. After that I enrolled some new Brownies and we helped them find their property in the loft and fasten endless bundles and then we set off to Sunday School at Fort St. John. On the way it got darker and darker and began to rain pretty steadily so when we reached the church and the children had gone in, the driver of their car seized me and said they must start home at once, or he wouldn't take the responsibility if the roads got wetter. Moreover, he wouldn't take all the children in his car, the road being as it was already. First I thought Adeline and I must take the rest ourselves in Eliza but when we looked at the greasy road and the storm wrack across the river we agreed in not wishing to take the responsibility of six or seven other people's little children. So we found a man said to be the best driver North of the river and directly after the Sunday School we loaded them up with sandwiches and cake and packed them all into the two cars with all their bedding and kit bundles to keep them warm. I think and hope the time was a great success in helping to strengthen friendships and perhaps in deepening all our sense of what Guides and Brownies really stand for.

I'm afraid you'll think us dreadfully poor spirited, but you see the roads here are so different to English roads. Being nothing but scraped mud they can be excellent in dry weather but in heavy rain they become like half-melted butter. Even on the level it is almost impossible to keep out of the ditch, while on hills the wheels have hardly any grip—even with chains on. The hills South of the river are very steep and tortuous and quite impassable in really bad weather, though an experienced man learns how to slither up and down them without going over the edge, IF they aren't too bad.

After this we walked home, had a quick lunch and rode to Baldonnel for the Sunday School and Service at St. John's. There we were joined by Cecilia who came up on Robin from her Sunday School at Taylor's Flats. Baldonnel we share, i.e., Cecilia takes girls, I take boys or infants. Cecilia goes to Taylor's in the morning. It is a nine mile ride for her and she starts at 8.30. Her school is at 10.30 and Brother Wolf. joins her for a Service at 11.30. Then she rides back to Baldonnel, eats her lunch and we join her about 2. But once a month instead of Baldonnel she goes to one of the little new schools called Braeside. After Baldonnel we all ride home together and after supper Adeline and I go on to Fort St. John for Evensong, but I generally succeed in preventing Cecilia from going because she has ridden at least eighteen miles (once a month twenty-six), held two Sunday Schools and attended two Services already. Meanwhile, Muriel takes the Fort St. John Sunday School in the morning, goes on two miles to another little one at Fish Creek in the afternoon, and plays the organ (i.e., my little portable harmonium) at Evensong. So you see everyone else does more than me, but the advantage is that it leaves me free to take the place of either of the other two in the morning when necessary. And just at present there is no school that we can reach on a Sunday and get back in time for the afternoon—no other—though there are one or two farther away that I hope to reach on Saturdays once or twice a month.

The following week was very domestic, partly because Muriel and Miss Claxton (the Red Cross nurse)[199] rode up the trail to Hudson Hope while the rest of us shared Muriel's week day duties, Guides, Brownies, etc., between us. Muriel took Miles and hoped to get back by Sunday.

The other main occupation of that week was the well. The ground is

awfully tough, sticky clay and they have only been able to scoop our
about seven feet deep which is not really enough to ensure any liquid
water in the winter so I shall have to get Beggs again next week to try to
scoop out two more. His pay is two dollars a day with all his meals, so
scooping out a dam is rather like scooping out your vitals. Yet is has to
be done if we are to get any water next year. When Beggs went, Slim dug
the well and the connecting trench and this introduced us to a new job,
i.e., hauling up the buckets of clay as fast as he can dig them. It's simple
enough, you just stand on a plank on the well and haul up and throw
away and lower again, but it's quite good exercise for the back. One
morning I had nearly three hours of it from fourteen feet down, which is,
of course, nothing and yet seems low enough. This was the first
sustained tête-a-tête I had ever had with Slim and the first time we had
ever talked about religion. He is a Dane, you know, and professes to be
an atheist (he says they all are), but like the Scandinavians he is
interested in the Thorvaldsen picture of Our Lord at Baldonnel and the
Norwegian words underneath, "Kommer til Mig."[200] From the bottom
of the well Slim began to explain to me the rather archaic form of these
words and especially the exact meaning of "Kommer." He said in his
very broken English, "I can't quite tell you how it means, but it means
more than when we say 'Come.' It is more strong, it means like so to say,
'Don't you think of nothing else, just you come to me straight now.'" Of
course that led on to why he was not a Christian and we had a most
wonderful direct talk about the foundations of belief and of unbelief, he
at the bottom and me at the top and punctuated by pauses for breath and
calls connected with the bucket. Later he acknowledges that "Christians
do sure seem very happy." Slim has borrowed two books. Will you pray
for him? He is a typical Scandinavian Canadian, honest and clean and
intelligent, and his religion so far is Physical Culture. He is awfully keen
to have a Young Men's Athletic Club at Baldonnel. So I told Brother
Wolf. and he had a meeting last Wednesday in the Church Hall. Twelve
young men turned up, headed by Slim, and they planned gymnastics of
all sorts. I think it will make a good link between Brother Wolf. and
these fine but aloof Scandinavians besides some of the other bachelors
who live such scattered and independent lives that they are pretty hard to
reach.

Actually there is already a little water in the well and as this is the
driest time of the year we begin to think we may be within reach of the
spring divined by Miss Penrose. But she said it might be 100 feet and we
have only dug fourteen so far. Won't it be wonderful if we do strike a
spring in less than twenty feet? I hardly dare speculate on it. But anyway
we shall have the dam ready for the snow and rain to fill next spring and
meanwhile we can get water hauled for us until the snow comes. Of
course the well will have to be cribbed and the trench from it to the dam
filled with gravel and stones to make a filter. For all this we hope to

collect the materials in Eliza when she is herself again. But at present she is in hospital, waiting this time for a new front spring. Finally I dream of endowing the well with a pulley wheel and rope to take the place of plain hand hauling over a hole. Then we shall feel just like Rochester or Kew, but all this is rather a vision of future glory.

The new Roman Catholic hospital in Fort St. John is in full swing now. It has twelve beds and is splendidly equipped and run by five nuns and one secular nurse. We visit there as often as possible and of course we went to see Mrs. Shortt[201] whose husband caught Robin and who was too full of his own news to do anything but keep on saying, "You girls want to go over and see my wife in hospital. She's just had a little daughter born."

Also I try to go every few days to see a little boy aged nine, called Leonard, whose leg was most dreadfully burned by a petrol iron. His family moved up here about a month ago, when he had already been six weeks in hospital in Calgary. Nearly all the skin of his leg was gone from the knee to the foot, and the knee itself doubling up from muscular contraction. Poor little boy. He has had weeks of suffering and even now may lose his leg. His father hopes to set up a tinker's shop here and has hauled his logs for building, but so far all the family time and savings have been devoted to Leonard and I fear they will soon be quite cleaned out. There are five other children and a fine, handsome mother with a face like a Roman cameo. I think she is a wonderfully plucky woman too.

One day that week we started the Women's Auxiliary at Baldonnel. It is a small branch at present, only eight or ten women, but they are very keen and friendly. They elected Mrs. Simpson as President and Cecilia Secretary, a good arrangement, as I am President and Muriel Secretary of the Branch at Fort St. John. Both branches are to meet once a month regularly, apart from extra meetings for special jobs. Last week they started in by making the two big pairs of curtains I have wanted so long for the church. These are made of darkish blue repp (which took ages to come from Edmonton and cost several fortunes when it did), and each pair is ten feet high and twenty-five feet wide. Their purpose is to hang like this:

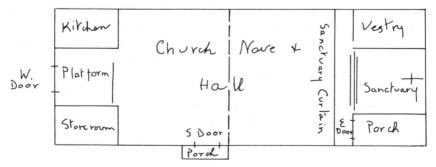

The Sanctuary curtain is closed all the week and open on Sundays. The church (western) curtain is to be open all the week and closed on Sundays unless a large congregation is expected. The purpose of it is to get more reverence, by getting people to confide their inevitable assembly and departure conversation to its Western side, thus getting a sort of big Narthex, while on the Eastern side of the curtain is real church and quiet. Of course, you'll hear all the noise clear enough on that side, but it will at least be more reverent than openly chatting before the altar. This curtain isn't up yet. It isn't quite easy to get everyone to see the need of it because chattering before and after Church in church is generally regarded as inevitable. Also, we have to get telegraph wire and to send out to Grande Prairie for big screw eyes and more harness rings (curtain rings being quite unobtainable). When all these parts are assembled and someone's husband can be snatched from thrashing to pierce the wall and stretch the wire taut—that little job will be finished and a great need supplied to the church.

Sunday the 27th was Harvest Festival, the first ever held up here of course, and a very great event. We didn't the least know how people would play up but [we] all went along on Saturday to our special places of worship to decorate as far as possible. Muriel had wired to say she couldn't get back, so Adeline went to St. Martin's (the Fort St. John church), I to Baldonnel, St. John's, and Cecilia to the school at Taylor's Flats. Both of them [were] very pleasantly surprised. The children brought quite a lot of stuff to Taylor's. Adeline found a keen crowd of W.A. ladies loaded with sheaves, turnips, carrots, iced cakes and red leaves, while at St. John's we were nearly overwhelmed. Sheaves and vegetables poured in all the afternoon—carrots, potatoes and marrows and cabbages, some of them spreading out as big as waggon wheels. Then of course there were eggs and loaves and the storekeeper gave a box of apples and oranges. And not only the W.A. and their children but also several men rolled up and rushed round training oats to grow up round the windows [sic], trailing rose leaves and balancing marrows at inaccessible places—all of course their own ideas and a new and rapturous form of self-expression. The oldest of all was most funny. He is a real old tough, not exactly what you would call God-fearing, though he says he used to sing in the choir of St. Paul's Hammersmith. He very seldom comes to church but when he does he sings louder than anyone else to make up for it. He brought the most enormous cabbage I have ever seen, several sheaves and a loaf just small enough to stand on the altar. Then he set to work making up little sheaves of wheat and nailing them to the lectern and prayer desk and as each one was fixed, he looked round at me with a wink of deep satisfaction.

Sunday itself was a great day. Muriel being still up the trail, I took

Sunday School at St. Martin's and Adeline took her new one at Fish Creek. Cecilia started off as usual at 8.30 for Taylor's. Brother Wolf. was South of the river that day taking Services for Canon Proctor who came up to take ours and brought with him Dr. Bate, the very nice Organising Secretary of the Colonial and Continental Society.

All the congregations were good except the evening one at St. Martin's, which was a little damped by a solid and freezing fog, the first I have seen in this country and much more disconcerting to these people than any amount of frost and snow. However, Dr. Bate realized that and was quite impressed with our singing of "We Plough the Fields and Scatter," which made it well worth while to have worked the children at it for three weeks as hard as if it were at least the B Minor Mass.

Part of the following week was spent in distributing the Harvest Festival offerings between the Roman Catholic hospital, the Red Cross (Miss Claxton) and various specially hard up families who for one reason or another were known to have no supply of vegetables. Meanwhile Muriel got back and she and Cecilia made a splendid lot of jam out of marrows chiefly, and also dried apricots. May has given us a fine lot of vegetables and we should be quite well stocked if it were not for the great trial of pack-rats in the cellar. Do you know pack-rats? They are the chief pest of this country and dreadfully hard to get rid of. We have now had three of them and between them they have eaten or spoilt most of our vegetable supply. They are very big and fat, rather handsome really, but they stink like badgers and steal and hide away what they can't eat. The Kellys lent us a horrible big iron trap which we set with cheese and most mornings found the cheese gone and the pack-rat too. But it's almost worse when they are caught because they have to be killed. Luckily Slim was here to kill the first and the heroic Adeline went down and killed the second, after which Harvey and I, less heroically, buried him. But the third one got out of the trap, leaving a leg behind, in revenge for which his appetite is at least equal to both the other two put together.

On October 1, the long-sought High School was opened at Fort St. John. It started with nine boys and girls in one of the farmers' shacks, but in time an old lumber house is to be moved and converted for the purpose. Where we come in is by having another boarder—Erving Foster. Erving lives eight miles away, which his mother felt was too far to ride each way daily through the winter. She was awfully keen for me to take him and I am willing enough because he really is a nice boy and will be a help to Harvey. They are a funny contrast—Erving is fourteen, very civilized and intelligent with charming manners and a responsive smile, altogether more like a good type of town boy. Harvey is twelve, very tall and fair and nice looking, but when he came he was almost incredibly slow and speechless. Poor boy, he has had hardly any chance to become anything else. His mother ran away when he was a baby and he has trailed about since after a silent father who is fond of him, but unable to provide him with any but the barest necessities of life. He lives six miles from the nearest school and had attended nowhere. Mr. Cheverton accepted instantly my offer to board Harvey in return for chores and since then he seems to have handed him over entirely. The boy arrived dressed neatly in overalls and carrying a sack. I took him to his little attic room and asked to see his kit. He shook out of the sack one grey blanket. Besides this he has a short overcoat and a cap and one clean shirt, nothing else at all, not even a change of socks. I had two night shirts made for him and presented him with the first last week. Evidently he had never seen such a thing before and was puzzled about it. But he is beginning to get the idea of it now and puts it on quite bravely after the statutory evening wash in our little hall which at night becomes the bath room. At first he was so shy as to be quite speechless and when he did speak it was through clenched jaws and teeth so you could hardly hear a word. But in these six weeks he has come on quite wonderfully and is now almost articulate and quite companionable. In theory he goes home to his father from Friday evening till Sunday evening, but lately he has stayed here for different events and come to Church and Sunday School with us. Of course he is fearfully backward at school and also can't bear reading. But I find he likes pictures, so let him cut out a lot of illustrated papers and decorate the wall over his bed. He has done this with the greatest enthusiasm and the most wonderful mixture of subjects—wild animals, historical scenes, sacred pictures and comics, all close packed on two or three square feet of rough boards. He is so keen that we are going to turn him on to making scrap books for little children, messy and a little agitating for the rest of us, but I think at present the perfect evening occupation for him. He and Erving clean out the stable before breakfast and fetch in all our wood and water, so they are quite useful, really, and awfully little trouble.

Muriel is a wonder. She cooks everything except breakfast (my share because it is always crushed wheat porridge and coffee, involving no skill); that is, prepares something for supper before she goes out in the morning and whoever gets in nearest to 6 P.M. lights the fire and heats it up. It's all so easy that I gasp to think of highly paid professionals working all day long to get our meals in England. Also housework is so simple. About an hour after prayers does all the beds and sweeping and dusting and that only leaves washing up which we do in rotation quite automatically after meals. Of course we only scrub the floor about once a month except in muddy weather when it is rather a trial, but on the whole I don't think we are dirty. Household washing, like sheets and towels, we have to send to Mrs. Kelly, because incidentally we do not have enough water for that. But domestic washing we do ourselves when possible, though I'm ashamed to say that Adeline nearly always does mine. Muriel also makes cookies (plain sort of biscuit) and excellent jam out of dried apricots. Last week she made carrot marmalade, but I can't say it was a very great success though you can eat it if VERY hungry and listening to someone telling a jolly good story.

Erving has now brought his horse to add to the party, so we are house and barn full, i.e., four women, and two boys, four horses and two kittens, and I am beginning to feel just like Abraham. I'm afraid you must get dreadfully bored with the horses. But you see in this part of the country horse problems exactly fill the place of servant problems at Home. They are the basis of our physical life, constantly giving trouble by quarreling, for instance, jibbing, falling ill, leaving without notice, or otherwise letting you down. All the same we love them and wouldn't change our problem for yours for any money.

Even now I don't believe our family is quite complete. There is a girl I dreadfully want to make room for, but I'll tell you about her next time. It would mean building on a room and I'm not sure that I can afford it, though I mean to if I can.

Last week Adeline and I rode up to the Blueberry River and visited the very last family settled Northward, about forty-five miles from here. We took our sleeping bag as before and slept very happily on the floor of three different houses. But all that you must get from Adeline's diary.

Diary to October 20.

I will run over the last fortnight, i.e., from October 4th. On that Sunday we had our first Celebration at St. John's Church (Baldonnel). It was in the afternoon, of course, because Brother Wolf. has Taylor's in the morning and Fort St. John at night. He took the Holy Communion Service in place of Evensong and invited everyone to stay till the end whether communicants or not. Hardly anyone communicated besides ourselves (only one or two grown-ups are confirmed, no children yet) but everyone remained to the end.

The plan is to have a Sunday Celebration at each church once a month and a week day one at St. Martin's in the intervening weeks. Hitherto this has been on Tuesday but I think it will settle down to Monday. After supper we went on to St. Martin's for the evening Service. This was rather an odd one because an elderly man had arrived in Fort St. John the day before with a waggon containing a magic lantern and a set of slides on the Life of Christ. He had come to give his lecture somewhere and was a nice old man. So Brother Wolf., with his admirable Franciscan brotherliness, immediately made him share his tiny shack with him and the Sunday Evening Service. We foolish virgins were a little dubious, feeling we all knew nothing about Mr. B. or his slides, but the event proved Brother Wolf. to be quite right. The church was full because everybody loves a lantern. Mr. B. was a dear old, shy farmer with no gift of speech but just a simple faith and most appalling slides (which they all loved), and after his lecture Brother Wolf. preached an excellent little sermon which summed it all up.

That night we had our first snow storm and woke up to a white world. There was frost of course but nothing to speak of, and the only tiresome effect was on the horses. They got excited by the sun and cold and broke away and in a moment they were all away with Kellys' fifty acres open to them, and it cost us the whole morning to round them up. In the afternoon we had an emergency meeting of the Baldonnel W.A. to work at the two pairs of church curtains, but owing to the snow, only one sewing machine turned up so we didn't get them finished after all.

Tuesday was a lovely day with nothing to prevent us going North, so we packed up the bed roll on Miles again, and two haversacks on Puck, and started off, Adeline and I, directly after dinner hour with the Fort St. John Cubs. We ate our sandwiches and then struck North up the old Montney trail. For the first two or three hours it crosses an Indian reserve where no white cultivation or building is allowed, a rough, bushy country, pretty earlier but now rather desolate, the grass being all burnt up and the trees leafless. There is a new, graded road, just finished, which runs straight North for fifteen miles, but we avoided that as you can well imagine—not because of the traffic, because there isn't any, but because fifteen miles of perfectly straight road is enough to break any English heart.

About 6 o'clock we reached a nice family called the Bells[202] who gave us supper, and then went on at once hoping to reach the Hold-up before dark. This is a tiny creek where there is a store and the last house before the trail goes into the bush for fourteen miles. So we meant to sleep there that night and go on first thing next morning. But as luck would have it we hit on the wrong trail and as night fell, found ourselves going steadily North East instead of North West. We couldn't leave the trail because the bush is so full of dead-fall and snags that you can't get along in the dark. So we could only follow the one we were on, taking our direction from the stars and hoping for a swing to the North West before long. But instead, after about two more miles the stupid trail ran straight into the bush and disappeared completely all of a sudden, and so with great disgust we had to turn round and retrace it two miles or more to where we had seen the last house. By this time it was so dark that only the horses could see the trail and when at last we reached a wire fence we saw nothing but walked straight into it. However, it was all right and we were led there by our Guardian Angel, for the people, whom Price and I had visited last year, were most welcoming, made us come in, showed us where to lay the bed roll, and we were soon all asleep. These people are a devout United Church family called Cairns, ready to back up any religious work. The father, mother and daughter run a little Sunday School and take quite a lot of trouble about it. They are old settlers for Montney, having been there two years already, and have quite a good two-room house, i.e., a kitchen-living room and two little bedrooms partitioned off from it by curtains. In these slept Mr. and Mrs. Cairns and the daughter Alma. We slept on the living room floor, while the son David, a tall, shy boy of about nineteen, slept on the little sofa modestly hidden from us by the rocking chair. Next morning the men went off to work early and after breakfast we had prayers with Mrs. Cairns before starting off again. Alma, the girl of eighteen, was very keen to be a Guide so she agreed to beat up one or two neighbours' girls and get them to the nearest school next afternoon in case we should get back in time, have a Sunday School, and then discuss Guides with them.

From there it was only about five miles to the Hold-up and thirteen or fourteen to the Blueberry River. But this last part of the trail was pretty fierce—in fact, nearly as bad as last year. It goes right through real forest, tall sombre spruce and pine trees, rather beautiful but very dark and melancholy and monotonous. The ground was still covered with snow because the sun could not get through to it, but the trail was one long swamp varied by deeper bogs and fallen logs, and the horses simply loathed it. However, we got through in a little under four hours which was better than my time last year. And of course it was quite a different thing altogether because of being with Adeline.

All the same you can't think how delightful it was, even after so short a time as that, to emerge into more or less open country again where there is grass and sunshine. We let the horses graze while we ate our sandwiches (Muriel's make of yesterday morning) and finally reached the river and Mrs. Mann. This lady was a widow last year, called Mrs. Rodgers, and she was the only woman living by the Blueberry. But since then she has married her hired man and this summer four families have penetrated the bush and settled up here. So we asked if we might sleep with her and hold a Sunday School for the children after supper, and then crossed the river (quite shallow) and went four miles farther to visit the two more Northerly families in the parish. Actually the Blueberry is just outside the Peace River Block, being forty miles North West of Fort

St. John, but as there is no settlement beyond it, these families must belong to our parish because they are at present on the edge of civilization. One of the families consists of a father, son and daughter only. The girl was in the little new shack and she was curiously shy and unresponsive. The other family was very different. The mother and daughter greeted us effusively and begged us to stay with them; failing that [they] hastened to produce a meal of tea and bread and butter and bottled fruit. Mrs. M. is middle aged and used to more conventional surroundings. They only arrived two or three months ago and are living in two tiny shacks of poplar with mud floors for lack of lumber. So she is a little desolate, especially for lack of neighbours—only the shy girl a mile away to the East, Mrs. Mann, four miles to the South, and in every other direction nobody at all, at present. The daughter, Myrtle, aged thirteen, was very bright and friendly, and jumped at the idea of being a Guide, even though it must mean almost a lone Guide unless she can occasionally ride down to the Hold-up and meet others who at present don't exist. After that Mr. M. came in and proved to be an International Bible Student which is apparently an excuse for holding all the most tiresome heresies. However, we parted amiably enough, though he did mention the "undoubted fact" that all Churches were the inventions of the devil—just as I accepted Mrs. M.'s pressing invitation to stay with them next time we come to the Blueberry River.

Then we crossed the river again and visited two families just in, called Smith. One of these has a tiny little crippled child of whom the Caravan workers had told me. So I took them particulars of an orthopaedic hospital at Winnipeg and hope that it may be possible to help them to get her out there for treatment. Finally we had a tiny Sunday School for the Rodgers' children—four little boys and a little girl. We had taken hymn books and picture cards and two big wall pictures and the mother and children were all very sweet and attentive. The eldest son and stepfather were away but Mrs. Mann says that boy is an atheist and cares for none of these things—rather sad at fourteen. Between 11 and 12 we went to bed, that is, Mrs. Mann and all the children retired to a tiny bunk-house outside and left us the shack to ourselves. It was a squalid little cabin but we were far too tired to bother and slept nearly as well as on the feather beds of Kew Palace.

In the cold, dim dawn the door burst open and one of the little boys, Melville, aged nine, came in and lit the stove. It seemed so odd and Dickensian to lie on the floor and watch this child kneeling like a little dark shadow before the stove and only his face lit up by a flickering glare as he tried to blow the embers into flame. Having succeeded, he went out again and we just had time to jump up and dress quickly before the door opened and the whole family trooped in ready for breakfast. It's marvelous how quickly all these people go to bed and get up. Each process takes less than two minutes, chiefly because no time is wasted in washing. At night no one washes at all, that seems to be quite unheard of. In the morning everyone, when fully dressed, gathers round a small tin basin in the kitchen and scrubs their faces and hands with a communal wash rag. The amazing thing is the effect is so good and everyone seems to be remarkably clean.

Mrs. Mann is an Anglican from Saskatchewan. She teaches the children herself with the help of correspondence lessons from Victoria. In spite of their unusual isolation they are a noticeably refined family. The little boys look and talk just like little Prep. school boys in England. She has had a sad life, too. She started as an orphan in a Home, was adopted by a man who brought her up most harshly and finally broke his wife's heart. She died and the girl married to escape from him. She had eight children and then the two oldest died from some kind of poison. After that the husband died, leaving her with six children, little ones, in Edmonton. She heard of this country and sold everything to come up here and take a homestead. Last summer, when she had been in a few weeks, her baby boy was drowned in the river. It was a little after that I visited her. Now she has married again and I hope it's all right.

We got off from there in good time, stopped for Matins under a tree (about 8.30) and pushed through the bush so quickly that we reached the Hold-up School just before their dinner hour at 12. Here we found four or five big girls most eager to be Guides, so spent the hour with them, gave them cards to go on learning from, and promised to try to come up about once a month if they would carry on and prepare to pass their Tenderfoot. Then we snatched some dinner in a house on the way farther South and reached the next school, Crystal Springs, just before 3.30. The teacher [Miss D.A. Tilton] was friendly and allowed us to hold a short Sunday School for which nearly all the children stayed. After that, Alma Cairns rolled up on horseback with another Guide—two other big girls—and we ended with another Guide meeting for eight keen recruits. In this school the teacher is prepared to help so that seems very hopeful for Guiding, though as regards Sunday School I can't do much because the Cairns already run one for the United Church.

We went to supper with a nice delicate Anglican woman whom we had also visited last year. She is keen and is teaching her little girl of nine all about the Prayer Book. Finally we groped our way back to the Cairns for a second night and they were as kind as before.

Next day we visited various new families including two Anglican ones, the first still living in a dreadfully small tent, the second just building their house. The wife there was great fun, enjoying it all so much. The father and son were just getting the logs into position so we stayed for half an hour to help haul on the rope. But our longest time was spent with a sweet little English woman called Mrs. Wait.[203] She comes from Sussex and is quite unchanged. She lost a little girl from scarlet fever last winter, a dreadful sorrow. But she still has seven little children and they are desperately poor. In fact, here as elsewhere, CLOTHES are the greatest need and any that you can send out to me marked, "Old Clothes for Free Distribution," will be most thankfully received and used. We didn't want to stay to dinner but she was so eager we couldn't refuse. So Adeline and I took turns to churn the butter in a little pail while she plucked and dressed two prairie chickens someone had given her. I think she and her family have been as hard up as anybody could be this year. She had no teapot and the children no shoes or stockings; but everything was bright and clean and she made no complaint. Only her eyes filled with tears when I spoke of the little girl who died and she could make no answer.

Towards evening, having seen all her very numerous family photographs, we started South once more but only got as far as the little Montney Post Office when darkness fell. Here live Mr. and Mrs. "Shorty" Long, he a Roman Catholic, she an Anglican, with one little boy of seven.

Mr. and [Mrs.] Long were most kind; gave us supper and found a place on the cabin floor (not without difficulty) where we could lay the bedroll. That night I was all hips—I can't think why. The floor was no harder than usual and I ought to have been in training instead of becoming a mass of resentful bony projections. Poor Adeline got the worst of it as usual, for a combined sleeping bag doesn't allow much independence of action—or inaction either.

Next morning we had a Sunday School lesson with little Vincent and morning prayers with Mrs. Long. Then we saddled up and Adeline hitched Puck to a carpenter's trestle while she was being shown the exact way we were to follow. Puck pulled the trestle and being loose it swung against his legs. The first I knew of it was a shout from Adeline and the sight of poor Puck in a frenzy of fear dashing round and round and kicking the trestle to pieces as it banged against his legs. Finally he dashed off into space and bolted for about half a mile, still dragging the bits of trestle behind him. Adeline and I had awful visions of ourselves chasing him to the North Pole or farther (there being no fence as far as we knew), but mercifully his fit of terror suddenly passed and left him so exhausted or dazed that when Miles eventually came up with him he let me catch him quite easily.

After that we had no more adventures or visits of any interest but a steady three and a half hours ride Southward brought us home on Saturday just in time for supper, to find the house still standing, and

Muriel and Cecilia, Erving and Harvey, Lucifer and Michael and Robin—all having made lots of hay while the old cats were away.

(Finished to October 10.)
Diary for October 11-31, Oh Dear . . .

    October 11 was observed here as Children's Day, a rather pointless festival but a good excuse for rounding up stragglers. The only difference we made at Baldonnel was to turn Sunday School more or less into a choir practice in preparation for Wolf.'s Service which was for grown-ups and children combined, the stress being laid on the children. But at the Evening Service at Fort St. John Muriel was much more ambitious. A boy and girl each read a lesson and all the children sang some special choruses (Church Sunday School Missions Productions) which have no literary or musical merit but seem to give immense happiness to the singers. They have, of course, simple sentiments and catchy tunes and the children certainly love them. Lots of parents came to hear them and the net result was the excellent congregation of seventy-two.

    Of the next Monday to Friday I can remember almost nothing except a Scout Rally on Monday at Fort St. John to meet the Edmonton Commissioner. On the return journey Brother Wolf. surpassed all records by carrying in his car, an ordinary Ford saloon five-seater, himself, the Commissioner and twenty-three boys. Having only so far taken fourteen in Eliza there is no more spirit in me and her nose is quite out of joint. On Friday Adeline and I crossed the Pine again for one night. It was a bright cold day with a high wind. The horses went well and we reached the nearer of the two schools in exactly three hours and arranged to take the Guides next morning at 10 and Sunday School afterwards. Then we had a blissful lunch in a clearing, spent too long over it and had to go straight on eight miles to Mrs. Spence for the night. She is a delightful woman and gave us such a warm welcome, her only regret being that her house is not yet finished and they are all still living in two rooms, i.e., kitchen and one bedroom. However, that was no matter as we had got our sleeping bag and could put it anywhere on the floor in the kitchen. So we sat and talked while she went through the rather grim process of plucking and drawing three prairie chickens for our supper. The wind had been against us or something—anyway I simply couldn't keep awake and my replies got more and more disjointed. Twice poor Mrs. Spence invited me to go and lie down on her bed. Twice I refused and bucked up for a few minutes. But the third time I was beaten so retired thankfully into the little family bedroom and in one minute was wrapped in swinish sleep. Next moment, as it seemed, but really an hour later, Mrs. Spence kindly woke me up to say that supper was ready and what was my surprise to find at my side, still quite unconscious, was Adeline who had succumbed just one minute later than me. Weren't we a pleasant pair of guests? Anyway we woke up for supper and tried to make up for it then and for several long hours afterwards sitting round the kitchen table with Mr. and Mrs. Spence, their seven children and a nice boy of nineteen who lives with them as a sort of extra son. At last the evening ended and we all went to bed. Raymond, the boy, slept outside somewhere to leave us the kitchen for ourselves. So we spread out the sleeping bag between the table and the cream separator while the nine Spences retired in mass formation upon their bedroom and were all in bed and asleep before we had our clothes off. Next morning before it was light we leapt up and dressed just before the whole Spence family emerged out from their fastness.

At 8.30 we set off with Jean, who is a tremendously keen little Guide, she riding a big farm horse saddled only with a blanket which was not girthed at all. We had a nice little meeting with the eight Guide recruits, followed by a Sunday School to which two or three more came, but oddly enough, no boys. This district has only three boys of school age and of these one lives too far away and the other two unluckily had to work on Saturday. So it is a girls' Sunday School and such a very different one to Baldonnel. After that we had lunch with the Framsts and left with Mrs. Spence the beautiful little red cross made for us by Crayford, a blue table cloth and some hymn books in hopes that she will carry on in some of the intervals of our monthly visit. Then we visited a pure Russian family, one of the few out here, and watched in rather pained admiration the mother as she made a MUD floor to the house and smoothed it flat with her hands. Then we turned homewards again, crossed the Pine once more and got back for supper just as the sun was setting.

Next day Brother Wolf. was South of the river doing duty for Canon Proctor so each of us had to take our own Services, Cecilia at Taylor's, Adeline and I at St. John's and Muriel at St. Martin's. Adeline read the lesson at St. John's and I played the "organ" and preached, taking as text the words "Come unto Me," which are under the picture of Our Lord over the altar. We all had goodish congregations but Muriel had a really splendid one in the evening st St. Martin's.

The next day, Monday, I had the Cubs at noon and then, with Adeline, rode over to Baldonnel for a Women's Auxiliary meeting. To our surprise we found quite a lot of new ladies there, chiefly from the region of the Flats. They were unduly smart and had produced an unduly smart "lunch" as they will call the refreshments, whether you have them at 4 in the afternoon or 11 at night. Suddenly we discovered that it was all really a feast in honour of Adeline. The ladies made little speeches about her, and in the middle of these ALL the school children walked in and presented her with a lovely little pair of beaded moccasins as a farewell gift. Wasn't it nice? Adeline was quite taken by surprise, but pleased, I think. It was all such a spontaneous expression of appreciation and that is not very common here.

On Tuesday Adeline and I rode over with Muriel to Fish Creek to enrol the first six of her little new Pack of Brownies there. It is one of the tiny schools of ten children, all very sweet and eager, and the teacher, a very charming girl of about twenty-one is most keen and welcoming too. Muriel goes there for Sunday School too on Sunday afternoons after her big one at Fort St. John in the mornings.

After our usual sandwiches together, Muriel went on to visit while Adeline and I rode home as fast as possible in order to carry out a daring plan. We had decided to have TWO HOURS OFF, that is, to do what we had longed to do ever since coming here—to walk down our own coulee as far as a certain lone spruce tree which stands up on a little hill in the middle—and see the view both ways from there. Up to now we had never had a chance, the world being too much with us late and soon. And this, besides being our first was our last chance, because Adeline was to leave on Friday, and after that the lone spruce would have to wait two years at least. So we took the two hours and climbed up through bush and dead fall to the top of the little hill. The view from there was delightful, half a mile straight North across the deep valley full of trees to this little house and barn looking like toys on the edge of a precipice, and one and a half miles South down the wandering coulee to the original old post and the broad curve of the Peace River looking as clear and still as its name.

We didn't stay long, being responsible for supper, but we just waited till the sun went off our little hill top and the shadow filled the coulee.

On Wednesday we went to the Baldonnel Guides, after which Mrs. Simpson joined us and we succeeded in putting up the Western pair of curtains.

After that we rode down to the Palings for Adeline to have a night there and say goodbye. We had a nice evening with them, chiefly playing the gramophone. Then we slept in a huge double bed, which after the sleeping bag, made me almost nervous, and were awakened by new tunes played by Mr. Paling and at the end he appeared with two cups of tea which made us feel absurdly luxurious and old-countrified. Then Mrs. Paling came in and talked to us so we couldn't get up and finally we didn't arrive at breakfast till 9 o'clock.

Afterwards we had to go and they loaded us with kindness in the form of a cauliflower, a piece of deer, and what is far more rare and wonderful, two sticks of BRUSSELS SPROUTS. I don't think anyone else grows them out here. So we hung all these in sacks round Puck because Robin always refuses to be treated as a pack-pony. The ride back was rather cold and snowy. We stopped for lunch with some people called Davis, she an Englishwoman and expecting an unmarried sister out shortly to live with them. The poor thing was dreading the sister's impressions of the new home. "She comes from Gloucestershire and has always lived in a very up to date bungalow with everything laid on."

We got home about 4 to find Mrs. Kelly had demanded that Adeline should go to tea so we went out again (rather reluctantly) and Adeline was rewarded by (a) a real afternoon tea, (b) a whole cooked chicken and some cake for her journey—rather nice, wasn't it?

Then we got back for supper and tried afterwards to pack peacefully and settle lots of things. But Miss Petter came in to say good-bye and Erving and Harvey wanted help with their homework and scrap books and so the last evening just muddled through like the others. Adeline took prayers and we sang "Praise My Soul, the King of Heaven."

Next morning, the 23rd, we had to be a little quicker than usual in order to drive in to Fort St. John by 7.30 for a Celebration specially arranged with Brother Wolf. We left the porridge and coffee ready for the boys who can perfectly look after themselves, and had our first early morning Service in the country. It was rather wonderful getting back to the dim morning hour for our last Communion all together for so long.

Brother Wolf. with his invariable consideration offered to drive us all to Pouce Coupé as the road was still snowy and when we refused that, insisted on our borrowing his car which is warmer than Eliza, being a saloon, and also younger and stronger in the vitals. So we came home to breakfast, finished packing, watered the horses and then all four drove to Pouce Coupé where Adeline was to catch the train that evening. We spent the afternoon visiting some of the ladies who run the local Guides, as I am Divisional Commissioner and Cecilia Divisional Secretary, and things seem always to be at sixes and sevens there. Then Miss Bertrand, the local Schoolmistress and Brown Owl, joined us for supper, and in no time the 7.30 train was gone.

Cecilia drove on the return journey and all went well till we had gone nearly sixty miles and crossed the ferry, when we got an awful and complete puncture. Then our luck turned—the jacks would not work, and the spanner would not turn the nuts. So after about an hour's gallant struggle under the frosty moonlight we retired in good order to sleep with the McKnights who were luckily only about a mile away.

End of Volume I, Diary 1931.

VOLUME II.

"With this new Volume of the Diary, I [Adeline Harmer] am venturing to add to the general appeal made lately, as I know more or less how things stand financially at Fort St. John.

Baldonnel, of course, owes its Church Hall to friends in England, and other lovely gifts of Altar Frontals, etc., for both Churches have been received. From time to time also a little windfall from a friend arrives to cheer the heart of Mr. Wolfendale, Monica, Muriel or Cecilia; and books and some clothes for distribution have been received.

But as far as I know the only money coming into the parish regularly is Mr. Wolfendale's salary. This is guaranteed by the Montreal Branch of the Fellowship of the West and is collected there by lantern lectures and by gifts from the Members. Most of these are young men, among whom at this time there is a tremendous amount of unemployment. It is therefore as much as the Fellowship can do to fulfil this obligation. The Women's Work in the parish gets no grant from any Society.

ST. MARTIN'S CHURCH, FORT ST. JOHN, owes its existence to several sources. Almost all the work on it was voluntary, the greater part being undertaken by Mr. Wolfendale and Mr. Whatmore. The building is finished and painted inside and out. A debt remains, however, on materials supplied locally; I do not know the amount.

On ST. JOHN'S CHURCH HALL, BALDONNEL, there is still owing some £12 or £13 on extras over and above the contract. Also the curtains have so far been paid for by Monica (about £11). The floor has yet to be stained or painted, and one day the building itself will have to be painted inside and out. For this, voluntary labour is sure to be forthcoming, but for such a big building the cost of paint will be considerable. This need, however, is not immediate.

The people there are doing their best to help. Collections at the services up to the time of the consecration paid for the chairs; and the heating and lighting arrangements for both buildings are being supplied by local effort. At Baldonnel a small salary is paid to the caretaker, but it is hoped that occasional letting of the hall will bring in a little money.

The SCOUTS AND GUIDES at Fort St. John and Baldonnel pay gradually for hats and belts, and some of the Guides for uniform material. Some

discarded hats and tunics have been received from a Guide company in
Toronto and from elsewhere. Money however would be very welcome
for initial expenses of ties, badges, and emblems for the outlying Patrols.
As these can only look for a meeting once a month it is essential also to
supply them with a certain amount of Guide literature to help them in
their work. BROWNIE Uniforms also have to be provided. These are lent
to the children and returned when they become Guides. Transport to
and from the Camps is another expense which cannot be covered by the
Camp fees paid by the Scouts and Guides.

Settlers and workers alike are fully conscious of, and most grateful for,
the tremendous help they have already received from England, and
realise that this is not the time to make a further appeal for funds.

But to Readers of the Diary I should like to make the following
suggestion:

The cost of materials for producing and issuing the diary comes to
about £7 a year, which would be covered by 2/- per head from those to
whom it is sent. This cost continues to be defrayed by someone (not
myself!) as a contribution towards the work at Fort St. John. The typing
also is voluntary.

We venture therefore to suggest that those who receive the Diary might
subscribe for 1932 AT LEAST TWO SHILLINGS (the normal price per annum
for a Missionary Magazine) and—either now or later—WHATEVER ELSE
THEY FEEL THEY COULD GIVE: and bear in mind the needs out there and
make them known to other people whom they may have interested in the
work. This request does not apply to those who have already responded
to the appeal made lately in the Diaries.

MONEY should be sent to
   MISS M. CAUSTON,
   BISHOPS SPARKFORD,
   ST. CROSS, WINCHESTER.

WARM CLOTHES or BOOKS should be sent direct to Monica (Fort St.
John, B.C., and parcels marked "USED CLOTHES" (or Books) "FOR FREE
DISTRIBUTION TO SETTLERS." If sent by rail the words "DAWSON CREEK
STATION" should be added.

Readers of the Diary will be glad to know that when I left at the end of
October, Monica seemed very well. Although of course the Winter with
its problems and hardships was before them, all the workers were
looking forward to the new developments of Church life throughout a
Parish of about 4000 square miles, cheered this year by fellowship
together, by the witness and usefulness of the two churches and by the
regular "ministry of the Word and Sacraments" now available, and
relying on the continuance of the prayers and encouragement of friends
at Home, which have been such a tremendous help since the work began.

(Signed) Adeline Harmer

Postscript

At the end of Monica's second year in Peace River Adeline Harmer returned to England, leaving Monica with Cecilia Goodenough to carry on the work begun. She also left Monica with her Church House—soon to be fondly called the Abbey—, two churches built, a strong ally in Brother Wolf., Sunday Schools in the newly opened schoolhouses, cubs and scouts, brownies and guides, and ever new homes to be visited. Monica was now established on her own, and committed to service in the North Peace. Her accounts of visits to infinitely lonely and cruelly burdened women, of many nationalities, and many faiths or none, suggest strongly that she was well on her way to becoming the Companion of the Peace.

Notes

It has been exceedingly difficult to identify some of the people mentioned in this manuscript and impossible in other cases. Where identification was possible, there was occasionally a wealth of material available on the individual, and here the book, *The Peacemakers of the North Peace* ([Fort St. John], 1973), by Cora Ventress, Marguerite Davies, and Edith Kyllo, proved invaluable. Much material was also gathered in the Provincial Archives in Victoria, British Columbia, and obtained by letters from various correspondents. Quite frequently, however, research provided nothing but a family name. The result, unfortunately, is an uneven mixture of footnote feast and famine.

1. Monica Storrs wrote her "diaries" as newsletters to be distributed among members of her family and interested friends. Miss Mabel Causton, a very close friend, had them reproduced, and it was she who labeled them as "extracts." The diaries which follow, therefore, are not selections culled from a larger volume, but, to use Monica's own description in a letter to R.D. Symons, appear as they were written "for home consumption."

2. The ship was the *Duchess of Bedford*, one of the Canadian Pacific steamships, which, being of shallow draft for the St. Lawrence River, rolled at sea and were consequently known as the "drunken Duchesses."

3. Miss Muriel Hooper, a friend of Monica's from St. Christopher's College, Blackheath, was on her way to join Miss Marguerite Fowler, O.B.E., at St. Faith's Mission in Swan River, Manitoba, which had been established in 1928. When Miss Fowler retired as head of the mission, Miss Hooper succeeded her. She is presently also retired but serving as sacristan for the Society of St. John the Evangelist in Bracebridge, Ontario.

4. Sylvia and Iris Tower were cousins of Monica.

5. Gundulf was a Sealyham terrier belonging to Monica and her friend Adeline Harmer. Adeline was the daughter of Bishop John Reginald Harmer of Rochester.

6. Margaret Robertson, together with Muriel Hooper, joined Miss Fowler at Swan River, Manitoba, as Bishop's Messengers of St. Faith's. Miss Robertson was the daughter of General Sir Phillip and Lady Robertson.

7. Exactly what a "Rothenburg Top" is seems uncertain, but according to Peter Storrs, Monica's nephew, it was probably one of the little wooden toys from Rottenburg, Germany, the craftsmanship of which Monica admired.

8. Havergal College for Girls, a private day and boarding school with Church of England connections, was established in Toronto, Ontario, in 1894.
9. Margaret E. Popham, C.B.E., a Storrs' family friend, who was appointed to Havergal College in 1923. She remained with the college until 1930 when she returned to England. She became head of the prestigious Cheltenham Ladies' College, where she remained until her retirement in 1953.
10. Canon Henry Pemberton Plumptre, rector of St. James' Cathedral and canon and sub-dean of St. Alban's Cathedral, Toronto, Ontario, 1909-35.
11. Sarah Trumbell Warren, honoured for her services with a C.B.E. in 1935.
12. "Swan" refers to Lillian Swanzy, a friend then working in Edmonton, Alberta.
13. The United Church of Canada came into being on 10 June 1925, a union of all of Canada's Methodist congregations, virtually all Congregationalists, and approximately two-thirds of the Presbyterians. In 1929, the year of Monica's encounter, there were 650,000 members with 1,500,000 persons considered under pastoral care. Those Presbyterians shunning union viewed this new denomination with some trepidation, as is obvious from the context of Monica's remark.
14. Mary Webb (1881-1927) wrote popular rustic novels set in Shropshire. Among the best known are *The Golden Arrow, The House in Dormer Forest*, and *Precious Bane*.
15. The Cathedral Church of the Redeemer was built in 1905; it was a pro-cathedral until 1948.
16. John Patrick Somers Cocks, later to become the 8th Baron Somers, was professor of compositional theory at the Royal College of Music. He was a cousin to Adeline Harmer and often stayed with the Harmers, where Monica came to know him.
17. Archdeacon Arthur Edward Burgett, D.D., 1869-1942, consecrated second bishop of Edmonton in 1932, was always a great source of help for Monica.

18. The railway reached Hythe in 1928, and it was incorporated as a village, population 328, the same year.
19. The memorial dedicated to Miss Hasell in St. Andrew's Church, Dacre, Cumberland, reads as follows: "Frances Hatton Eva Hasell, younger daughter of John and Maud Hasell of Dalemain, Member of the Order of the British Empire, Doctor of Divinity, Officer of the Order of Service of Canada, who for over 50 years was the life spring of The Western Canada Caravan Mission, to which she devoted her entire life. Born: 13th December, 1886. Died: 3rd May, 1974."
   Miss Hasell's companion from 1926 was Iris Eugenie Friend Sayle (1894-1973), daughter of George and Emily Sayle. Together these indomitable ladies traversed the rural areas of Canada as one unit of the Caravan Mssion until 1972, when Miss Hasell was eighty-four years old and Miss Sayle, seventy-eight. Miss Hasell suggested the Peace River to Monica for her work not only because she perceived a need for Christian education but also because there was "another great need . . . for someone to look after the young people and provide wholesome recreation such as Guides and Scouts." She complained that "girls of eleven and twelve went to the local dances," as Monica was soon to discover (F.H. Eva Hasell, *Canyons, Cans and Caravans* [London: Society for the Propagation of Christian Knowledge, 1930], p. 199). She also arranged for Monica to stay the first winter with May Birley.
20. The hotel was operated by Mr. and Mrs. George Hart. A Vancouver *Province* article of 5 October 1930 entitled "An Optimistic Town"— the buildings were being moved back seventeen feet on either side to make Main Street one hundred feet wide— saw the hotel as a focal point. "If you know Pouce Coupé you will know its landmarks, and you will recall the hotel, perched on the brow of a hill, overlooking the Pouce Coupé Valley. . . ."
21. Frank J. Clark was the road engineer for the whole district. He lived at Rolla for some years and then moved

to Pouce Coupé. For further information, see Hasell, *Canyons, Cans and Caravans*, p. 193. In F.C. Gaylor's article "First Car Trip to Hudson Hope," Mr. Clark is credited with making the eight-hour trip from Fort St. John possible (Vancouver *Province*, 20 October 1929).

22. The matron of the Red Cross Hospital from 1923 to 1935 was Ida S. Crook. She is described in Esme Tuck's *A Brief History of Pouce Coupé Village and District* (Pouce Coupé: Women's Institute, 1954). Miss Crook told some pioneer stories in *Pioneers All! Human Interest Sketches* (n.p.,n.d.). The Red Cross Hospital had twelve beds and cost $7,000 to build. The expenses were shared by the Alberta Red Cross, the British Columbia government, and the community. In 1931 the public ward rates were $1.50 for taxpayers and $4.00 for non-taxpayers; private rooms were $3.00 and $5.00 (see C.A. Dawson and R.M. Murchie, *The Settlement of the Peace River Country: A Study of a Pioneer Area* [Toronto: Macmillan, 1934], pp. 215-16.

23. Miss May Birley. May, her sister Nína, and brother Kenneth were born in Brisbane, Australia, but the family moved to the Isle of Man when the children were quite young. May was a graduate nurse and served in France in World War I. She was decorated for her outstanding service, receiving the *Croix de Guerre*. Kenneth Birley took his discharge from the R.N.W.M.P. in 1909 and worked for Revillon Frères thereafter. In 1914 he took up farming. After the war May came to Fort St. John to settle near her brother and later Nina joined them. Another brother also came to Fort St. John, but he died shortly after his arrival (Ventress, Davies, and Kyllo, *Peacemakers*, p. 154).

24. Letitia Petter later married Braden Herron of the Fort St. John area. She was tragically killed in an airplane accident a few years later.

25. In this period the majority of the Peace River schools were taught by inexperienced female teachers who had come to this outlying part of the province in order to obtain a year's experience that would fit them for a position closer to the larger centres.

The schools themselves were of the crudest possible structure—usually built of logs—consisting of four bare walls with no ceiling, no ventilation except doors and windows, and no heating arrangements except an unjacketed stove which provided excessive warmth in some parts of the room and insufficient warmth in others. There were no blinds and in most cases it was impossible to open the windows. The blackboards usually consisted of painted beaverboards, or in some instances, just plain tarpaper. There were no cloakrooms and the back of the room was used as a storage place for coats, hats, rubbers and surplus stove-wood. No screen doors or windows were provided so it was customary during the mosquito season to be unable to see across the class-room because of the smoke from the smudge that was used to keep out the mosquitoes.

Toilet facilities were of the worst imaginable kind. In the winter the children were forced to use the open toilets in temperatures of thirty or forty degrees below zero; in summer, the open toilets provided a gathering place for all the flies and mosquitoes of the neighbourhood. No toilet paper was supplied, and it was usual to find in place of this, a Simpson's or Eaton's catalogue.

Drinking water was in almost every case provided by the melting of snow during the winter and from unsanitary scoopouts in the summer.

In all schools there was a general scarcity of equipment. In most schools there was a lack of supplementary textbooks, and the reading library usually consisted of two or three battered and obsolete novels that were unfit for juveniles to use. In the majority of schools no playground equipment was supplied, and no attempt was made to provide for extracurricular activities. In many of the school districts no barns were supplied for the horses which the pupils rode to school, with the consequence that the horses had to be tied to the school fence, or allowed to wander at will around the schoolyard (William A. Plenderleith, "An Experiment in the Reorganization and the Administration of a Rural Inspectoral Unit in British Columbia" [Ph.D. thesis, University of Toronto, 1937]).

26. The hotel is presumably the ten-room establishment owned by Maizie and Claire Stokke. They soon sold it to a man named Ross, and it was later managed by Mrs. Stokke's uncle, Leslie Hunter (Marguerite Davies and Cora Ventress, *Fort St. John Pioneer Profiles* [Fort St. John: Alaska Highway News, 1971], p. 16).

27. Field Marshall Sir Douglas Haig (1861-1928), commander of the British armies in France, 1915-19. The horse of the "ill-fated memorial" on Whitehall in London is a most striking example of equine superciliousness.

28. In fact, males outnumbered females 185 to 100 in the Peace River Block as late as 1931. Despite Monica's experience, the excess was particularly marked in the age group over thirty with the many prospectors and trappers (see Dawson and Murchie, *Settlement of the Peace River Country*, p. 62).

29. Monica drew a sketch at this point, but it was not reproduced in the typescript.

30. The Society for the Propagation of Christian Knowledge was established in 1699 and emphasized schools, medical missions, and the publication of books and tracts on Christian issues (See W.K. Lowther Clark, *A History of the S.P.C.K.* [London: S.P.C.K., 1959]).

31. Sir Ronald Storrs, Monica's eldest brother, military, then civil governor of Jerusalem, 1917-25, became governor of Cyprus in 1926. In 1931, during an unexpected outburst of violence on the island, the wooden Government House where Storrs was in residence was burned down, completely destroying the books and works of art which were such a source of pleasure to him. For more information on Sir Ronald, see *Dictionary of National Biography, 1952-1960*, p. 931.

32. Tommy Hargreaves was known for his sense of humour and his ingenuity. Besides operating the garage in Fort St. John and driving the first

taxi, he also owned land at Rose Prairie.

33. The use of the term "punctured" for a broken blister is an example of Monica's picturesque and slightly exaggerated speech. The incident is also illustrative of her resolution, for she blistered the inside of her knees in her determination to learn to ride "like the Canadians." During the coming years she was to do a great deal of riding, and one of the nicknames affectionately given to her and her companions by the settlers was "God's Galloping Girls."

34. Helen McDonald (or possibly MacDonald) became a close friend. At that time she and her husband Jack had three children, Harold, Helen, and Jack. The fourth, Billy, arrived in 1931. Mrs. McDonald had been a schoolteacher and undertook the Sunday School by Post marking and mailing as a volunteer. The materials were prepared and published by the General Board of Religious Education and were sent out to isolated children, usually free of cost, either every four weeks or every quarter, depending on the courses being taken. The children were encouraged to take annual examinations and were awarded certificates of promotion when passing from one level to the next. In some areas the Sunday School by Post was also used to prepare candidates for confirmation. Its work still continues in some areas under the title "Church at Home."

35. Mrs. Millar joined her children Billy, Ann, Florence, and Sarah in the 1920's. The daughters had come from Hammond, Ontario, to join their brother in 1920. Sarah married Gilbert Howe; Florence, Cecil Warren; and Ann, a man named Garside, who homesteaded at Baldonnel. He may be the Pete mentioned below.

36. The policeman was Joseph Clark Devlin of the British Columbia Provincial Police.

37. R.D. Symons writes: "Their inability to sing was not so much due to vocal weakness as to these children's cultural environment. Among men and boys singing was considered to be

'sissy,' and if little girls did sing they were looked on with scorn by their brothers. . . . Also, children who never hear a grownup sing do not sing by nature. These children had little knowledge of music or reading, and so rather suddenly evolved from infants to knowledgeable and practical farm hands, scorning anything imaginative."

38. Pierre LeClerc joined his brother and eldest son, Art, in Peace River in the spring of 1921. His wife, Alexina, and family joined him in the summer. The older daughters, Marie and Yvonne, were already married. The girl referred to here was Alice, and the other two brothers were Alphonse and Bert.

39. James Travis was the district agriculturist at Pouce Coupé in 1929. He was considered a better-than-average authority on cereal grains and forage crops, especially in relation to growing them in the heavy clay and grey-wooded soils of the area.

40. According to local history a small band of Indians, led by their chief Muckithay, was camping in the area bordered by Fort St. John on the south, North Pine and Rose Prairie to the east, and the Blueberry River to the north, when the first settlers arrived. Realizing the land bore Muckithay's name but being unable to pronounce it, the newcomers gradually shortened it to Montney (Ventress, Davies, and Kyllo, *Peacemakers*, p. 248). Elsewhere this chief is called "Montegue," and R.D. Symons believed Montney came from "Montagnais." In Davies and Ventress, *Fort St. John Pioneer Profiles*, p. 9, Mrs. Birley gives the name as Montaigne, Monica uses various phonetic spellings in the diaries, but for the sake of clarity the present usage has been adopted throughout.

41. Jean Bell came to Charlie Lake from the coast in 1929 and boarded with the Somans, mentioned later. In 1931 she married Frank Gross.

42. Son of Mr. and Mrs. Dominic Chiulli. Friends in Italy raised money for Dominic Chiulli to emigrate, and he was in the district for a number of years before his family could join him.

43. One of the sons of Carl and Anna Donis. There were also three daughters. They came in the early 1920's and first lived at Taylor Flat. Later they built a store in Fort St. John. John Donis began freighting on the Nelson Trail at the age of thirteen, a characteristic example of the responsibilities these children undertook.

44. Taylor's Flats, Taylor Flats or simply Taylor, derived its name from Donald Herbert Taylor, who came in the area in 1912.

45. The scout law and the scout promise to obey the law are at the heart of scouting. The boy must promise that he will do his best to do his duty to God and his country and to help other people at all times.

46. Clarke Mackenzie Finch was born near Aylmer, Ontario, came west with his family, and arrived in Fort St. John in 1913. He worked at first for Revillon Frères under Ken Birley and then built his own store. He married Mary Kelly Brooks, who had children from a previous marriage, in 1931.

47. William Simpson, a local homesteader, who acted as lay reader at Monica's services. The Simpsons had three sons, the youngest was named Johnnie and one of the older boys was called Benny.

48. It has so far proved impossible to find out even Mr. Ritchie's first name. He lived at Taylor's Flats, according to Mrs. Cora Ventress, and insisted that the boys take "sun baths"! At the time when Monica was writing, however, he evidently lived between May Birley's home and Fort St. John.

49. A singing game played like "London Bridge."

50. Probably George Cushway, one of the eight children of Samuel and Marie Cushway who came to Baldonnel in 1919.

51. The priest was Rev. Luc Beuglet, O.M.I., who arrived in the Fort St. John area in December 1929, and by 1931 he had established both a church and a hospital.

52. The order of "Black Sisters" refers to the Sisters of Providence, a congregation founded in Kingston, Ontario, in

1861, which was, in turn, a branch of the Sisters of Charity of Providence of Montreal, founded in 1843. The first sisters in Fort St. John in early 1931 were Sisters Agatha, Marie Gilbert, and Catherine de Bologne, joined in September of the same year by Miss Laura Murphy, R.N., later to become Sister Marcellina, and by Sisters Alfred of the Cross and Gerard Majella. See Ventress, Davies, and Kyllo, *Peacemakers*, p.400, for more information.

53. Ellesmere, in Shropshire, England, was the family home of Monica's mother, Lucy Anna Maria Cust. Mrs. Storrs' sister continued to live in Ellesmere, on the estate of their cousin, the third Earl Brownlow. When he died without issue, the earldom became extinct, but Monica's uncle, Adelbert S.C. Cust, became the fifth Baron Brownlow. Obviously, Monica's relations in the Ellesmere area took a keen interest in her work.

54. The Girls' Friendly Society was founded in 1875 with its stated objectives: "To band together in one Society, ladies as Associates and girls and young women as Members, for mutual help (religious and secular), for sympathy and prayer. To encourage purity of life, dutifulness to parents, faithfulness to employers, temperance, and thrift."

55. Sir James Hopwood Jeans, *The Universe around Us* (Cambridge: University Press, 1930). Mostly scientific, the book concludes with some comments on the relationship of science and faith. In a review in the *Edmonton Journal*, 28 May 1931, his conclusion that "the universe begins to look more like a great thought than a great machine" is quoted.

56. This trustee, variously described as a Swede and a Dane by Monica, was R.H.A. Neilson, who came to Fort St. John in 1919. He later moved to Taylor's Flats where he had a store and continued to work as telegraph agent and linesman. His daughters Joyce and Violet were among Monica's guides (see Ventress, Davies, and Kyllo, *Peacemakers*, pp. 36ff).

57. To be "M.D." at cards was to be mentally deficient in Monica's terms.

58. In Dumb Crambo one team chooses a word to be guessed and gives a rhyming word to the other team; the latter then pantomimes its guess as to the original word.

59. Alice LeClerc later married Len Byrnes and went to live at Grande Prairie.

60. Monica Hardcastle, daughter of Archdeacon Edward Hoare Hardcastle of Canterbury, was a good friend of Monica's and frequently sent her parcels and supplies.

61. Mr. and Mrs. E.J. Paling lived east of Baldonnel on the lower bench of the Peace River. Eventually they moved into Fort St. John.

62. Sandy Taylor writes of his mother: "Charlotte Taylor was very friendly but exceedingly shy. She would entertain . . . her own [children] by the hour as she had learned English and some French at the Mission School near Peace River. Except for her story telling and conversation with the children she much preferred her native Cree. Hence, although she handled the Post Office work most competently when alone, she invariably left Herbie and the children to attend to the customers" (Ventress, Davies, and Kyllo, *Peacemakers*, p. 38). The Taylors had eight children: Harriet, Dave, Charlie, Mabel, Maggie, Sandford, Walter, and Joan.

63. Mr. and Mrs. Leo Pickell operated the telegraph office. They had three sons, Bill, Cecil, who is mentioned later in the diaries, and Owen. Mr. Pickell was also the postmaster and government agent, and it was his stable where Monica left Rama on Saturday nights.

64. Church of England was the religion of 14.9 per cent of the population of the Peace River in 1931. Other denominations were: Roman Catholic, 22.9 per cent; United Church, 25.3; Presbyterian, 9.8; and Lutheran, 15.5 (Dawson and Murchie, *Settlement of the Peace River Country*, p. 193).

65. J.M. Barrie, *The Old Lady Shows Her Medals* (London: Hodder and Stoughton, [1923]).

66. The ethnic origin of the settlers in the Peace River in 1931 was: British, 50.2

per cent; Scandinavian, 12.2; North and West European, 16.29; Central and Southeastern European, 13.9; Others, 6.7. Of the farm operators, 23 per cent came from the United States (Dawson and Murchie, *Settlement of the Peace River Country*, pp. 66–69.

67. These three women have not been identified, but they evidently aroused interest throughout the district. Mary Percy Jackson, a pioneer doctor in the eastern part of the Block, met the "three mad Englishwomen" on skis in December 1929 (*On the Last Frontier: Pioneering in the Peace River Block* [London: Sheldon Press; Toronto: General Board of Religious Education, 1933], p. 61).

68. The Red Cross commissioner for the province of British Columbia was Mr. J.S. Corry Wood.

69. Evelyn Gedge, mentioned in the introduction, was a daughter of Canon Edward L. Gedge. She took great interest in Monica's work and contributed both time and money to have the diaries distributed as widely as possible.

70. The English nurse was Angharad Meiron Roberts, usually called "Anne." She held a medical, surgical, and C.M.B. certificate, and Miss Eva Hasell, who "produced" her, also helped pay her expenses. Thor Thorsen, the storekeeper at Grandhaven, gave his log house for the outpost. In 1931 Miss Roberts married James Young, but she continued to nurse and delivered many of the area's residents. She died in 1973. For further information, see Ventress, Davies, and Kyllo, *Peacemakers*, pp. 293ff; Hasell, *Canyons, Cans and Caravans*, p. 291.

71. *Mary Rose*, a play written by Sir James Matthew Barrie in 1920 (London: Hodder and Stoughton, 1924).

72. Clumps is a team game in which two players from opposing teams agree upon an object and then join the opposite group, which tries to guess the object by asking questions which are answered "yes," "no," and "I don't know."

73. J.M. Barrie, *A Kiss for Cinderella* (London: Hodder and Stoughton, 1920).

74. Miss H. is possibly the head Fort St. John teacher at the time, Miss House, and Mr. H. may be Alwin Holland.

75. The boys referred to here are probably Donald and Leslie Hunter.

76. Mr. and Mrs. Charles Ohland. Their sons were Roy, Harvey, and Bob.

77. Even before coming to Canada Monica was active in the Bishop's Messengers, a name used by groups of women in England who had taken part in the Mission of Repentance and Hope during World War I and after. Miss Fowler used the name for her missionary workers in Manitoba, and it was also applied to Monica and her helpers by Bishop Rix. The Messenger Cross refers to the symbol of this organization.

78. Mr. and Mrs. Robert Ogilvie originally homesteaded across the river from the old fort where he had come in 1913. Later they homesteaded in what became the southeast portion of Fort St. John. They had one son, Jim, and three daughters, Kathleen, Eunice, and Margaret. Mr. Ogilvie became the first magistrate.

79. Possibly the store built by a man named Spanner and later purchased and run by George Arnott (Ventress, Davies, and Kyllo, *Peacemakers*, p. 215).

80. A game like jackstraws or modern "pick-up sticks," where the player tries to remove sticks from a pile one at a time without disturbing the others.

81. William B. Hole prepared *The Holy Bible with Coloured Illustrations*, which was published in London in 1927 by Eyre and Spottiswoode.

82. Eileen is the daughter of Mary Kelly Brooks Finch, the Fort St. John storekeeper. After Clarke Finch's death, Eileen and her mother moved to California.

83. Children of Gilbert and Sarah Millar Howes (see Ventress, Davies, and Kyllo, *Peacemakers*, pp. 168–69).

84. Although the origins of the name "Charlie Lake" are obscure, it appears that it was named after an Indian chief. It is situated north of the junction of the Moberly and Peace rivers, and there is now a provincial campground there.

85. Joseph and Mabel Soman came to Peace River from Wisconsin at the urging of her brother Walter "Red" Powell in 1924. In 1927 Soman advertised his store as "a First-Class Restaurant and Stopping Place, with plenty to eat for man and beast" (Ventress, Davies, and Kyllo, *Peacemakers*, p. 138).

86. The Timothy Eaton Company is a reputable Canada-wide department store chain, formerly a mail-order house as well, and the expression refers to the mail-order aspects of the firm rather than to any inferences of cheapness or inferiority.

87. One of St. Catherine of Alexandria's torments during her martyrdom was being placed on a wheel which was intended to tear her apart.

88. Genesis 32:31.

89. Mabel Causton, although approximately ten years older than Monica, was one of her dearest friends. It was she who compiled the diaries as they presently exist, who helped collect funds for the Peace River work, and who supported Monica in every way she possibly could.

90. B.H. Streeter, ed., *Adventure: The Faith of Science and the Science of Faith* (London: Macmillan, 1927). "Reality" refers to an earlier book by Streeter, *Reality: A New Correlation of Science and Religion* (London, Macmillan, 1926). The other book mentioned is T.R. Glover, *The Jesus of History*, first published in 1917 and based on lectures given in India, 1915-16. It was reprinted by Hodder and Stoughton, London, in 1965.

91. There were six Alexander brothers who came first to Taylor Flat and then moved to Peace View, Jim, Sam, Bert, Bob, Will, and Ed. They were the sons of Lancelot (Lant) and Margaret Jane Hudson Alexander, originally from Exeter and Kincardine, Ontario. At one time the Peace View School had thirty-five pupils, with thirty of them Alexanders, so Monica's problems became obvious. Only one sister, Irene, came with them. She was married to Jim Pratt. There were thirty-eight children all together, all but three being Alexanders.

92. This may be the family of Harry and Laura Large who had three children when they arrived in the District in 1928. According to Ventress, Davies, and Kyllo, *Peacemakers*, pp. 276-77, however, they had moved to Fish Creek by this time.

93. Lucina (Lucy) was the daughter of John and Christina Lohman, who came from Illinois in 1929 and settled two miles from the centre of Fort St. John. Christina died of cancer in 1931. The other four children were Irene, Lawrence, Sylvia, and Mary Ann.

94. Probably Ernest McKnight.

95. Grande Prairie was still somewhat smaller than Monica indicates; its population in 1931 was 1,464 (Dawson and Murchie, *Settlement of the Peace River Country*, p. 51). The weekly newspaper referred to below was the *Herald*.

96. Canon William Charles John James returned to England in 1932.

97. Canon Thomas David Proctor, L.Th., was rural dean and superintendent of the Peace River District, 1929-43. The Colonial and Continental Society was the result of the union in 1851 of the Colonial Church Society and the Church of England Society for Newfoundland and the Colonies. Until 1861 its name was the Colonial Church and School Society. Its object was "to send Clergyman, Catechists, and Schoolmasters to the Colonies of Great Britain, and to British Residents in other parts of the world."

98. The schoolmaster in Pouce Coupé in 1929-30 was Mr. M.C. Simmons, according to the records of the British Columbia Department of Education and that is the name Monica later gives. "McC", therefore, is probably a typographical error.

99. *Chétif* is a French word meaning a "puny, stunted shrub." The English variant "chaitif" or more commonly "caitiff" means "of little value, wretched, sorry, miserable." Monica obviously did not like the little poplars!

100. Margaret Beaton Mikkleson was the daughter of Frank Beaton and a sister to Mrs. Ken Birley. Her husband was

Carl Mikkleson.

101. Although Dr. O'Brien practised medicine in Grande Prairie, Alberta, he attended the banquet marking the opening of the new Providence Hospital in Fort St. John in 1931. The following day he was called upon to perform emergency surgery, the first in the hospital.

102. The priest was Rev. Geoffrey Guiton, one of the founders of the Fellowship of the West. He was ordained to the priesthood in 1929 and in 1932 went to Lahore, India, as a missionary. The student, Dick, worked as his helper, according to the policy of the Fellowship of the West, as explained in the introduction.

103. The boy scouts hold a world jamboree approximately every four years, where thousands of scouts gather from countries all over the world. However, the term "jamboree" is sometimes also used to denote national or intersectional gatherings of boy scouts.

104. "In July 1927 a Measure was passed in the (Anglican) Church Assembly for the purpose of authorizing the use of a Prayer Book which had been deposited with the Clerk of the Parliaments, and was referred to in the Measure as 'The Deposited Book.'" The House of Commons, however, in 1928 defeated the resolution directing that this measure be presented for the royal signature, and the Deposited Book remained unauthorized (see *The Book of Common Prayer with the Additions and Deviations Proposed in 1928* [Oxford: The University Press, 1928], V).

105. Helen Price came from a well-known and wealthy Quebec family. In assigning her to Miss Hasell's van mission, Iris Sayle wrote, "her great great grandfather was sent over to Quebec by the Admiralty in the Napoleonic Wars to buy masts for the battle ships. . . . Her Mother's brother is Sir John Gilmour."

106. Jean-Baptiste-Marie Vianne (1786-1859), canonized in 1925, was known as the Curé d'Ars.

107. "The Bishop" was the Right Rev. George Alexander Rix (1865-1945). He was consecrated bishop in 1928, and although resident in Prince Rupert, which was then a long and tedious travelling distance from Fort St. John, he was very encouraging to Monica and gladly gave her the recognition necessary to continue her work.

108. R.D. Symons notes: "East Fort St. John, a school and post office, was then on the 'main road' from Dawson Creek to Fort St. John. Later it was renamed Baldonnel and it was here that a church hall, which could be used for services or community meetings, was built in memory of [Monica's] father."

109. The Bishop of Montreal was the Right Rev. John Cragg Farthing, consecrated bishop of Montreal in 1909. The dean is Dean Arthur Carlisle, dean of Montreal and rector of Christ Church Cathedral, Montreal, Quebec, 1922-39. He was consecrated bishop of Montreal in 1939.

110. The body of Mike Monasterski (or Ministyrski) was found under a manure pile a long while after his disappearance. His son, Nick, was charged with the murder on 7 June 1929, the crime being alleged to have taken place at Kleskun Hill 16 May 1928. He was acquitted by a jury of six on 14 June 1930 after a trial which lasted from 11 to 13 June 1930 and during which over forty witnesses were called (*Edmonton Journal,* 16 June 1930; and Office of the Clerk of the Court and Sheriff, Attorney General of Alberta).

111. The sister is, of course, Nina Birley, mentioned in the introduction.

112. Rev. Reuben Kenneth Naylor was one of the founders and original team members of the Fellowship of the West. He was priested in 1913 and became a professor in the Montreal Diocesan Theological College in 1925. Later he served as canon of Christ Church Cathedral, Montreal, as lecturer in divinity at McGill University, and as archdeacon of Montreal.

113. The name used in the diary is "Snoden," but this seems to be an error. The name "Sowden" occurs in the district, however, and it seems probable that Monica was referring to

this family. Among the children were Ruth, Alan, Roy, Dorothy, and Wilfred.

114. Frank W. Beaton, born in the Orkney Islands, served the Hudson's Bay Company from 1883 until his retirement in 1925. He married Emma Shaw, whose father was a Hudson's Bay factor and whose mother was a Cree, and twelve children were born to them, not eleven as Monica indicates. One of the two daughters was Mary, Kenneth Birley's wife. For further information see Ventress, *Peacemakers*, pp. 13, 75, and Gordon F. Bowes, *Peace River Chronicles* (Vancouver: Prescott Publishing Co., 1963), p. 357ff. Several volumes of Mr. Beaton's handwritten day-books are in the B.C. provincial archives in Victoria, British Columbia. He is referred to as the *last* factor in Davies and Ventress, *Fort St. John Pioneer Profiles*, p. 8.

115. R.D. Symons writes, "When Bishop Rix of Caledonia went to the Lambeth Conference in England . . . he found that Rochester friends of John Storrs had suggested a Church Hall be built . . . in his memory . . . As a result a meeting was held at Knights' Place, Rochester (a private home) and a subscription was started."

116. Mr. F. may be Fred Fraser who held the office of government agent at Pouce Coupé for many years. (John M. Imrie, *Peace River in the Making* [Edmonton *Journal*, 1930]).

117. The Canadian general election of 1930, in which the government of W.L. Mackenzie King was defeated by the Conservative party under R.B. Bennett.

118. John Masefield, *Captain Margaret* (London: G. Richards, 1908) is indeed highly romantic in style, hardly to Monica's taste.

119. Giovanni Papini's, *Storia di Cristo* (Firenze: Vallecchi, [1922, c. 1921]) was translated by Dorothy Canfield Fisher (New York: Harcourt Brace, [1923]). The Bampton Lectures for 1920 were given by the Rev. Arthur Cayley Headlam, bishop of Gloucester, and published under the title *The Doctrine of the Church and*

Christian Reunion (London: J. Murray, 1920).

120. Among the families referred to here are the Ohlands, the Hadlands, and the Spences; the C's could be the Colpitts or the Cushways, and the M's may be either the McDonalds or the Mattsons. All of these families had children in the Baldonnel school and most in the scouts.

121. A "tweenie" is a domestic servant who assists two others, usually the cook and the housemaid.

122. Monica's brother, Christopher Storrs, then chaplain and sub-warden, St. George College, Perth. In 1946 he became bishop of Grafton, New South Wales. He died in 1977.

123. Reverend Charles E. Rogers (1884-1964) came from Sexsmith, Alberta, near Grande Prairie. He became the United Church minister in Rolla in 1929 and remained until 1934. He was chairman of the Grande Prairie presbytery and visited in the district from time to time, but mainly services were held in various homes by lay readers (*United Church of Canada Yearbooks*).

124. Dr. W.A. Brown, his wife, and five children came to Fort St. John from Toronto in 1930. One pioneer said of him: "He was just the right man for the job at that time—the right mixture of qualities—a friendly man who liked the North and didn't feel isolated here" (Ventress, Davies, and Kyllo, *Peacemakers*, p.192). He later became Indian agent.

125. Tommy Flatt was always known as "Captain Flatt" in the district. He had served with the British regulars in Egypt. His wife Margo was from Northampton. Their house was regarded as a "Halfway House" between Fort St. John and Hudson's Hope. Their son Tony came to live with Monica and her companions in 1932 in order to attend high school in Fort St. John.

126. George Freer came to the Peace River country in 1914, followed by his wife Edith and four children in 1915. The family had previously lived in Missouri and North Dakota, and according to Lukin Johnston they had homesteaded at Fort George as early

as 1909 (*Beyond the Rockies* [Toronto: Dent, 1929], p. 195). Three more children were born after they arrived. They lived in a tent for the first summer and winter, but they had become well established by the time Monica met them.

127. This is the Canadian name of the shrub or small tree *Amelanchier canadensis*. Its fruit is also called Juneberry, shadberry, and service berry.

128. John and Emily Augusta Robinson from Kent County, Ontario, followed their son Allan into the Peace River in 1921. Both John and Allan, as well as the younger son, Eden, were said to be "very ingenious and inventive."

129. In 1919 Philip F. Tompkins, from Brockville, Ontario, and his English wife, Emily, came to a homesite selected by his brother, Stuart Ramsay Tompkins, the preceding year. They planned a partnership, but after serving in Siberia with the Canadian Expeditionary Force, teaching in Lethbridge, and acting as superintendent of schools in the Yukon, Stuart Tompkins became a distinguished Russian historian in the United States. Philip and his wife had seven children, and many stories relating to them are to be found in *Peacemakers*. According to Bowes, *Peace River Chronicles*, p. 411, Tompkins imported a married hired man from the Old Country, possibly the G's, in order to have enough children for a school. Since the twins were only three, the other children living with them probably made up the required number.

130. John [Jack] Ardill married his wife Betty in Holland after World War I. They came up the Peace River on the sternwheeler *The Pine Pass of Winnipeg*, on which Betty Ardill shared a cabin with May Birley. Their story is told in some detail in Ventress, Davies, and Kyllo, *Peacemakers*, pp. 75ff. Their four children were John, Betty, Dick, and Tommy.

131. This couple may be Barnett and Sadie Dopp. They had come to Bear Flat in 1917, and he earned his living in the summer by haying and clearing land (see ibid., p. 54).

132. John and Bertha MacDougall. Jack MacDougall was a fur trader who became Hudson's Bay factor at Hudson's Hope in 1915 and later farmed at Lynx Creek. The five sons were Wilfred, Gilbert, Jack, Donald, and Colin; the daughters, Bessie and Jean.

133. Jimmy R. is probably Jim Ruxton, who stayed in the area until 1934, "trapping, surveying, writing articles on the area and its people for the magazine section of the Vancouver Province and northern stories for an English magazine" (Ventress, Davies, and Kyllo, *Peacemakers*, p. H41). Ruxton had been a member of the P.G.E. survey and his articles combine geographical description with vague optimism about the region. His six articles in 1930 (16 February, 9 March, 23 March, 24 May, 25 June, and 28 December), for instance, cover the areas of Crooked River, Finlay River, the Pine Pass, the "Upper Peace," the Peace River canyon, and Hudson Hope.

134. Mrs. R. is probably Mrs. Myrtle Robison, who arrived in 1921 to join her trapper husband Guy. She had remained in the United States to raise her five daughters. One of them, Iva Blair, came with her children, June, Dick, and Ruth, to live with them at the "Gates."

135. The hotel was built by Bob Ferguson and stood until it was destroyed by fire in 1957. The C.P.R. and C.N.R. had jointly purchased the railways that were to make up the Northern Alberta Railways in 1929, and their surveyors as well as those for the P.G.E. and those despatched by the dominion government early in 1930 to survey land being taken up by squatters were frequently encountered (F.H. Kitto, *The Peace River Country* [Ottawa, 1930], pp. 61, 99; and Ventress, Davies, and Kyllo, *Peacemakers*, p. H65).

136. This was the family of Elizabeth and Jim Beattie, who came to 20-Mile (later known as Gold Bar) in 1919. Their children were Louise, Mary, Clarisse, Bob, Olive, Ruth, Jim, and Bill (Ventress, Davies, and Kyllo, *Peacemakers*, pp. H42ff.; see also Johnston, *Beyond the Rockies*, p. 180). In later years Monica and her

friends were to visit with them.

137. The stopping place was run by Mr. and Mrs. James McKnight. He advertised it as "Taylor's Landing Hostelry—Accommodation for Man and Beast at all hours and at all seasons" (Ventress, Davies, and Kyllo, *Peacemakers*, p. 47). They had come to Taylor Flat with their son Ernest in 1920, and Mr. McKnight was well known as a builder. May Birley's was one of the homes he built.

138. Mr. and Mrs. Ross Darnall had arrived at what is known as Fish Creek in 1928. Ross Darnall hauled groceries from Hythe to Fort St. John. Among the neighbouring children who attended Sunday schools arranged by Monica Storrs were members of the Reid, Large, Middleton, and Boyko families, and they are probably referred to here.

139. Mr. and Mrs. William Lea and their children Jimmy and Muriel arrived in the area known as Pineview in April 1929. Muriel was blinded when her eyes were pierced by scissors.

140. Anton and Lillian Framst came to the area in 1930. At the time Monica met them they were living in the cabin of Harry Downey, and Anton Framst—who was a Swede, not a Dane—was building their homestead at Cecil Lake. Mr. Framst was later killed by a falling tree, and Mrs. Framst was for a time the teacher at Cecil Lake. The children were Muriel, Audrey, Doreen, and Elli. For further information, see Ventress, Davies, and Kyllo, *Peacemakers*, pp. 381–83.

141. The little boy was named Vincent; the father, George ("Shorty") Long.

142. Holdup, now known as Murdale and forming part of the Montney district, during Monica's time consisted of a post office and several trading posts. One of the traders was robbed at gunpoint, hence the name "Holdup." Monica hyphenates the name, and although this is not common usage, it has been left that way in this publication.

143. Probably Mrs. Dorothy MacDougall, who taught at the new Montney school in 1930 and at Transpine in 1931. Later she became Mrs. Joe Hatt.

144. This area is better known as the North Pine district, covering the valley of Indian Creek and the slope down to the Beatton or North Pine River.

145. Mrs. J. is likely Mrs. Belle Jarvis, whose two-bedroom home was large enough for her to host teas and Christmas concerts. She came to the Peace River district in 1930, and the first school teacher, Amy Stewart, boarded with her that year.

146. Probably the farm of Mr. Stinson, the local veterinary surgeon.

147. Monica probably refers to the teacher in the first Holdup School, Thelma Paynter. It is likely that she stayed with the Erwin Tuckers.

148. M. Slyman and F. Nassar started a store *cum* trading-post in Murdale in 1929.

149. Mrs. Rodgers (Rogers) came to the Peace River country in 1930. The hired man, whom she later married, was Bill Mann.

150. Absalom's story is told in 2 Samuel. The comparison here may be to the manner of his death!

151. Bishop George A. Rix, already referred to in the diary.

152. The boy was Bertrum ("Buddy") Thompson. See Ventress, Davies, and Kyllo, *Peacemakers*, p. 283.

153. Mrs. Harmer was, of course, wife of Bishop John R. Harmer of Rochester and Adeline's mother.

154. Joseph and Annie Babchuck were murdered at their cabin on the southern end of Cecil Lake in mid-August 1930. Their bodies were found by Constable Devlin on 3 September. Babchuck was considered to be wealthy because of the amount of possessions he brought with him and because he hired men to clear his land. Michael Sowry of Hythe, among whose belongings were found the rifle used in the crime and articles of Babchuck's clothing, was convicted at Prince George and executed at New Westminster 14 August 1931 (*Prince George Citizen*, 14 May and 16 August 1931).

155. George Hedley Wolfendale attended Montreal Diocesan Theological College and was ordained deacon before going to the Peace River country in 1931. In August of that same year he was priested by Bishop

George Rix of Caledonia and became the first rector of St. Martin-in-the-Fields, Fort St. John. He served in the Peace River until 1935 when he and his wife returned to Quebec. When war was declared, he enlisted as a stretcher-bearer but was subsequently appointed chaplain. In 1944 he was awarded the O.B.E. He died of wounds on 11 June 1944 while a prisoner of war.

156. The Premonstratensians, called White Canons in England, are a Roman Catholic order of canons regular, following the Rule of St. Augustine. Founded in 1120 by St. Norbert at Prémontré in Aisne, a site shown to him in a vision, they were noted for their secluded and austere lives.

157. Karl Anderson arrived in the Peace River country in 1928, driving a 1917 Buick touring car. He homesteaded in the Baldonnel area but never married, and upon retirement he returned to his native Sweden.

158. Daniel 2:31-45.

159. Walter ("Red") Powell, his wife Evelyn, and their three children arrived in the area on the old steamer, the *D.A. Thomas*, in 1921. Six more children were born between 1922 and 1933. Powell started the first shingle mill at Charlie Lake in 1924 and added a lumber mill in 1927. For further information, see Ventress, Davies, and Kyllo, *Peacemakers*, p. 142ff; Vera Kelsey, *British Columbia Rides a Star* (Toronto: Dent, 1958), pp. 91-94.

160. Mrs. Emily L. Crawford was a unique pioneer. She raised polled Hereford cattle on her "XY" Farm and acquired a buffalo cow from the federal government for experimental cross-breeding purposes. She loved horses and rode her own horse, Congo, everywhere. Not surprisingly, she habitually wore a riding habit—a strange sight in pioneer country.

161. Madge Jones, wife of Charlie Jones. They lived at Carbon River, twelve miles from the Beattie family. He had arrived in the area in 1910 and settled at Carbon River in 1911 to trap, prospect, and fish (Ventress, Davies, and Kyllo, *Peacemakers*, pp. H12, 36).

He brought his wife out in 1919, and they remained in the area until 1935 when they moved to Victoria. Monica visited them in 1932 after Mrs. Jones's year-long visit to England and was impressed by the number of books in their home. In fact, they started the "Gold Bar Library," later moved to the Beatties, with discarded books from the Vancouver Public Libraries (ibid., p. H36). For further information, see Johnston, *Beyond the Rockies*, pp. 178-80.

162. Nurse Roberts had by this time married Jim Young of Rose Prairie. He had been that area's first settler in 1928 and was postmaster and mail carrier there for many years.

163. The incident is reported in the *Edmonton Journal*, 26 May 1931, and the *Prince George Citizen*, 4 June 1931. Constable A.J. Pomeroy, who was wounded in the chase, had a warrant for the arrest of Charles Watt (alias R.F. Stewart) on a charge of issuing false cheques. There is no indication that the man was apprehended, and there is no mention of the girl.

164. Alwin Holland came originally from Ontario. He opened a number of schools in the district, and he was also a qualified surveyor. After doing pioneer missionary work for the Presbyterian church, he later taught Sunday school and served as an elder in the Burch Presbyterian Church.

165. Thor Thorsen came to the North Peace in the early 1920's from Grandhaven, North Dakota. His original house became the Red Cross Outpost hospital. In advertising his Mountain View Trading Company, he stated that he outfitted "Trappers, Tramps and Homesteaders" (Ventress, Davies, and Kyllo, *Peacemakers*, p. 112).

166. This was Mark's Cafe, operated for many years by Mark Wah.

167. An early example of the "Bennett buggy" of the depression years.

168. Otto Hoffstrom was a sawmill operator who experienced great personal tragedy when the car in which he and his daughters were returning from a stampede in Dawson Creek slipped into the river after crossing on

the ferry. The children, Lily, Florence, Olga, and Agnes, all Sunday school students of Monica Storrs, were drowned. A church in their memory was erected at Taylor's Flat.

169. The car here inexplicably changes gender, from "Elijah" and "he" to "Eliza" and "she."

170. The Church Army was established in 1882 and was intended as an evangelistic arm of the Church of England. Church Army evangelists were to be drawn from working men and women and had many kinds of social work missions among workers.

171. Judges 7:8.

172. William Colpitts came to the district in 1919. He married a neighbour, Annie Cushway, and they had four children, Ken, Marjorie, Louise, and Charles.

173. Probably Henry and Harriet McLeod. He was a well-known freighter and for a time had the Hudson's Bay Company contract (Ventress, Davies, and Kyllo, *Peacemakers*, p. 91).

174. A charabanc is a bus, especially one with open sides, used on sightseeing tours or pleasure trips.

175. By Giovanni da Fiesole (1387-1455) called Fra Angelico. The painting referred to is probably *Christ as Pilgrim Received by Two Dominicans*, a fresco in the cloister, San Marco, Florence.

176. Cecilia Goodenough, the daughter of Admiral Sir William and Lady Goodenough, distinguished supporters of Monica's work. Monica wrote of her: "Cecilia Goodenough, who came out to us in August, 1931, was a very brilliant student from Oxford, a fine art needle-worker, a good cook and horsewoman, a tremendously keen Christian, and most loyal companion. She loved this country."

177. Genesis 13-18.

178. Petronella, Monica's young sister, who married Dr. Frewin Moor. She died in 1978.

179. Hans Memling (1430?-95), Flemish painter. The original of the Floreins triptych with the *Adoration of the Magi* is in Bruges. Two of Fra Angelico's paintings of the Crucifixion, both done in the early 1440's,

hang in the convent of San Marco in Florence.

180. Crayford, near London but in the diocese of Rochester. It is possible, according to Mrs. Petronella Moor, that the red dorsal and curtains mentioned in the diary were sent by the girls of the Crayford G.D.A., who knew Monica from her work among them before she went to Canada.

181. Lady Darnley was the wife of Ivo Francis Walter, the 8th Earl of Darnley, a cousin of Monica's mother. Lady Darnley, an Australian by birth, was a close friend of Mrs. Storrs.

182. The Danish sculptor Bertel Thorvaldsen (1768-1849) was regarded as a leader of the classical school. The marble statue is in the Cathedral of Our Lady, Copenhagen, and a bronze in L'Eglise de la Paix, Potsdam.

183. Eaton Square refers to St. Peter's Church, Eaton Square, London, where Monica's father was vicar before going to Rochester.

184. One of the Rider (or Ryder) daughters, Rose, married a Baldonnel schoolmate, George Cushway, in the first wedding to be conducted in the hall (Ventress, Davies, and Kyllo, *Peacemakers*, p. 216.)).

185. The Victoria League, now known as the Victoria League for Commonwealth Friendship, was organized in 1901 to promote closer union between different parts of the British Empire (now Commonwealth).

186. The hospital was in fact opened by Monsignor J. Guy from Grouard, and the opening was attended by Dr. Watson from Pouce Coupé and Dr. O'Brien from Grande Prairie (Ventress, Davies, and Kyllo, *Peacemakers*, p. 401).

187. Braeside was a school just opened in 1931 with Miss E.M. Smedley as teacher.

188. Presumably Filippo Lippi, known as Filippino (1457?-1504), son of Fra Filippo Lippi. His *Angel Adoring* was painted c. 1485 and hangs in the National Gallery, London.

189. Probably Mrs. Harry Davis, an early settler at the area now called Sunrise-Two Rivers.

190. Eli Stanley Jones, *The Christ of Every Road: A Study in Pentecost* (New

York: Abingdon Press, 1930).

191. Probably Mrs. Marion Fell, wife of Fletcher Fell. Amongst their children were Bob, Vera, Don, Stan, Harold, and Millie. Vera was the first child born in the Red Cross Outpost.

192. Jack and Peggy Kirkpatrick came to the Baldonnel area in 1928. Their children were Neil, Kenneth, and Molly.

193. Mrs. Cesare Copes. Her husband had come to the Cecil Lake district in 1928 and did custom threshing. He also picked out the road on the hill above the Beatton River (Ventress, Davies, and Kyllo, *Peacemakers*, p. 366, 377).

194. Mr. and Mrs. Russell Budd homesteaded in the far west of the Cecil Lake district on the Beatton River. Their son, Stanley, was the first child born in the area (ibid., p. 382). Victor and Lena Kostick with their son Lloyd came to the Peace River in 1931 from Saskatchewan, not the States, forced to move by the Depression. They arrived with thirty-three horses, wagons, their household goods, and thirty-five cents (ibid., pp. 371-72). Later Vic trapped and the family moved into Fort St. John.

195. The George Kemp family. They had arrived from Humboldt, Saskatchewan, in 1929. The friend who came with them was Herman Mair, and their son was Stanley Kemp. The Kemps frequently played at the schoolhouse dances. For further information, see ibid., p. 363ff.

196. Albert and Elizabeth Spence came to Cecil Lake with their seven children from the area south of Edmonton in 1930. The four oldest girls, who attended school at Baldonnel for a time, were Jean, Marjorie, Marion, and Lorna, and the three younger children were Albert, Sheila, and Gordon. Pat, Dennis, and Lucy were born in the Peace. During that first rainy summer, which Monica described earlier, all nine of them lived with the Kemps.

197. George and Lila Maginnis came to Cecil Lake with their daughter Dorothy from Saskatchewan in 1930. A friend, Rudy Weiberg was with them (Ventress, Davies, and Kyllo, *Peacemakers*, pp. 353, 365).

198. The difficulty of identifying people from Monica's references to them is evident here. It is possible that the first family referred to is that of Dewey and J.B. Simmons. Their younger daughter's name was Lois; and the elder was Alice. However, there were two younger children, both boys (ibid., pp. 366-67). The Nova Scotians might be Mr. and Mrs. Ralph Hiltz (ibid., p. 368). It is impossible to identify the "Russian" families among the many eastern and central European names in the district.

199. Miss Elinor Claxton took charge of the Red Cross outpost at Grandhaven, about two miles west of Fort St. John, when Miss Roberts married Jim Young and moved to Rose Prairie. In 1935 Miss Claxton became head of the Gough Memorial Red Cross Hospital with which Monica was connected. She died in 1937.

200. The imperative form of the "high" Norwegian, which is essentially Danish, would be "Kom til Mig." The form given, "Kommer til Mig," is much softer, according to Professor H. Bessason of the University of Manitoba.

201. Mr. and Mrs. Everett Shortt homesteaded on Taylor's Flats in 1929.

202. There were a number of Bells in the district, among them Ralph, John D., and Pat, but this reference is probably to Mr. and Mrs. Alexander Bell who came to the Montney in 1929. Their children were Mildred, Ada, Douglas, Jean, and Jack.

203. The Harry Waites arrived in the Montney in 1930. Their seven children were Jim, Harold, Clifford, Ralph, Joyce, Connie, and Mary. According to Davies and Ventress, *Fort St. John Pioneer Profiles*, the name was originally spelt Wait.

Index

Alaska Highway, xxiii
Alberta, xx, xxii
Alexander, Jim, 90, 193f.
Ambrose, Harry, 166
Anderson, Cecil, 133
Anderson, Karl, 186, 188, 201, 211, 216, 221-24, 232, 234f., 240
Anderson, Mabel, 24f., 40f., 45, 73, 97, 136, 186
Ardill, John, 157
Athabaska, diocese of (Anglican), xx, xxviii
Aulneau, Fr. Jean Pierre, xix

Babchuck, Joseph, 179-80
Barrie, Sir James Matthew, 59, 66, 68
Beaton, Frank W., xli, 138-40
Beaton, Mrs. Frank W., 138-40, 225
Beaton, Freddy, 138-40, 165
Beattie, Jim, 160
Beaver Indians, xvii, xix, xxi
Beggs, Earl, 253, 256, 268
Bell, Alexander, 274
Bell, Jean, 21, 25, 50, 84, 86
Bernard, Barbara H., 163
Besanzon, A.M., xxiii
Beuglet, Rev. Luc, 33
Birley, Douglas, 34f., 37, 69, 70, 76, 81, 83, 87, 108, 116
Birley, Frank, 34-35, 96
Birley, Harold, 34-35, 88
Birley, Kenneth, xli, 11, 13f., 16, 19f., 22f.,

27, 30f., 35f., 40f., 47, 49, 57, 74f., 81, 87, 89, 93, 96, 98, 105, 108, 117, 132-35, 138, 141, 143, 146, 148-52, 162, 180, 184, 193, 199, 201, 211, 229, 248, 251, 253
Birley, Mrs. Kenneth (née Mary Beaton), xli, 57, 131, 134, 138f., 141, 147, 151, 199, 236
Birley, May, xxxi, xli, 10-15, 18, 20-23, 27, 30f., 34, 37, 39-41, 44, 46f., 50-55, 57, 59f., 63-69, 71f., 74, 76, 81, 83, 89, 93, 96-98, 100, 104-9, 114-18, 120-23, 127-35, 137, 140-46, 148, 150-52, 162, 176f., 180-84, 186-89, 194, 201, 203-5, 207, 209, 211, 214, 218, 221, 224, 240, 244, 248, 271
Birley, Nina, xli, 151, 183
Bishop's Messengers, xxvi, xxxvii, xxxix, 73, 206
Bompas, Bp. W. C., xix
Bowyer, Mildred, 242
British Columbia, xixf., xxii
Brooks, Eileen, 77
Brown, Bp. R. F., xxv
Brown, Dr. W. A., 176f., 186, 194f., 200, 208f., 241, 247
Brown, Mrs. W. A., 152
Brownies, 17, 180-82, 185, 190, 198, 200f., 205, 215, 265-67, 281, 284f.
Budd, Mrs. Russell H., 259
Burgett, Archd. Arthur Edward, 7, 75, 94f., 136, 138, 178, 180, 237
Butler, Capt. William F., xxi

Byrnes, Hugh, 95, 203, 215

Cairns, Alma, 275, 277
Cairns, David, 275
Caledonia, diocese of (Anglican), xx, xxviii
Calgary, 7
Canadian Northern Railway, xxii
Canadian Pacific Railway, xx-xxii
Carlisle, Bp. Arthur, xxviii, 124
Causton, Mabel, xii, 88, 284
Cheverton, Harvey, 228, 246f., 249, 256f.,
    271f., 279, 281
Chipewyan Indians, xix, xxi
Chiulli, Dave, 21, 25, 95
Chiulli, Dominic, 84
Chiulli, Mrs. Dominic, 25f., 92f., 212f.
Chiulli, Donella, 213
Chiulli, Steve, 213
Clark, Frank J., 8, 10
Clarke, Charlie, 200f., 206, 212, 217, 227
Claxton, Elinor, 267, 271
Cocks, John Patrick Somers, 7
Colpitts, William, 221, 224, 227, 229, 231
Copes, Cesare, 258-60, 262, 264
Cran, Duncan, xli
Crawford, Emily L., 189-91, 216, 249, 253,
    265
Cree Indians, xvii, xix, xxi
Crook, Ida S., 9
Cushway, George, 32

Darnall, Mrs. Ross, 163
Darnley, Lady, 236
Davis, Mrs. Harry, 250
Dawson, G. M., xxi
Dawson Creek, 125
Devlin, Joseph Clark, 176
Devlin, Mrs. Joseph Clark, 19, 32f., 43, 63,
    67, 70, 79, 86-88, 98f., 104, 152
Donis, John, 21, 88, 95

Earl, Jack, 263
Edmonton, xxiif., xlviii, 178
Edmonton, diocese of (Anglican), xx,
    xxviii
Edmonton, Dunvegan and British
    Columbia Railway. *See* Northern
    Alberta Railway

Faraun, Fr. Henri, xix
Farthing, Bp. John Cragg, xxviii, 124, 136
Fell, Marion, 251f.
Fellowship of the Maple Leaf, xxvii, xliv

Fellowship of the West, xxviif., xli, 113,
    146, 283
Finch, Clarke Mackenzie, 26, 220, 241
Flatt, Tommy, 153f.
Fort Chipewyan, xviiif.
Fort St. John (town), xxiii, xlvii, xlix, llf.
Fort St. John (trading post), xviiif., 132,
    139, 225
Fort Vermilion, xviiif., xxi
Foster, Aubrey, 195, 197, 206
Foster, Clarke, 194f.
Foster, Erving, 54, 77, 92, 194-97, 206, 247,
    271-73, 279, 282
Foster, Herman, 194-97
Fowler, Marguerite, xxvii, 2, 6
Framst, Anton, 280
Framst, Lillian, 166, 258, 262
Freer, Edith, 154f.

Galloway, Capt. J. T. O., xxiii
Gedge, Mrs. Evelyn, xxxvif.
Geological Survey of Canada, xxi
Girls' Diocesan Association, xxvi, xxxix,
    219
Goodenough, Cecelia, lii, 230, 232f., 237-
    40, 242f., 245, 248-50, 252, 254, 256f.,
    261, 265, 267, 269-71, 279f., 282f., 285
Goodenough, Lady, 233, 237, 242
Grand Haven, 192
Grand Trunk Pacific Railway, xxii
Grande Prairie, 101
Greenhithe Girls' Friendly Society, 38
Guides, xif., xxvi, xxxix, 4f., 16, 18, 21, 25,
    45, 49, 55f., 60, 62, 68f., 73, 77, 80-83,
    96f., 106-8, 116, 120f., 126, 130-32,
    134f., 137f., 151, 181-83, 185, 189f.,
    198-201, 205, 207f., 212f., 215f., 218-20,
    226f., 239, 242f., 252, 259, 261, 267,
    277, 280, 283-85
Guiton, Rev. Geoffrey, xxvii, 113-15, 117-
    33, 136, 146f., 181, 189, 200-204, 206f.,
    209f., 212, 214-17, 226f.
Guy, Msgr. J., 248

Hardcastle, Monica, 54
Hargreaves, Tommy, 15, 26, 31f., 35, 40, 50,
    52-55, 57, 60, 67f., 98-100, 109f., 117f.,
    134, 138, 140, 146, 181, 183, 187, 190,
    197, 203, 207f., 217, 224, 226f., 230
Harmer, Adeline, xxv, xxxiiif., xliv, lii,
    123, 178, 180-84, 186-97, 200, 202-40,
    243, 245-49, 253f., 256-67, 270f., 273-
    75, 278-85
Harmer, Bp. John Reginald, xxxiii
Harmer, Mrs. John Reginald, 178, 236

Hart, George, 142
Hasell, Frances Hatton Eva, xxv-xxviii, xl,
    8, 13, 64, 96, 119, 138, 142, 168, 176, 183
Haslam, Muriel, lii, 181, 183f., 186f., 193,
    197, 205f., 210, 212, 218-23, 228-30,
    232f., 236-41, 243, 245f., 248, 254,
    256f., 265, 267, 269-73, 279-81
Hoffstrom, Otto, 200, 210, 237, 242
Holland, Alwin, 190-92
Hooper, Muriel, 1-6
House, Ethel, 96-99, 107
Howes, Roddy, 78f.
Howes, Thelma, 78f.
Hudson Hope, xviii, 160
Hudson's Bay Company, xviif., xxi, xli
Hunter, Donald, 71
Hunter, Leslie, 71
Hythe, 8

James, Can. William Charles John, 102,
    110
Jarvis, Belle, 168
Jones, Eli Stanley, 251
Jones, Madge, 189f.

Kelly, George, 104f.
Kelly, Jim, 225f.
Kelly, Robert, 104f.
Kemp, George, 260-63
Kirkpatrick, Mrs. Jack, 253
Kostick, Victor, 259

Large, Laura, 90f., 101f.
Lea, William, 164
LeClerc, Alexina, 196, 198
LeClerc, Alice, 50, 82, 97
LeClerc, Alphonse, 198
LeClerc, Art, 198
LeClerc, Pierre, 21, 197f.
Lewinski, David (né Arwed), xxxvi, xlii
Littlewood, Hope, 142
Lloyd, Bp. George E., xxvii
Lohman, Christina, 93
Lohman, Lucina, 92
Long, George, 278
Long, Mrs. George, 167f.

McDonald, Harold, 77
McDonald, Helen (daughter), 37, 51, 77,
    235
McDonald, Helen (mother), 18, 36, 116,
    147, 229
McDonald, Jack (father), 36, 147

McDonald, Jack (son), 54, 77, 115, 235
McDonald, William, 235
MacDougall, Dorothy, 168
MacDougall, John, 158f.
Mackenzie, Alexander, xviii
McKnight, Ernest, 94
McLeod, Henry, 225
McLeod's Fort, xviii

Macoun, James, xxiii
Macoun, John, xxi, xxiii
Maginnis, Mrs. George, 262f.
Mann, Mrs. Bill (formerly Rodgers), 173f.,
    275-77
Marquis wheat, xxiv
Masefield, John, 144
Mikkleson, Margaret Beaton, 109f., 165f.,
    189, 258
Monasterski, Mike, 125
Montney District, 21, 167
Moodie, Susanna, xlviii

Naylor, Rev. Reuben Kenneth, xxvii, 136,
    146, 148, 150f.
Neal, G. M., 295
Neilson, Joyce, 207
Neilson, R. H. A., 40, 48, 59, 135
Neilson, Violet, 207f.
North West Company, xviif.
Northern Alberta Railway, xxiif., xlvi

Oblate fathers, xl
Ogilvie, Robert, 73f.
Ohland, Charles, 72, 92, 127
Ohland, Mrs. Charles, 208f., 247

Pacific Great Eastern Railway, xxiii
Paling, E. J., 54, 60, 63, 65, 250f., 281f.
Paling, Mrs. E. J., 64f., 144-48, 151, 162,
    250f.
Papini, Giovanni, 145
Paynter, Thelma, 171
Peace River, xi, xv, xvi, xvii-xxi, xl, xlv-
    xlix
Peace River Block, xxii
Peace River Crossing, xxi
Petter, Sir Ernest, 186
Petter, Letitia, 10, 13, 20, 22-24, 27f., 30f.,
    40f., 46f., 49f., 52-55, 57, 59, 63, 66, 81,
    83, 89, 92, 97, 99, 107, 118, 122, 127,
    130-32, 151, 162, 186, 282
Phillips, Harry, 263
Pickell, Cecil, 88, 95, 123, 126f.

Pickell, Leo, 56, 175, 177, 217
Pickell, Mrs. Leo, 123
Pike, Warburton, xxi
Pine Point Railway, xxiii
Plumptre, Can. Henry Pemberton, 4
Pomeroy, A. J., 190
Popham, Margaret E., 4, 92, 108
Pouce Coupé, xlvii, 8f., 142, 203
Powell, Walter, 188
Price, Helen, 118f., 124-32, 138, 142, 144, 147, 151f., 154-57, 160-65, 169, 172, 175-77, 275
Proctor, Can. Thomas David, 102, 122, 124f., 144f., 180, 239-42, 246, 271, 280

Revillon Frères, xxi, xli
Rix, Bp. George A., xxviii, xli, 102, 119, 175-77, 228-30, 234, 238-42
Roberts, Angharad Meiron (later Mrs. James Young), 64, 96, 118, 121, 146, 190f.
Robertson, Margaret, 2, 4, 5
Robinson, Emily Augusta, 155
Robinson, Bp. Henry, xl
Robison, Myrtle, 159
Rocky Mountain House, xviii
Rodgers, Melville, 276
Rodgers, Myrtle, 276
Rogers, Rev. Charles E., 151
Rolla, 112
Rose Prairie, 170
Ruxton, Jim, 158

St. John's Church Hall, Baldonnel, xlii, 202, 210, 229, 235-37, 241, 273, 283
St. Martin-in-the-Fields, Fort St. John, xlii, 201f., 210, 230, 241, 273, 283
Sayle, Iris Eugenie Friend, xxviii, xl, 8
Schramm, Hubert (né Horst), xxxvi, xlii
Scott, Rev. Elton, xxvii
Scouts, xif., xxvi, 16-18, 20f., 23, 25, 28f., 44-46, 49, 52f., 55f., 59-61, 68, 77, 80, 83, 90-92, 96f., 102, 106-8, 111, 115, 126, 131f., 137, 181-83, 185, 198, 200f., 212f., 215-17, 226, 253, 283-85
Shortt, Everett, 265
Shortt, Mrs. Everett, 269
Simmons, M. C., 102, 182
Simpson, John, 45, 92, 215
Simpson, William, 27, 29, 32f., 38f., 42, 44f., 47f., 54f., 58, 64, 67f., 74, 76, 81, 90, 92, 94, 99, 109, 117, 122, 130f., 141, 147, 179-81, 186, 188, 197f., 204, 208, 215f., 229

Simpson, Mrs. William, 81, 182, 245, 269, 279-81
Sisters of Providence, 34
Slyman, M., 172-74
Soman, Dolores, 85f.
Soman, Joseph, 84-86
Soman, Richard, 85f.
Spence, Albert, 261
Spence, Jean, 280
Storrs, Bernard, xxv
Storrs, Bp. Christopher, xii, xxv, xxxi-xxxiii, xliii, 149, 153, 177
Storrs, Francis, xxv
Storrs, Mrs. Francis, xxvii
Storrs, Rev. John (father), xxiv, xxxi
Storrs, Rev. John (son), xv, xxiv-xxvi, xxxii, xxxviiif., 3, 240
Storrs, Monica Melanie, xi-xiii, xv-xvii, xix, xxii-xliv, xlix, lii
Storrs, Petronella (later Mrs. Frewin Moor), xiii, xxv, xxxvi, xliv, 233, 249
Storrs, Sir Ronald, xxv, xxxi, xxxix, 14
Sunday School, xif., xxvi, 13, 16, 18-20, 22, 25f., 29f., 43, 54, 58, 64, 67, 70f., 75, 79f., 87f., 94, 104f., 108f., 133, 142f., 146, 150, 152, 156, 159f., 168, 173, 183f., 187-89, 197, 207, 223, 227f., 252, 262, 267, 275, 277, 280, 285
Sunday School by Post, xxvii, xl, 17f., 51, 105, 116, 153, 157, 247, 259
Swanzy, Lillian, 5-7, 110
Symons, Hope (née Onslow), xxxi, xxxiiif.
Symons, R. D., xii, xxixf.

Taylor, Herbie, 55f., 68f., 73, 91, 100
Taylor, Mrs. Herbie, 55f., 68f., 73, 80
Taylor, Sandy, 90f.
Taylor's Flats, 24, 213f.
Thompson, Bertrum, 176
Thorsen, Thor, 64, 192
Thorvaldsen, Bertel, 236f., 268
Tilton, D. A., 277
Tompkins, Philip F., 155f.
Tower, Iris, xxxix, 1
Tower, Sylvia, 1
Travis, James, 21
Tucker, Erwin, 171f.

Victoria League, 247
Village Evangelists, xxvi, xxxvii, xxxix, xliv

Waites, Mrs. Harry, 278

Warren, Sarah Trumbell, 4f.
Watt, Charles, 190
Western Canada Sunday School Caravan
    Mission Fund, xxviii, xl
Wood, J.S. Corry, 63f.
Wolf-cubs, 13f., 16, 23, 68, 91f., 97, 181, 185,
    199-201, 285
Wolfendale, Rev. George Hedley, xxviii,
    xli, 181, 184, 189, 200-202, 206-10, 213,
    217, 223f., 229f., 234f., 237-39, 241,
    243-47, 252f., 257, 262, 267f., 271,
    273f., 279f., 282f., 285
Women's Auxiliary, 255f., 269f., 280f.

Young, James, 190f.